23895

In appreciation for ... ...'s experience at M.U.S. this volume is given by Dr & Mrs. ... ...

Oct 1987

DATE DUE

APR 2 8 2003			

LUTHER'S WORKS

American Edition

VOLUME 31

Published by Concordia Publishing House

and Fortress Press in 55 volumes.

General Editors are Jaroslav Pelikan (for vols. 1–30)

and Helmut T. Lehmann (for vols. 31–55)

LUTHER'S WORKS

VOLUME 31

Career of the Reformer: I

EDITED BY

HAROLD J. GRIMM

GENERAL EDITOR

HELMUT T. LEHMANN

FORTRESS PRESS / PHILADELPHIA

Library of Congress Catalog Card Number 55-9893

ISBN 0-8006-0331-1

Fifth printing 1987

3273I87   Printed in the United States of America   1–331

GENERAL EDITORS' PREFACE

The first editions of Luther's collected works appeared in the sixteenth century, and so did the first efforts to make him "speak English." In America serious attempts in these directions were made for the first time in the nineteenth century. The Saint Louis edition of Luther was the first endeavor on American soil to publish a collected edition of his works, and the Henkel Press in New Market, Virginia, was the first to publish some of Luther's writings in an English translation. During the first decade of the twentieth century, J. N. Lenker produced translations of Luther's sermons and commentaries in thirteen volumes. A few years later the first of the six volumes in the Philadelphia (or Holman) edition of the *Works of Martin Luther* appeared. But a growing recognition of the need for more of Luther's works in English has resulted in this American edition of Luther's works.

The edition is intended primarily for the reader whose knowledge of late medieval Latin and sixteenth-century German is too small to permit him to work with Luther in the original languages. Those who can will continue to read Luther in his original words as these have been assembled in the monumental Weimar edition (*D. Martin Luthers Werke*. Kritische Gesamtausgabe; Weimar, 1883–). Its texts and helps have formed a basis for this edition, though in certain places we have felt constrained to depart from its readings and findings. We have tried throughout to translate Luther as he thought translating should be done. That is, we have striven for faithfulness on the basis of the best lexicographical materials available. But where literal accuracy and clarity have conflicted, it is clarity that we have preferred, so that sometimes paraphrase seemed more faithful than literal fidelity. We have proceeded in a similar way in the matter of Bible versions, translating Luther's translations. Where this could be done by the use of an existing

v

English version—King James, Douay, or Revised Standard—we have done so. Where it could not, we have supplied our own. To indicate this in each specific instance would have been pedantic; to adopt a uniform procedure would have been artificial—especially in view of Luther's own inconsistency in this regard. In each volume the translator will be responsible primarily for matters of text and language, while the responsibility of the editor will extend principally to the historical and theological matters reflected in the introductions and notes.

Although the edition as planned will include fifty-five volumes, Luther's writings are not being translated in their entirety. Nor should they be. As he was the first to insist, much of what he wrote and said was not that important. Thus the edition is a selection of works that have proved their importance for the faith, life, and history of the Christian church. The first thirty volumes contain Luther's expositions of various biblical books, while the remaining volumes include what are usually called his "Reformation writings" and other occasional pieces. The final volume of the set will be an index volume; in addition to an index of quotations, proper names, and topics, and a list of corrections and changes, it will contain a glossary of many of the technical terms that recur in Luther's works and that cannot be defined each time they appear. Obviously Luther cannot be forced into any neat set of rubrics. He can provide his reader with bits of autobiography or with political observations as he expounds a psalm, and he can speak tenderly about the meaning of the faith in the midst of polemics against his opponents. It is the hope of publishers, editors, and translators that through this edition the message of Luther's faith will speak more clearly to the modern church.

J. P.
H. T. L.

CONTENTS

C. R.   — *Corpus Reformatorum*, edited by C. G. Bretschneider
        and H. E. Bindseil (Halle, 1834-1860).

CL   — *Luthers Werke in Auswahl*, edited by Otto Clemen *et
        al*. (Bonn, 1912-1933; Berlin, 1955-1956).

EA   — *D. Martin Luthers sämmtliche Werke*
        (Frankfurt and Erlangen, 1826-1857).

LW   — American edition of *Luther's Works*
        (Philadelphia and St. Louis, 1955-   ).

MA³   — *Martin Luther*. Ausgewählte Werke
        (München, 1948-   ).

Migne   — *Patrologiae, Series Latina*, 221 vols. in 222
        (Paris, 1844-1904), J. P. Migne, editor.

PE   — *Works of Martin Luther* (Philadelphia, 1915-1943).

St. L. — *D. Martin Luther's sämmtliche Schriften*, edited by
        Johann Georg Walch. Edited and published in
        modern German, 23 vols. in 25
        (St. Louis, 1880-1910).

WA   — *D. Martin Luthers Werke*. Kritische Gesamtausgabe
        (Weimar, 1883-   ).

WA, Br — *D. Martin Luthers Werke*. Briefwechsel
        (Weimar, 1930-1948).

WA, TR — *D. Martin Luthers Werke*. Tischreden
        (Weimar, 1912-1921).

WA, DB — *D. Martin Luthers Werke*. Deutsche Bibel
        (Weimar, 1906-   ).

INTRODUCTION TO
Career of the Reformer

Luther, in the introduction to the first volume of the first edition of his Latin works,* apologized for the fact that his writings were poorly written and badly organized. He explained this by calling attention to the course of events which had dictated the time and circumstances of these writings, stating that the events themselves were disorganized and without reason or logic. He also called attention to the fact that he had been "forced into the tumult" of the controversy with ecclesiastical and political authorities, that is, into the career of a reformer, entirely against his will, for he preferred peace to strife and was greatly concerned over the fact that he was engaged in a bitter strife concerning the Word of God.

Because Luther's works, particularly those which emanated from the first critical years of his career as a reformer, were written in the midst of a bitter struggle against formidable opposition, they are both autobiographical and confessional. They provide the best introduction to the study of this remarkable man, who made the preaching and teaching of the gospel his sole concern.

The succession of events which catapulted Luther into fame as a reformer often bewildered him, for what he had done as a young monk, district vicar of the order of Augustinian Eremites, preacher, and professor he had done in the first instance to solve his own personal religious problems. His career as a reformer did not begin with his attacks upon the corruption in the church but with questions raised concerning his own salvation in the quiet of his monastery cell. It was there that he found an unequivocal and satisfying answer to the question which had long perturbed him and many of his contemporaries: "How may I be certain of salvation?"

---

* WA 54, 179-187. Cf. p. 184. This Latin edition of Luther's works was published in 1545, a year before his death. LW 34, 279-288.

The answer to this question concerning salvation depended primarily upon his interpretation of the words, "righteousness of God," which had always frightened him. When, after a long and earnest study of the Psalms and the letters of St. Paul, he came to the conclusion that this term was not to be interpreted in a formal or active sense, namely that God pronounced judgment upon man according to man's just deserts, but in a passive sense, namely that he imputed his righteousness to a believer, he entered "the gates of paradise."† This doctrine of justification by faith and not by works, which became the fundamental principle of Protestantism, he had found in the Bible and not in the textbooks of the medieval schoolmen. Therefore he turned from the works of men to the Word of God and enunciated the second evangelical principle which formed the basis of Protestantism: the recognition of the Bible as the sole authority in religious matters. When, finally, he came to the conclusion that the ecclesiastical hierarchy as it had developed in the Middle Ages hindered rather than aided the Christian in his personal, direct approach to God, he formulated the third fundamental principle of the Protestant Reformation: the universal priesthood of believers.

Once Luther had developed a basically evangelical theology, it was only a matter of time before an occasion would present itself which would bring him into direct conflict with ecclesiastical authorities. That occasion presented itself when he nailed the *Ninety-five Theses* on the door of the Castle Church in Wittenberg, October 31, 1517. When these theses, which contained Luther's questions regarding the abuses in the indulgence traffic of his day, were widely published in the Latin original and in translations, Luther could no longer devote himself solely to expounding Scripture to his fellow Augustinians, students, and Wittenberg citizens. He was now compelled to defend his views on indulgences and also his fundamental evangelical doctrines against all those who believed that the authority of the church in general and the papacy in particular was at stake.

All the significant and representative writings of Luther which are concerned with his career as a reformer, from the *Disputation*

---

† *Ibid.*, p. 186.

Against Scholastic Theology in 1517 to *The Italian Lie Concerning Luther's Death* in 1545, are included in this and the following three volumes. Most of them appear in English translation for the first time. In them one may read the account of the stirring events in the life of this courageous reformer in his own words and relive with him the critical events which greatly influenced not only his career but the fate of Germany and all Europe. Furthermore, it will be possible through these works to probe the depth of that faith which enabled a humble monk to defy the authority of the pope, the church councils, the church fathers, canon law, and the emperor, and utter in effect upon every critical occasion, "I cannot do otherwise."

When reading Luther's works, however, it is necessary to follow his advice and accept them for what they were. Luther was often too close to the line of battle to see the issues in all their ramifications. Furthermore, when he reminisced about his early years, he naturally gave them, despite his overwhelming sense of honesty, an interpretation which was colored by subsequent events and years of experience as an active leader. To present his writings in conformity with all the data concerning the highly complicated events as they unfolded during the first half of the sixteenth century, the editors have drawn upon the critical apparatus of each of the important editions of Luther's works, other contemporary documents, and the interpretations of recent students of Luther and the Reformation.

The most comprehensive bibliography of works on the Reformation is that by Karl Schottenloher, *Bibliographie zur deutschen Geschichte im Zeitalter der Glaubensspaltung*, 6 vols. (Leipzig, 1933-39). Vol. 7, *Das Schrifttum von 1938-1960* (Stuttgart, 1962), is an important supplement. The International Committee of Historical Sciences has published seven fascicles of its *Bibliographie de la réforme 1450-1648* (Leiden, 1958-70), listing works on the Reformation published in Europe and the United States from 1940 to 1955.

The following are helpful bibliographies in English: R. H. Bainton, *Bibliography of the Continental Reformation* (Chicago, 1935), and "Survey of Periodical Literature in the United States, 1945-1951," *Archiv für Reformationsgeschichte*, 43 (1952); Harold J. Grimm, *The Reformation in Recent Historical Thought*, A.H.A. Service Center for Teachers of History (New York, 1964); and Wilhelm

Pauck, "The Historiography of the German Reformation in the Past Twenty Years," *Church History*, 9 (1940).

Among the widely used single-volume books on the Reformation are R. H. Bainton, *The Reformation of the Sixteenth Century* (Boston, 1952), in paperback; H. Daniel-Rops, *The Protestant Reformation*, tr. from the French (London, 1961); A. G. Dickens, *Reformation and Society* (London, 1966), in paperback; G. R. Elton, *Reformation Europe 1517-1559* (Cleveland and New York, 1963), in paperback; Harold J. Grimm, *The Reformation Era* (New York, 1965); Hans J. Hillerbrand, *Men and Ideas in the Sixteenth Century* (Chicago, 1969), in paperback; Hajo Holborn, *History of Modern Germany*, Vol. 1: *The Reformation* (New York, 1959); Philip Hughes, *Popular History of the Reformation* (Garden City, N. Y., 1960), in paperback; and Preserved Smith, *The Age of the Reformation* (New York, 1920), in paperback.

Important recent biographies of Luther in English are those by R. H. Bainton, *Here I Stand: A Life of Martin Luther* (Nashville, 1950), in paperback; Heinrich Bornkamm, *Luther's World of Thought*, tr. from the German (St. Louis, 1958); V. H. H. Green, *Luther and the Reformation* (London, 1964); Franz Lau, *Luther*, tr. from the German (Philadelphia, 1963); James Mackinnon, *Luther and the Reformation*, 4 vols. (London, 1925-30); Gerhard Ritter, *Luther: His Life and Work* (New York and Evanston, 1963); and E. G. Schwiebert, *Luther and His Times* (St. Louis, 1950).

Luther's early development as a reformer is discussed by Heinrich Boehmer, *Road to Reformation*, tr. from the German (Philadelphia, 1946); Ernst Bizer, *Fides ex auditu: Eine Untersuchung über die Entdeckung der Gerechtigkeit Gottes durch Martin Luther* (Neukirchen, 1958); Jaroslav Pelikan, *Luther the Expositor* (St. Louis, 1959); E. G. Rupp, *Luther's Progress to the Diet of Worms* (London, 1951); U. Saarnivaara, *Luther Discovers the Gospel* (St. Louis, 1951); Otto Scheel, *Martin Luther: Vom Katholizismus zur Reformation*, 2 vols., 3rd. ed. (Tübingen, 1921-30); Reinhard Schwarz, *Fides, spes und caritas beim jungen Luther* (Berlin, 1962); Carl Stange, *Die Anfänge der Theologie Luthers* (Berlin, 1957); and P. S. Watson, *Let God be God* (Philadelphia and London, 1947).

Indispensable as an aid in locating Luther's writings in all the major editions is Kurt Aland, et al., *Hilfsbuch zum Lutherstudium* (Berlin, 1957). Among the many bibliographical aids for the study of Luther are the following: *Luther-Jahrbuch* (1925-29; 1957-   ), an annual publication of the Luther-Gesellschaft; *Luther-Forschung Heute*, ed. Vilmos Vajta (Berlin, 1958), which contains summaries of Luther research in various countries; John Dillenberger, "Literature in Luther Studies, 1950-1955," *Church History*, 25 (1956), and "Major Volumes and Selected Periodical Literature in Luther Studies, 1956-1959," *Church History*, 30 (1961); Harold J. Grimm, "Luther Research Since 1920," *Journal of Modern History*, 32 (1960); W. von Loewenich, "Die Lutherforschung in Deutschland seit dem 2. Weltkrieg," *Theologische Literaturzeitung*, 81 (1956). Current literature is reviewed in *Luther*, journal of the Luther-Gesellschaft (1929-   ); *Archiv für Reformationsgeschichte* (1903-44; 1951-   ), an international journal; and *Renaissance News* (since 1948).

Useful works of reference are the *New Catholic Encyclopedia*, 15 vols. (New York, 1967); *New Schaff-Herzog Encyclopedia of Religious Knowledge*, 13 vols. (Grand Rapids, Mich., 1949-50), with two supplementary volumes prepared by American scholars (Grand Rapids, Mich., 1955); *Die Religion in Geschichte und Gegenwart*, 6 vols., 3rd ed. (Tübingen, 1957-62); *Lexikon für Theologie und Kirche*, 8 vols., 2nd ed. (Freiburg i. Br., 1957-63); and *Dictionnaire de Théologie Catholique*, 15 vols. (Paris, 1925-50).

H. J. G.

INTRODUCTION TO VOLUME 31

The writings of Luther selected for this volume depict his emergence as a reformer. By 1517 he had lectured on Psalms (*WA* 3, 1-652; 4, 1-462), Romans (*WA* 56 and 57), and Galatians (*WA* 57^{II}). In that same year he delivered his lectures on Hebrews (*WA* 57^{III}), wrote and published *The Seven Penitential Psalms with a German Exposition* (*WA* 1, 154-220), wrote *The German Exposition of the Lord's Prayer for the Laity* (*WA* 2, 74-130) and *The Ten Commandments . . . with a Short Exposition* (*WA* 1, 247-256), prepared for public debate the *Disposition Against Scholastic Theology* (*WA* 1, 220-228) and the *Ninety-five Theses* (*WA* 1, 229-238), and wrote innumerable sermons and letters. After years of intensive study he now considered himself prepared to come to grips with the traditional scholastic theologians and to apply his evangelical doctrines to conditions as they existed in the church of his day. His writings, which kept three Wittenberg printers busy and provided work for many others, soon brought him a large following throughout Germany and in much of Europe; but they also aroused such considerable opposition that the preparation of polemical writings soon occupied much of his time.

It was in the *Ninety-five Theses* that Luther applied his evangelical doctrines to the indulgence traffic, specifically to Johann Tetzel's sale of indulgences in the neighborhood of Wittenberg. The indulgence which Tetzel sold was for the purpose of supplying money for the building of the new St. Peter's in Rome and at the same time reimbursing Archbishop Albrecht of Mainz for expenses involved in obtaining a costly dispensation to enable him to hold three sees and gain the palium, or symbol of his office as archbishop. Although Luther's theses were primarily questions raised for discussion among theologians, they obtained a wide circulation and adversely affected Tetzel's sale of indulgences.

Tetzel immediately began his attacks upon Luther. Archbishop Albrecht reported him to Rome, but Pope Leo X (1513-1521), considering the resulting disturbance a mere monkish quarrel between the Augustinian Eremites, to which Luther belonged, and the Dominican order, to which Tetzel belonged, did not at first take a hand in the matter. Tetzel and others of his order, however, soon influenced persons close to the pope. Meanwhile Dr. Johann Eck (1486-1543), professor of theology and chancellor of the University of Ingolstadt in Bavaria, canon of Eichstätt, and preacher at Augsburg, published his *Obelisks* (literally, little daggers used for marking notes).* In this pamphlet this former friend of Luther called attention to the fact that the Wittenberg theologian's views were similar to those of John Huss, who had been burned as a heretic in 1415. Sylvester Cardinal Prierias, or Mazzolini (1456?-1523), a Dominican theologian, master of the sacred palace, adviser of Leo X, grand inquisitor, and censor of books, also accused him of heresy. Luther answered these charges by publishing his *Explanations of the Ninety-five Theses* (1518).

Leo X, finally aware of the seriousness of Luther's criticism of the church and the papacy, ordered the general of the Augustinians "to quiet the man." The general in turn instructed Johann Staupitz, Luther's superior as vicar general of the order in Germany who had been helpful in finding a solution to his religious problems, to compel the errant brother to recant. Luther accordingly attended the meeting of the general chapter of the Saxon province at Heidelberg, in session during April and May, 1518. He refused to recant, but resigned his position as district vicar. The *Heidelberg Disputation* of April 26 gave him an opportunity to present to his brothers his new evangelical theology and win many friends.

Meanwhile the Dominicans had induced the pope to summon Luther to Rome within sixty days to answer for his heresy as defined by *The Dialogue Against the Presumptuous Conclusions of Martin Luther†* of Prierias, one of the three judges of the Roman Curia who considered his case. Luther received the citation August 7, 1518. Realizing the implications of this step, he requested that Frederick the Wise (1486-1525), his prince, intervene. Frederick, one of the

---

* Eck's theses, called *Obelisks*, have not been published since they were incorporated and answered by Luther in his *Asterisks*, WA 1, 278-316.
† St. L 18, 310-345.

seven electors of the Empire, whose political importance was becoming apparent during the meeting of the Diet of Augsburg in the summer of 1518, determined to do all he could for the professor who was bringing fame to his university. Frederick entered into negotiations with Cardinal Cajetan, or Thomas de Vio of Gaeta (1469-1534), general of the Dominican order and papal legate at the Diet of Augsburg. Cajetan agreed to have the citation to Rome replaced by an interview between him and Luther in the city of Augsburg. Despite his fatherly attitude, this learned theologian could not compel Luther to recant.

Returning to Wittenberg from his three appearances before the cardinal, Luther was disappointed that he had not been given an opportunity to defend himself against the attacks of his enemies and the objections of Cajetan to his books. He therefore published the *Proceedings at Augsburg (1518)* and then made his daring appeal for a hearing before a general church council. This appeal was published December 11 without his consent and contrary to the wishes of Frederick the Wise. The elector, aware of the political maneuvering attending the serious illness of Emperor Maximilian, believed that he could still obtain a fair hearing for Luther. He therefore urged Luther to remain in Wittenberg.

Leo X, eager to influence the choice of a successor to Maximilian, made a significant attempt to gain the good will of Frederick the Wise. He sent Karl von Miltitz, a Saxon nobleman who was serving as papal chamberlain and secretary in the papal Curia, to present Frederick with the Golden Rose, a symbol of papal blessing awarded annually to an outstanding ruler, and to induce him to turn Luther over to Rome if he would not recant. Having learned that the elector would not accede to the pope's wishes, Miltitz went beyond his instructions by dealing directly with Luther at Altenburg from January 4 to 6, 1519. At this interview Luther agreed to refrain from further attacks, provided his opponents did likewise; to write the pope a humble letter offering to recant if his errors were pointed out to him; to submit his case to the archibishop of Salzburg; and to urge the people to obey and honor the Roman Church. Dissatisfied with Luther's letter to the pope, Miltitz substituted one which gave the pope the impression that Luther would submit without further ado. The overjoyed Leo was now eager to welcome the one-time "son of perdition" to his arms as "his beloved son." Since Luther was highly dissatisfied with the interview, Miltitz' trick would have had unpleasant repercussions if it had not been for the death of Maximilian on January 12 and the preoccupation of the pope and German princes in the election of the new emperor.

The election of Charles I of Spain as Charles V was not concluded until June 28. Meanwhile Luther considered himself attacked by Eck who had been exchanging theses on free will and the authority of Scripture with Andreas Bodenstein von Karlstadt, one of Luther's colleagues at the University of Wittenberg. When Karlstadt, who held a benefice directly from the pope, was reluctant to answer one of Eck's extreme assertions concerning papal supremacy, Luther entered the fray by publishing his twelve theses against Eck. In the last thesis, which became the thirteenth in a revised edition, he made the startling statement that papal authority rested solely on flimsy papal decrees of the preceding four centuries and was contradicted by the Bible, the decrees of the Council of Nicaea, and the first eleven centuries of the history of the church.

Already noted for his ability as a debater, Eck longed to enhance his reputation by meeting Luther in a public disputation. He seized the opportunity presented by Luther's attack upon papal authority and challenged both Karlstadt and him to a debate at Leipzig in ducal Saxony. Luther's account of the Leipzig Debate (June 27 to July 16, 1519) to Georg Spalatin, his close friend, secretary and chaplain of Frederick the Wise, and the go-between of Luther and the elector, shows how cleverly Eck had succeeded in calling attention to those of Luther's doctrines which were especially detested by the ecclesiastical authorities. Luther on his part courageously asserted that the pope held his authority by human and not divine right; that church councils could and did err, as the Council of Constance had erred in condemning all the articles of John Huss; and that Scripture was the ultimate authority in matters of doctrine.

Although Luther virtually despaired of having his religious convictions discussed calmly, the debate marked an important step in his career as reformer. He now relied more than ever on the Bible as the source of all religious knowledge and doctrine and came to the realization that his break with the "mother church" was inevitable. When Eck went to Rome in the spring of 1520, the pope appointed a commission including him and Cajetan to examine Luther's doctrines. It drafted a bull condemning forty-one specific errors ascribed to Luther. Officially issued on June 15, 1520, under the title, *Exsurge Domine*, or *Arise, O Lord*, it demanded that he retract his heresies within sixty days after publication of the bull in Germany on pain of excommunication, and warned all Christians to reject these heresies and burn Luther's books.‡

Luther formally and ceremoniously answered the papal attack on the morning of December 10, 1520, toward the close of the sixty-day period of grace. Together with a number of colleagues and students he proceeded to a place just outside the Elster Gate of Wittenberg where a bonfire was built, and consigned to the flames a number of books which supported papal supremacy, including a copy of the canon law. Finally, as though acting on a sudden impulse, he tossed into the fire a copy of the bull, *Exsurge Domine*. Soon thereafter he published in German his pamphlet *Why the Books of the Pope and His Disciples Were Burned*. As far as Luther was concerned, the die was cast.

Meanwhile Luther continued to carry out his many responsibilities as a professor and preacher and to instruct the people outside Wittenberg by his many publications. One of the most significant of a number of important works written in the year 1520 was his *The Freedom of a Christian*. Published in Latin and German, it portrayed his inner spirituality and evangelical faith in a positive form. At the request of Miltitz, Luther wrote Leo X a letter stating that he had never attacked the pope personally but had always wished him well, and enclosed the pamphlet, *The Freedom of a Christian*, to show him the kind of devotional writing he could do if his enemies would allow him the time. Leo, of course, did not answer the letter. In the face of Luther's refusal to recant and his bold self-assurance as evinced in the revolutionary pamphlets of 1520—*The Address to the Christian Nobility of the German Nation* and *The Babylonian Captivity of the Church*—Leo felt

‡ Cf. Carl Mirbt, *Quellen zur Geschichte des Papsttums und des römischen Katholizismus* (2d. ed., Tübingen and Leipzig, 1910), pp. 183-185. *LW* 32, 7-99.

compelled to excommunicate the reformer. The bull of excommunication, the *Decet Pontificem,* or *It Is Fitting That the Pope,* was officially promulgated in Rome on January 3, 1521 and was published in a revised form at Worms on May 6. With this act Luther's break with Rome was made official. He now faced the task of ordering the affairs of the church based upon an evangelical faith.

The selections of Luther's writings incorporated in this volume consist of disputations, treatises, letters, a sermon, and a preface to a book.

The disputation was frequently used in Luther's day. This was a debate in syllogistic form between a person who proposed a set of theses or propositions and one who responded. It was commonly used in medieval universities to sharpen the intellect of students, raise and clarify questions among the learned, and instruct audiences. Luther was so pleased with the weekly disputations held at Erfurt that he introduced them at the new University of Wittenberg. The theses of a disputation were carefully worked out so that the logical conclusion of one would be related to the conclusion of another and that the entire series would clarify the main thesis by a marshaling process. Luther prepared the theses here translated for himself and for his students.

Luther was one of the first persons to make extensive use of printed pamphlets and broadsides, carrying his cause directly to the people in their own tongue. To make them more attractive they were given catchy titles and were provided with woodcuts illustrating their contents. The invention of printing by movable type in the middle of the fifteenth century, the development of paper, and the rise in literacy made these pamphlets and broadsides influential.

The voluminous writing of letters by the humanists continued into the sixteenth century. Like the humanists, Luther carried on an extensive correspondence. Although a few of his letters are included in this volume to make the account of his development as a reformer complete, the bulk of his correspondence will be published in subsequent volumes.

By far the most effective means of spreading the Reformation was preaching. In his sermons Luther carried his evangelical theology directly to the people in a popular vernacular and by the use of a simple homiletical method. Although he carefully prepared these sermons, he and his contemporaries invariably preached *ex tempore*, frequently using notes. According to our present usage, the word "sermon" refers to this preaching, designated in German by the word *Predigt*. In Luther's time it also meant the formal exposition of a Scripture text for publication, designated in Luther's German by the word *Sermon*, in Latin by the word *sermo*. One of the best examples of the latter is the sermon, *Two Kinds of Righteousness*, included in this volume.

Since the invention of printing, scholars published many works of the ancients, church fathers, and medieval writers which up to that time had existed only in manuscript form, adding to these works prefaces of their own. Luther brought the reading public a number of such works, including Aesop's *Fables;* Augustine's *The Spirit and the Letter*, which he published in 1518 and to which he refers in the *Heidelberg Disputation;* and the work of a German mystic which he called *A German Theology*.

The selections in this volume have been translated directly from the Latin and German documents in the Weimar Edition, *D. Martin Luthers Werke*, Weimar, 1883, hereafter cited as *WA*. The *Briefwechsel* (correspondence) will be cited as *WA*, Br; *Die Deutsche Bibel* (The German Bible) as *WA*, DB; and the *Tischreden* (Table Talk) as *WA*, TR. These documents have in a number of instances been compared with those in *D. Martin Luthers sämmtliche Schriften*, edited by Johann Georg Walch (24 vols., Halle, 1740-1753), and edited and published in modern German, 23 vols. in 25, by Concordia Publishing House, St. Louis, Mo., 1880-1910, cited as *St L.; Luthers Werke in Auswahl*, edited by Otto Clemen *et al.* (8 vols.; Bonn, 1912-1933; Berlin, 1955-1956), cited as *CL;* and *Martin Luther, Ausgewählte Werke* (München, 1948-   ), cited as *MA³*. A number of the documents were published in English translation in *Works of Martin Luther*, 6 vols., Philadelphia, 1915-1943 (Philadelphia Edition), cited as *PE*. There are a number of Luther's letters in *Luther's Correspondence and other Contemporary Letters*, translated and edited by Preserved Smith, Vol. I (Philadelphia, 1913), Vol. II, in collaboration with C. M. Jacobs (Philadelphia, 1918). References to the canon law are to the recent edition *Corpus Iuris*

Canonici, edited by Aemilius Friedberg, Vols. I and II (Graz, 1955). Quotations from the church fathers are usually taken from J. P. Migne, ed., *Patrologiae, Series Latina,* 221 vols. in 222 (Paris, 1844-1904), cited as Migne.

The preparation of this volume would not have been possible without the generous assistance of many colleagues and friends. The editorial duties were a pleasure because of the able co-operation of the translators, Professor Lewis W. Spitz of the Department of History at the University of Missouri, Columbia, Mo.; Professor Lowell J. Satre of the Department of New Testament at the Luther Theological Seminary, St. Paul, Minn.; and the Reverend Carl W. Folkemer of St. John's Lutheran Church, Linthicum Heights, Maryland. I am also indebted to Professor Ralph E. Cleland, Dean of the Graduate School of Indiana University, for providing research assistance; the Reverend George S. Robbert, my research assistant, for help in checking sources, reading proof, and preparing the index; and to Miss Colleen Newby and Mrs. Sharon Helfrich for typing parts of the manuscript. Finally, I am grateful to Professor Robert H. Fischer of the Lutheran School of Theology at Chicago and Professor Jared Wicks of Bellarmine School of Theology, North Aurora, Illinois, for their helpful suggestions for improving the translations.

H.J.G.

LUTHER'S WORKS

VOLUME 31

DISPUTATION AGAINST SCHOLASTIC THEOLOGY

1517

Translated by Harold J. Grimm

INTRODUCTION

Luther's studies soon led him to the conclusion that there was an irreconcilable conflict between his evangelical theology and scholasticism. By means of Aristotelian logic the schoolmen sought a synthesis of all things, divine and human. By means of reason they would explain their faith. In search of principles for achieving this, they studied the philosophical writings of ancient philosophers from Plato to Boethius; for them the prince of them all was Aristotle.

The most remarkable synthesis of the medieval schoolmen was that of St. Thomas Aquinas (1225-1274), a Dominican scholar whose *Summa Theologica (Summary of Theology)** best illustrates the scholastic form or argument with its lists of authorities, syllogisms in defense of theses, statements of contrary theses, refutations, distinctions, conciliations, and conclusions.

By Luther's time, however, scholasticism had already run its course, having been weakened from without and within. From without it was largely the humanists who disliked its highly rationalistic, logically-involved approach to religious and secular problems. Within scholasticism there developed two extreme schools of thought which became mutually antagonistic: realism and nominalism. There had always been those who, like Plato, had taught that ultimate reality lay in ideas, or universals. This realism, as it was called, triumphed in the great synthesis of St. Thomas, for by means of it one could attempt to explain logically such important Christian doctrines as that of the Trinity and transubstantiation. Another group followed Aristotle in maintaining that ideas, or universals, existed in name only. According to the nominalists, as they were called, ideas resulted only from experience with things, or particulars.

---

* The *Summary of Theology*, most complete scholastic synthesis of all learning, was and remains an important authority in Roman Catholic theology in our day. A good modern edition is the *Summa Theologica of St. Thomas Aquinas*, trans. by fathers of the English Dominican Province (2d and rev. ed.; London, New York, Cincinnati, Chicago, San Francisco, no date).

The most brilliant scholastic following St. Thomas was a Scottish Franciscan educated at Oxford, Duns Scotus (d. 1308), called "the subtle doctor." By his brilliant logic, however, he tended to weaken scholasticism by exposing errors in the conclusions of other scholastics, including St. Thomas; reducing the method of absurdity by writing highly involved treatises; and emphasizing the importance of a constant re-examination and investigation of knowledge.

William of Ockham (1280-1349), an English Franciscan also educated at Oxford, embraced an extreme form of nominalism. Convinced that the logical method of even the greatest schoolmen could not provide incontestable proof of religious doctrines, he maintained that these should be accepted entirely by faith in revelation. Reason had validity only in the realm of nature. Gabriel Biel (d. 1495), an influential professor at the University of Tübingen, revived Ockhamism in Germany where it was taught in most universities. Luther studied its methods and tenets at the University of Erfurt.

Although Luther thought highly of Ockham and Biel, he could not accept their doctrines of freedom of the will, good works, and justification. Ockham and Biel believed that man by nature could will to love God above all things and prepare the way for God's saving grace. Since, according to them, Christ's work of atonement became operative only after man had proven himself worthy of it, Luther could not be certain that he would be saved. Such certainty came only with his discovery of justification by faith alone. This basic insight led him to repudiate scholasticism as a whole. Because he believed that it actually hindered God's work of saving man he vehemently attacked the schoolmen, Aristotle, and reason.

In 1517 Luther was working on a commentary on the first book of Aristotle's *Physics* for the purpose of dethroning the god of the scholastics. Although nothing of this commentary is extant, the *Disputation Against Scholastic Theology* undoubtedly grew out of its preparation. He wrote his theses for Franz Günther, who defended them at the University of Wittenberg on September 4, 1517, in fulfillment of the requirements for the degree of bachelor of Holy Scripture, with Luther, dean of the Faculty of Theology, presiding. Christopher Scheurl of Nürnberg, to whom Luther sent a copy, believed that this disputation would "restore the theology of Christ." Although no separate printings of the disputation have come down to us, it was included in a collection of disputations published in Wittenberg in 1520. The following translation is made from the Latin in WA 1, 221-228, which, in turn, is based on the reliable printed copy of 1520. It is printed in a new German translation in St. L. 18, 18-27.

There is an excellent analysis of the disputation in C. Stange, "Die ältesten ethischen Disputationen Luther," *Quellenschriften zur Geschichte des Protestantismus* (Leipzig, 1904), 1:35-50. Stange discusses the breakthrough of Pauline theology in Luther in *Die Anfänge der Theologie Luthers* (Berlin, 1957). Reinhard Schwarz presents a detailed analysis of Luther's opposition to scholasticism in *Fides, spes und caritas beim jungen Luther* (Berlin, 1962). Heiko A. Oberman has made substantial contributions to our knowledge of late medieval thought by the publication of *The Harvest of Medieval Theology: Gabriel Biel and Late Medieval Nominalism* (Cambridge, Mass., 1963), and *Forerunners of the Reformation: The Shape of Late Medieval Thought* (New York, 1966).

DISPUTATION AGAINST SCHOLASTIC THEOLOGY

1. To say that Augustine exaggerates in speaking against heretics is to say that Augustine tells lies almost everywhere. This is contrary to common knowledge.

2. This is the same as permitting Pelagians[1] and all heretics to triumph, indeed, the same as conceding victory to them.

3. It is the same as making sport of the authority of all doctors of theology.

4. It is therefore true that man, being a bad tree, can only will and do evil [Cf. Matt. 7: 17-18].

5. It is false to state that man's inclination is free to choose between either of two opposites. Indeed, the inclination is not free, but captive. This is said in opposition to common opinion.

6. It is false to state that the will can by nature conform to correct precept. This is said in opposition to Scotus[2] and Gabriel.[3]

7. As a matter of fact, without the grace of God the will produces an act that is perverse and evil.

8. It does not, however, follow that the will is by nature evil, that is, essentially evil, as the Manichaeans[4] maintain.

---

[1] Pelagius (360?-420?), a native of Britain, denied original sin. He held that justifying grace is given according to merit and regarded sinless perfection possible after baptism. His teachings were vigorously attacked by St. Augustine (354–430), bishop of Hippo.

[2] John Duns Scotus (d. 1308) was the leader of the Scotist school which taught freedom of the will and the superiority of the will over the intellect. He denied the real distinction between the soul and its faculties.

[3] Gabriel Biel (1425?-1495) was "the last of the scholastics" and the first professor of theology in the newly founded University of Tübingen. He was the author of The Canon of the Mass which Luther studied diligently as a young man.

[4] Manichaeism is a form of religious dualism consisting of Zoroastrian dualism, Babylonian folklore, and Buddhist ethics superficially combined with Christian elements. It was founded in the latter half of the third century by the Persian prophet Mani (215?-276?). According to Mani, everything material and sensual is created evil and must be overcome.

9. It is nevertheless innately and inevitably evil and corrupt.

10. One must concede that the will is not free to strive toward whatever is declared good. This in opposition to Scotus and Gabriel.

11. Nor is it able to will or not to will whatever is prescribed.

12. Nor does one contradict St. Augustine when one says that nothing is so much in the power of the will as the will itself.

13. It is absurd to conclude that erring man can love the creature above all things, therefore also God. This in opposition to Scotus and Gabriel.

14. Nor is it surprising that the will can conform to erroneous and not to correct precept.

15. Indeed, it is peculiar to it that it can only conform to erroneous and not to correct precept.

16. One ought rather to conclude: since erring man is able to love the creature it is impossible for him to love God.

17. Man is by nature unable to want God to be God. Indeed, he himself wants to be God, and does not want God to be God.

18. To love God above all things by nature is a fictitious term, a chimera, as it were. This is contrary to common teaching.

19. Nor can we apply the reasoning of Scotus concerning the brave citizen who loves his country more than himself.

20. An act of friendship is done, not according to nature, but according to prevenient grace. This in opposition to Gabriel.

21. No act is done according to nature that is not an act of concupiscence against God.

22. Every act of concupiscence against God is evil and a fornication of the spirit.

23. Nor is it true that an act of concupiscence can be set aright by the virtue of hope. This in opposition to Gabriel.

24. For hope is not contrary to charity, which seeks and desires only that which is of God.

25. Hope does not grow out of merits, but out of suffering which destroys merits. This in opposition to the opinion of many.

26. An act of friendship is not the most perfect means for accomplishing that which is in one.[5] Nor is it the most perfect means

---

[5] "To do what is in one" is a scholastic phrase which implies that a Christian can do meritorious works agreeable to God.

10

for obtaining the grace of God or turning toward and approaching God.

27. But it is an act of conversion already perfected, following grace both in time and by nature.

28. If it is said of the Scripture passages, "Return to me, . . . and I will return to you" [Zech. 1:3.], "Draw near to God and he will draw near to you" [Jas. 4:8], "Seek and you will find" [Matt. 7:7], "You will seek me and find me" [Jer. 29:13], and the like, that one is by nature, the other by grace, this is no different from asserting what the Pelagians have said.

29. The best and infallible preparation for grace and the sole disposition toward grace is the eternal election and predestination of God.

30. On the part of man, however, nothing precedes grace except indisposition and even rebellion against grace.

31. It is said with the idlest demonstrations that the predestined can be damned individually but not collectively. This in opposition to the scholastics.

32. Moreover, nothing is achieved by the following saying: Predestination is necessary by virtue of the consequence of God's willing, but not of what actually followed, namely, that God had to elect a certain person.

33. And this is false, that doing all that one is able to do can remove the obstacles to grace. This in opposition to several authorities.

34. In brief, man by nature has neither correct precept nor good will.

35. It is not true that an invincible ignorance excuses one completely(all scholastics notwithstanding);

36. For ignorance of God and oneself and good work is always invincible to nature.

37. Nature, moreover, inwardly and necessarily glories and takes pride in every work which is apparently and outwardly good.

38. There is no moral virtue without either pride or sorrow, that is, without sin.

39. We are not masters of our actions, from beginning to end, but servants. This in opposition to the philosophers.

40. We do not become righteous by doing righteous deeds but, having been made righteous, we do righteous deeds. This in opposition to the philosophers.

41. Virtually the entire *Ethics* of Aristotle is the worst enemy of grace. This in opposition to the scholastics.

42. It is an error to maintain that Aristotle's statement concerning happiness does not contradict Catholic doctrine. This in opposition to the doctrine on morals.

43. It is an error to say that no man can become a theologian without Aristotle. This in opposition to common opinion.

44. Indeed, no one can become a theologian unless he becomes one without Aristotle.

45. To state that a theologian who is not a logician is a monstrous heretic—this is a monstrous and heretical statement. This in opposition to common opinion.

46. In vain does one fashion a logic of faith, a substitution brought about without regard for limit and measure. This in opposition to the new dialecticians.

47. No syllogistic form is valid when applied to divine terms. This in opposition to the Cardinal.[6]

48. Nevertheless it does not for that reason follow that the truth of the doctrine of the Trinity contradicts syllogistic forms. This in opposition to the same new dialecticians and to the Cardinal.

49. If a syllogistic form of reasoning holds in divine matters, then the doctrine of the Trinity is demonstrable and not the object of faith.

50. Briefly, the whole Aristotle[7] is to theology as darkness is to light. This in opposition to the scholastics.

51. It is very doubtful whether the Latins comprehended the correct meaning of Aristotle.

---

[6] Luther refers to the Cardinal of Cambrai, Pierre d'Ailly (1350-1420), a French theologian, a commentator on the *Sentences* of Peter Lombard and guiding spirit of the conciliar movement which led to the calling of the Council of Constance (1414-1418).

[7] The logical and metaphysical writings of Aristotle were well known in the Middle Ages and were incorporated in scholasticism. His scientific writings became known to Europeans in the late Middle Ages and caused much concern because they contained statements contrary to Christian doctrine. It is to these writings that Luther refers in his phrase "the whole Aristotle."

52. It would have been better for the church if Porphyry[8] with his universals had not been born for the use of theologians.

53. Even the more useful definitions of Aristotle seem to beg the question.

54. For an act to be meritorious, either the presence of grace is sufficient, or its presence means nothing. This in opposition to Gabriel.

55. The grace of God is never present in such a way that it is inactive, but it is a living, active, and operative spirit; nor can it happen that through the absolute power of God an act of friendship may be present without the presence of the grace of God. This in opposition to Gabriel.

56. It is not true that God can accept man without his justifying grace. This in opposition to Ockham.[9]

57. It is dangerous to say that the law commands that an act of obeying the commandment be done in the grace of God. This in opposition to the Cardinal and Gabriel.

58. From this it would follow that "to have the grace of God" is actually a new demand going beyond the law.

59. It would also follow that fulfilling the law can take place without the grace of God.

60. Likewise it follows that the grace of God would be more hateful than the law itself.

61. It does not follow that the law should be complied with and fulfilled in the grace of God. This in opposition to Gabriel.

62. And that therefore he who is outside the grace of God sins incessantly, even when he does not kill, commit adultery, or become angry.

63. But it follows that he sins because he does not spiritually fulfil the law.

64. Spiritually that person does not kill, does not do evil, does not become enraged when he neither becomes angry nor lusts.

---

[8] Porphyry (233-303) was a Neoplatonic follower of Plotinus and a bitter opponent of Christianity.
[9] William of Ockham (ca. 1280-1349) was a Franciscan schoolman, a nominalist who stated that reason could not be applied to theology. He published commentaries on Aristotle and Porphyry.

65. Outside the grace of God it is indeed impossible not to become angry or lust, so that not even in grace is it possible to fulfil the law perfectly.

66. It is the righteousness of the hypocrite actually and outwardly not to kill, do evil, etc.

67. It is by the grace of God that one does not lust or become enraged.

68. Therefore it is impossible to fulfil the law in any way without the grace of God.

69. As a matter of fact, it is more accurate to say that the law is destroyed by nature without the grace of God.

70. A good law will of necessity be bad for the natural will.

71. Law and will are two implacable foes without the grace of God.

72. What the law wants, the will never wants, unless it pretends to want it out of fear or love.

73. The law, as taskmaster of the will, will not be overcome except by the "child, who has been born to us" [Isa. 9:6].

74. The law makes sin abound because it irritates and repels the will [Rom. 7:13].

75. The grace of God, however, makes justice abound through Jesus Christ because it causes one to be pleased with the law.

76. Every deed of the law without the grace of God appears good outwardly, but inwardly it is sin. This in opposition to the scholastics.

77. The will is always averse to, and the hands inclined toward, the law of the Lord without the grace of God.

78. The will which is inclined toward the law without the grace of God is so inclined by reason of its own advantage.

79. Condemned are all those who do the works of the law.

80. Blessed are all those who do the works of the grace of God.

81. Chapter Falsas concerning penance, dist. 5,[10] confirms the fact that works outside the realm of grace are not good, if this is not understood falsely.

---

[10] *Decretum Magistri Gratiani, Decreta Secunda Pars,* causa XXXIII, ques. III, dist. V, cap. 6. *Corpus Iuris Canonici,* ed. Aemilius Friedberg (Graz, 1955), I, col. 1241. Cf. Migne 187, 1636.

82. Not only are the religious ceremonials not the good law and the precepts in which one does not live (in opposition to many teachers);

83. But even the Decalogue itself and all that can be taught and prescribed inwardly and outwardly is not good law either.

84. The good law and that in which one lives is the love of God, spread abroad in our hearts by the Holy Spirit.

85. Anyone's will would prefer, if it were possible, that there would be no law and to be entirely free.

86. Anyone's will hates it that the law should be imposed upon it; if, however, the will desires imposition of the law it does so out of love of self.

87. Since the law is good, the will, which is hostile to it, cannot be good.

88. And from this it is clear that everyone's natural will is iniquitous and bad.

89. Grace as a mediator is necessary to reconcile the law with the will.

90. The grace of God is given for the purpose of directing the will, lest it err even in loving God. In opposition to Gabriel.

91. It is not given so that good deeds might be induced more frequently and readily, but because without it no act of love is performed. In opposition to Gabriel.

92. It cannot be denied that love is superfluous if man is by nature able to do an act of friendship. In opposition to Gabriel.

93. There is a kind of subtle evil in the argument that an act is at the same time the fruit and the use of the fruit. In opposition to Ockham, the Cardinal, Gabriel.

94. This holds true also of the saying that the love of God may continue alongside an intense love of the creature.

95. To love God is at the same time to hate oneself and to know nothing but God.

96. We must make our will conform in every respect to the will of God (in opposition to the Cardinal);

97. So that we not only will what God wills, but also ought to will whatever God wills.

In these statements we wanted to say and believe we have said nothing that is not in agreement with the Catholic church and the teachers of the church.

1517

NINETY-FIVE THESES

or

DISPUTATION ON THE POWER AND EFFICACY OF INDULGENCES

1517

Translated by C. M. Jacobs

Revised by Harold J. Grimm

INTRODUCTION

From Luther's day to the present, October 31, 1517 has been considered the birthday of the Reformation. At noon on this Eve of All Saints' Day, Luther nailed on the Castle Church door, which served as a bulletin board for faculty and students of the University of Wittenberg, his *Ninety-five Theses*, as his *Disputation on the Power and Efficacy of Indulgences* has commonly been called. That he intended these theses to serve as a basis for a scholarly discussion with his colleagues at the University of Wittenberg and other learned men can be gathered not only from his own words and those of his colleagues, but also from the fact that they were written in Latin. His act may have been prompted by the circumstance that people were gathering in Wittenberg to adore the remarkable collection of religious relics of Frederick the Wise on All Saints' Day and to receive indulgences for their act of piety.

In the *Ninety-five Theses* Luther applied his evangelical theology to indulgences. He hoped thereby to find an answer to a practical problem which had disturbed him and other sincere Christians for a long time. As a pastor he had noted the bad effects of indulgences upon the members of his own congregation, many of whom were going to nearby Jüterbog and Zerbst in Brandenburg to buy indulgence slips from Johann Tetzel. This practical question raised for him a deeper one, the question of their efficacy. He did not as yet deny the validity of indulgences or the sacrament of penance out of which they had grown. He did not even mention justification by faith in these theses, although the implications of that doctrine are present and were not lost upon his enemies.

The indulgence, or permission to relax or commute the satisfaction or penance of a contrite sinner, was a medieval development connected with the history of the sacrament of penance. Originally the right to grant an indulgence was exercised by the congregation. A penitent sinner who had been excommunicated by the congregation could show sorrow for his sins *(contritio cordis)*, confess them orally *(confessio oris)*, render the penitential acts *(satisfactio operis)* determined by the congregation in accordance with the penitential canons or rules established by the church, and then receive pardon (*absolutio*) and be reinstated in the congregation.

After private penance, administered by the clergy, had gradually been substituted for public penance and had become a part of the sacramental system of the church, the popes began to use it to enhance their power and wealth. The Crusades, beginning at the close of the eleventh century, contributed greatly to this development. Indulgences were granted first only to the crusaders, but later also to those who substituted money for actual participation in the movement.

As the crusading fervor diminished, indulgences came to be granted for visiting shrines at Rome during jubilee years. In the Jubilee of 1300 Pope Boniface VIII granted a plenary indulgence, or complete remission of all temporal punishment remaining after absolution, to every penitent pilgrim in this and all subsequent jubilee years. By the end of the fourteenth century plenary indulgences were granted to all persons who paid the papacy for them.

Another important development which followed the conversion of penance into a sacrament consisted of granting absolution before the penitent had rendered satisfaction. The practical effect of this was that the sinner realized that absolution removed both the guilt and the eternal punishment but did not free him from temporal punishment on earth or in purgatory. To explain this, scholastic theologians drew a distinction between guilt and penalty, and classified sins as venial and mortal. Venial, or insignificant, sins merited only small penalties. A sinner who had committed a mortal sin which had not been absolved, however, would suffer eternal punishment. If it was absolved he was freed of the guilt as well as the eternal penalty in hell, but he still had to render satisfaction, that is, the temporal penalty, here on earth or, if he had not done enough here, in purgatory.

During the thirteenth century scholastic theologians also formulated the doctrine concerning the treasury of merits in order to explain how the pope could relax a penalty which God had demanded. This treasury was a storehouse of merits of Christ and the saints who had done more than God had required of them. The pope as the successor of Peter, to whom Christ had given the power of the keys, could draw upon this treasury when granting indulgences. To make sure that the pope's authority over the sinner did not end with the latter's death, Pope Sixtus IV declared in 1477 that the pope exercised authority over souls in purgatory, but only by way of intercession for them. The ordinary Christian could not readily distinguish between intercession and complete jurisdiction and therefore freely bought indulgences for the dead.

Another important change occurred when theologians discovered a distinction between contrition and attrition. Realizing that true contrition, prompted by one's love of God, was difficult to achieve, they stated that attrition, prompted by such an unworthy motive as fear of punishment, might be substituted for contrition and then transformed into it by absolution in the sacrament of penance. The bad ethical effects of this are obvious, for a man fearing eternal punishment could in one transaction with an indulgence hawker convert his attrition into contrition and his eternal sin into a temporal sin, be freed of his guilt, and buy a plenary indulgence remitting all temporal penalty. Many uneducated people innocently confused temporal and eternal punishment and the guilt and penalties of sin, actually believing that they could buy their salvation, despite the fact that the distinctions were made in the papal bulls promulgating indulgences.

The indulgence with which Luther came into direct contact through his parishioners was the jubilee indulgence announced by Pope Julius II for the year 1510, the proceeds of which were to be used in building the new basilica of St. Peter in Rome. After the death of Julius II in 1513, Leo X revived this indulgence. In March, 1515, he commissioned Albrecht of Hohenzollern, archbishop of Mainz and of Magdeburg and bishop of Halberstadt, to sell the indulgence in his sees and in certain Brandenburg lands. Albrecht, who was heavily indebted to the papacy for the dispensation to hold the three sees and for the pallium, the symbol of his episcopal authority in Mainz, borrowed the money from the banking house of the Fuggers. In return for selling the indulgence the Fuggers and he were to get half of the proceeds while the other half was to go to the papal treasury. Albrecht appointed as subcommissary Johann Tetzel, a Dominican monk who had sold indulgences for the papacy and the Fuggers since 1504.

Although Luther did not know the details concerning the bargaining at Rome among the pope, Archbishop Albrecht, and the Fuggers, he knew the provisions of the papal bull and of Albrecht's instructions to the indulgence salesmen. The purchasers were assured that this indulgence would grant plenary remission of temporal sin and its penalties in purgatory upon absolution by a confessor of the purchaser's own choice. An indulgence slip would be given the purchaser which would compel a priest to grant him absolution or be subject to excommunication by Tetzel. Furthermore, one could obtain plenary remission of all penalties for the dead in purgatory without confession or contrition. The official doctrines of the church were stated by Tetzel and the other indulgence sellers, but their mercenary approach gave the impression that money would remit the guilt and the penalties of the worst crimes and would immediately transfer souls suffering in purgatory to heaven.

Luther had repeatedly warned people of the danger of being misled by indulgences and of the necessity of sincere repentance.° In the *Ninety-five Theses* he organizes all his arguments with reference to Albrecht's instructions and the claims of the indulgence sellers, not in his usual logical arrangement. He begins with the thesis which embodies the core of all the others, namely, that penance is not a mechanical act but a permanent inner attitude. On the same day that he posted the theses, he sent a copy to Archbishop Albrecht with an accompanying letter advising him to stop the sale of indulgences. He hoped that no copies would be circulated among the people at this time, for he did not want to involve his prince, Frederick the Wise, in difficulties, since Frederick had already spoken against the indulgence preached by Tetzel and had forbidden its sale in his lands.

The first printing of the *Ninety-five Theses* was made for Luther by Johann Grünenberg of Wittenberg on a folio sheet for posting on the door of the Castle Church and distribution among his friends and opponents. Only a few reprints made by Hieronymus Hölzel

---

° See Luther's sermons of July 27, 1516, October 31, 1516, and February 24, 1517 in WA 1, 63-65; 94-99; and 138-141, respectively.

in Nürnberg, Jacob Thanner Herbipolensis in Leipzig, and Adam Petri in Basel are extant. The following translation is a revision of C. M. Jacob's translation in *PE* 1, 25-38. It in turn was made from the Latin in *WA* 1, 233-238. There is another English translation in *Reformation Writings of Martin Luther*, Vol. I, translated and edited by Bertram Lee Woolf (New York, 1953), pp. 32-43. *MA*³ 1, 31-38, contains a recent revision of the German translation made by Luther's colleague Justus Jonas. It is included in *St. L.* 18, 72-81.

Indispensable for the study of the Ninety-five Theses and the indulgence controversy are Walther Köhler, *Dokumente zum Ablassstreit von 1517*, 2nd ed. (Leipzig, 1934), and *Luthers 95 Theses samt seinen Resolutionen sowie den Gegenschriften von Wimpina-Tetzel, Eck und Prierias und den Antworten Luthers darauf* (Leipzig, 1903), and Theodor Brieger, *Das Wesen des Ablasses am Ausgange des Mittelalters* (Leipzig, 1897). Hans Volz, in his *Martin Luthers Thesenanschlag und dessen Vorgeschichte* (Weimar, 1959), argued that the posting of the Ninety-five Theses took place November 1, 1517, not October 31, since Luther subsequently referred to All Saints Day as the date. The Catholic historian Erwin Iserloh, in his *Luthers Thesenanschlag—Tatsache oder Legende?* (Wiesbaden, 1962), published in English translation as *The Theses Were Not Posted: Luther between Reform and Reformation* (Boston, 1968), stated that Luther did not post the Theses but only sent them to Archbishop Albert of Mainz and Bishop Jerome Schulz of Brandenburg, the appropriate representatives of the church, for their approval. Iserloh's contention was supported by Klemens Honselmann in his *Urfassung und Drucke der Ablassthesen Martin Luthers und ihre Veröffentlichung* (Paderborn, 1966). Among the scholars who challenged the views of Volz, Iserloh, and Honselmann are Franz Lau, in "Die gegenwärtige Diskussion um Luthers Thesenanschlag," *Luther Jahrbuch*, 34 (1967), Heinrich Bornkamm, in *Thesen und Thesenanschlag Luthers* (Berlin, 1967), and Kurt Aland, whose *Martin Luthers 95 Thesen* (Hamburg, 1965) was published in English translation as *Martin Luther's 95 Theses* (St. Louis and London, 1967).

NINETY-FIVE THESES

or

DISPUTATION ON THE POWER AND EFFICACY OF INDULGENCES

Out of love and zeal for truth and the desire to bring it to light, the following theses will be publicly discussed at Wittenberg under the chairmanship of the reverend father Martin Lutther,[1] Master of Arts and Sacred Theology and regularly appointed Lecturer on these subjects at that place. He requests that those who cannot be present to debate orally with us will do so by letter.[2]

In the Name of Our Lord Jesus Christ. Amen.

1. When our Lord and Master Jesus Christ said, "Repent" [Matt. 4:17],[3] he willed the entire life of believers to be one of repentance.

2. This word cannot be understood as referring to the sacrament of penance, that is, confession and satisfaction, as administered by the clergy.

3. Yet it does not mean solely inner repentance; such inner repentance is worthless unless it produces various outward mortifications of the flesh.

---

[1] Luther spelled his name Lutther in this preamble.
[2] There was actually no debate, for no one responded to the invitation. The contents of the ninety-five theses were soon widely disseminated by word of mouth and by the printers, and in effect a vigorous debate took place that lasted for a number of years.
[3] The Latin form, *poenitentiam agite*, and the German, *tut Busse*, may be rendered in two ways, "repent," and "do penance."

25

4. The penalty of sin[4] remains as long as the hatred of self, that is, true inner repentance, until our entrance into the kingdom of heaven.

5. The pope neither desires nor is able to remit any penalties except those imposed by his own authority or that of the canons.[5]

6. The pope cannot remit any guilt, except by declaring and showing that it has been remitted by God; or, to be sure, by remitting guilt in cases reserved to his judgment. If his right to grant remission in these cases were disregarded, the guilt would certainly remain unforgiven.

7. God remits guilt to no one unless at the same time he humbles him in all things and makes him submissive to his vicar, the priest.

8. The penitential canons are imposed only on the living, and, according to the canons themselves, nothing should be imposed on the dying.

9. Therefore the Holy Spirit through the pope is kind to us insofar as the pope in his decrees always makes exception of the article of death and of necessity.[6]

10. Those priests act ignorantly and wickedly who, in the case of the dying, reserve canonical penalties for purgatory.

11. Those tares of changing the canonical penalty to the penalty of purgatory were evidently sown while the bishops slept [Matt. 13:25].

12. In former times canonical penalties were imposed, not after, but before absolution, as tests of true contrition.

13. The dying are freed by death from all penalties, are already dead as far as the canon laws are concerned, and have a right to be released from them.

14. Imperfect piety or love on the part of the dying person necessarily brings with it great fear; and the smaller the love, the greater the fear.

---

[4] Catholic theology distinguishes between the "guilt" and the "penalty" of sin.

[5] The canons, or decrees of the church, have the force of law. Those referred to here and in Theses 8 and 85 are the so-called penitential canons.

[6] Commenting on this thesis in the *Explanations of the Ninety-five Theses* (p. 114), Luther distinguishes between temporal and eternal necessity. "Necessity knows no law." "Death is the necessity of necessities." Cf. WA 1, 549.

15. This fear or horror is sufficient in itself, to say nothing of other things, to constitute the penalty of purgatory, since it is very near the horror of despair.

16. Hell, purgatory, and heaven seem to differ the same as despair, fear, and assurance of salvation.

17. It seems as though for the souls in purgatory fear should necessarily decrease and love increase.

18. Furthermore, it does not seem proved, either by reason or Scripture, that souls in purgatory are outside the state of merit, that is, unable to grow in love.

19. Nor does it seem proved that souls in purgatory, at least not all of them, are certain and assured of their own salvation, even if we ourselves may be entirely certain of it.

20. Therefore the pope, when he uses the words "plenary remission of all penalties," does not actually mean "all penalties," but only those imposed by himself.

21. Thus those indulgence preachers are in error who say that a man is absolved from every penalty and saved by papal indulgences.

22. As a matter of fact, the pope remits to souls in purgatory no penalty which, according to canon law, they should have paid in this life.

23. If remission of all penalties whatsoever could be granted to anyone at all, certainly it would be granted only to the most perfect, that is, to very few.

24. For this reason most people are necessarily deceived by that indiscriminate and high-sounding promise of release from penalty.

25. That power which the pope has in general over purgatory corresponds to the power which any bishop or curate has in a particular way in his own diocese or parish.

26. The pope does very well when he grants remission to souls in purgatory, not by the power of the keys, which he does not have,[7] but by way of intercession for them.

27. They preach only human doctrines who say that as soon

---

[7] This is not a denial of the power of the keys, that is, the power to forgive and to retain sin, but merely an assertion that the power of the keys does not extend to purgatory.

as the money clinks into the money chest, the soul flies out of purgatory.

28. It is certain that when money clinks in the money chest, greed and avarice can be increased; but when the church intercedes, the result is in the hands of God alone.

29. Who knows whether all souls in purgatory wish to be redeemed, since we have exceptions in St. Severinus and St. Paschal,[8] as related in a legend.

30. No one is sure of the integrity of his own contrition, much less of having received plenary remission.

31. The man who actually buys indulgences is as rare as he who is really penitent; indeed, he is exceedingly rare.

32. Those who believe that they can be certain of their salvation because they have indulgence letters will be eternally damned, together with their teachers.

33. Men must especially be on their guard against those who say that the pope's pardons are that inestimable gift of God by which man is reconciled to him.

34. For the graces of indulgences are concerned only with the penalties of sacramental satisfaction[9] established by man.

35. They who teach that contrition is not necessary on the part of those who intend to buy souls out of purgatory or to buy confessional privileges[10] preach unchristian doctrine.

36. Any truly repentant Christian has a right to full remission of penalty and guilt,[11] even without indulgence letters.

---

[8] Luther refers to this legend again in the *Explanations of the Ninety-five Theses* below, p. 178. The legend is to the effect that these saints, Pope Severinus (638-640) and Pope Paschal I (817-824), preferred to remain longer in purgatory that they might have greater glory in heaven.

[9] Satisfaction is that act on the part of the penitent, in connection with the sacrament of penance, by means of which he pays the temporal penalty for his sins. If at death he is in arrears in paying his temporal penalty for venial sins, he pays this penalty in purgatory. Indulgences are concerned with this satisfaction of the sacrament of penance—they permit a partial or complete (plenary) remission of temporal punishment. According to Roman Catholic theology, the buyer of an indulgence still has to confess his sins, be absolved from them, and be truly penitent.

[10] These are privileges entitling the holder of indulgence letters to choose his own confessor and relieving him, the holder, of certain satisfactions.

[11] To justify the placing of absolution before satisfaction, contrary to the practice of the early church. theologians distinguished between the guilt and the penalty of sins.

37. Any true Christian, whether living or dead, participates in all the blessings of Christ and the church; and this is granted him by God, even without indulgence letters.

38. Nevertheless, papal remission and blessing are by no means to be disregarded, for they are, as I have said [Thesis 6], the proclamation of the divine remission.

39. It is very difficult, even for the most learned theologians, at one and the same time to commend to the people the bounty of indulgences and the need of true contrition.

40. A Christian who is truly contrite seeks and loves to pay penalties for his sins; the bounty of indulgences, however, relaxes penalties and causes men to hate them—at least it furnishes occasion for hating them.

41. Papal indulgences must be preached with caution, lest people erroneously think that they are preferable to other good works of love.

42. Christians are to be taught that the pope does not intend that the buying of indulgences should in any way be compared with works of mercy.

43. Christians are to be taught that he who gives to the poor or lends to the needy does a better deed than he who buys indulgences.

44. Because love grows by works of love, man thereby becomes better. Man does not, however, become better by means of indulgences but is merely freed from penalties.

45. Christians are to be taught that he who sees a needy man and passes him by, yet gives his money for indulgences, does not buy papal indulgences but God's wrath.

46. Christians are to be taught that, unless they have more than they need, they must reserve enough for their family needs and by no means squander it on indulgences.

47. Christians are to be taught that the buying of indulgences is a matter of free choice, not commanded.

48. Christians are to be taught that the pope, in granting indulgences, needs and thus desires their devout prayer more than their money.

49. Christians are to be taught that papal indulgences are use-

ful only if they do not put their trust in them, but very harmful if they lose their fear of God because of them.

50. Christians are to be taught that if the pope knew the exactions of the indulgence preachers, he would rather that the basilica of St. Peter were burned to ashes than built up with the skin, flesh, and bones of his sheep.

51. Christians are to be taught that the pope would and should wish to give of his own money, even though he had to sell the basilica of St. Peter, to many of those from whom certain hawkers of indulgences cajole money.

52. It is vain to trust in salvation by indulgence letters, even though the indulgence commissary, or even the pope, were to offer his soul as security.

53. They are enemies of Christ and the pope who forbid altogether the preaching of the Word of God in some churches in order that indulgences may be preached in others.

54. Injury is done the Word of God when, in the same sermon, an equal or larger amount of time is devoted to indulgences than to the Word.

55. It is certainly the pope's sentiment that if indulgences, which are a very insignificant thing, are celebrated with one bell, one procession, and one ceremony, then the gospel, which is the very greatest thing, should be preached with a hundred bells, a hundred processions, a hundred ceremonies.

56. The treasures of the church,[12] out of which the pope distributes indulgences, are not sufficiently discussed or known among the people of Christ.

57. That indulgences are not temporal treasures is certainly clear, for many [indulgence] preachers do not distribute them freely but only gather them.

58. Nor are they the merits of Christ and the saints, for, even without the pope, the latter always work grace for the inner man, and the cross, death, and hell for the outer man.

59. St. Laurence said that the poor of the church were the

---

[12] The treasury of merits is a reserve fund of good works accumulated by Christ and the saints upon which the pope could draw when he remitted satisfaction in indulgences.

treasures of the church, but he spoke according to the usage of the word in his own time.

60. Without want of consideration we say that the keys of the church,[13] given by the merits of Christ, are that treasure;

61. For it is clear that the pope's power is of itself sufficient for the remission of penalities and cases reserved by himself.

62. The true treasure of the church is the most holy gospel of the glory and grace of God.

63. But this treasure is naturally most odious, for it makes the first to be last [Matt. 20:16].

64. On the other hand, the treasure of indulgences is naturally most acceptable, for it makes the last to be first.

65. Therefore the treasures of the gospel are nets with which one formerly fished for men of wealth.

66. The treasures of indulgences are nets with which one now fishes for the wealth of men.

67. The indulgences which the demagogues acclaim as the greatest graces are actually understood to be such only insofar as they promote gain.

68. They are nevertheless in truth the most insignificant graces when compared with the grace of God and the piety of the cross.

69. Bishops and curates are bound to admit the commissaries of papal indulgences with all reverence.

70. But they are much more bound to strain their eyes and ears lest these men preach their own dreams instead of what the pope has commissioned.

71. Let him who speaks against the truth concerning papal indulgences be anathema and accursed;

72. But let him who guards against the lust and license of the indulgence preachers be blessed;

73. Just as the pope justly thunders against those who by any means whatsoever contrive harm to the sale of indulgences.

74. But much more does he intend to thunder against those

---

[13] The office of the keys: the preaching of the gospel, the celebrating of the sacraments, the remitting of sins to the penitent, and the excommunicating of impenitent sinners.

who use indulgences as a pretext to contrive harm to holy love and truth.

75. To consider papal indulgences so great that they could absolve a man even if he had done the impossible and had violated the mother of God is madness.

76. We say on the contrary that papal indulgences cannot remove the very least of venial sins as far as guilt is concerned.

77. To say that even St. Peter, if he were now pope, could not grant greater graces is blasphemy against St. Peter and the pope.

78. We say on the contrary that even the present pope, or any pope whatsoever, has greater graces at his disposal, that is, the gospel, spiritual powers, gifts of healing, etc., as it is written in I Cor. 12 [:28].

79. To say that the cross emblazoned with the papal coat of arms, and set up by the indulgence preachers, is equal in worth to the cross of Christ is blasphemy.

80. The bishops, curates, and theologians who permit such talk to be spread among the people will have to answer for this.

81. This unbridled preaching of indulgences makes it difficult even for learned men to rescue the reverence which is due the pope from slander or from the shrewd questions of the laity,

82. Such as: "Why does not the pope empty purgatory for the sake of holy love and the dire need of the souls that are there if he redeems an infinite number of souls for the sake of miserable money with which to build a church? The former reasons would be most just; the latter is most trivial."

83. Again, "Why are funeral and anniversary masses for the dead continued and why does he not return or permit the withdrawal of the endowments founded for them, since it is wrong to pray for the redeemed?"

84. Again, "What is this new piety of God and the pope that for a consideration of money they permit a man who is impious and their enemy to buy out of purgatory the pious soul of a friend of God and do not rather, because of the need of that pious and beloved soul, free it for pure love's sake?"

85. Again, "Why are the penitential canons, long since abrogated and dead in actual fact and through disuse, now satisfied by

the granting of indulgences as though they were still alive and in force?"

86. Again, "Why does not the pope, whose wealth is today greater than the wealth of the richest Crassus,[14] build this one basilica of St. Peter with his own money rather than with the money of poor believers?"

87. Again, "What does the pope remit or grant to those who by perfect contrition already have a right to full remission and blessings?"[15]

88. Again, "What greater blessing could come to the church than if the pope were to bestow these remissions and blessings on every believer a hundred times a day, as he now does but once?"[16]

89. "Since the pope seeks the salvation of souls rather than money by his indulgences, why does he suspend the indulgences and pardons previously granted when they have equal efficacy?"[17]

90. To repress these very sharp arguments of the laity by force alone, and not to resolve them by giving reasons, is to expose the church and the pope to the ridicule of their enemies and to make Christians unhappy.

91. If, therefore, indulgences were preached according to the spirit and intention of the pope, all these doubts would be readily resolved. Indeed, they would not exist.

92. Away then with all those prophets who say to the people of Christ, "Peace, peace," and there is no peace! [Jer. 6:14].

93. Blessed be all those prophets who say to the people of Christ, "Cross, cross," and there is no cross!

94. Christians should be exhorted to be diligent in following Christ, their head, through penalties, death, and hell;

95. And thus be confident of entering into heaven through many tribulations rather than through the false security of peace [Acts 14:22].

1517

---

[14] Marcus Licinius Crassus (115-53 B.C.), also called Dives ("the Rich"), was noted for his wealth and luxury by the classical Romans. Crassus means "the Fat."

[15] See Theses 36 and 37.

[16] The indulgence letter entitled its possessor to receive absolution once during his lifetime and once at the approach of death.

[17] During the time when the jubilee indulgences were preached, other indulgences were suspended.

HEIDELBERG
DISPUTATION

1518

Translated by Harold J. Grimm

INTRODUCTION

The disputation to which Luther had invited participants by posting his *Ninety-five Theses* never materialized. Instead, a storm of protest arose and Luther was assailed as a heretic. Leo X, hoping to silence Luther through regular channels, asked Gabriel della Volta, or Venetus, general of the Augustinian Eremites, to do this. Volta in turn transmitted the request to Johann von Staupitz, vicar of the German congregation of the order.

The general chapter of the Augustinians of Germany met as a rule triennally on Jubilate Sunday, that is, the third Sunday after Easter. In 1518 it convened at Heidelberg, April 25. Luther obediently left Wittenberg April 11, against the advice of most of his friends. Provided with letters of introduction by Frederick the Wise, he set out on foot with his fellow Augustinian, Leonhard Beier. At Würzburg the two joined the Erfurt group with whom they rode to Heidelberg, arriving there three or four days before the opening of the meeting.

Staupitz apparently made known Volta's wishes, but there is no record of any official action having been taken by the chapter. We know, however, that Luther agreed to complete and publish his *Resolutions,* or *Explanations of the Ninety-five Theses,* and send it to the pope with a letter of apology. More important for the course of the Reformation, however, was the fact that Staupitz asked Luther and Beier to participate in a disputation at the Augustinian monastery on April 26 to acquaint the brothers with the new evangelical theology. To avoid arousing animosity against Luther, Staupitz asked him not to debate controversial subjects but to prepare theses concerning sin, free will, and grace—topics which had been debated in the *Disputation Against Scholastic Theology.* Although the older theologians were not convinced by Luther, most of the younger men, including Martin Bucer, Johann Brenz, and Theobald Billikan, who later spread the Reformation in Strassburg, Württemberg, and Nördlingen, respectively, were highly receptive and immediately wrote enthusiastic accounts concerning him to their friends. Bucer was particularly impressed by Luther's reliance upon the Bible, his familiarity with the church fathers, his courtesy in answering questions, his willingness to listen to others, and his courage in expressing his views.*

Luther prepared the twenty-eight theological and twelve philosophical theses for the *Heidelberg Disputation* before the debate, as was customary. He also drew up short proofs for the theological theses and a special explanation of the sixth thesis.† Leonhard Beier debated the theses with Luther presiding.

The following English translation is made from the Latin in *WA* 1, 353-374. There are German translations in *St. L.* 18, 36-71, and *MA*³ 1, 125-138. For accounts in English of the Augustinian chapter meeting, see E.G. Schwiebert, *Luther and His Times,* pp. 326-330, and H. Boehmer, *Road to Reformation,* pp. 206-210. For an analysis of the disputation, see C. Stange, "Die ältesten ethischen Disputationen Luthers," *Quellenschriften zur Geschichte des Protestantismus* (Leipzig, 1904), I, 50.

---

* See the letter of Martin Bucer to Beatus Rhenanus, written May 1, 1518, *Luther's Correspondence and Other Contemporary Letters,* translated and edited by Preserved Smith, I, 83.

† Cf. p. 58, n. 15. Vogelsang, in *CL* 5, 376, maintains that this was an exposition which probably is to be regarded as a preliminary draft for the entire disputation.

HEIDELBERG
DISPUTATION

Brother Martin Luther, Master of Sacred Theology, will preside, and Brother Leonhard Beier, Master of Arts and Philosophy, will defend the following theses before the Augustinians of this renowned city of Heidelberg in the customary place. In the month of May, 1518.[1]

THEOLOGICAL THESES

Distrusting completely our own wisdom, according to that counsel of the Holy Spirit, "Do not rely on your own insight" [Prov. 3:5], we humbly present to the judgment of all those who wish to be here these theological paradoxes, so that it may become clear whether they have been deduced well or poorly from St. Paul, the especially chosen vessel and instrument of Christ, and also from St. Augustine, his most trustworthy interpreter.

1. The law of God, the most salutary doctrine of life, cannot advance man on his way to righteousness, but rather hinders him.

2. Much less can human works, which are done over and over again with the aid of natural precepts, so to speak, lead to that end.

3. Although the works of man always seem attractive and good, they are nevertheless likely to be mortal sins.

4. Although the works of God always seem unattractive and appear evil, they are nevertheless really eternal merits.

5. The works of men are thus not mortal sins (we speak of works which are apparently good), as though they were crimes.

6. The works of God (we speak of those which he does through man) are thus not merits, as though they were sinless.

---

[1] This is an approximate date. The disputation actually took place April 26, 1518.

7. The works of the righteous would be mortal sins if they would not be feared as mortal sins by the righteous themselves out of pious fear of God.

8. By so much more are the works of man mortal sins when they are done without fear and in unadulterated, evil self-security.

9. To say that works without Christ are dead, but not mortal, appears to constitute a perilous surrender of the fear of God.

10. Indeed, it is very difficult to see how a work can be dead and at the same time not a harmful and mortal sin.

11. Arrogance cannot be avoided or true hope be present unless the judgment of condemnation is feared in every work.

12. In the sight of God sins are then truly venial when they are feared by men to be mortal.

13. Free will, after the fall, exists in name only, and as long as it does what it is able to do, it commits a mortal sin.

14. Free will, after the fall, has power to do good only in a passive capacity, but it can always do evil in an active capacity.

15. Nor could free will endure in a state of innocence, much less do good, in an active capacity, but only in its passive capacity.

16. The person who believes that he can obtain grace by doing what is in him[2] adds sin to sin so that he becomes doubly guilty.

17. Nor does speaking in this manner give cause for despair, but for arousing the desire to humble oneself and seek the grace of Christ.

18. It is certain that man must utterly despair of his own ability before he is prepared to receive the grace of Christ.

19. That person does not deserve to be called a theologian who looks upon the invisible things of God as though they were clearly perceptible in those things which have actually happened [Rom. 1:20].

20. He deserves to be called a theologian, however, who comprehends the visible and manifest things of God seen through suffering and the cross.

21. A theologian of glory calls evil good and good evil. A theologian of the cross calls the thing what it actually is.

22. That wisdom which sees the invisible things of God in

---

[2] Cf. p. 10, n. 5.

40

works as perceived by man is completely puffed up, blinded, and hardened.

23. The law brings the wrath of God, kills, reviles, accuses, judges, and condemns everything that is not in Christ [Rom. 4:15].

24. Yet that wisdom is not of itself evil, nor is the law to be evaded; but without the theology of the cross man misuses the best in the worst manner.

25. He is not righteous who does much, but he who, without work, believes much in Christ.

26. The law says, "do this," and it is never done. Grace says, "believe in this," and everything is already done.

27. Actually one should call the work of Christ an acting work and our work an accomplished work, and thus an accomplished work pleasing to God by the grace of the acting work.

28. The love of God does not find, but creates, that which is pleasing to it. The love of man comes into being through that which is pleasing to it.

PHILOSOPHICAL THESES

29. He who wishes to philosophize by using Aristotle without danger to his soul must first become thoroughly foolish in Christ.

30. Just as a person does not use the evil of passion well unless he is a married man, so no person philosophizes well unless he is a fool, that is, a Christian.

31. It was easy for Aristotle to believe that the world was eternal since he believed that the human soul was mortal.

32. After the proposition that there are as many material forms as there are created things had been accepted, it was necessary to accept that they all are material.

33. Nothing in the world becomes something of necessity; nevertheless, that which comes forth from matter, again by necessity, comes into being according to nature.

34. If Aristotle would have recognized the absolute power of God, he would accordingly have maintained that it was impossible for matter to exist of itself alone.

35. According to Aristotle, nothing is infinite with respect to ac-

tion, yet with respect to power and matter, as many things as have been created are infinite.

36. Aristotle wrongly finds fault with and derides the ideas of Plato, which actually are better than his own.

37. The mathematical order of material things is ingeniously maintained by Pythagoras, but more ingenious is the interaction of ideas maintained by Plato.

38. The disputation of Aristotle lashes out at Parmenides' idea of oneness[3] (if a Christian will pardon this) in a battle of air.

39. If Anaxagoras posited infinity as to form, as it seems he did, he was the best of the philosophers, even if Aristotle was unwilling to acknowledge this.

40. To Aristotle, privation, matter, form, movable, immovable, impulse, power, etc. seem to be the same.

PROOFS OF THE THESIS DEBATED IN THE CHAPTER AT HEIDELBERG, MAY, 1518, A.D.

1

The law of God, the most salutary doctrine of life, cannot advance man on his way to righteousness, but rather hinders him.

This is made clear by the Apostle in his letter to the Romans (3 [: 21]): "But now the righteousness of God has been manifested apart from the law." St. Augustine interprets this in his book, *The Spirit and the Letter (De Spiritu et Littera)*: "Without the law, that is, without its support." [4] In Rom. 5 [:20] the Apostle states, "Law intervened, to increase the trespass," and in Rom. 7 [:9] he adds, "But when the commandment came, sin revived." For this reason he calls the law a law of death and a law of sin in Rom. 8 [:2]. Indeed, in II Cor. 3 [:6] he says, "the written code kills,"

---

[3] Parmenides was a well-known Greek philosopher who, with Zeno, headed the Eleatic school and taught a monistic cosmology.

[4] In *Basic Writings of St. Augustine*, trans. P. Holmes, ed. Whitney J. Oates (2 vols.; New York, 1948) I, 461-518. Cf. Migne 44, 199-246.

which St. Augustine throughout his book, *The Spirit and the Letter,* understands as applying to every law, even the holiest law of God.

2

Much less can human works which are done over and over again with the aid of natural precepts, so to speak, lead to that end.

Since the law of God, which is holy and unstained, true, just, etc., is given man by God as an aid beyond his natural powers to enlighten him and move him to do the good, and nevertheless the opposite takes place, namely, that he becomes more wicked, how can he, left to his own power and without such aid, be induced to do good? If a person does not do good with help from without, he will do even less by his own strength. Therefore the Apostle, in Rom. 3 [:10-12], calls all persons corrupt and impotent who neither understand nor seek God, for all, he says, have gone astray.

3

Although the works of man always seem attractive and good, they are nevertheless likely to be mortal sins.

Human works appear attractive outwardly, but within they are filthy, as Christ says concerning the Pharisees in Matt. 23 [:27]. For they appear to the doer and others good and beautiful, yet God does not judge according to appearances but searches "the minds and hearts" [Ps. 7:9]. For without grace and faith it is impossible to have a pure heart. Acts 15 [:9]: "He cleansed their hearts by faith."

The thesis is proven in the following way: If the works of righteous men are sins, as Thesis 7 of this disputation states, this is much more the case concerning the works of those who are not righteous. But the just speak in behalf of their works in the following way: "Do not enter into judgment with thy servant, Lord, for no man living is righteous before thee" [Ps. 143:2]. The Apostle speaks likewise in Gal. 3 [:10], "All who rely on the works of the law are under the curse." But the works of men are the works of the law, and the curse will not be placed upon venial sins. Therefore they are mortal sins.

In the third place, Rom. 2. [:21] states, "You who teach others not to steal, do you steal?" St. Augustine interprets this to mean that men are thieves according to their guilty consciences even if they publicly judge or reprimand other thieves.

4

Although the works of God always seem unattractive and appear evil, they are nevertheless really eternal merits.

That the works of God are unattractive is clear from what is said in Isa. 53 [:2], "He had no form of comeliness," and in I Sam. 2 [:6], "The Lord kills and brings to life; he brings down to Sheol and raises up." This is understood to mean that the Lord humbles and frightens us by means of the law and the sight of our sins so that we seem in the eyes of men, as in our own, as nothing, foolish, and wicked, for we are in truth that. Insofar as we acknowledge and confess this, these is no form or beauty in us, but our life is hidden in God (i.e. in the bare confidence in his mercy), finding in ourselves nothing but sin, foolishness, death, and hell, according to that verse of the Apostle in II Cor. 6 [:9-10], "As sorrowful, yet always rejoicing; as dying, and behold we live." And that it is which Isa. 28 [:21] calls the alien work of God that he may do his work (that is, he humbles us thoroughly, making us despair, so that he may exalt us in his mercy, giving us hope), just as Hab. 3 [:2] states, "In wrath remember mercy." Such a man therefore is displeased with all his works; he sees no beauty, but only his ugliness. Indeed, he also does those things which appear foolish and disgusting to others.

This ugliness, however, comes into being in us either when God punishes us or when we accuse ourselves, as I Cor. 11 [:31] says, "If we judged ourselves truly, we should not be judged" by the Lord. Deut. 32 [:36] also states, "The Lord will vindicate his people and have compassion on his servants." In this way, consequently, the unattractive works which God does in us, that is, those which are humble and devout, are really eternal, for humility and fear of God are our entire merit.

44

5

The works of men are thus not mortal sins (we speak of works which are apparently good), as though they were crimes.

For crimes are such acts which can also be condemned before men, such as adultery, theft, homicide, slander, etc. Mortal sins, on the other hand, are those which seem good yet are essentially fruits of a bad root and a bad tree. Augustine states this in the fourth book of *Against Julian (Contra Julianum).*[5]

6

The works of God (we speak of those which he does through man) are thus not merits, as though they were sinless.

In Eccles. 7 [:20], we read, "Surely there is not a righteous man on earth who does good and never sins." In this connection, however, some people[6] say that the righteous man indeed sins, but not when he does good. They may be refuted in the following manner: "If that is what this verse wants to say, why waste so many words?" or does the Holy Spirit like to indulge in loquacious and foolish babble? For this meaning would then be adequately expressed by the following: "There is not a righteous man on earth who does not sin." Why does he add "who does good," as if another person were righteous who did evil? For no one except a righteous man does good. Where, however, he speaks of sins outside the realm of good works he speaks thus [Prov. 24:16], "The righteous man falls seven times a day." Here he does not say, "A righteous man falls seven times a day when he does good." This is a comparison. If someone cuts with a rusty and rough hatchet, even though the worker is a good craftsman, the hatchet leaves bad, jagged, and ugly gashes. So it is when God works through us.

7

The works of the righteous would be mortal sins if they

---

[5] Migne 44, 641-880.
[6] By "some people" Luther means St. Jerome above all.

*would not be feared as mortal sins by the righteous them-
selves out of pious fear of God.*

This is clear from Thesis 4. To trust in works, which one ought to
do in fear, is equivalent to giving oneself the honor and taking it
from God, to whom fear is due in connection with every work. But
this is completely wrong, namely to please oneself, to enjoy oneself
in one's works, and to adore oneself as an idol. He who is self-confident and without fear of God, however, acts entirely in this
manner. For if he had fear he would not be self-confident, and for
this reason he would not be pleased with himself, but he would be
pleased with God.

In the second place, it is clear from the words of the Psalmist
[Ps. 143:2], "Enter not into judgment with thy servant," and Ps. 32
[:5], "I said, 'I will confess my transgressions to the Lord,'" etc.
But that these are not venial sins is clear because these passages
state that confession and repentance are not necessary for venial
sins. If, therefore, they are mortal sins and all the saints intercede
for them, as it is stated in the same place, then the works of the
saints are mortal sins. But the works of the saints are good works,
wherefore they are meritorious for them only through the fear of
their humble confession.

In the third place, it is clear from the Lord's Prayer, "Forgive
us our trespasses" [Matt. 6:12]. This is a prayer of the saints, therefore those trespasses are good works for which they pray. But that
these are mortal sins is clear from the following verse, "If you do
not forgive men their trespasses, neither will your father forgive
your trespasses" [Matt. 6:15]. Note that these trespasses are such
that, if unforgiven, they would condemn them, unless they pray this
prayer sincerely and forgive others.

In the fourth place, it is clear from Rev. 21 [:27], "Nothing unclean shall enter into it" [the kingdom of heaven]. But everything
that hinders entrance into the kingdom of heaven is mortal sin (or
it would be necessary to interpret the concept of mortal sin in another way). Venial sin, however, hinders because it makes the soul
unclean and has no place in the kingdom of heaven. Consequently,
etc.

8

By so much more are the works of man mortal sins when they are done without fear and in unadulterated, evil self-security.

The inevitable deduction from the preceding thesis is clear. For where there is no fear there is no humility. Where there is no humility there is pride, and where there is pride there are the wrath and judgment of God, for God opposes the haughty. Indeed, if pride would cease there would be no sin anywhere.

9

To say that works without Christ are dead, but not mortal, appears to constitute a perilous surrender of the fear of God.

For in this way men become certain and therefore haughty, which is perilous. For in such a way God is constantly deprived of the glory which is due him and which is transferred to other things, since one should strive with all diligence to give him the glory— the sooner the better. For this reason the Bible advises us, "Do not delay being converted to the Lord."[7] For if that person offends him who withdraws glory from him, how much more does that person offend him who continues to withdraw glory from him and does this boldly! But whoever is not in Christ or who withdraws from him withdraws glory from him, as is well known.

10

Indeed, it is very difficult to see how a work can be dead and at the same time not a harmful and mortal sin.

This I prove in the following way: Scripture does not speak of dead things in such a manner, stating that something is not mortal which is nevertheless dead. Indeed, neither does grammar, which says that "dead" is a stronger term than "mortal." For the gram-

---

[7] This quotation is from Sirach 5:8. The Vulgate Bible contained the apocryphal books.

marians call a mortal work one which kills, a dead work not one that has been killed, but one that is not alive. But God despises what is not alive, as is written in Prov. 15 [:8], "The sacrifice of the wicked is an abomination to the Lord."

Second, the will must do something with respect to such a dead work, namely, either love or hate it. The will cannot hate a dead work since the will is evil. Consequently the will loves a dead work, and therefore it loves something dead. In that act itself it thus induces an evil work of the will against God whom it should love and honor in this and in every deed.

11

Arrogance cannot be avoided or true hope be present unless the judgment of condemnation is feared in every work.

This is clear from Thesis 4. For it is impossible to hope in God unless one has despaired in all creatures and knows that nothing can profit one without God. Since there is no person who has this pure hope, as we said above, and since we still place some confidence in the creature, it is clear that we must, because of impurity in all things, fear the judgment of God. Thus arrogance must be avoided, not only in the work, but in the inclination also, that is, it must displease us still to have confidence in the creature.

12

In the sight of God sins are then truly venial when they are feared by men to be mortal.

This becomes sufficiently clear from what has been said. For as much as we accuse ourselves, so much God pardons us, according to the verse, "Confess your misdeed so that you will be justified" [Cf. Isa. 43:26], and according to another [Ps. 141:4], "Incline not my heart to any evil, to busy myself with wicked deeds."

13

Free will, after the fall, exists in name only, and as long as it does what it is able to do, it commits a mortal sin.

The first part is clear, for the will is captive and subject to sin.

Not that it is nothing, but that it is not free except to do evil. According to John 8 [:34, 36], "Every one who commits sin is a slave to sin. . . . So if the Son makes you free, you will be free indeed." Hence St. Augustine says in his book, *The Spirit and the Letter*, "Free will without grace has the power to do nothing but sin";[8] and in the second book of *Against Julian*, "You call the will free, but in fact it is an enslaved will,"[9] and in many other places.

The second part is clear from what has been said above and from the verse in Hos. 13 [:9], "Israel, you are bringing misfortune upon yourself, for your salvation is alone with me," [10] and from similar passages.

14

Free will, after the fall, has power to do good only in a passive capacity,[11] *but it can always do evil in an active capacity.*

An illustration will make the meaning of this thesis clear. Just as a dead man can do something toward life only in a passive capacity, so can he do something toward death in an active manner while he lives. Free will, however, is dead, as demonstrated by the dead whom the Lord has raised up, as the holy teachers of the church say. St. Augustine, moreover, proves this same thesis in his various writings against the Pelagians.

15

Nor could free will endure in a state of innocence, much less do good, in an active capacity, but only in its passive capacity.

The Master of the *Sentences*,[12] quoting Augustine, states, "By these

---

[8] Chap. 3, par. 5, Migne 44, 203.

[9] Chap. 8, par. 23, Migne 44, 689.

[10] This is a free rendering of the passage, "I will destroy you, O Israel; who can help you?"

[11] This is Luther's way of stating that the free will could before the fall determine to do good. That it could do so after the fall would seem likely because of its name, but not in actual fact.

[12] Peter Lombard. Migne 192, 519-964. The chapter to which Luther refers is in col. 586.

testimonies it is obviously demonstrated that man received a right-eous nature and a good will when he was created, and also the help by means of which he could prevail. Otherwise it would appear as though he had not fallen because of his own fault." He speaks of the active capacity, which is obviously contrary to Augus-tine's opinion in his book, *Concerning Reprimand and Grace* (*De Correptione et Gratia*), where the latter puts it in this way: "He re-ceived the ability to act, if he so willed, but he did not have the will by means of which he could act."[13] By "ability to act" he understands the passive capacity, and by "will by means of which he could," the active capacity.

The second part, however, is sufficiently clarified by the Master in the same distinction.

16

The person who believes that he can obtain grace by doing what is in him adds sin to sin so that he becomes doubly guilty.

On the basis of what has been said, the following is clear: While a person is doing what is in him, he sins and seeks himself in every-thing. But if he should suppose that through sin he would become worthy of or prepared for grace, he would add haughty arrogance to his sin and not believe that sin is sin and evil is evil, which is an exceedingly great sin. As Jer. 2 [:13] says, "For my people have committed two evils: they have forsaken me, the fountain of living waters, and hewed out cisterns for themselves, broken cis-terns, that can hold no water," that is, through sin they are far from me and yet they presume to do good by their own ability.

Now you ask, "What then shall we do? Shall we go our way with indifference because we can do nothing but sin?" I would reply, By no means. But, having heard this, fall down and pray for grace and place your hope in Christ in whom is our salvation, life, and resurrection. For this reason we are so instructed—for this reason the law makes us aware of sin so that, having recognized our sin, we may seek and receive grace. Thus God "gives grace to the

---

[13] Migne 44, 915-946.

humble" [I Pet. 5:5], and "whoever humbles himself will be exalted" [Matt. 23:12]. The law humbles, grace exalts. The law effects fear and wrath, grace effects hope and mercy. "Through the law comes knowledge of sin" [Rom. 3:20], through knowledge of sin, however, comes humility, and through humility grace is acquired. Thus an action which is alien to God's nature results in a deed belonging to his very nature: he makes a person a sinner so that he may make him righteous.

17

Nor does speaking in this manner give cause for despair, but for arousing the desire to humble oneself and seek the grace of Christ.

This is clear from what has been said, for, according to the gospel, the kingdom of heaven is given to children and the humble [Mark 10:14, 16], and Christ loves them. They cannot be humble who do not recognize that they are damnable whose sin smells to high heaven. Sin is recognized only through the law. It is apparent that not despair, but rather hope, is preached when we are told that we are sinners. Such preaching concerning sin is a preparation for grace, or it is rather the recognition of sin and faith in such preaching. Yearning for grace wells up when recognition of sin has arisen. A sick person seeks the physician when he recognizes the seriousness of his illness. Therefore one does not give cause for despair or death by telling a sick person about the danger of his illness, but, in effect, one urges him to seek a medical cure. To say that we are nothing and constantly sin when we do the best we can does not mean that we cause people to despair (unless they are fools); rather, we make them concerned about the grace of our Lord Jesus Christ.

18

It is certain that man must utterly despair of his own ability before he is prepared to receive the grace of Christ.

The law wills that man despair of his own ability, for it leads him into hell and makes him a poor man and shows him that he is a sinner in all his works, as the Apostle does in Rom. 2 and 3 [:9], where he says, "I have already charged that all men are under the power of sin." However, he who acts simply in accordance with his ability and believes that he is thereby doing something good does not seem worthless to himself, nor does he despair of his own strength. Indeed, he is so presumptuous that he strives for grace in reliance on his own strength.

19

That person does not deserve to be called a theologian who looks upon the invisible things of God as though they were clearly perceptible in those things which have actually happened [Rom. 1:20].

This is apparent in the example of those who were "theologians" and still were called fools by the Apostle in Rom. 1 [:22]. Furthermore, the invisible things of God are virtue, godliness, wisdom, justice, goodness, and so forth. The recognition of all these things does not make one worthy or wise.

20

He deserves to be called a theologian, however, who comprehends the visible and manifest things of God seen through suffering and the cross.

The "back" and visible things of God are placed in opposition to the invisible, namely, his human nature, weakness, foolishness. The Apostle in I Cor. 1 [:25] calls them the weakness and folly of God. Because men misused the knowledge of God through works, God wished again to be recognized in suffering, and to condemn wisdom concerning invisible things by means of wisdom concerning visible things, so that those who did not honor God as manifested in his works should honor him as he is hidden in his suffering. As the Apostle says in I Cor. 1 [:21], "For since, in the wisdom of God, the world did not know God through wisdom, it pleased God through the folly of what we preach to save those who believe." Now it is not sufficient for anyone, and it does him no good to recognize God in his glory and majesty, unless he recognizes

52

him in the humility and shame of the cross. Thus God destroys the wisdom of the wise, as Isa. [45:15] says, "Truly, thou art a God who hidest thyself."

So, also, in John 14 [:8], where Philip spoke according to the theology of glory: "Show us the Father." Christ forthwith set aside his flighty thought about seeking God elsewhere and led him to himself, saying, "Philip, he who has seen me has seen the Father" [John 14:9]. For this reason true theology and recognition of God are in the crucified Christ, as it is also stated in John 10 [John 14:6]: "No one comes to the Father, but by me." "I am the door" [John 10:9], and so forth.

21

A theologian of glory calls evil good and good evil. A theologian of the cross calls the thing what it actually is.

This is clear: He who does not know Christ does not know God hidden in suffering. Therefore he prefers works to suffering, glory to the cross, strength to weakness, wisdom to folly, and, in general, good to evil. These are the people whom the apostle calls "enemies of the cross of Christ" [Phil. 3:18], for they hate the cross and suffering and love works and the glory of works. Thus they call the good of the cross evil and the evil of a deed good. God can be found only in suffering and the cross, as has already been said. Therefore the friends of the cross say that the cross is good and works are evil, for through the cross works are destroyed and the old Adam, who is especially edified by works, is crucified. It is impossible for a person not to be puffed up by his good works unless he has first been deflated and destroyed by suffering and evil until he knows that he is worthless and that his works are not his but God's.

22

That wisdom which sees the invisible things of God in works as perceived by man is completely puffed up, blinded, and hardened.

This has already been said. Because men do not know the cross and hate it, they necessarily love the opposite, namely, wisdom, glory, power, and so on. Therefore they become increasingly blinded and hardened by such love, for desire cannot be satisfied by the acquisition of those things which it desires. Just as the love of money grows in proportion to the increase of the money itself, so the dropsy of the soul becomes thirstier the more it drinks, as the poet says: "The more water they drink, the more they thirst for it." The same thought is expressed in Eccles. 1 [:8]: "The eye is not satisfied with seeing, nor the ear filled with hearing." This holds true of all desires.

Thus also the desire for knowledge is not satisfied by the acquisition of wisdom but is stimulated that much more. Likewise the desire for glory is not satisfied by the acquisition of glory, nor is the desire to rule satisfied by power and authority, nor is the desire for praise satisfied by praise, and so on, as Christ shows in John 4 [:13], where he says, "Every one who drinks of this water will thirst again."

The remedy for curing desire does not lie in satisfying it, but in extinguishing it. In other words, he who wishes to become wise does not seek wisdom by progressing toward it but becomes a fool by retrogressing into seeking folly. Likewise he who wishes to have much power, honor, pleasure, satisfaction in all things must flee rather than seek power, honor, pleasure, and satisfaction in all things. This is the wisdom which is folly to the world.

23

The law brings the wrath of God, kills, reviles, accuses, judges, and condemns everything that is not in Christ [Rom. 4:15].

Thus Gal. 3 [:13] states, "Christ redeemed us from the curse of the law"; and: "For all who rely on works of the law are under the curse" [Gal. 3:10]; and Rom. 4 [15]: "For the law brings wrath"; and Rom. 7 [:10]: "The very commandment which promised life proved to be the death of me"; Rom. 2 [:12]: "All who have sinned without the law will also perish without law." Therefore he who boasts that he is wise and learned in the law boasts in his confusion, his damnation, the wrath of God, in death. As Rom. 2 [:23] puts it: "You who boast in the law."[14]

24

Yet that wisdom is not of itself evil, nor is the law to be evaded; but without the theology of the cross man misuses the best in the worst manner.

Indeed the law is holy [Rom. 7:12], every gift of God good [I Tim. 4:4], and everything that is created exceedingly good, as in Gen. 1 [:31]. But, as stated above, he who has not been brought low, reduced to nothing through the cross and suffering, takes credit for works and wisdom and does not give credit to God. He thus misuses and defiles the gifts of God.

He, however, who has been emptied [Cf. Phil. 2:7] through suffering no longer does works but knows that God works and does all things in him. For this reason, whether man does works or not, it is all the same to him. He neither boasts if he does good works, nor is he disturbed if God does not do good works through him. He knows that it is sufficient if he suffers and is brought low by the cross in order to be annihilated all the more. It is this that Christ says in John 3 [:7], "You must be born anew." To be born anew, one must consequently first die and then be raised up with the Son of Man. To die, I say, means to feel death at hand.

25

He is not righteous who does much, but he who, without work, believes much in Christ.

For the righteousness of God is not acquired by means of acts frequently repeated, as Aristotle taught, but it is imparted by faith, for "He who through faith is righteous shall live" (Rom. 1 [:17]), and "Man believes with his heart and so is justified" (Rom. 10 [:10]). Therefore I wish to have the words "without work" understood in the following manner: Not that the righteous person

---

[14] The editor has followed the text in CL 5, 390 rather than WA 1, 363.

does nothing, but that his works do not make him righteous, rather that his righteousness creates works. For grace and faith are infused without our works. After they have been imparted the works follow. Thus Rom. 3 [:20] states, "No human being will be justified in His sight by works of the law," and, "For we hold that man is justified by faith apart from works of law" (Rom. 3 [:28]). In other words, works contribute nothing to justification. Therefore man knows that works which he does by such faith are not his but God's. For this reason he does not seek to become justified or glorified through them, but seeks God. His justification by faith in Christ is sufficient to him. Christ is his wisdom, righteousness, etc., as I Cor. 1 [:30] has it, that he himself may be Christ's action and instrument.

26

The law says, "do this," and it is never done. Grace says, "believe in this," and everything is already done.

The first part is clear from what has been stated by the Apostle and his interpreter, St. Augustine, in many places. And it has been stated often enough above that the law works wrath and keeps all men under the curse. The second part is clear from the same sources, for faith justifies. "And the law (says St. Augustine) commands what faith obtains." For through faith Christ is in us, indeed, one with us. Christ is just and has fulfilled all the commands of God, wherefore we also fulfil everything through him since he was made ours through faith.

27

Actually one should call the work of Christ an acting work and our work an accomplished work, and thus an accomplished work pleasing to God by the grace of the acting work.

Since Christ lives in us through faith so he arouses us to do good works through that living faith in his work, for the works which he does are the fulfilment of the commands of God given us through faith. If we look at them we are moved to imitate them. For this reason the Apostle says, "Therefore be imitators of God, as beloved children" [Eph. 5:1]. Thus deeds of mercy are aroused by the works through which he has saved us, as St. Gregory says: "Every act of Christ is instruction for us, indeed, a stimulant." If his action is in us it lives through faith, for it is exceedingly attractive according to the verse, "Draw me after you, let us make haste" [Song of Sol. 1:4] toward the fragrance "of your anointing oils" [Song of Sol. 1:3], that is, "your works."

28

The love of God does not find, but creates, that which is pleasing to it. The love of man comes into being through that which is pleasing to it.

The second part is clear and is accepted by all philosophers and theologians, for the object of love is its cause, assuming, according to Aristotle, that all power of the soul is passive and material and active only in receiving something. Thus it is also demonstrated that Aristotle's philosophy is contrary to theology since in all things it seeks those things which are its own and receives rather than gives something good. The first part is clear because the love of God which lives in man loves sinners, evil persons, fools, and weaklings in order to make them righteous, good, wise, and strong. Rather than seeking its own good, the love of God flows forth and bestows good. Therefore sinners are attractive because they are loved; they are not loved because they are attractive. For this reason the love of man avoids sinners and evil persons. Thus Christ says: "For I came not to call the righteous, but sinners" [Matt. 9:13]. This is the love of the cross, born of the cross, which turns in the direction where it does not find good which it may enjoy, but where it may confer good upon the bad and needy person. "It is more blessed to give than to receive" [Acts 20:35], says the Apostle. Hence Ps. 41 [:1] states, "Blessed is he who considers the poor," for the intellect cannot by nature comprehend an object which does not exist, that is the poor and needy person, but only a thing which does exist, that is the true and good. Therefore it judges according to appearances, is a respecter of persons, and judges according to that which can be seen, etc.

THE END

EXPLANATION TO THESIS 6[15]

Is the will of man outside the state of grace free or rather in bondage and captive?

THESIS (PART 1)

Outside of grace, the will of man is not free with reference to actions which are either contrary or contradictory to each other; the will is necessarily in bondage and captive even if it is free of all compulsion.

As proof of this thesis it must be noted, in the first place, that contrary actions of the will are willing and being unwilling [*velle et nolle*], either of which is positive in its position, whereas contradictory actions are willing and not willing [*velle et non velle*], also being unwilling and not unwilling [*nolle et non nolle*]; that is, at one time it wills, at another, however, it neither wills nor does not will, but remains indecisive and without action. It must be noted, in the second place, that we speak of the freedom of the will with respect to merit and lack of merit. With respect to other things inferior to these, I do not deny that the will is free, or indeed considers itself free, with respect to contrary as well as contradictory actions.

With these presuppositions as a basis, I shall now prove the first part of the thesis that the will is without a doubt not free in contradictory actions. Because if it is free not to choose what it wills, it follows that it would also be free to be on its guard against every future sin. But that is false, indeed heretical and contrary to the statement of St. Gregory: "Sin which is not washed away by repentance soon leads to another by its own weight." But if the will is free, it can prevent itself from being led to another sin. To put it an-

---

[15] The exact thesis to which this refers cannot be established with certainty. The "Explanation" apparently stems from the year 1518 and further clarifies Luther's view concerning freedom of the will.

other way, if the will cannot avoid the attraction, it is not free. I can prove this also by using the common saying that the will outside grace cannot long endure without mortal sin, therefore also not without losing its freedom. Finally, I can prove this through the statement of the Apostle in II Tim. 2 [:25, 26]: "God may perhaps grant that . . . they may escape from the snare of the devil, after being captured by him to do his will." But it is the will of the devil that they will and do evil.

THESIS (PART 2)

That the will is not free in contrary actions I will prove by the word of the Lord in Gen. 8 [:21]: "The imagination and thought of man's heart are inclined to evil at all times." But if it is at all times inclined to evil, then it is never inclined to good, the contrary of evil. That this, however, takes place freely and at the same time necessarily, I shall prove in the following manner: The natural will possesses its willing or being unwilling no less than every natural thing possesses its own inherent function, and it is no more deprived of its function than any other thing. But it is impossible that willing is constrained and not free. Consequently it is of necessity free and of necessity wills with freedom. Therefore either of the following is true:

Falling man is not able to fall by means of his own power.
Falling man is unable not to fall by means of another's power.

Thus the will outside grace or in falling is unable not to fall and not to will evil by its own power. It is able, by the grace of God, not to fall or to stop falling. With that I shall lay aside the thesis as having been proven within brief compass.

I deduce the following corollary: Since there is no righteous person on earth who in doing good does not sin, the unrighteous person sins that much more when he does good.

This is proven by the following authorities: First through the verse in Isa. 64 [:6]: "We have all become like one who is unclean, and all our righteous deeds are like a polluted garment." If righteous deeds are unclean, how will the unrighteous be? And Eccles. 7 [:20]: "Surely there is not a righteous man on earth who does good and never sins"; and· Jas. 3 [:2]: "For we all make many mistakes"; and Rom. 7 [:22-23]: "For I delight in the law of God, in my inmost self, but I see in my members another law at war with the law of my mind and making me captive to the law of sin [which dwells in my members]"; and Ps. 21 [Ps. 32:2]: "Blessed is the man to whom the Lord imputes no iniquity."

COROLLARY

That the righteous man also sins while doing good is clear from the following: First, from the verse Eccles. 7 [:20]: "Surely there is not a righteous man on earth who does good and never sins." In this connection, however, some people say that the righteous man indeed sins, but not when he does good. They may be refuted in the following manner: If that is what this verse wants to say, why waste so many words? Or does the Holy Spirit like to indulge in loquacious and foolish babble? For this meaning would then be adequately expressed by the following: "There is not a righteous man on earth who does not sin." Why does he add "who does good," as if another person were righteous who did evil? For no one except a righteous person does good. Where, however, he speaks of sins outside the realm of good works, he speaks thus [Prov. 24:16], "The righteous man falls seven times a day." He does not say, "The righteous man falls seven times a day when he does good." This is a comparison. If someone cuts with a rusty and rough hatchet, even though the worker is a good craftsman, the hatchet leaves bad, jagged, and ugly gashes. So it is when God works through us, etc.

Secondly, from the verse of the Apostle in Rom. 7 [:19]: "For I do not do the good I want, but the evil I do not want is what I do," and below: "I delight in the law of God, in my inmost self; but I see in my members another law at war with the law of my mind" [Rom. 7:22-23]. See how he delights in and at the same time is displeased with the law of God; at one and the same time he wishes good according to the spirit and yet does not do it, but does the contrary. Consequently this contrary is a certain "not-willing," which is always present when the will is present. Through this he does well and through that evil. The "not-willing" is of the flesh and the willing is of the spirit. Therefore there is as much sin present as there is unwillingness, difficulty, constraint, resistance; and there is as much merit present as there is will, inclination, freedom, cheerfulness; for these two are found together in our entire life and work. But if there is total unwillingness there already are mortal sin and aversion. There is no such thing as a total will in this life. Therefore we constantly sin while doing good, sometimes less and sometimes more. That is the reason why there is no righteous person on earth who does good and does not sin. Such a righteous person exists only in heaven. Just as, therefore, man is not without this unwillingness, so he does not act without it, and for this reason he is not without sin. For how can he act without it since he cannot live without it? Scripture also says, "Who can boast of having a pure heart?" [Cf. Prov. 20:9]. Likewise Gal. 5 [:17] states, "The desires of the flesh are against the Spirit, and the desires of the Spirit are against the flesh; for these are opposed to each other, to prevent you from doing what you would," and so on.

In the third place through Ps. 143 [:2]: "Enter not into judgment with thy servant: for no man living is righteous before thee." Here I ask whether that righteous person, who is imagined righteous since he already actually finds himself in a state of glorious merit, is also to be counted among the living? If he is among the living, then he is not righteous. How would this be possible if he does not sin in his merit?

This I shall prove by means of reason: Whoever does less than he ought, sins. But every righteous person in doing good does less than he ought. Well, then, I shall prove the minor premise in the following way: Whoever does not do good out of complete and perfect love of God does less than he ought. But every righteous man is that kind of a person. I shall prove the major premise through the commandment: "You shall love the Lord your God with all your soul, and all your might" etc. [Deut. 6:5], of which the Lord says in Matt. 5 [:18], "Not an iota, not a dot, will pass from the law until all is accomplished." Therefore we must love God with all our might, or we sin. But the minor premise, that we do not love him with all our might, has been proven above, for the unwillingness in the flesh and in the members hinders this perfection so that not all members or powers love God. This unwillingness resists the inner will which loves God.

But those persons say: "God does not demand of us this perfect law." I ask: Of whom does he then demand it? Of stone and wood? Or of cattle? This is an error, for it is stated in Rom. 3 [:19], "Now we know that whatever the law says it speaks to those who are under the law." Therefore it is a command for us and is demanded of us. Through that entirely false interpretation of the following word, "God does not demand perfection," the opinion was spread that no sin is involved if a person does something with less than perfect love, since God does not demand it because he pardons it, not because he permits it and it is not sin. If this had been the case, he could have altered his commandment, which is contrary to his own statement, that "Not an iota, not a dot, will pass from the law until all is accomplished" [Matt. 5:18].

Now I shall raise my objections against this:

In the first place, John states in his canonical epistle that "No one born of God commits sin" [I John 3:9]. Similarly God gave Abimelech evidence in Gen. 20 [:6] that he acted in the simplicity of his heart and consequently did not sin. In Ps. 86 [:2] it is written, "Preserve my life, for I am godly." There are other passages which can be applied here.

I answer: Each is true for he who is born of God does not sin and also sins. Unless perhaps Paul was not born of God (Rom. 7). Or did indeed John contradict himself when he said: "If we say we have no sin . . . the truth is not in us" [I John 1:8]? Actually, he sins in the same act because of the will of the flesh; he does not sin because of the contrary will of the spirit.

Thus you say, "How do we fulfil the law of God?" I answer, Because we do not fulfil it, therefore we are sinners and disobedient to God. Nor is this a venial sin according to its essence and nature, for nothing impure will enter the kingdom of heaven [Rev. 21:27]. For this reason damnation is demanded for every sin, for Christ says that not an iota, not a dot shall pass before all is accomplished [Matt. 5:18]. Therefore St. Augustine quite correctly states in chapter 19 of the first book of his *Retractations:* "All divine com-

mands are fulfilled when whatever does not occur is pardoned." [16]
Therefore the commands of God are fulfilled when God pardons
for his mercy's sake rather than when man acts through his own
righteousness, for the mercy of God is greater than the righteousness of man. Thus it is that those people say, "God does not demand perfection," whereas they should say, "God pardons." But
whom? Those who feel secure and those who do not believe that
they sin? Not at all. Rather he pardons those who say, "Forgive us
our sins," those who recognize and hate their wickedness with a
true heart, as in Ezek. 20 [:43], "And you shall loathe yourselves
for all the evils that you have committed," and so on.

That is also what the Lord says in Ps. 32 [:6], "Therefore let
every saint offer prayer to thee." If he is a saint, then he has no
impiety except that which is forgiven him in his sin. For what then
does he pray? Certainly the saint prays for that sin which is to be
forgiven, for he gives thanks above all for the sin which is forgiven.
Then he ought not to say "every saint," but rather, "every sinner
will pray for them," if he wants to speak of past sins. For holy is
he whose sins are forgiven, and a holy man prays for forgiveness
of his sin. A wonderful statement, which cannot be solved by means
of their foolish and carnal interpretation, that a saint prays for
past sins. The prophet does not speak of himself, but of those whom
he saw sanctified and holy by virtue of the forgiveness of sins. And
nevertheless he says that they pray for forgiveness, unless perchance
the prophet either lies or flatters when he calls those people holy
whose sins were not forgiven. But then he should say that they
pray "that they might be forgiven" or "for the forgiveness of sins."

Therefore, it is the sweetest righteousness of God the Father
that he does not save imaginary, but rather, real sinners, sustaining
us in spite of our sins and accepting our works and our lives which
are all deserving of rejection, until he perfects and saves us. Meanwhile we live under the protection and the shadow of his wings
and escape his judgment through his mercy, not through our
righteousness.

---

[16] Migne 32, 615.

Hence, away with arguments which are like so much smoke: "One and the same action cannot be accepted and unaccepted by God. For it follows that it would be good and not good at the same time." I answer: Can man then at the same time fear justice and hope for mercy? I therefore say that every good deed is both accepted and not unaccepted, and, on the other hand, that it is not accepted but unaccepted. It is accepted through pardon, and thus not rejected, for he forgives through mercy that which is less worthy of being accepted. This, however, is unaccepted, that is, sin, insofar as it is an action of the malice of the flesh.

God nevertheless pardons sin in his time and demands a good deed now as well as in the future. For there is no action which God accepts without reserve (such expressions are fictions of the human heart), but he pardons and deals sparingly with all our actions. Those opponents of ours, however, imagine that there might be someone whom he would accept without pardon, which is false. When therefore he pardons, he neither accepts nor does not accept, but he pardons. And thus he accepts his own mercy in our works, that is, the countenance of Job, namely the righteousness of Christ for us [Job 42:8]. For this is the mercy seat of God who forgives and makes pardonable our actions so that we substitute his fulness for that which is deficient in us. For he alone is our righteousness until we are made to conform with his image.

I prove this anew:

1. "Nothing good dwells within me, that is, in my flesh" [Rom. 7:18]. Much less will there be any good in those who are entirely flesh and blood. The Apostle speaks of himself and of all righteous people. If therefore these, insofar as they do what is beyond them and according to grace, do not yet do what they should, no matter how much they exert themselves, how much more will those, who act without grace according to their ability and do not exert themselves, do the opposite of that which they should! But then they say, "It is true, they do it imperfectly, but this imperfection is not sin." I answer: According to its nature it is sin, but those who lament it, God does not hold accountable for it.

2. Through Gen. 6 [:5; 8:21]: "Every imagination of a man's heart is inclined to evil from his youth." Here he does not say "imagination," but "every imagination," and whatever man thinks,

is evil, because he seeks those things which are to his advantage. Nor can he do otherwise without the grace of God.

3. I Cor. 13 [:5]: Here it is said of love only that it does not insist on its own way. Without it, as the Apostle shows in Phil. 2 [:21], all persons "look after their own interests," not those of Christ. But seeking one's own interests is mortal sin.

4. Hos. 13 [:9]: "Your destruction is certain, that is, destruction is your lot, O Israel. Your salvation is alone with me."[17] He does not say, "righteousness," but "destruction," is yours. By yourself you accomplish nothing but destruction.

5. "A bad tree cannot bear good fruit" [Matt. 7:18].

6. "He who is not with me is against me" [Luke 11:23]. But to be against Christ is a mortal sin. And not to be with him is to be beyond grace.

7. "If a man does not abide in me, he is cast forth as a branch and withers; and the branches are gathered, thrown into the fire and burned" [John 15:6]. See, to be outside Christ means to deserve fire and thoroughly wither. In any case, doing whatever is done surely cannot be understood as venial sin.

8. Were not the foolish virgins rejected [Matt. 25:1 ff.], not because they had not worked, but because they had worked without oil? They did good in itself but not out of grace, for they sought their own glory. Man cannot possibly be free from this vice without grace.

9. "God sends rain on the good and on the ungrateful" [Cf. Matt. 5:45]. But that person is ungrateful who does not return thanks for the gifts of God as received from God, which is a mortal sin. Thus works are of necessity beyond grace.

10. "Every one who commits sin is a slave of sin" [John 8:34]. How is it possible that a slave of the devil and a captive of the sin he serves can do anything else but sin? How can he do a work of light who is in darkness? How can he do the work of a wise man who is a fool? How can he do the work of a healthy person who is ill? And more examples could be given. Therefore all things which he does are works of the devil, works of sin, works of darkness, works of folly.

---

[17] Hos. 13:9 reads: "I will destroy you, O Israel; who can help you?"

11. If the being of man is under the power of darkness, why are not also his actions? The tree is under the tyranny of the devil, and it cannot be denied that its fruits are under the same tyranny.

12. That verse in Ps. 94 [:11] which the Apostle adduces: "The Lord knows the thoughts of man, that they are vain"; and Ps. 33 [:10]: "The Lord brings the counsel of the nations to nought; he frustrates the plans of the peoples and rejects the counsel of the princes." Here I ask: Do you understand the thoughts of man to be those which man thinks up by himself? If so, you hear that they are rejected and not only dead but displeasing in the judgment of God. If they are thoughts, however, which man does not think up by himself but out of an evil inclination, God should not call them thoughts of man. It is certain that he sees through those counsels which men give by virtue of natural reason, otherwise he would have preferred to call them follies. Now God rejects that which is the wisdom of man; how much more should he reject folly!

13. Prov. 3 [:5]: "Do not rely on your own insight." This is to be understood either in general or in particular. If in general, no dictate of reason is unrejected or uncondemned. If in particular, as many think, then it is also occasionally permitted to rely upon oneself and one's reason, which is contrary to this specific text.

14. If man can do something good of himself without sin, then he can also rightly give himself honor according to the measure of the good done by him. Then he may say that he is good, wise, strong, and the flesh may boast in the sight of God against the Apostle, who specifically says: "Let him who boasts, boast of the Lord" [I Cor. 1:31].

15. Psalm 81 [:12]: "So I gave them over to their stubborn hearts." See, this is the punishment of sin, that man is left at the mercy of his heart; therefore it is a mortal sin. But "his heart" is also in every way his will outside grace. Otherwise he would have said, "I gave them over to the desires of the enemy, and they wander about according to the counsel of the enemy, but not according to their own."

16. Romans 14 [:23]: "For whatever does not proceed from faith is sin." St. Augustine understands this as referring to faith in Christ, although others interpret it as referring to the con-

science. Nevertheless, faith in Christ is a good conscience, as Peter says: "As an appeal to God for a good conscience" [I Pet. 3:21], that means that it thoroughly confides in God. If therefore a work without faith were not a mortal sin, it would follow that Paul would greatly concern himself with a venial sin, which is false, since no one can live without venial sin. Therefore, everything that does not proceed from faith is a mortal and damnable sin, because it is also contrary to the conscience, the conscience, I say, of faith in Christ, because man does not act with confidence in Christ. For he does not believe that he pleases God in order thereby to merit something, and nevertheless he acts in such lack of faith and according to his conscience.

17. The condition of the sinner would be better than that of the righteous person, for the righteous person sins venially in his work and the godless does not sin. Therefore it is necessary that one concede that he sins more than venially. Likewise: The righteous persons fear their works [Job 9:28]. How much more are the works of the godless to be feared! Actually then, the condition of the godless is better than that of the righteous, since this one fears, while that one feels secure.

18. If grace is given to that person who acts according to his own ability, then man can know that he is in grace. This is proven in the following way: Man either knows whether he does what is in him, or he does not know it. If he knows it, then he knows that he has grace, since they say that grace is certainly given to him who does what is in him. If he does not know it, this doctrine is erroneous and his consolation ceases. For whatever work he has done, he does not know whether he has done what is in him. Consequently he always remains in doubt.

19. The question is raised: What kind of a work is it which a man does when he does what is in him? If none can be pointed out, why teach that a man should do what he does not know? But if there is such a work, let it be pointed out. Some specify the act of loving God above all else as such a work.

Here (if I may digress a little) I say, in the first place: Such teachers attribute nothing to the grace of God except a certain embellishment of our works, not that it may heal the sick but adorn the strong. We can do works, but without embellishment. Thus grace is the most despised thing and a gift which is not necessary for us, but exists only because of the will and the intention of the one who demands it, as they say. What Christian will stand for such blasphemy? Christ therefore died for us in vain, for he suffered only because of the intention of God. We did not need him, but only the intention of God who demanded it. If indeed we could have fulfilled the law, God was still not satisfied, for in addition to the law, he wanted to exact his grace from us. And thus it is not Pelagius who reappears, but a blasphemer worse than Pelagius. So we find that God is naturally to be loved above all things, and one is not ashamed to say "above all things."

But I still answer: If the act of loving God is doing as much as is in a man, it still remains true that man does not know when he loves and therefore not when he acts according to what is in him, or how and what he must do in order to do what is in him, or he must be sure of grace, which all agree is impossible.

If you say: Man should strive to do that which is in him, I would counter with the question whether he knows that he is striving and how he strives and what he must do in order to strive? If he knows it, he is indeed certain. If he does not know it, the doctrine is entirely worthless. Indeed, this striving is either the same as doing what is in one, and the same question recurs, or it is something else. Therefore man by not doing what is in him, but by striving to do as much as is in him, does what is in him. Therefore by doing what is in him he does not yet do what is in him.

20. Let us stop this senseless talk and consult experience. Let anyone do what is in him while he is angry, irritated, and tempted; indeed, let him prepare himself for clarification concerning that which he does not know and let us see if he accomplishes it. Let him work, I beg, and begin, and let us see what he does and accomplishes.

21. If man receives grace by doing what is in him, it seems impossible that not everyone or at least the majority of men might be saved. I ask: When man is proud, sins, etc., does he do such a work by himself or is it done by another? Of course, he himself does it. Or does he do it himself and by his own strength? Or does

another do it and by strength other than his own? He does it himself and by his own strength. Therefore, if a man sins, he does what is in him. Therefore, on the contrary, if he does what is in him, he sins.

But here it is said: I am speaking of a person and of powers which are by nature good, not of powers which are abused, for they are diseased. Created man is indeed good, but he is also weak. He does not act apart from his diseases but he acts as one who has become infected with a disease. Therefore he can only do imperfect things, even though he is good. He is like a rusty hatchet which is made of iron, but works only as a rusty one, even though it is made of iron.

22. Why therefore do we grant that evil lust is invincible? Do what is in you and do not lust. But you cannot do that. Therefore you also do not by nature fulfil the law. But if you do not fulfil it, much less will you fulfil the law of love. Likewise, do what is in you and do not become angry with him who offends you. Do what is in you and do not fear danger.

23. Do what is in you and do not fear death. I ask, what man does not shudder, does not despair, in the face of death? Who does not flee it? And yet because God wishes that we endure it, it is apparent that we by nature love our will more than the will of God. For if we should love the will of God more, we should submit to death with joy, indeed, we should consider it a gain, just as though we considered it to be our will. Therefore we are discussing figments of our imagination. He loves God less than himself, even hates him, who hates or does not love death (that is, the will of God). We are all like that. Where now is the love of God above all things? See, we do not love God more than our life and our will. What shall I then say about hell? Who does not hate it?

24. The Lord's Prayer itself is sufficient proof that we are poor laborers throughout our lives. For imagine someone, who does what is in him, deciding whether to pray: "hallowed be thy name, thy will be done"; or to pray: "it is hallowed; it has been done." By saying "may it be hallowed," he thereby confesses that it is defiled. If he says "may it be done," he thereby confesses dis-

obedience. But if this takes place among sons of God and saints, how much more so among the godless!

In the year 1518

A STATEMENT CONCERNING THE HEIDELBERG DISPUTATION, MADE BY LUTHER APPARENTLY SOON AFTER ITS CONCLUSION.[18]

These theses were discussed and debated by me to show, first, that everywhere the Sophists of all the schools have deviated from Aristotle's opinion and have clearly introduced their dreams into the works of Aristotle whom they do not understand. Next, if we should hold to his meaning as strongly as possible (as I proposed here), nevertheless one gains no aid whatsoever from it, either for theology and sacred letters or even for natural philosophy. For what could be gained with respect to the understanding of material things if you could quibble and trifle with matter, form, motion, measure, and time—words taken over and copied from Aristotle?

---

[18] WA 9, 170.

PREFACE TO THE COMPLETE EDITION OF A GERMAN THEOLOGY

1518

Translated by Harold J. Grimm

INTRODUCTION

During his formative years Luther was much impressed by the writings of the late-medieval German mystics, particularly by their emphasis upon the necessity of a spiritual rebirth of despair before one could be united with God. When he came upon an incomplete manuscript copy of a book by an unknown mystic, a member of the Teutonic Knights of Sachsenhausen near Frankfurt, he was so pleased with its evangelical content and assistance to him in his religious struggle that he published it under the title, *A Spiritually Noble Little Book,* in 1516 (WA 1, 153). He stated in the short preface which he wrote for this, his first publication, that only God knew who the author was and added that he felt certain that the person had belonged to the school of mystics led by John Tauler (1300-1361). He had bought an edition of Tauler's sermons published in 1508 and had annotated it with great care.

By 1518 Luther had clarified his doctrine of justification by faith and had gained assurance that his earlier despair and anguish had served as indispensable prerequisites for the grace of a loving God who had never deserted him. Moreover, he had discarded all references to man's own merits in obtaining salvation. The use of scholastic authorities by his opponents during the indulgence controversy now made him particularly appreciative of the simple evangelical approach of the German mystics which he called "a wisdom of experience" *(sapientia experimentalis)* rather than "a wisdom of theology" *(WA 9, 98)*.

Like the mystics, Luther was most concerned that the sinner should find a way out of sin and to salvation in communion with God—in other words, that he should annihilate his own personality and substitute God's. He agreed, for example, with Tauler's instructions that the sinner should be humble, faithful, penitent, joyful in poverty, and eager to return to God by whom he had been created.

Yet one looks in vain in Luther's writings for doctrines of the mystics. Unlike these, he never became subjective in his approach, but continued to emphasize at every step the doctrine which had resulted from his own experience and study, namely, justification by faith. Christ's redemptive act always remained for him a reality, appropriated by a sinner solely by faith through the mercy of God. Similarly Luther rejected the mystic conception of love as essentially "the sweetness" of the loved one and stressed the active love which suffers and labors for the loved one. This emphasis upon the moral activity of a child of faith stands in sharp contrast to mystical passivity (*Gelassenheit*), contemplation, and ecstasy.

When Luther came across a complete, though less accurate, manuscript copy of the little work by the anonymous German mystic, he published it in June, 1518, under the title *A German Theology* (*Ein deutsch Theologie*) with the German preface translated in the following pages. It was published in Wittenberg by Johann Grünenberg. A reprint was published by Silvanus Otmar in Augsburg in September of the same year under the title, *Theologia Deutsch,* by which the book was thenceforth commonly known. The popularity of the book can be seen from the fact that four more reprints appeared by 1520. To date about 170 printed editions have been identified. The Grünenberg copy is the one edited for *WA* 1, 378-389 and *MA*³ 1, 140-141. The English translation in this volume is from the text in *WA*.

For a detailed appraisal of the influence of mysticism on Luther, see R. H. Fife, *The Revolt of Martin Luther* (New York, 1957), pp. 217-221, 232-233.

PREFACE TO THE
COMPLETE EDITION OF
A GERMAN THEOLOGY

One reads that St. Paul, although he was an unimportant and a despised person, nevertheless wrote powerful and courageous letters [II Cor. 10:10] and gloried in the fact that his language was not embellished with ornate and flowery words [I Cor. 1:17], yet was richly endowed with literary art and wisdom. When one contemplates God's wonders it is obvious that brilliant and pompous preachers are never chosen to spread his words. As it is written, *Ex ore infantium*, "By the mouth of babes and infants," that is, of those who are not eloquent, "thou hast chanted thy glory in the best manner" [Ps. 8:2]. Likewise, "The wisdom of God makes the tongues of the inarticulate most articulate" [Cf. Prov. 10:20]. Furthermore, God punishes persons with high opinions of themselves who become offended and angered by those simple people. *Consilium inopis*, etc.: "You have dishonored good counsel and doctrine because they were given you by poor and unprepossessing persons" [Cf. Ps. 14:6], etc.

I say the above because I wish to warn everyone who reads this book not to harm himself and become irritated by its simple German language or its unadorned and unassuming words, for this noble little book, poor and unadorned as it is in words and human wisdom, is the richer and more precious in art and divine wisdom. To boast with my old fool,[1] no book except the Bible and St. Augustine has come to my attention from which I have learned more about God, Christ, man, and all things. I now for the first time become aware of the fact that a few of us highly educated Wittenberg theologians speak disgracefully, as though we want to

---

[1] Faith in Christ, Luther maintained with Paul, makes one a fool in Christ.

75

undertake entirely new things,[2] as though there had been no people previously or elsewhere. Indeed, there have been others, but God's wrath, aroused by our sin, has prevented us from being worthy enough to recognize or hear them. It is obvious that such matters as are contained in this book have not been discussed in our universities for a long time, with the result that the holy Word of God has not only been laid under the bench but has almost been destroyed by dust and filth.

Let anyone who wishes read this little book, and then let him say whether theology is original with us or ancient, for this book is certainly not new. But some may say, as in the past, that we are German theologians. We shall let that stand. I thank God that I hear and find my God in the German tongue, whereas I, and they with me, previously did not find him either in the Latin, the Greek, or the Hebrew tongue. God grant that this little book will become better known. Then we shall find that German theologians are without a doubt the best theologians. Amen.

Doctor Martin Luther,
Augustinian at Wittenberg

---

[2] Luther refers to his new evangelical theology. On numerous other occasions he voices his concern over the question, "Am I the only wise one?"

EXPLANATIONS OF
THE NINETY-FIVE THESES

or

EXPLANATIONS OF THE
DISPUTATION CONCERNING
THE VALUE
OF INDULGENCES

1518

INTRODUCTION

Luther's detailed *Explanations of the Ninety-five Theses* is one of the most important documents written during his formative years, for it was written and revised over a period of several months and illustrates how inexorably his doctrine of justification by faith alone was compelling him to break with the past. His new evangelical convictions, when applied to the indulgence traffic, had brought him into conflict with his superiors whose authority he still respected with sincere humility. Both he and his opponents, however, now viewed the question of indulgences in a broader theological and ecclesiastical context. In explaining his theses Luther now applied his newly developed "theology of the cross," already enunciated in *The Heidelberg Disputation,* and challenged the authority of the church when it was in opposition to this new theology. His opponents correctly pointed to his deviations from scholastic theology and his actions in defiance of ecclesiastical authorities.

Notable throughout the *Explanations* is Luther's strong inner conflict, already voiced in his *Preface to A German Theology.* He writes respectfully of the pope but questions his primacy as bishop of Rome; he quotes the church fathers and canon law but treats the Bible as the primary—but not yet sole—authority in religious matters; he recognizes the ultimate authority of general church councils in matters of faith but opposes the burning of heretics, as was done at the Council of Constance; he still accepts purgatory and "the treasure of the church" but interprets them in an evangelical fashion; he dislikes tumult and disobedience but asks in unmistakable terms for a reformation of the church.

Luther planned his *Explanations* late in 1517, especially since he had learned that his opponents were misinterpreting a number of his statements. He was working on it early in 1518 and was ready to publish it in February. Its publication was held up, however, by the fact that Bishop Hieronymus Schulz (Scultetus), his superior, forbade it. Despite this prohibition, he turned the manuscript over to his publisher in April, but his trip to Heidelberg postponed its publication. Having promised Staupitz at Heidelberg that he would complete it, he resumed work on it after his return to Wittenberg. The revised form was finally published toward the end of August, 1518. Luther then sent copies and accompanying letters to his three ecclesiastical superiors, Bishop Schulz [WA, Br, 1, 138-140], Vicar Staupitz [WA 1, 525-527], and Pope Leo X [WA 1, 527-529]. The pope received his copy while initiating the formal process against Luther. Although it in no way altered the pope's intentions, it greatly clarified the issues at stake in the indulgence controversy.

The *Explanations*, written in Latin, was first published by Johann Grünenberg in Wittenberg. The following English translation is based on this copy as edited in WA 1, 525-628. It was published in German for the first time in the Leipzig Edition. This translation was included in volume 18, pages 299-533 of *Dr. Martin Luther's sämmtliche Schriften*, edited by Johann Georg Walch (24 vols., Halle, 1740-1753), but the one in *St.L.* 18, 102-269 was made from the Latin in WA. The German translation in MA³ 1, 142-295 was based on the German in volume 18 of Walch's edition, but the editor collated it with the Latin in WA and incorporated the corrections in the latter made by Theodor Brieger in *Zeitschrift für Kirchengeschichte*, XVII, 175ff. Cf. W. Köhler, *Dokumente zum Ablassstreit* (Leipzig, 1903), and Otto Clemen, "Beiträge zur Lutherforschung," *Festschrift für Theodor Brieger* (1912).

EXPLANATIONS OF
THE NINETY-FIVE THESES

or

EXPLANATIONS OF THE
DISPUTATION CONCERNING
THE VALUE
OF INDULGENCES

DECLARATION

Because this is a theological disputation, I shall repeat here the declaration usually made in the schools in order that I may pacify the individuals who, perhaps, are offended by the simple text of the disputation.

First, I testify that I desire to say or maintain absolutely nothing except, first of all, what is in the Holy Scriptures and can be maintained from them; and then what is in and from the writings of the church fathers and is accepted by the Roman church and preserved both in the canons and the papal decrees. But if any proposition cannot be proved or disproved from them I shall simply maintain it, for the sake of debate, on the basis of the judgment of reason and experience, always, however, without violating the judgment of any of my superiors in these matters.

I add one consideration and insist upon it according to the right of Christian liberty, that is, that I wish to refute or accept, according to my own judgment, the mere opinions of St. Thomas, Bonaventura, or other scholastics or canonists which are maintained without text and proof. I shall do this according to the advice of Paul to "test everything, hold fast to that which is good" [I Thess. 5:21], although I know the feeling of Thomists who want St. Thomas to be approved by the church in everything. The weight of St. Thomas' authority is known well enough. From this declaration I believe that it is made sufficiently clear that I can err, but also that I shall not be considered a heretic for that reason, no matter how much those who think and wish differently should rage or be consumed with anger.

1

When our Lord and Master Jesus Christ said, "Repent" [Matt. 4:17], he willed the entire life of believers to be one of repentance.

This I assert and in no way doubt.

1. Nevertheless, I shall prove the thesis for the sake of those

who are uninformed, first from the Greek word *metanoeite* itself, which means "repent" and could be translated more exactly by the Latin *transmentamini*, which means "assume another mind and feeling, recover one's senses, make a transition from one state of mind to another, have a change of spirit"; so that those who hitherto have been aware of earthly matters may now know the spiritual, as the Apostle says in Rom. 12 [:2], "Be transformed by the renewal of your mind." By this recovery of one's senses it happens that the sinner has a change of heart and hates his sin.

It is evident, however, that this recovery or hatred of oneself should involve one's whole life, according to the passage, "He who hates his soul in this life, preserves it for eternal life" [Matt. 10:39]. And again, "He who does not take his cross and follow me, is not worthy of me" [Matt. 10:38]. And in the same chapter, "I have not come to bring peace, but a sword" [Matt. 10:34]. In Matt. 5 [:4], "Blessed are those who mourn, for they shall be comforted." And Paul in Romans 6 and 8 and in many other places orders us to mortify the flesh and members of the body which are upon earth. In Gal. 5 [:24] he teaches us to crucify the flesh with its lustful desires. In II Corinthians 6 he says, "Let us show ourselves in much patience, in many fastings, etc." [Cf. II Cor. 6:4-5]. I produce these citations so extensively because I am dealing with those who are unacquainted with our teachings.

2. I shall prove this thesis also according to reason. Since Christ is the master of the spirit, not of the letter, and since his words are life and spirit [John 6:63], he must teach the kind of repentance which is done in spirit and in truth, but not that which the most arrogant hypocrites could do openly by distorting their faces in fasts and by praying in streets and heralding their giving of alms [Matt. 6:16]. Christ must teach a repentance, I say, which can be done in every walk of life, a repentance which the king in purple robes, the priest in his purity, and the princes in their dignity can do just as well as the monk in his rituals and the mendicant in his poverty, just as Daniel and his companions did in Babylon [Dan. 1 and 3]. For the teaching of Christ must apply to all men, that is, to men in every walk of life.

3. We pray throughout our whole life and we must pray "for-

give us our debts" [Matt. 6:12]; therefore, we repent throughout our whole life and are displeased with ourselves, unless anyone may be so foolish as to think he must only pretend to pray for the forgiveness of debts. For the debts for which we are commanded to pray are real and not to be treated lightly; and even if they were venial, we could not be saved unless they were remitted.

2

This word cannot be understood as referring to the sacrament of penance, that is, confession and satisfaction, as administered by the clergy.

I assert and prove this thesis also.

1. I assert it, first, because sacramental penance is temporal and cannot be done all the time; otherwise one would have to speak with the priest continually and do nothing else but confess one's sins and perform the satisfaction which has been imposed. Therefore sacramental penance cannot be the cross which Christ bids us bear [Matt. 16:24]; nor is it a mortification of the passions of the flesh.

2. Sacramental penance is only external and presupposes inward penance without which it has no value. But inward penance can exist without the sacramental.

3. Sacramental penance can be a sham, inward penance cannot exist unless it is true and sincere. And if penance were not sincere, it would be hypocritical and not that which Christ teaches.

4. There is no teaching of Christ concerning sacramental penance but it is legally instituted by the popes and the church (at least with respect to its third part, namely satisfaction), and is thereby changeable by the will of the church. But evangelical penance is a divine law, never changeable; for it is unceasingly the sacrifice which is called a contrite and humble heart [Ps. 51:17].

5. The scholastic teachers with one accord distinguish at this point between real penance and sacramental penance, considering real penance as the material or the subject of sacramental penance.

3

Yet it does not mean solely inner repentance; such inner re-

pentance is worthless unless it produces various outward mortifications of the flesh.

I assert and maintain this thesis also.

First, in Rom. 12 [:1], the Apostle enjoins us to offer our bodies as a living sacrifice, holy and pleasing to God; and how this may happen, he sets forth clearly and extensively in the passages that follow, in which he teaches us to be wise and humble, to serve one another, to esteem one another highly, to persist in prayer, to have patience, etc. [Rom. 12:3-21]. In the same manner also in II Corinthians 6 he says, "Let us conduct ourselves in much patience, in fastings and watchings etc." [Cf. II Cor. 6:4-5]. But in Matthew 5 and 6 Christ also teaches us to fast rightly, to pray, to give alms. Likewise, in another place, he says, "Of whatever you have, give alms, and behold all things are clean for you" [Cf. Luke 11:41].

Thus it follows that the three parts of satisfaction (fasting, prayer, and alms) do not pertain to sacramental penance as far as the essence of the deeds is concerned, since these things are the command of Christ. But they do pertain to sacramental penance as far as the exact manner and time of these satisfactions are concerned (which the church prescribes for this penance), namely, how long one must pray, fast, and give alms, as well as how much one must give for charity. But since these satisfactions are related to evangelical penance, fasting consists of all chastenings of the flesh apart from the choice of food or difference in clothes. Prayer includes every pursuit of the soul, in meditation, reading, listening, praying. The giving of alms includes every service toward one's neighbor. Thus by fasting a Christian may serve himself, by prayer he may serve God, and by the giving of alms he may serve his neighbor. By means of fasting he may conquer concupiscence of the flesh and live soberly and purely. By means of prayer he may conquer the pride of life and live in a godly manner. By means of giving alms he may conquer concupiscence of the eyes and live righteously in this world. Therefore all mortifications which the conscience-stricken man brings upon himself are the fruit of inner penance, whether they be vigils, work, privation, study, prayers, abstinence from sex and pleasures, insofar as they minister to the spirit. The Lord himself showed forth these fruits of the spirit as did all his saints. Jesus commanded, "Let your light so shine before men, that they may see your good works" [Matt. 5:16]. Without doubt good works are the outward fruits of penance and of the Spirit, although the Spirit makes no sound except that of the turtledove, that is, the groaning of the heart which is the root of good works.

Against these three theses of mine, some shameful individual, going about as an ass under the cloak of a babbling lion, has maintained that it is a mistake for anyone to say that the word "penance" is not to be understood as referring to the sacrament of penance. First, it is not my purpose to refute his specific propositions. They are so foolishly and ignorantly composed that I cannot believe that the man under whose name they are published[1] and the man who has composed them[2] understand them. This fact is very evident to anyone who is fairly intelligent and well versed in the Scriptures.

Yet in order to show this man his ignorance (if he is capable of grasping the truth), I will make this first distinction. I admit that the term "penance" can be applied even to the penance of Judas, also to the penance which God requires, even to illusory penance, and, as the logicians are accustomed to distinguish, to a penance with respect to the essence of penance and secondly with respect to the intention behind it, and also with respect to the sacrament, that is, satisfaction. And who would deny that hitherto many theologians have been permitted to corrupt almost the whole Scripture with their daring distinctions and double meanings recently fabricated, so that for Paul and Christ we read patchworks of Paul and patchworks of Christ? I have spoken about the true and real significance of the word *metanoeite* which Christ intended, or at least the meaning which John the Baptist intended, who himself had no authority to institute the sacrament and yet came preaching a baptism of repentance, saying, "Repent" [Matt. 3:2; 4:7]. Christ repeated that word, and so I believe it is sufficiently understood that he did not speak of the sacrament of penance. Yet

---

[1] Johann Tetzel.
[2] Conrad Wimpina.

granting for the sake of argument that the nonsense of my refuter is true, let us see what follows from this.

Christ is without doubt a divine lawgiver and his doctrine is divine law, which no authority can change or dispense with. But if the penance taught by Christ signifies sacramental penance (satisfaction), and if the pope can change this and actually does change it according to his own will, then either the pope has divine law under his authority or else he is a most wicked adversary of his God, causing the command of God to be of no effect. If these false theologians dare to assert the former (these men who boast that they speak out on behalf of the revelation of truth and the suppression of errors to the glory of God, the defense of the catholic faith, and the honor of the holy apostolic throne), and if they so honor the church and defend the faith (these men who wish to appear as inquisitors of heretical perversity, a title which they boast of in a terrifying and insane—I almost said "inane"—manner), what, I ask, is left for these most insane heretics, since they also blaspheme and make accusations against the pope and the apostolic throne? With a free voice I would pronounce them not inquisitors but ingrafters of heretical perversity. Of such a nature and so intelligently stated are almost all the counter-theses which that most distinguished and most innocent paper is circulating indiscriminately, not willing to be subject to vanity [Rom. 8:20]. If I wanted to refute all of them a large volume would be necessary and nearly the entire chaos of the fourth book of the *Sentences*,[3] along with its commentators, would have to be unraveled. But you, my reader, be free and honest, in order that you may discern the fallacies of all the other theses from this one.

4

The penalty of sin remains as long as the hatred of self, that is, true inner repentance, until our entrance into the kingdom of heaven.

I also assert and examine this thesis.

---

[3] Peter Lombard. Migne 192, 519-964. In the fourth book, Lombard discusses eschatological subjects and the sacraments.

1. A definite corollary follows from what has been said. If a person's whole life is one of repentance and a cross of Christ, not only in voluntary afflictions but also in temptations of the devil, the world, and the flesh, and more especially also in persecutions and sufferings, as is clear from what has been said previously, and from the whole of Scripture and from examples of the Saint of saints himself and all the martyrs, then it is evident that the cross continues until death and thereby to entrance into the kingdom.

2. This is evident also in the case of other saints. St. Augustine had copies prepared of the seven penitential psalms, prayed them with tears in his eyes and meditated upon them, declaring that even a bishop, no matter how righteously he may have lived, should not leave this world without penance. St. Bernard also, while he was in agony, shouted, "I have lived in a reckless manner for I have wasted my time; I have nothing, but I know that because my heart is contrite and humble, O God, Thou wilt not despise me" [Ps. 51:17].

3. This thesis is evident from reason. The cross of repentance must continue until, according to the Apostle, the body of sin is destroyed [Rom. 6:6] and the inveterate first Adam, along with its image, perishes, and the new Adam is perfected in the image of God. But sin remains until death, although it diminishes daily through the renewing of the mind.

4. At least the punishment of death remains in every case. This is the fear of death, which is surely the punishment of punishments and is itself worse than death in most cases, to say nothing of the fear of judgment and hell, the qualms of conscience, etc.

5

The pope neither desires nor is able to remit any penalties except those imposed by his own authority or that of the canons.

I discuss this thesis and humbly seek instruction. And as I have asked in the preface so I ask here, that if there is anyone who can instruct me, let him offer me a helping hand and consider my motives.

1. First I shall list the kinds of punishment which faithful believers can suffer.

The first punishment is eternal punishment, the hell of the damned, with which this thesis is not concerned. This punishment is certainly not in the power of the highest or the lowest bishop, as everybody throughout the whole church believes. God alone remits punishment through the remission of guilt.

The second punishment is that of purgatory which we shall consider later as a separate thesis. Meanwhile we accept the belief that purgatory does not come under the power of the pope or of any man.

The third punishment is that voluntary and evangelical punishment which is put into effect by spiritual penance in accordance with I Cor. 11 [:31]: "If we were to judge ourselves surely we should not be judged by the Lord." This is the cross and mortification of suffering which is mentioned in Thesis 3. Since, however, this suffering has been commanded by Christ both with respect to the nature of spiritual penance and certainly with respect to the need of salvation, under no circumstances has the priest any power at all to increase or diminish it. For it depends not upon the authority of man but upon grace and the Holy Spirit. Nay, this punishment of the cross of mortification and suffering is even less in the power of the pope than all other punishments, whatever they may be. Accordingly, the pope is able to annul the eternal, purgatorial, and self-mortifying punishment, at least by prayer to God, just as he is able to obtain justifying grace for the sinner; but he is not able to remove this punishment of mortification and suffering even by prayer. Instead he should procure this punishment for the sinner and impose it no less than he procures grace, that is, he should announce that it has been imposed. Otherwise he would invalidate the cross of Christ [I Cor. 1:17] and unite the remnants of the Canaanites with his own sons and daughters, and he would not utterly destroy the enemies of God (sins). However, if he should see that some, with too much zeal, afflict themselves more than they should for their salvation and for the needs of others, he should not only remit but prohibit it, as St. Paul says to Timothy, "No longer drink only water," etc. [I Tim. 5:23].

The fourth punishment is God's correction and scourging, concerning which Psalm 89 says: "If, however, his children shall sin and not keep my law, I will punish their iniquities with the rod and their sins with the scourges of men" [Cf. Ps. 89:30-33]. Who would doubt that this punishment is beyond the power of popes? For Jer. 49 [:12] says that God imposes it upon the innocent: "If those who did not deserve to drink the cup must drink it, will you go unpunished? You shall not go unpunished, but you must drink." And that same prophet says (Jer. 25 [:29]), "Behold, I begin to work evil at the city which is called by my name, and shall you go unpunished? You shall not go unpunished." Then St. Peter says (I Pet. 4 [:17]), "For the time has come for judgment to begin with the household of God; and if it begins with us, what will be the end of those who do not believe the gospel?" Revelation 3 [:19] says, "Those whom I love, I punish." Hebrews 12 [:6] says, "Moreover, he chastises every son whom he receives." But if the pope desires to remit God's correction or if sinners should believe that it is remitted, they would certainly become bastards and illegitimate children, as it is recorded in Heb. 12 [:8], "If you are left without discipline, in which all have participated, then you are illegitimate children and not sons." For John the Baptist and those who were the greatest of the saints endured chastisement.

Yet I will admit that through the prayers of the church some such punishments could be lifted from the weak, namely, sickness, cares, plagues, and fevers; for St. James taught the elders of the church to bring in and anoint the sick one in order that the Lord might relieve him through the prayer of faith [Jas. 5:14-16]. But why do I delay, as if there should be any doubt in the mind of a Christian that the rod of God can be removed, not by the power of the keys, but by tears and prayers, and by imposition of more punishments rather than by their remission, as for example in the case of the Ninevites who humbly scourged themselves by their penances and thereby managed to avert the rod of destruction intended for them [Jonah 3:6-10]. Otherwise, if a priest of the church, whether he be of high or low rank, can remove God's punishment by the power of the keys, then he also drives away plagues, wars, insurrections, earthquakes, fires, murders, thefts, as well as the

91

Turks, Tartars, and other infidels; none but a poor Christian would fail to recognize in these the lash and rod of God. For Isa. 10 says, "Ah, Assyria, the rod of my anger, the staff of my fury! In its hand is my indignation" [Cf. Isa. 10:5]. Many, however, even the "big wheels" in the church, now dream of nothing else than war against the Turk. They want to fight, not against iniquities, but against the lash of iniquity and thus they would oppose God who says that through that lash he himself punishes us for our iniquities because we do not punish ourselves for them.

The fifth punishment which the pope cannot remit is the canonical punishment, which is instituted by the church. There is no doubt that this rightfully belongs in the hand of the pope, but only in such a way that there is (as they say) a valid reason for their remission and that the bearer of the keys does not err. Yet in my brazenness I would not accept this "valid reason" as cut-and-dried, as many are accustomed to do. The pious desire of the pope seems to be sufficient, and this may be a valid enough reason. Nor do I see how a mistake of the keys affects this remission, or if it does affect it, what harm it does, since the soul may nevertheless be saved even if punishments of that sort are not remitted because of error.

More attention must be given to this canonical punishment since the pope, in plenary remission, does not remit all punishments stipulated in canon law. For example, he does not remit either free or forced entrance of persons into a monastery, a punishment not unknown in canon law. Nor does he remit the civil, or rather, the criminal punishments which are imposed by civil law, although his legates may do this wherever they personally are present. He seems, therefore, to remit only those which are imposed concerning fasts, prayers, alms giving, and other works and disciplines, some for seven years, some for less, some for more. And in this category of punishments which the pope does not remit I include also that which a priest of the church imposes in accord with his own judgment. Look now and teach me, you who can. He cannot remit the first four; what else does he remit except punishment which is canonical and arbitrary?

Here again my opponent snarls at me in that lion skin,[4] saying the punishment exacted by divine justice or to be cleansed in purgatory is remitted. To him I answer that it is most wicked to assume that the pope has authority to change the divine law and to relax that which divine justice imposes. For God does not say, "Whatever I shall have bound, you shall loose," but rather "whatever you loose, shall be loosed, although you shall not loose everything that is bound, but only that which is bound by you, not that which is bound by me" [Cf. Matt. 16:19]. They, however, understand it to mean, "Whatever you shall have loosed either in heaven or on earth, shall be loosed," whereas Christ has purposely added the words "on earth" to restrict the power of the keys to earth, for he knew that otherwise they would perforate heaven itself.

The sixth punishment which I wish to consider as one which the pope cannot remit, unless I am taught otherwise, is that which they say divine justice requires in order that it may be satisfied. If this punishment is different from the third and fifth, as it must be if it is to be the sixth, it is impossible to imagine in what respect, unless it is because the third and fifth were not sufficient, so that additional punishment has to be imposed in the form of more prayer, fasting, alms giving. Therefore this sixth punishment is distinguished from the fifth or the third only by the degree of intensity. It cannot be understood as punishment according to civil law, for the pope does not remit this (as I have already said); otherwise the letters of indulgences of the church could remove all gallows and racks. Nor can it have reference to punishment according to canon law actually (de facto) imposed by the judgment of a law court dealing with matters in dispute, since the pope does not remit excommunications, interdicts, or other ecclesiastical penalties which have been meted out, as is evident enough from experience. All that remains, therefore, is that which I said I would consider [the punishment that divine justice requires]. But I am absolutely convinced that there is no such punishment. First, because by no authority of Scripture, of teachers, or of the accepted interpretation of the canons can it be taught that there is such punishment; and

---

[4] Luther here evidently has in mind Aesop's familiar fable, *The Ass in the Lion Skin.*

it is utterly absurd to teach anything in the church for which a basis cannot be found in the Scriptures, in teachers, in the canons, or at least in human reason. Secondly: granted there were some such punishment, it would nevertheless not pertain to the remission granted by the pope, for it has been imposed voluntarily over and beyond the canons, indeed not imposed at all but undertaken voluntarily. Therefore it is a different punishment from punishments which have been imposed, as I have mentioned above in my discussion of the fifth punishment.

But if you should say, "In what way does a person satisfy divine justice if for some reason the canonical or priestly punishment were not sufficient?", my answer would be that one does quite enough by means of the third and fourth punishment to a degree which is known to God alone. It is not recorded anywhere that God has required any other than the third and sometimes the fourth, as in the case of David and the children of Israel, recorded in the books of Judges and Kings.

But God is nearly always satisfied with a contrite heart and with the punishment of the third type. Hence I wonder at the negligence of some people, who, in order to add satisfaction, say that Christ absolved the adulteress in the Gospel without satisfaction, but that he did not absolve Mary Magdalene without satisfaction, and so the Master must be imitated in the case of Mary, but not in the case of the adulteress, since the sin of no one may be remitted without satisfaction. For these people say that Jesus did not cleanse the lepers without requiring that they should satisfy the law and show themselves to the priest [Luke 17:12-19]. This is, therefore, the punishment which divine justice requires beyond those punishments already mentioned.

I reply by saying that, in my opinion, the adulteress endured more punishments and made greater satisfaction than Mary Magdalene. Indeed she already suffered death and saw nothing but the severest judgment. So she was crucified exceedingly and grieved far more than Mary, for whom judgment of death was not imminent. Therefore, her punishment was of the fourth and third types, because she endured the sting of death with a contrite heart. Mary Magdalene, on the other hand, paid the punishment of the third type; and it is evident that her punishment can not be shown to have been different. But concerning the lepers I say that they were commanded to show themselves, not for satisfaction, but for testimony; for leprosy was not a sin but simply signified sin. Moreover, as everyone knows, satisfaction does not consist in showing the sin but in seeking to obtain the judgment of the priest, all of which is well known.

2. I prove the thesis in this manner. The two powers of binding and loosing are equal and they relate to the same matter. But the pope has no power to bind and loose any punishment beyond that of canonical law or the fifth punishment. Therefore he does not have any power to loose and remove them, otherwise it would have to be said that these two powers are unequal in extent. But if they are said to be unequal no one is required to believe it, since it is proved nowhere by the Scripture and canons, and since the text is clear where Christ gives power to bind on earth and loose on earth, by measuring and extending each power equally.

3. I shall prove my thesis from the fifth book of the *Decretals* of Gregory IX where the chapter "Concerning Penance and Remission," beginning with the words, *Quod autem,* expressly says that remissions which have not been made by a judge are not valid for individuals, since no one can be bound or loosed by his own judgment alone.[5] It is certain that a man is not under the jurisdiction of the pope in the first, second, third, fourth, and sixth punishments, but only in the fifth, as is clearly evident and will become more evident later.

DEDUCTION

It follows that satisfaction is not sacramental simply because it makes satisfaction for guilt (because the third and fourth punishments make satisfaction for guilt), but because it makes satisfaction for guilt according to the statutes of the church. The greatest satisfaction one makes to God is through a new life, etc. And it must also be proved by Scripture that no other satisfaction is required for sins.

---

[5] *Decretalium D. Gregorii Papae IX Lib. V. tit. XXXVIII, cap. 4. Corpus Iuris Canonici,* II col. 885.

And then there is John the Baptist, who was sent according to the plan and decree of God for the purpose of preaching repentance. He also said "Repent" [Matt. 3:2], and again, "Bear fruits that befit repentance" [Luke 3:8]. John himself explained these words; for after the crowd had asked what they should do, he answered, "He who has two coats, let him share with him who has none; and he who has food, let him do likewise" [Luke 3:11]. Do you not see that he imposes no penance except that of observing the commands of God, and that he therefore desires that penance be understood as nothing except conversion and the change to a new life? But this is seen even more clearly in the passage where the tax collectors came to him and said, "Teacher, what shall we do?" And he said, "Nothing more than you have been commanded to do" [Cf. Luke 3:12-13]. Has he in any way said here, "It is necessary for you to make satisfaction for past sins?" He said the same thing to the soldiers: "Terrify no one by threats, accuse no one falsely, and be content with your wages" [Cf. Luke 3:14]. Has he in any way imposed anything here other than the ordinary commands of God? But if this teacher of repentance, who has been raised up by God for this purpose, does not teach us that we must make satisfaction, doubtless he has deceived us and has not taught us enough about the duty of repentance.

The second passage is Ezekiel 18: "If a wicked man turns from his wickedness and does what is lawful and right, he shall surely live and shall not die" [Cf. Ezek. 18:21]. Behold, he imposes nothing except justice and righteousness, and these things must be done in every aspect of his life, according to that passage which says, "Blessed are they who observe justice, and do righteousness at all times" [Ps. 106:3]. Has this prophet also deceived us?

The third passage is Micah 6 [:8]: "I will show you, O man, what is good; and what does the Lord require of you but to do justice, and to love kindness, and to walk humbly with your God." You see what satisfaction God requires of man. In short, Micah speaks forth ridiculing those who wish to make satisfaction through works, saying, "What shall I offer that is worthy of the Lord? Shall I ever offer him burnt offerings and calves a year old? Can he ever be pleased with thousands of rams or with thousands of he-goats?

Shall I give my first-born for my transgression, the fruit of my body for the sin of my soul?" [Mic. 6:6, 7]. This implies that we should say, "No," for God requires no such things because of sin, but rather he requires justice, compassion, and fear. This, as I have said, means a new life.

6

The pope cannot remit any guilt, except by declaring and showing that it has been remitted by God; or, to be sure, by remitting guilt in cases reserved to his judgment. If his right to grant remission in these cases were disregarded, the guilt would certainly remain unforgiven.

The first part of this thesis is so evident that some have even admitted that a figurative manner of speech is employed when it is said that the pope grants remission of guilt. Others admit that they do not understand it. But everyone confesses that the guilt is remitted by God alone, according to the passage in Isa. 43 [:25], "I, I am He who blots out your transgressions for my own sake, and I will not remember your sins." And John 1 [:29], "Behold, the Lamb of God, who takes away the sin of the world." And Ps. 130 [:3, 4], "If thou, O Lord, shouldst mark iniquities, Lord, who could stand? But there is forgiveness with thee." And farther on, "With the Lord there is steadfast love, and with him is plenteous redemption. And he will redeem Israel from all his iniquities" [Ps. 130:7-8]. And Ps. 51 [:10], "Create in me a clean heart, O God, etc." There are many other references of this kind in the Scriptures. And St. Augustine in so many of his writings against the Donatists maintains absolutely that sins are remitted by God alone.

The second part of the thesis is likewise clear enough, for he who would reject reserved cases would surely have no guilt remitted. "He who rejects you," Jesus says, "rejects me" [Luke 10:16]. Indeed, God does not remit the guilt of anyone who does not at the same time have respect for the office of the keys. Since everybody concedes the truth of this thesis, it is not necessary to support it by my statement. However, I will indicate here what moves me to do so, and once more I will confess my ignorance, if anyone thinks it worth while to enlighten me and to make this matter clearer.

The first part of this thesis seems to be a figurative manner of speech or an idea inconsistent with the wording of the Gospel, since it says that the pope looses, that is, declares that the guilt is loosed and approves the loosing. For the text does not say, "Whatever I shall loose in heaven, you shall loose on earth." But on the contrary it says, "Whatever you shall loose on earth, I may loose or it shall be loosed in heaven," so that what is meant is that God approves that which the priest looses rather than the opposite. With regard to the second part of this thesis it is certain that those cases which the pope looses God also looses, and that no one can be reconciled to God unless he is first reconciled to the church, at least by desire. Nor is an offense against God removed while it still remains an offense against the church. But it is questionable whether a man is also reconciled to God as soon as he is reconciled to the church. The text certainly says that all things loosed in the church are also loosed in heaven, but it does not seem to follow that therefore absolutely all things are loosed in heaven, but merely those things which are loosed in the church. In my opinion these two questions are not unimportant questions concerning which I shall perhaps disclose my judgment more fully in the following thesis.

7

God remits guilt to no one unless at the same time he humbles him in all things and makes him submissive to his vicar, the priest.

I maintain this thesis. And since it has been thoroughly approved by the consensus of everyone, it does not require further discussion and proof. Yet I am still trying to understand it and I shall voice my understanding of it in simple terms. This thesis maintains, along with the preceding thesis, that God does not remit guilt unless there is a prior remission by the priest, at least by desire, as the text clearly indicates: "Whatsoever you loose, etc." [Matt. 16:19]. And that passage in Matt. 5 [:24] says, "First go and be reconciled to your brother and then come and offer your gift." And this, "Render therefore to Caesar the things that are Caesar's and to God the things that are God's" [Matt. 22:21]. And in the Lord's Prayer it says, "Forgive us our debts as we also forgive our debtors" [Matt. 6:12]. In all these passages remission is indicated as taking place on earth before it takes place in heaven. One is right in asking how these things can take place before the infusion of grace, that is, before the remission of God, for man cannot have his guilt forgiven or the desire to seek remission without first of all having the grace of God which remits.

So it seems to me, and I declare: When God begins to justify a man, he first of all condemns him; him whom he wishes to raise up, he destroys; him whom he wishes to heal, he smites; and the one to whom he wishes to give life, he kills, as he says in I Kings 2 [I Sam. 2:6], and Deut. 32 [:39], "I kill and I make alive, etc." He does this, however, when he destroys man and when he humbles and terrifies him into the knowledge of himself and of his sins, in order that the wretched sinner may say, "There is no health in my bones because of my sins; there is no soundness in my flesh because of thy indignation" [Ps. 38:3].

For thus do the mountains fall away before the face of the Lord. Thus does he send his arrows and scatter them, "at thy rebuke, O Lord, and at the breath of the spirit of thy wrath" [Ps. 18:15]. Thus sinners are turned to hell and their faces are filled with shame. David often experienced such consternation and trembling, as he confesses with groans in many different psalms. However, in this consternation is the beginning of salvation, for the "fear of the Lord is the beginning of wisdom" [Ps. 111:10]. Nahum says that when the Lord cleanses, he makes no one innocent: "His way is in whirlwind and storm, and the clouds are the dust of his feet" [Nah. 1:3]. Here his lightnings flash, the earth sees it and is moved; here his arrows fly and stick fast, the voice of his thunder rolls, that is, rolls all around, the waters see and tremble; here, in short, God works a strange work in order that he may work his own work. This is true contrition of heart and humility of spirit, the sacrifice most pleasing to God. Here is the sacrificial victim cut into pieces and the skin drawn and kindled for the burnt offering. And here (as they say) grace is infused, as Isa. 41 [:3] says, "He pursues them and passes on safely." And in Isa. 66 [:2]: "My spirit rests upon him, but only upon that one who is humble and contrite in spirit, and trembles at my word." And in Isa. 38 [:16] Hezekiah says, "O Lord, if in such things is the life of my spirit, restore me to health and make me live."

Actually man knows so little about his justification that he believes he is very near condemnation, and he looks upon this, not as infusion of grace but as a diffusion of the wrath of God upon him. Blessed is he, however, if he endures this trial, for just when he thinks he has been consumed, he shall arise as the morning star. However, as long as he remains in this wretched, perplexed state of conscience, he has neither peace nor consolation, unless he flees to the power of the church and seeks solace and relief from his sins and wretchedness which he has uncovered through confession. For neither by his own counsel or his strength will he be able to find peace; in fact, his sadness will finally be turned into despair. When the priest sees such humility and anguish, he shall, with complete confidence in the power given him to show compassion, loose the penitent and declare him loosed, and thereby give peace to his conscience.

To be sure, the person who is to be absolved must guard himself very carefully from any doubt that God has remitted his sins, in order that he may find peace of heart. For if he is uncertain of the anguish of his conscience (as it must always be if it is a true sorrow), yet he is constrained to abide by the judgment of another, not at all on account of the prelate himself or his power, but on account of the word of Christ who cannot lie when he says, "Whatever you loose on earth" [Matt. 16:19]. For faith born of this word will bring peace of conscience, for it is according to this word that the priest shall loose. Whoever seeks peace in another way, for example, inwardly through experience, certainly seems to tempt God and desires to have peace in fact, rather than in faith. For you will have peace only as long as you believe in the word of that one who promised, "Whatever you loose, etc." [Matt. 16:19]. Christ is our peace, but only through faith. But if anyone does not believe this word, even though he be pardoned a million times by the pope himself, even though he confess before the whole world, he shall never know inner peace.

This peace, therefore, is that sweetest power, for which, from the depth of our hearts, we ought to give the greatest thanks to God, who has given such power to men—that power which is the only consolation for sins and for wretched consciences, if only men will believe that which Christ has promised is true. Thus the question raised above is now clear, namely, that even if the remission of guilt takes place through the infusion of grace before the remission of the priest, this infusion is of such a nature and is so hidden under the form of wrath that man is more uncertain about grace when it is present than when it was absent; for the Scripture says, "accordingly his footprints are not recognized" [Ps. 77:19], and "by paths his feet have not trod" [Isa. 41:3].

So as a general rule we are not sure of the remission of guilt, except through the judgment of the priest, and not even through him unless you believe in Christ who has promised, "Whatever you shall loose, etc." [Matt. 16:19]. Moreover, as long as we are uncertain, there is no remission, since there is not yet remission for us. Indeed, one would perish woefully unless it should become certain, for he would not believe that remission had taken place for him.

Thus Christ spoke to Simon, the leper, concerning Mary Magdalene, "Her sins . . . are forgiven" [Luke 7:47], by which he certainly incidated that she had already received grace. But she did not recognize this infusion of grace, since there was no peace in her bones because of her sins, until he turned to her and said, "Your sins are forgiven" [Luke 7:48]. "Your faith has saved you" [Luke 7:50], that faith, namely, by which she believed him who forgave her sins. Therefore the words, "Go in peace" [Luke 7:50] followed. And the sins of the adulteress [John 8:3-11] had already been forgiven before Christ raised her. But she did not recognize this, since there were so many accusers around her, until she heard the voice of the bridegroom who said, "Woman, . . . has no one condemned you? . . . Neither do I condemn you" [John 8:10, 11]. And surely David, after he had sinned and, by the command of

God, had been reprimanded by the prophet Nathan [II Sam. 12:1-15], would have been struck dead immediately, when, moved by the justifying grace of God, he cried out, "I have sinned" (for this is the voice of the righteous when they first accuse themselves), if Nathan had not pardoned him immediately by saying, "The Lord has also put away your sin, you shall not die" [II Sam. 12:13]. For why did he add, "You shall not die," if it were not that he saw him overwhelmed by the terror of his sin and in despair? Hezekiah, also, when he heard that he was to die, would have died if he had not accepted comfort and the sign from Isaiah that he would enter the house of the Lord again [Isa. 38:4-8]; when he believed him he received at the same time both peace and remission of sins, as he says: "You have cast all my sins behind you." And, generally speaking, how could those in the Old Testament have had any confidence in the mercy of God and in the remission of sins, if God had not shown them by revelations, inspirations, burnt offerings, providing a cloud, and other signs, that whatever they sacrificed was pleasing to him. And he desires to accomplish that same thing now by the word and judgment of the priests.

Therefore, God's remission effects grace, but the priest's remission brings peace, which is both the grace and gift of God, since it is faith in actual remission and grace. It is my opinion that this grace is what our teachers declare is conferred efficaciously through the sacraments of the church. It is not, however, the first justifying grace which adults must have before the sacrament, but, as Rom. 1 [:17] has it, "faith for faith." For one who approaches God must believe [Heb. 11:6]. But one who has been baptized must also believe that he had believed and approached properly, or else he shall never have that peace which is gotten only through faith. Therefore Peter did not loose before Christ did, but declared and disclosed the loosing by Christ. Whoever believes this confidently has truly obtained the peace and remission of God (that is, he is sure that he is pardoned), not by the certainty of the process but by the certainty of faith, according to the infallible word of the one who has mercifully promised, "Whatever you shall loose, etc." [Matt. 16:19]. Thus we read in Rom 5 [:1] that, having been justified freely by his grace, we have peace with God through faith, certainly not through the process itself, etc.

But if I discern rightly and truly, then it is not wrong or improper to say, as my opponents want to say, that the pope remits guilt. Indeed, the remission of guilt is far better than the remission of any kind of punishment, though they preach only the latter and do so in such a manner that they make the remission of guilt of little significance in the church, while actually it is just the opposite. For when a man through the remission of guilt (which he cannot bestow upon himself, for no one should believe in himself unless he prefers to make two disorders out of one) has found peace through the acceptance of faith in absolution, every punishment is to him as no punishment at all. For anxiety of conscience makes the punishment harmful, but cheerfulness of conscience makes punishment desirable.

And we see that this understanding which the people have concerning the power of the keys is adequate when they seek and receive absolution in simple faith. But certain intellectuals, by their contritions, works, and confessions, endeavor to find peace for themselves but do nothing more than go from restlessness to restlessness because they trust in themselves and their works, while, if they feel torment of conscience, they should believe in Christ who says, "Whatever you shall loose, etc." [Matt. 16:19]. More recent theologians, however, contribute entirely too much to this torment of conscience by treating and teaching the sacrament of penance in such a way that people learn to trust in the delusion that it is possible to have their sins cancelled by their contritions and satisfactions. This most vain conceit can accomplish nothing more than it did for the woman in the Gospel who had a flow of blood and whose whole fortune was used up for doctors [Mark 5:25-34]—so as to make the situation even worse. The people must first be taught faith in Christ, the gracious bestower of remission. Then they must be persuaded to despair of their own contrition and satisfaction so that, when they have been strengthened by confidence and joy of heart over the compassion of Christ, they finally may despise sin cheerfully, become contrite, and make satisfaction.

Also the jurists have given encouragement to that torture of conscience. In extolling the power of the pope they placed more value and awe upon the power of the pope than they did respect for the word of Christ in faith. People must be taught that if they really want to find peace for their consciences they should learn to place their confidence, not in the power of the pope, but in the word of Christ who gives the promise to the pope. For it is not because the pope grants it that you have anything, but you have it because you believe that you receive it. You have only as much as you believe according to the promise of Christ.

Moreover, if the power of the keys would have no such value for peace of heart and remission of guilt, then, indeed (as some say) indulgences would be of little value. For what matter of great importance is conferred if remission of punishments is granted, since Christians ought to despise even death?

By the same token, why did Christ say, "If you forgive the sins of any, they are forgiven" [John 20:23], except that they are not forgiven to anyone unless he believes that they are forgiven for him through the remission of the priest? Thus the power is conferred in the words, "If you forgive the sins of any," but in the words, "they are forgiven," the sinner is challenged to faith in the remission; just as the power is given in the words, "whatever you shall loose," and our faith is aroused in the words, "they shall be loosed." For Christ could have said, "If you forgive punishments or chastisements of any, you shall remit," if he wanted us to understand it that way. But he knew that conscience, already justified by grace, would by its own anxiety cast out grace if it had not been aided by faith in the presence of grace, through the ministry of the priest. Indeed the sin would have remained if he had not believed that it was remitted. For the remission of sin and the gift of grace are not enough; one must also believe that one's sin has been remitted. And this is the witness that the Spirit of God gives to our spirit, that we are children of God [Rom. 8:16]; for to be a child of God is so great a mystery (for he may appear to himself to be an enemy of God) that if one does not believe it to be so, it cannot be so. The Lord causes his saints to marvel in such a way that no one would have confidence in the one who justifies and heals him, if he did not believe that he was justified

104

and healed; just as the sick man would not believe that the doctor cuts his body out of a desire to heal his infirmity, if he were not so persuaded by good friends.

Therefore I am not concerned whether the priest is a necessary cause for the remission of sins or whether there is some other cause, as long as it is somehow clear that the priest truly remits sins and guilt, just as a sick man's health is truly attributed to his friends because it was by their persuasion that the sick man believed in the doctor who operated on him.

This is not the place to consider the question, "What if the priest should err?" since that remission rests not upon the priest, but upon the word of Christ. So regardless of whether the priest should do it for the sake of money or honor, you should only desire remission without assuming anything, and should believe in Christ who promises it. Indeed, even if the priest should pardon you in a spirit of levity, nevertheless you shall obtain peace from your faith. When he also administers baptism or the eucharist, your faith receives the full benefit of the sacrament, regardless of whether he should seek money or be in a mood of levity and play. So great a matter is the word of Christ and man's faith in him. For we read in the history of the martyrs that a certain actor, in spirit of jest and for the purpose of ridiculing baptism, desired to be baptized, and becoming converted during the rite, was truly baptized by his pagan fellow actors and immediately crowned by them with martyrdom. Likewise when St. Athanasius was a boy, he baptized boys whom the bishop of Alexandria afterwards declared baptized, as recorded in church history. Indeed, St. Cyprian censured a peace bestowed rashly by a certain bishop, Therapius, but he wanted it to be approved. Therefore, we are justified by faith, and by faith also we receive peace, not by works, penance, or confessions.

With respect to my sixth and seventh theses, that ass of ours in lion's skin[6] triumphs with glory. Indeed he sings a hymn of victory over me before the victory is won, and from that bilge water of opinions[7] he draws another distinction between a satisfying and avenging punishment on the one hand, and a healing and curing

---

[6] Cf. Thesis 5.
[7] That is, scholastic argumentation.

punishment on the other, as if it were necessary to believe in people who dream up these things. Yet they very wisely conceal this distinction from the people. Otherwise indulgences, rather the money, would decrease if the people should realize that such trifling and useless avenging (that is, fabricated) punishments were remitted. Then in order to show everybody that he does not know what is of the old or of the new priesthood, he introduces another obscurity of words and draws another distinction of the keys, namely, among those of authority, superiority, and office. So our illustrious masters, inquisitors of the inquisition and defenders of the Catholic faith, have learned nothing except what they have imbibed from the confusing and obsolete questions of the fourth book of the *Sentences*.[8] Perhaps they wish that whatever Christ shall loose with the keys of superiority in heaven (for on earth he himself does not loose) shall be loosed by God in a "superheaven." Then, in order that the pope may be God, some other higher God must be invented, who looses in the higher heaven whatever the pope has loosed with the keys of authority.

But away with such nonsense. We know of only one type of keys, namely, those which are given to earth. Now my opponents contend this: "He therefore errs who says that the priest of the new law looses only by confirmation and declaration." That was the office of the Jewish priesthood. What sagacity of spirit and monstrous weight of erudition this is! And they are the ones who are considered most worthy to try heretics and defend the Catholic faith, however against stones and sticks. How much more accurately did the Apostle Paul assert that the old priesthood consisted in judging lepers, the administration of justice, and purifications of the flesh, in food, drink, clothing and festival days, etc. Justification of spirit and purity of heart which Christ worked in the church by the ministry of the new priesthood were signified by these figures of speech. I have not advanced the sixth thesis enthusiastically, as I have mentioned, but for the sake of the feelings of others. These adversaries of mine and all their masters up to the present time cannot show how the priest remits guilt unless they do so by advancing that heretical but usual opinion which says that the sac-

---

[8] Peter Lombard, *op. cit.*

raments of the new law give justifying grace to those who place no obstacle in the way. But it is impossible to proffer the sacrament in a salutary manner except to those who already believe and are just and worthy. The one who approaches the sacrament must believe [Heb. 11:6]. Therefore it is not the sacrament, but faith in the sacrament, that justifies. No matter what these arrogant sophists may chatter, it is much more plausible to say that the priest of the new law only declares and confirms the absolution of God, that is, points it out, and by this pointing out of his and by his judgment calms the conscience of the sinner, who is bound to believe and have peace by this judgment of the priest. In the same manner the priest of the old law calmed those whom he judged clean in body and clothing, though he himself could make no one clean, not even himself. For what that does for the body, this does for the conscience. Just so does the spirit respond to the letter and the truth to the symbol. And I am waiting to see how those defenders of the Catholic faith could explain the power of the keys in any other way, without becoming snarled in heresy.

8

The penitential canons are imposed only on the living, and, according to the canons themselves, nothing should be imposed on the dying.

I shall examine this thesis, although there are many people who wonder why it should be open to question.

1. The first proof of this thesis is that passage in Rom. 7 [:1]: "The law is binding on a person only during his life." Although the Apostle interprets this to mean the divine law, this statement of Scripture is even more applicable to human law, as the Apostle says in the same chapter, "If her husband dies a woman is discharged from the law concerning the husband" [Rom. 7:2]. To an even greater extent one who is dead is discharged from the law which applies to the one who is still alive. The Apostle makes his proof from the lesser to the greater. If he who is alive is released from the law through the death of the other, then even more

so is the dead person released from the same law which releases the one who is alive.

2. Canon laws, like all other man-made laws, are, according to chapter 29,[9] bound by the circumstances of time, place, and persons, as everybody knows. It is only about the word of Christ that it has been said, "Thy word, O Lord, endures forever, thy truth to all generations" [Cf. Ps. 119:89-90], "And his righteousness endures forever" [Cf. Ps. 111:3]. The word and righteousness of men, however, remain only for a time. Therefore when these circumstances are changed the laws also cease, unless one should say that after a city has been destroyed the deserted place that remains is still obliged to do everything which the city did before. This is absurd.

3. Justice requires that the living be released from the canon laws and that the law be changed when the circumstances back of the law cease or when the law inclines toward injustice. Pope Leo says that the law should not militate against love because it is for the sake of love that the law is established. Then surely that which begins to militate against unity, peace, etc. must cease. If the living are released from the laws, how much more should the dead be released! In the latter case, not only the circumstances back of the law cease, but the person himself ceases. And it is for him and for the conditions of his life that the laws were originally established.

4. The very words of the law prove this thesis for in the law the days and years, fasts, watches, labors, pilgrimages, and so forth are clearly stipulated. All these stipulations clearly belong to this life and end with death. At death a person passes into an entirely different life, at which time he neither fasts, weeps, eats, nor sleeps, since he no longer has a body. It is for this reason that Jean Gerson[10] dared to condemn indulgences which were bestowed as being valid for many thousands of years. And I cannot help wondering what happened to the inquisitors of heresy that they have not burned this heretic even after his death, for he condemned indulgences which entitled recipients to many thousand years and

---

[9] *Ibid.*, Book 4.
[10] Cf. p. 262, n. 8.

he spoke out so confidently against the custom of every pilgrimage station in the city [Rome]. He spoke out also against the practice of that squanderer of indulgences, Sixtus IV, as a result of which the latter warned his prelates that it was their duty to correct and give careful attention to these indulgence practices. He referred to the claims of these indulgences as foolish and superstitious, etc.

5. When one considers the intention of the legislator of the canons, it is evident that he did not once think that canons of this sort should be imposed upon the dying. Suppose we were to ask this question of the pope who imposes such canons: "Whom do you understand, Holy Father, to be included in your law, the living or the dead?" What answer will he give except this: "Why the living, of course. For what could I do with the dead who have been removed from my jurisdiction?"

6. A priest of Christ would act most cruelly if he did not set his brother free from the law, as he would wish for himself. And there is no reason why he should not do it, for it is in his power to do so.

7. If the penitential canons apply to the dead, then by the same token all the other canons apply. Therefore the dead should observe the festivals; keep the feasts, fasts, and watches; observe the canonical hours; on certain days eat no eggs, milk, meat but only oil, fish, fruit, vegetables; wear black or white clothes according to the different days; and bear other exceedingly heavy burdens which oppress that wretched church of Christ which formerly was most free. There is no reason why some canons should cease because of time, and not all. If the canons which are good and beneficial to life cease, why should not those cease even more which afflict men and are unprofitable and a hindrance? Or do we even here imagine that a transposition has been made and that, just as the dead suffer certain punishments which are in proportion to what they deserve, just so they perform certain works which are in proportion to what they deserve and thereby that one might say of them that they observe the canonical hours?

8. As a matter of fact, penitential as well as moral canons are waived for those who are sick in body and not on the verge of

death. A sick priest, for example, is not obligated to say public prayers and celebrate public worship. Therefore others also are not obligated to fast, watch, or abstain from meat, eggs, milk. And not only are sick people free from all these obligations, but they are forbidden to do all those things which formerly they were ordered to do when they were in good health. Indeed one should say to them now that the hand of the Lord has already touched them! "Why do you, like God, pursue me? Why are you not satisfied with my flesh (that is, my sickness)?" [Job 19:22]. Therefore I contend that the canons are not imposed upon the sick, but upon the healthy and the strong, thus much less upon the dead than upon the living. And if those who are on the verge of death and those who have already died are not free, why then are not the sick also oppressed and tormented by the same canons? And after these individuals have finally regained their health, if they are not obligated to make up for their omissions during their period of sickness, how is one to believe that after death the canons must be made up or fulfilled?

But at this point some people say, "Suppose some healthy person will have omitted performing the imposed penances and will confess this when he is about to die? In this case it appears that such a person must of necessity pay these penances in purgatory, even if no other penances needed to be imposed or would be imposed." My answer is: Not at all, for by such an omission he has done nothing more than sin against the precepts of the church, and for that he must grieve. He must not be required to make up and fulfil the canons for that which concerns the past, but only for that which is to come. "Let the day's own trouble be sufficient for the day, tomorrow will be anxious for itself" [Matt. 6:34]. But if the transgression of every law remains to be satisfied, so that no transgression remains, even more should transgressions of the divine laws be made up. Yet it is impossible for adultery to be an act in which chastity is not lost.

9. Whoever submits to a greater punishment than that which has been imposed upon him, deservedly and by natural right receives remission of lesser punishments, but the one who is about to die submits to the last, the highest, and the greatest punishment

of all, namely, death. Therefore in the face of death every other punishment should be waived, since scarcely anyone is strong enough for this one punishment. And imagine if one who is about to die were to present himself before a legislator at death, would not that legislator immediately retract his punishment?

10. Certain distinguished teachers in the church say that any Christian may be the richest of men because through a voluntary death he could discharge every debt and immediately fly to heaven, for nothing could be greater than a death voluntarily undertaken for the sake of God. It is therefore useless for the pope to reserve the punishments of canon law until after death. William of Paris[11] and Gerson[12] shared this opinion, and many rational individuals agree with them.

11. If death is not sufficient punishment unless the one who is dead suffers also the punishments which the canons impose, then the punishment of the canons will be greater than the punishment of death, since the former continues even beyond death and will work harm to the death of Christians, concerning which death the Scripture says, "Precious in the sight of the Lord is the death of his saints" [Ps. 116:15].

12. Imagine that the sinner might be snatched away and immediately suffer martyrdom because he confesses Christ before he has satisfied the canons. This is said to have happened to the martyr, St. Boniface. Will purgatory then detain such a person, preventing him from being with Christ? Can he then be prayed for in the church as a martyr?[13] But every person who dies voluntarily (it is that type of person we are talking about, that is, a Christian) also dies according to the will of God.

13. Why do not the civil laws also remain to be enforced after death, since they too are binding before God and in heaven, not by virtue of their own strength but by the testimony of Christ and the apostles Peter and Paul, who teach that one must be brought

---

[11] Since there were a number of scholastic theologians by this name, we do not know to whom Luther refers.

[12] Cf. p. 262, n. 8.

[13] According to Roman doctrine a martyr does not go to purgatory but immediately enters heaven. For this reason he is prayed to immediately, but one does not pray for him.

into subjection to them in spirit and with respect to conscience, for such is the will of God? [Matt. 22:21; Rom. 13:1-7; I Pet. 2:13-17].

14. The punishments of canon law cease when a penitent layman changes his position, when, for example, he becomes a priest, or when a priest becomes a bishop or a monk. And if this cessation of canonical punishment takes place in this life, should it not take place when a change is brought about by death? What is more absurd than this?

15. The opinion that punishments stipulated by canon law must be satisfied after death has absolutely no authority in Scripture, the canons, or acceptable reason, but appears to have been introduced purely by the slothfulness and negligence of the priests, as have many other superstitions.

16. To prove our point we have examples from the ancient fathers, of whom Cyprian is probably the most exacting observer of ecclesiastical censures and disciplines. In his Letter 17, Book III,[14] he bids us give peace to those who are exposed to the danger of death, so they may come to the Lord in peace after they have made confession either to the presbyter or the deacon, as he says in the same passage. This giving of peace, however, is nothing more than that which is now called "plenary remission," as anyone can see who has given any thought to this work.

We do conclude, therefore, that punishments stipulated by canon law must be imposed only upon the living and even then only upon those who are healthy and strong; actually only upon the sluggards and those who of their own accord do not wish to lead a better life. I certainly would not have drawn out this discussion so far if it weren't for the fact that certain individuals oppose me too strenuously with their assertions which they can in no way prove. If I wanted to deal with the wise and learned, I would keep quiet rather than speak.

At this point someone may say, "When you speak in this manner you cheapen indulgences exceedingly, that is, when you say that only canonical punishments are remitted and not all punishments, and even they are remitted only for this life." I answer that

---

[14] This letter of Cyprian was addressed to the presbyters and deacons informing them of the action they should take in re-admitting the lapsed into the church.

it is better to cheapen indulgences than to make the cross of Christ of no effect. And it is better for one to hold indulgences of little value than to teach some fiction in the church which could be discussed in such a manner that the church is confused. To be sure, I confess quite frankly and declare publicly that I do not care much for indulgences as a remission of punishments, in which my opponents glory. However, I particularly respect, cherish, and rejoice in them as a remission of guilt in the sense in which I set this forth previously, but they think very little of it.

One leaden dagger opposes this eighth thesis, because it is found in the laws that even the dead are excommunicated, as the chapter, *A Nobis*, in the work [of Pope Gregory IX], *Concerning the Sentence of Excommunication*, especially proves.[15] Oh, how afraid I was that my opponents would say that they had also discovered that reasonable punishments and satisfactions would be imposed upon the dead! It is good that they said the dead would only be excommunicated. No one denies that the dead are also absolved. But what does this absolution have to do with the remission of punishments? Is this that most subtle dialectic, without which, they teach, no one may become a theologian? Perhaps the conclusion which follows contains a fifth figure[15a] which says, "A person is absolved from excommunication, therefore, the punishments of satisfaction are remitted to him." Why, then, do these hucksters bestow indulgences so indiscriminately if the person who is absolved from sin soon has remission of punishments also? If, however, satisfaction still remains for those who are absolved, how can absolution be profitable for the dead or remove punishment? Therefore such reasoning as this is hopeless, for just as excommunication extends to those who are dead so also does remission of punishments.

The jurists themselves say that excommunication of the dead does no harm to the dead, just as absolution does them no good. But all these things are done to terrorize us, and the church does not pray publicly for one who has been excommunicated. Therefore a person suffers no more from this type of excommunication than

---

[15] *Decretalium, D. Gregorii Papae IX* Lib. v. tit. XXXIV, cap. 28. *Corpus Iuris Canonici*, II, cols. 899-900.
[15a] Medieval logic knew only four figures.

a house or garment suffers if it is excommunicated. By the same token a person is not helped by absolution. But I will put an end to the refutation of such babbling contradictions, since nothing more is contained in them than scholastic opinions which are founded neither on the Scriptures, church fathers, nor church law. My opponent always begs the question or, if he does not do that, he rages like mad women with such words as: "He errs, he rages, he is insane, an error, to err." He desires the sum total of his wisdom and knowledge to appear to consist of these words.

9

Therefore the Holy Spirit through the pope is kind to us insofar as the pope in his decrees always makes exception of the article of death and of necessity.

This thesis is more a proof for the preceding thesis. It is certain that if the pope wishes to make an exception in cases of temporal necessity, he will make an even greater exception in the case of eternal necessity which one experiences through death. On the other hand, one who is sick or recognized by law as handicapped is bound only by a temporal impotence. And even if the pope makes no exception in the case of necessity, nevertheless it is understood that an exception is made in that case, since necessity knows no law. Death alone is the absolute necessity and the last and greatest hindrance of all.

10

Those priests act ignorantly and wickedly who, in the case of the dying, reserve canonical penalties for purgatory.

1. This thesis is an obvious deduction of the eighth thesis. Certainly there must be many who wonder if the priests really do these things. To be sure they do. Since to do this is to place greater value upon obedience to the canons than obedience to the call of God and to prefer the cheap works of the canons to the most

precious reward that Christians receive through death, I do not know whether those who hold such an opinion have the right type of faith.

2. It is well known and often repeated by most distinguished teachers in the church that if God should reveal his will to a person through a trance or some particular form of enlightenment at the moment that person is doing works of obedience to the church, then that individual is obligated to discontinue the work, relinquish obedience to the church, and "obey God rather than men" [Acts 5:29]. Indeed, our teachers say that in the canonical hours themselves one must violate the command of the church and turn aside from the usual words in the event that heavenly enlightenment or ecstasy should possess him. If, therefore, the laws of the church cease to apply in such divine summons, why should they not cease to apply in so great a summons and moment of rapture as that of death? Or perhaps one ought to follow that great multitude of lunatics who depend so much on their ceremonial works that, to satisfy these works, they often put off obvious obedience to God and men and really believe they have done rightly when they have observed ceremonial works only, and neglected obedience to God.

3. Surely the church would act wickedly if by its inferior jurisdiction it should retain one whom God already calls before his highest tribunal. When does the pope allow a defendant to be bound by the law and rules of the inferior jurisdiction of a bishop or prelate after he has been summoned to appear before his own jurisdiction? Or does he require something from his subordinates which he himself, being a man, does not concede to God who is his superior? Can man force the hand of God when one man cannot force the hand of another? Far be it. But surely if he imposes the punishments stipulated by canon law upon one who is about to die, it is evident that he judges and punishes that one according to his own jurisdiction.

Therefore there are almost twenty reasons which have caused me (I hope not arrogantly) to doubt this matter of canonical punishments. On the other hand, there is no authority to support it, either from canon law, reason, or the common practice of the church. The only support for it is the abuse of some individuals.

11

Those tares of changing the canonical penalty to the penalty of purgatory were evidently sown while the bishops slept [Matt. 13:25].

Here I ask that no one think I am slandering the most worthy bishops when I say that they were asleep. These are not my words but the words of the Gospel, only in the Gospel the word "men" is used instead of "bishops" [Matt. 13:25]. Yet it is certain that the word "men" referred to the superiors and leaders of the church, unless you take this word to refer to the rule of every person's spirit and mind over his body. Therefore the popes of the church do not even teach that canonical punishments apply to purgatory, for, as I have said, there is no canon or statute from which it could be taught. Therefore certain canonists labor in vain if they try to point out by such means how many years and forty-days fasts must be spent in purgatory, since there are actually none, or at least it cannot be proved that there are any. The error consists in the fact that they do not regard the canons as given only for this life and binding upon earth, just as anyone who changes his residence from one city to another thereby also changes his citizenship. Before making the change he must make satisfaction for any debts he may have. Therefore, absolutely nothing should be imposed upon those about to die, nor should the dying be given up to purgatory while still in arrears with penances (as Gerson asserts in one place), but rather (as he teaches more correctly elsewhere), they should surrender to death with steadfastness and resignation according to God's will.

At this point we must regard that fabrication and worthless sophistry of the indulgence sellers as an effort to frighten us in the same manner as men desire to frighten little children by the use of masks, namely, by saying that, since the priest does not know the amount of repentance required for absolution and thereby, perhaps, does not impose as great a satisfaction as divine justice requires, therefore this disparity must be satisfied either by a special work or by indulgences.

1. Consider how like oracles their empty words sound when

they have no proof, even though the prophet says, "God utters no word without revealing his secret to his servants and the prophets" [Cf. Amos 3:7]. For it is incredible that this God of ours, who teaches us those things which are profitable for us, as he says through the prophet [Mic. 6:8], would nowhere have revealed this demand of his justice also.

2. I do not know whether or not those who speak in such a manner want to make God a usurer or dealer, one who remits nothing to us gratis but who expects us to make a satisfaction as payment for the remission. Or do these men desire, perhaps, that we should bargain with the justice of God regarding our sins, before which justice no man can be justified?

3. If the latter is the case, then why does the pope make full absolution, since he likewise does not know the amount of contrition necessary and is not able to make up the contrition that is lacking? Furthermore, perfect contrition does not need his absolution. Nor does he have power of another kind which is different from that of any other priest, but only of another degree. The pope remits everyone's sins, other priests remit only the sins of some. The amount of satisfaction they remit for some, he is able to remit for all, and nothing more than that, for otherwise the church would be some monster which consists of different types of power.

4. Furthermore, the early church did not know the amount of contrition necessary or the importance of personalities; nevertheless it gave plenary remission for sins after penance had been done, although, according to the opinions of these opponents of ours, the church could not know whether the penance was sufficient or not.

5. Another fantasy stems from the fact that our opponents base the remission of sins not upon faith and upon the word of the compassionate Christ, but upon the work of man who seeks and strives, for they imagine that plenary remission can only be given to those who have perfect contrition, which no one has in this life. Yet they concede that plenary remission can be given by the pope, even to those who have imperfect contrition.

6. Whatever the justice of God requires is already beyond

the jurisdiction of the church, which can change nothing that God wills or imposes. For that injunction still holds: "My counsel shall stand, and I will accomplish all my purpose" [Isa. 46:10].

By the same token, that which others say is also disproved, namely, that canonical punishments are declarations of the punishments required by divine justice. In the first place there is no proof for this opinion. Therefore it may be condemned very easily. If God declares something, then it is impossible for the church to relax the same, since the church does not do the imposing but simply declares those things which have been imposed by God. Otherwise these men are compelled to say the word of Christ must be read in this way: "Whatever I shall have bound, you shall loose."

12

In former times canonical penalties were imposed, not after, but before absolution, as tests of true contrition.

This twelfth thesis again proves the eighth, for canonical punishments are so temporal that they have absolution itself as their goal. However, since anyone who is about to die should be pardoned (other things being equal), it is evident that not only must no punishments be imposed, but also those which have been imposed, as well as those which should be imposed, must be remitted. And if the former custom of the church had been preserved, this error would not have arisen to the extent that it exists today. But now that absolution precedes punishments [satisfaction], it has developed that they disgrace absolution by sending people to death without absolution and thereby create a type of monstrosity, and at the same time they do not absolve by absolving and by the very same voice bind the one who is absolved.

1. This thesis is proved by that use of the solemn penance described in the canons, an example or remaining trace of which is still treated under the homicidal penance. Why do they, who are so strict with those who are on the verge of death, absolve him who lives from punishment and not direct him to perform other penances in life?

118

2. St. Jerome writes that his Fabiola is pardoned after satisfaction is made. In the same manner St. Ambrose pardons his Theodosius. Finally, one reads of this practice in no author more frequently than in the glorious martyr Cyprian, in the third book of his letters. The same thing is found in the *Ecclesiastical History* [of Eusebius] [16] and the *Tripartite History* [of Cassiodorus].[17] The status of penitents and demoniacs is likewise described by Dionysius in his work, *The Ecclesiastical Hierarchy*.[18] In all these references we see that at that time sinners did not receive grace and absolution before penances were performed.

3. Christ did not pardon Mary Magdalene and the adulteress, until after they had shed tears, anointed him, and chastened themselves most ardently and humbly.

4. Thus we read in Genesis 44 that Joseph chastened his brothers with many tests in order to find out whether their affection for him and Benjamin was sincere, and after he was sure of this he made himself known to them and received them graciously.

13

The dying are freed by death from all penalties, are already dead as far as the canon laws are concerned, and have a right to be released from them.

This thesis sums up that which has been said previously and is clear enough. It would be a very strange thing, if one who is about to die is released from all works and laws, from responsibility to men, even from those laws of God himself, especially where almsgiving, prayer, fasting, a cross, work, and whatever can be performed by the body are demanded. And finally, it would be very strange if one who is about to die is released from the works of holy love toward his neighbor (a love which in itself never dies),

---

[16] *Ecclesiastical History, Nicene and Post-Nicene Fathers*, eds. Henry Wace and Philip Schaff (Oxford and New York, 1890) I, 81-400. A more recent translation is that by Kirsopp Lake in the Loeb Classical Library (2 vols.; London and New York, 1926-1932).

[17] *Historia ecclesiastica vocata tripartita*. Migne 9, 879-1214.

[18] Dionysius, the Areopagite, referred to in Acts 17:34, probably was not the author of this work.

only to be confronted with requirements of the canons from which he cannot be released. Then the Christian would be even more miserable than all the heathen, because the laws of living torment him even in death, while, as a matter of fact, he is of such a nature that, even though dead he ought to be free through Christ in whom he lives.

Now, finally, let us draw together our conclusions to discover how many men there are whose punishments are remitted through indulgences. Six types of men seem to me to be excepted, because they need no indulgences: first, the dead or those about to die, second, the sick, third, those who have lawful hindrances, fourth, those who have not committed crimes, fifth, those who have not committed public crimes, sixth, those who mend their ways. We shall prove that these need no indulgences and at least make our reasons plausible.

1. The first proof is that which perhaps has the greatest offense, namely, that indulgences are necessary only for public crimes such as adultery, homicide, usury, fornication, drunkenness, rebellion, etc. If such sins were kept secret, the canons would not appear to apply to them. First, because the canons establish public penances and the church has no authority to judge publicly concerning secret things. Second, because just as a secret sin ought not to be punished publicly, so it does not need to be remitted publicly. Yet indulgences are public remissions and take place in the presence of the congregation, as is evident. Indeed there are some who think there is a distinction between indulgences by public bulls and those given privately under the judgment of conscience. Third, the church is offended, not by secret sins, but only by public ones. Therefore, they who sin in secret are not required to make amends for offenses committed and thus to rebuild that which has been destroyed. Fourth, at the present time the jurists do not condemn criminals publicly unless they have been recognized as such by law, while on the other hand they tolerate those who are recognized as criminals by deed. I certainly do not condemn their opinion, nor does it appear to me to be erroneous, since it gives no one the right to judge, condemn, or despise another regardless of how great a sinner he may be, unless he has the authority to judge him, lest

it be said of him, "Who are you to pass judgment on the servant of another" [Rom. 14:4]. Nevertheless, prelates must be blamed as much as subordinates for the neglect of love, since they permit those who are recognized as criminals by deed to act freely and do not care whether they become recognized as such by law, in spite of that command of Christ, "Tell it to the church; if he refuses to listen even to the church, etc." [Matt. 18:17].

2. I believe it is evident to everyone that canonical punishments are imposed only for crimes. Therefore indulgences (if they are remissions of the canons) apply only to criminals. So those who lead an ordinary life, which is not done without venial sins, have no need of indulgences, especially since no punishment may be imposed for venial sins; nor is there any obligation even to confess these sins. It is even less necessary for those who lead an ordinary life to purchase indulgences. Otherwise, canonical punishments would have to be borne by everyone at every moment, since no one, as I have said before, lives without committing venial sins. I add further that it is not necessary to purchase indulgences for every mortal sin and I prove that in this manner: No one is sure that he does not always sin mortally because of the most secret vice of pride. If, therefore, canonical punishments should apply to every mortal sin, then the whole life of the faithful, over and beyond the cross referred to in the gospel, would be nothing more than a torture chamber of canonical punishments. Therefore one must continually purchase indulgences and do nothing else. But if this seems absurd, it is clear that indulgences apply only to sins punished by the canons. Yet no sins can be punished by the canons except those which are certain and public crimes, or if I should be urged to go further, at least those which one is sure are crimes, as I have said about adultery, theft, homicide, etc., that is, deeds which are recognized as such publicly. Therefore consent to any mortal sin is not included in canonical punishment, either to be imposed or remitted. A sin committed by word of mouth is also not included, unless it becomes the occasion for a future deed, as is also clear from the words of the canons.

3. The canons are imposed for crimes in such a way that punishments cease if one mends his ways, for example, if he enters

a monastery or devotes himself to the service of the poor and the sick, or if he suffers for Christ's sake or dies according to the will of God, or if he does something similar to or greater than these things. In these cases it is clear that canonical punishments do cease, and indulgences have no value for them. Hence punishments are imposed only upon those who are lazy and who are indifferent toward penances, that is, those sinners who are spoiled by indulgences. Therefore indulgences appear to be granted especially and only to those whose hearts are hardened and to those who are without feeling.

4. It is to be understood, without any doubt, that punishments are not imposed upon those who are hindered, for a very just reason, from being able to bear the punishments, for example, if one were captured by the Turks or unbelievers, or if he is the slave of some master to whom he is constrained to give obedience according to the precept of the gospel, or even to perform services which he ought to perform to serve his wife and children by working with his hands and gaining a livelihood. Whoever is hindered by such things is not obligated to give them up, rather he is not only obligated to do them but also to ignore the canons and obey God. Therefore the person who is thus hindered has no need of the remissions of those things which he was incapable of having imposed upon him.

5. The canons impose nothing upon the sick; therefore the only one in question is the one who is healthy and who is not numbered among those who say, "The hand of God has touched me" [Job 19:21]. These sick people do not deserve to have punishments imposed upon them but rather to be visited and to receive comfort, according to that word of Christ, "I was . . . sick . . . and you did not visit me" [Matt. 25:43]. Moreover, it will be said to the popes, "For they persecute him whom thou hast smitten, and they have added to the pain of my wounds" [Cf. Ps. 69:26], and according to that word of Job, "Why do you, like God, pursue me?" [Job 19:22]. Therefore indulgences are not necessary for these people.

6. What is true concerning the sick is also true concerning the dead and those who are about to die, of whom I have already spoken.

You see, therefore, how many Christians there are for whom indulgences are neither necessary nor useful. But I will return to this thesis in order to bring this matter to a conclusion and to stab them with their own sword.

It is maintained by everyone in the church that in the agony and moment of death every priest is a pope and therefore remits everything for the one who is about to die. And if the priest is absent, certainly the longing of the dying man for the priest is sufficient. For this reason, since the dying man is pardoned for everything which can be pardoned by the pope, the indulgences for the dead seem to confer absolutely nothing, for whatever can be loosed is loosed by death. From this it is likewise evident that the distinction in gradations and laws is to be understood as applying only to the living and those who are in good health. Therefore indulgences evidently apply only to criminals and to the living who are healthy and strong, who have no hindrances and who have no desire to mend their ways. If I am wrong in this, let him correct me, whoever is able and knows.

One might ask, however, "From which punishments, then, are souls released, or what punishments do they suffer in purgatory if they do not suffer anything which is included in the canonical law?" My response is, If I knew the answer to that, why would I need to discuss it or ask about it? I am not experienced enough to know what God does with souls who have departed, at least not as experienced as those innumerable redeemers of souls who make such sure pronouncements about everything as though it were impossible for them to be mere men. Added to this difficulty is the fact that there are teachers who think that souls suffer nothing from the fire but only in the fire, so that the fire is not a tormentor but only the prison of souls. Therefore I am dealing here with a matter that is especially doubtful and debatable, and I offer what I have observed about these things.

14

Imperfect piety or love on the part of the dying person necessarily brings with it great fear; and the smaller the love, the greater the fear.

This is particularly pointed out by that passage in I John 4 [:18]: "There is no fear in love, but perfect love casts out fear. For fear has to do with punishment." Therefore if perfect love casts out fear, then of necessity a love which is not perfect does not cast out fear, and in this way fear remains in imperfect love. But where would one find that perfect love? And (to digress a little) what man is there who has no fear of death, judgment, or hell? For in every man, no matter how holy he may be, there are the remains of the old man, and of sin, and the vestige of the former Adam remains, just as the children of Israel in their day were not able to erase entirely the influence of the Jebusites, the Canaanites, and the rest of the heathen. Moreover, this old man consists of error, concupiscence, wrath, fear, apprehension, despair, evil conscience, horror of death, etc. Those are characteristics of the old, carnal man. They diminish, however, in the new man, but they are not extinguished until he himself is extinguished by death, just as the Apostle says, "Though our outer nature is wasting away, our inner nature is being renewed every day" [II Cor. 4:16]. Therefore these evil remains of the old man are not removed by indulgences or by contrition which has begun to take place in a person. Rather the process of removal has begun, and as a person increases in spiritual health these evils are removed. This spiritual health is nothing more than faith in or love in Christ.

Having made that statement, the thesis is clear enough. If anyone is snatched away by death before he has attained that perfect love which drives out fear, he necessarily dies in fear and trembling until love is perfected and able to cast out fear. This fear which I mention is that conscience which is evil and disturbed because of a weak point in faith. As the Apostle says, the blood of Christ frees our consciences from dead works [Heb. 9:14]. And also in Heb. 10 [:22] we read, "Our hearts are sprinkled clean from an evil conscience in the full assurance of faith."

Briefly, if I can prove that the reason for dread and fear is distrust, and that the reason for assurance, on the other hand, is faith, I believe it has been proved at the same time that the person who dies with an imperfect faith necessarily fears and trembles.

Furthermore, distrust is often referred to in the gospel as the reason for terror, despair, and condemnation. In the first place this becomes clear on the occasion when Peter commanded the Lord to depart from him, saying, "for I am a sinful man" [Luke 5:8]. The second case in point is given when Peter began to sink because of his little faith [Matt. 14:30]. A third instance is referred to when the disciples wanted to cry out in dismay when they thought Christ was a ghost walking on the sea [Matt. 14:26]. And a fourth occurrence is referred to when the distraught disciples thought they saw a spirit as Christ entered their midst through the closed doors [Luke 24:37]. In all these cases distrust is portrayed as the reason for fear and dread. Therefore all fear and trembling arises from distrust, every feeling of assurance arises from faith in God. Faith, however, arises out of love, since the person must be like the one in whom he puts his trust.

15

This fear or horror is sufficient in itself, to say nothing of other things, to constitute the penalty of purgatory, since it is very near the horror of despair.

I say nothing about the fire and place of purgatory, not because I deny them, but because that discussion is another one which I do not undertake to bring up at this time. Furthermore I do not know where the place of purgatory is, even though St. Thomas thinks it is beneath the earth. Meanwhile, I remain in agreement with St. Augustine, namely, in the belief that the places of refuge for souls are hidden and so obscure that we know nothing about them. I mention these things in order that the Picard heretic [19] may not appear to have drawn from my statement that there is no purgatory because I confess that its location is unknown, or that

---

[19] The term "Picard" is derived from the name "Beghard," which refers to a variety of mystical religious movements in Flanders and the Rhineland during the thirteenth, fourteenth, and fifteenth centuries. Luther probably refers to the spiritual descendants of the Picardi in Bohemia, whom the moderate Hussites considered heretics.

the Roman church errs because it does not reject the opinion of St. Thomas. I am positive that there is a purgatory, and it does not bother me much what the heretics babble, for St. Augustine, more than eleven hundred years ago, in the ninth book, thirteenth chapter, of his *Confessions*, [20] prayed for his mother and father and requested that intercession be made for them. And when that same saintly mother of his was dying (as he records), she wanted him to remember her at the altar of the Lord, although, as St. Augustine relates, this was done by St. Ambrose. But even if there had been no purgatory at the time of the apostles (as the disgusting Picard prides himself in), must, therefore, any credence be given a heretic who was born scarcely fifty years ago? And must it be contended that the faith of so many centuries has been false, especially since the Picard does nothing more than say, "I do not believe it," and by that means assumes that he has proved all his assertions and condemned all of ours, as though sticks and stones believe? But these matters pertain to his own work and time.

Therefore it has been conceded that souls feel dread. Now I shall prove that such dread is a punishment of purgatory, indeed the greatest punishment.

1. Everyone concedes that the punishments of purgatory and of hell are the same except that they differ in the fact that the latter is for eternity. But Scripture describes the punishments of hell as fear, trembling, dread, and flight, as it says in Ps. 1 [:4], "The wicked are not so, but are like chaff which the wind drives away." And also in Job, Isaiah, and many other places, the wicked are compared to the rubble and chaff which is snatched up and scattered by the whirlwind, a figure of speech which Scripture uses to be sure to symbolize the horrible flight of the damned. The same thought is found in Ps. 2 [:5]: "Then he will speak to them in his wrath, and terrify them in his fury." And in Isa. 28 [:16] we read, "He who believes in him will not be confounded," that is, will not hasten away, will not tremble, will not flee like one who is confused and disturbed; at any rate the prophet wishes to say that non-believers will be confounded and will tremble. Proverbs 1 [:33] says: "He who listens to me will dwell secure and will be at ease, without

---

[20] Migne 32, 778-780.

dread of evil." And Psalm 111 [112:7] says: "He will not be afraid of evil things." In these and in other places in Scripture terror, dread, trembling, fear, and quaking are expressed as the punishment of the wicked, while Scripture asserts the opposite of these for the godly. Finally, St. James says that "even the demons believe—and shudder" [Jas. 2:19]. And Deut. 28 [:65] clearly states that the punishment of the wicked is trembling, when it says, "The Lord will give you there a trembling heart." If there were no trembling, neither death nor hell nor any punishment would be trouble-some, as we read in the Song of Solomon [8:6], "For love is strong as death, jealousy is cruel as hell." This fact was ade-quately proved by the martyrs, as the Holy Spirit says about the wicked in Ps. 13 [:5], "There they trembled with fear" [Cf. Ps. 14:5], where there was no fear, and in Proverbs 28, "The wicked flees when no one pursues, but the righteous, bold as a lion, shall be free from terror" [Cf. Prov. 28:1]. Otherwise, why is it that one person fears death and grieves over it, while another regards it lightly, if it were not for the fact that the one who is inwardly lack-ing in faith in the righteousness [of God] is afraid exactly at the point where he should not be afraid?

2. In the next place, II Thess. 1 [:8-9] states, "Those who do not believe the gospel, will suffer the punishments of eternal de-struction and exclusion from the presence of the Lord and from the glory of his might." By the strength of his might alone God tortures and afflicts those to whom he is intolerable. Therefore the wicked shall flee and not escape, but shall be seized with anxiety. As that passage in the Book of Wisdom says, "It shall soon appear dread-ful to you" [Wis. of Sol. 6:6]. And in Ps. 20 [Ps. 21:9] we read, "You will make them as a blazing oven when you appear." Other-wise, whence came that voice, "O mountains, fall upon us, and hills, cover us" [Hos. 10:8], and that passage in Isa. 2 [:10], "Enter into the rock, and hide in the dust from before the terror of the Lord, and from the glory of his majesty," or that passage in Job, "Oh that thou wouldest hide me in Sheol, that thou wouldest conceal me until thy wrath is past." It therefore is clear that the greatest punishment for the wicked consists in being in the presence of the Lord, where they are put to shame because their

most foul impurity stands in sharp contrast to such sublime purity.

3. Moreover, the church, in behalf of souls, sings and groans, as in Ps. 6 [:2-3], "My bones are troubled, my soul also is sorely troubled." And Ps. 114 [Cf. Ps. 116:3] says, "The sorrows of death encompassed me and the pangs of Sheol laid hold on me." Therefore the most common prayer we make for these wicked people is the desire that they may have rest, particularly since we know that they are restless. However, it is not the punishments which produce the restlessness, as is evident from the martyrs and from those men who have been steadfast, but rather the dread of and the flight from punishments, both of which arise from frailty of trust in God. As a person believes, so it will be with him; and as he himself is, so punishments and all things will be to him. Therefore whatever may happen to the righteous man does not disturb him, as Proverbs states [Prov. 12:21]. On the other hand, the sound of a driven leaf terrifies the wicked [Lev. 26:36]. And in Isa. 57 [:20-21] we read, "The wicked are like the tossing sea; for it cannot rest, and its waters toss up dirt and mire. There is no peace for the wicked, says the Lord God."

4. Some individuals have tasted these punishments in this life, especially those of hell. Therefore we must believe even more that they are imposed upon the dead in purgatory. For David, a man of experience, said, "If the Lord had not been my help, my soul would soon have dwelt in hell" [Ps. 94:17]. And elsewhere he says, "My soul is full of troubles and my life has drawn near to Sheol" [Ps. 88:3]. And again he says, "Our bones are scattered at the mouth of Sheol" [Ps. 141:7], and "I become like those who go down to the Pit" [Ps. 28:1]. And again David says, "How many great and evil tribulations hast thou shown me, and then led me back again from the depths of the earth" [Ps. 71:20]. Indeed Hezekiah says, "I said, 'in the noontide of my days I must depart . . . to the gates of Sheol'" [Isa. 38:10]. And further on he says: "Like a lion he breaks all my bones" [Isa. 38:13], which surely cannot be understood in any other way except as an occurrence of unbearable horror.

5. How many there are even today who taste those punishments! For what else does John Tauler teach in his German ser-

mons than the sufferings of these punishments of which he also cites some examples?[21] Indeed, I know that this teacher is unknown to the schools of theologians and is probably despised by them; but even though he has written entirely in the German vernacular, I have found in him more solid and sincere theology than is found in all the scholastic teachers of all the universities or than can be found in their propositions.

I myself "knew a man" [II Cor. 12:2] who claimed that he had often suffered these punishments, in fact over a very brief period of time. Yet they were so great and so much like hell that no tongue could adequately express them, no pen could describe them, and one who had not himself experienced them could not believe them. And so great were they that, if they had been sustained or had lasted for half an hour, even for one tenth of an hour, he would have perished completely and all of his bones would have been reduced to ashes. At such a time God seems terribly angry, and with him the whole creation. At such a time there is no flight, no comfort, within or without, but all things accuse. At such a time as that the Psalmist mourns, "I am cut off from thy sight" [Cf. Ps. 31:22], or at least he does not dare to say, "O Lord, . . . do not chasten me in thy wrath" [Ps. 6:1]. In this moment (strange to say) the soul cannot believe that it can ever be redeemed other than that the punishment is not yet completely felt. Yet the soul is eternal and is not able to think of itself as being temporal. All that remains is the stark-naked desire for help and a terrible groaning, but it does not know where to turn for help. In this instance the person is stretched out with Christ so that all his bones may be counted, and every corner of the soul is filled with the greatest bitterness, dread, trembling, and sorrow in such a manner that all these last forever.

To use an example: If a ball crosses a straight line, any point of the line which is touched bears the whole weight of the ball, yet it does not embrace the whole ball. Just so the soul, at the point where it is touched by a passing eternal flood, feels and imbibes nothing except eternal punishment. Yet the punishment does not remain, for it passes over again. Therefore if that punishment of hell, that

---

[21] John Tauler was born at Strassburg about 1300 and died June 16, 1361. Cf. p. 73.

is, that unbearable and inconsolable trembling, takes hold of the living, punishment of the souls in purgatory seems to be so much greater. Moreover, that punishment for them is constant. And in this instance the inner fire is much more terrible than the outer fire. If there is anyone who does not believe that, we do not beg him to do so, but we have merely proved that these preachers of indulgences speak with too much audacity about many things of which they know nothing or else doubt. For one ought to believe those who are experienced in these matters rather than those who are inexperienced.

6. In addition to this there is the authority of the church, which chants, "Free them from the lion's mouth, lest hell engulf them"[22] [Ps. 22:21], as well as the words, "from the gate of hell."[23] These words certainly appear to indicate that souls are, as it were, already at the gate, at the threshold of condemnation and at the entrance of hell, which, as I have said, is near despair. And I do not believe the words of the church are empty words.

16

Hell, purgatory, and heaven seem to differ the same as despair, fear, and assurance of salvation.

Whoever shall have accepted the two preceding theses as true, easily admits this one also. Indeed, since we believe that peace, joy, and confidence reign in heaven in the light of God, we also believe that in hell despair, grief, and terrible flight rage[24] in the realms of outer darkness. It is clear that purgatory is the middle between both extremes, in such a way, however, that it is nearer hell than heaven, for in purgatory there is a despair, a longing to escape, dread, and grief. Souls in purgatory have no joy or peace, in fact they share nothing from heaven, since the punishment of purgatory is considered the same as that of hell, differing only in duration. But in speaking of despair I have added, "near despair," for

---

[22] Cf. *Officium et Missae pro Defunctis. Offertorium 2.* In *Liber usualis Missae et Officii* (Paris, Tornaci, Rome, 1929) p. 1886.

[23] *Ibid.* A versicle: *Ad Vesperas* and *Laudes,* p. 1149, *et al.*

[24] The Latin word in the Weimar edition is *servire* (to serve). Here I have read it *saevire* (to rage), with EA 2, 182, and CL 1, 58.

that type of despair finally comes to an end. Moreover, the soul, as long as it is in purgatory, feels nothing but despair, not because it despairs, but because it is so disturbed and perplexed with anxiety that it does not feel capable of hope. The Spirit alone helps them in their weakness [Rom. 8:26], as much as it is possible, by interceding for them in groans that are too deep for words. So those who have such temptations in this life do not know whether to hope or despair. Indeed, they appear to despair with only a groan for help remaining. By this sign, others, but not they, know that they still have hope. But I am not going to speak more extensively about this matter which is really most abstruse, lest the indulgence hawkers throw up to me the fact that I speak without proof, although, unlike them, I do not assert that which I know nothing about, but discuss, question, and contend that their presumptuous assurance is of a doubtful quality, indeed worthless.

17

It seems as though for the souls in purgatory fear should necessarily decrease and love increase.

This thesis is dependent upon the three preceding theses. Nevertheless, we shall explain this thesis and propose (as we started to do) three types of dying souls.

1. The first type consists of those who have no faith at all (that is, those who are condemned). These individuals must face death with the greatest dread and despair, according to that passage of Scripture which says, "Let evil take hold of the godless in death" [Ps. 140:11]. And also, "The death of sinners is the worst of all" [Ps. 34:22], for since they have no faith in God, the wrath of God lays hold of them.

The second type consists of those who have complete faith and are perfect (that is, those who are blessed). These individuals must face death with the utmost confidence and joy, according to the Scripture which says, "Although the righteous fall, he shall not be cast headlong, for the Lord is the stay of his hand" [Ps. 37:24]. And also, "Precious in the sight of the Lord is the death of his saints" [Ps. 116:15], and again, "If the just man shall be snatched by death, he shall be at rest" [Wis. of Sol. 4:7]. Both the just and the unjust have found a reason for death. The unjust man finds that which he feared, namely death and punishment. Moreover, he has always feared them. The just man, on the other hand, who is tired of this life, desires especially to be released, and so his desire is granted to him. The former has not lived out half his days [Ps. 55:23], the latter has prolonged the time of his dwelling in the body beyond his appointed goal. Therefore what the former dreads, the latter longs for. And since each of them is motivated by an entirely different desire, what is to the former the greatest dread is to the latter the highest gain and joy.

The third type of souls who are dying consists of those whose faith is imperfect, ranging anywhere from complete faith to no faith at all. I do not believe anyone denies that some people die with a faith that is imperfect; but we shall prove that point more fully a little later. Therefore, since imperfection of faith is nothing more than imperfect newness of life in the spirit and still a remnant of the old flesh and the old Adam (for if faith were perfect it would not fear punishment, face death reluctantly, or depart with earthly affection for this life), it seems clear that souls must not only remove the punishments, but also add the perfection of a new life and remove the remains of the old (that is, the love of this life and the fear of death and judgment). However much the punishment might be removed (if that were possible), the soul would not thereby be healthy simply because of its removal. In the same manner a person does not become better in this life simply by taking away punishments, but also by adding grace and removing sin. Therefore, before everything else, sin must be removed, that is, the imperfection in faith, hope, and love.

2. No punishment is overcome by running away or by fear. For the proverb is true which says, "He who is afraid of hell, goes there." Indeed, if one is afraid of the hoarfrost, the snow will fall upon him (Job 6 [:16]); that is, more will fall upon him than he feared. Every punishment is increased and strengthened by the fear of it, and by the same token, it is diminished and weakened by love. Moreover, punishment is overcome by love and affection for it; for no punishment is grievous as long as it has been overcome.

Therefore to him who loves punishments and death they are not grievous but sweet, because they have been overcome by love and the Spirit. On the other hand, to him who is afraid, they are grievous, because they are dominated by fear and the letter of the law. Therefore, if purgatory afflicts a soul and anxiety is a burden to him, it is clear that he lacks love and the spirit of freedom, and the letter and fear are present. I call this defect of love an imperfect spiritual health. Moreover, since no one shall enter heaven without perfect spiritual health, I conclude that for him love and health must be increased, just as dread must be decreased.

3. If anyone should deny these things or disbelieve them and should maintain that souls are perfected in spiritual life there [purgatory] and only pay previous debts of punishments, I answer first that those individuals should prove their opinion which I myself deny. I am positive that they shall prove their opinions either with no reasons at all or else with very weak ones. Now then, secondly, I ask whether they deny that three-fold division of dying souls mentioned above. If they admit the third type, they should explain with respect to what has been said previously, how timidity of spirit and fear is removed, since the perfect man, like his Father, God, fears nothing, can do all things, bears all things, rejoices and delights in all things. If they do not admit this third type, but think that faith is made perfect in death, that only the punishments remain to be paid, and that purgatory is only the reckoning of accounts of punishments which are due, then I shall proceed still further, in a persuasive manner, beyond that very strong and irrefutable argument which I have already advanced, namely, that they cannot prove their opinion by any passage of Scripture or by any rational argument. For this is what those conjecturers do, as well as those who follow blindly after them.

First of all, why does God want those who are perfect in spirit to be punished? Is it for satisfaction? Quite the contrary; beyond all satisfaction is the satisfaction of love, for by means of punishment God himself requires nothing else except that love should be perfected. For, unless the Apostle lies, "love covers a multitude of sins" [I Pet. 4:8]. But it has been established that the love these individuals have is perfect.

Second, where one is lacking in ability, satisfaction is made to God especially through the will, as the whole church believes along with St. Augustine. But if these individuals have perfect love, of necessity they possess such a will, and yet they do not have the ability with a life that is defective. Therefore, of necessity they make adequate satisfaction by the will alone.

Third, they who are perfect return to God whatever they owe, because they owe nothing more than the offering of their total selves along with their inmost will. God requires of man nothing more than his total self, as he says: "My son, give me your heart" [Prov. 23:26]. Indeed, through punishment he compels man to offer his whole self. In what way, then, do punishments remain after this has been done? For what purpose do they compel?

4. Consider, for example, a soul with perfect faith and love in the hour of death, which may still be obliged to keep a seven-day fast or satisfy some other canonical punishment. Is God so cruel that the soul which thirsts for him with the greatest love, and loves him most fervently above everything else, which has fully forgiven its neighbor all things, and desires most fervently that it itself may be forgiven all things, which because of these things has deserved forgiveness before God and men (for such is the soul of one who dies with pure love), here, I say, is God so cruel that he does not remit those seven days for the sake of the greatest love and humility toward Him and his neighbor, which is the greatest charity of all?

And yet this is the same God who says in the gospel to those who give alms not from the heart but from the abundance of the things which they possess that all things are remitted and cleansed [Luke 11:41], and who freely forgave the whole debt to the servant who did nothing but ask and promise [Matt. 18:23-28]. Does not God consider at all that it is so easy to grant such things to those who are living and in no danger of dying; and should it be so difficult to remit such little sins in exchange for so great a love to those who are about to die and are already burdened with the greatest danger of death? Who will believe that? Or how will they convince us of that? Therefore, either they should cease preaching their doctrines so confidently or else give better support for them and refute those which I have advanced. Meanwhile we shall conclude that the souls in purgatory labor on in punishment, not for the sake of punishment alone but because of a defect in love, since they had no desire to work towards perfection here on earth; or else, if they are perfect, we shall conclude that they are free, since all punishments are overcome by love.

It is not my understanding of the goodness of God that, in view of perfect and eternal love, he shall not remit to certain persons punishment of the shortest duration, when he, on the basis of very little love, at times remits eternal punishment to all. Furthermore, it is not my understanding that God, who often forgives all punishments in this life for the sake of one work of beginning love, shall never remit in death some punishments for the sake of every work of perfect love. I have, nevertheless, debated these matters because "God is marvelous in his sanctuary" [Ps. 68:35]. We would do better to leave such doubtful matters alone and teach people other things which are more certain. God is able to deal with them, not because of this or that opinion—for they have not been subjected to our judgment but to his—but because he is able and free to punish them there in order that he may show the glory of his grace, just as he did to Job and Paul.

5. Nevertheless, I speak in favor of this thesis for a fifth reason. If purgatory is only a workshop of punishment, why not call it "punitory" rather than purgatory? For the meaning and force of the term "purgatory" imply a cleansing which can only be understood as pertaining to the remains of the old nature and sin, because of which those persons are unclean who in their affection for earthly things have hindered the purity of faith. But if by the use of a new ambiguity (for they are prompted to make distinctions) they shall say that cleansing here is the same as payment, so that then they are said to be cleansed when the punishments have been paid, I answer: It is despised as easily as it is proved. But if they shall also despise the idea that the meaning of the term includes the cleansing of faults, let it be so. I do not dispute it. Nevertheless, it has been demonstrated that both meanings are doubtful. For that reason the first meaning has been scattered abroad among the people in a distorted manner and with the greatest of certainty, especially since the basic meaning of the term does not agree with their opinion.

6. The remark of Gregory I [d.604] in the *Decretals* (dist. XXV), in the chapter called *Qualis*, [25] also supports this thesis. There he says that not only punishments, but guilt, are remitted in the future life, that is, venial sins, as he points out by examples in that text. But the remission of guilt does not take place without the infusion of grace, and the dread of death is for saints a venial sin but not a small one.

18

Furthermore, it does not seem proved, either by reason or Scripture, that souls in purgatory are outside the state of merit, that is, unable to grow in love.

1. This is my strongest argument against the opinion for which I am reproached and which is taught without authority. Moreover, our opinion rests securely upon that authority which says that without the adding of grace no fear is dispelled, for perfect love alone casts out fear [I John 4:18]. Moreover, this thesis anticipates the argument of those who will say against me, "They are no longer able to earn merit, therefore the three preceding theses are false."

However, to continue with my opinion and disputation without asserting anything absolutely, as I started to do, I say if purgatory is only a workshop for paying punishments and souls are there because of their affection for that which is unclean (as I myself feel) and are not cleansed of that evil, then purgatory would become the same as hell, where punishment obtains and guilt remains. For the souls in purgatory there is guilt, namely, the fear of punishment and the lack of love, while, according to Isa. 8 [:13], the righteous man should fear nothing except God alone. Therefore they sin continuously as long as they dread punishments and seek rest. I prove this by the fact that they seek what is their own more than the will of God, which is contrary to love. But if they do love God, they love with the love of concupiscence (that is, with a faulty love), although even in the midst of their punishments they should please and glorify God and endure them steadfastly. And

---

[25] *Decretum Magistri Gratiani, Prima Pars,* dist. XXV, cap. 4. *Corpus Iuris Canonici,* I, col. 94. Migne 187, 148.

in order to assert something, even among so many thorny problems of this disputation, I confess freely that I don't believe anyone is redeemed from the punishments of purgatory on account of fear, until, having laid fear aside he begins to love the will of God in such punishment and loves the will of God more than he fears punishment—indeed loves the will of God alone and despises the punishment or even loves it as God's will. For he must love righteousness before he is saved.

But the righteousness is God who administers this punishment. Hence that statement of Christ, "He who does not take his cross (that is, bearing it willingly and lovingly) and follow me is not worthy of me" [Matt. 10:38]. But that punishment is the cross of souls. Since these things are so, and I believe they are absolutely true, let anyone who is able tell me how the love of punishment can take the place of fear without the infusion of a new grace. I confess that I do not know, unless you should say, contrary to what was said previously, that purgatory does not contain any dread of punishment, and for that reason is not similar to hell. In that case we pray in vain for those who, we understand, look forward to and love their punishments without any fear at all.

2. I prove that the souls in purgatory grow in love. The Apostle says, "To those who love God all things work for good" [Rom 8:28]. This good can only be understood as the increase of the good which one already possesses. Therefore purgatory also increases that good which is love for God, indeed, increases that most of all. And just as "jealousy is cruel as the grave" [Song of Sol. 8:6] and takes delight in such great evils, and just as the furnace proves gold to be gold [Prov. 27:21], just so punishment proves love to be love.

3. Strength is made perfect in weakness [II Cor. 12:9]. If love is present, every punishment is salutary and beneficial; for the most precious and most fruitful love does not permit anything in itself to be worthless. Since the greatest weakness exists in purgatory, therefore purgatory perfects love most of all.

4. It is impossible to stand still in the way of God. Moreover, the way of God is love reaching out towards God. Therefore it is evident that souls must either advance toward or fall away from the love of God, since they have not yet reached the end or seen God.

5. It is impossible for a created thing to persevere unless it continually receives more and more strength. For that reason certain thinkers say that the preservation of a thing is its continued creation. But to create is always to make new, which is clear even in brooks, rays, heat, and cold, especially when they are beyond their source. Therefore also in the case of spiritual warmth, that is, the love for God, souls must continually be preserved (until they become absorbed into their divine source) and, by the same token, necessarily grow, even if they perchance have been perfected, although to be outside of God and not to have attained to him and to have been perfected are ideas opposed to each other.

But it is worth while to see what moves my opponents to deny that souls may earn merit or what moves them to prove that it must be denied.

The first reason is that very well-known saying of St. Augustine: "All merit is acquired in this life; after death no merit is acquired."[26] Therefore, they say, purgatory is not a place for gaining merit.

My answer is this: St. Augustine and all other fathers who have spoken in a similar manner speak from the authority and by the use of Scripture, which speaks much more strongly in favor of this opinion. For example, that passage in the sixth chapter [:10] of Galatians: "As we have opportunity, let us do good." And Christ says in John 9 [:4]: "Night comes when no one can work." And the Apostle says: "For their deeds follow them" [Rev. 14:13]; and that particularly clear reference in Heb. 9 [:27] says: "It is appointed for men to die once, and after that comes judgment," then the end. Galatians 6 [:7] says: "For whatever a man sows, that he will also reap." Likewise: "We must all appear before the judgment seat of Christ, so that each one may receive good or evil, according to what he has done in the body" [II Cor. 5:10]. And there are many other passages which together make it appear as if, after death, there is a judgment according to which each one will receive in proportion as one has done, that is, deserved in this life, according to that passage in Ecclesiastes: "In the place where the tree falls, there it will lie" [Eccles. 11:3].

---

[26] *De praedestinatione sanctorum,* cap. 12. Migne 44, 977; *CL* 1, 64, note.

All these passages in like manner militate against the whole idea of purgatory because they do not establish an intermediary state between the dead who have been condemned and those who are saved. Therefore if purgatory is justly defended in spite of those things, it can also be defended that grace is increased in the souls in purgatory, notwithstanding that which is said, namely, that all merit is acquired in this life. Nothing is said about purgatory, just as the passages cited also say nothing about purgatory but speak only of heaven and hell. So neither side refers to purgatory. Therefore those words of Augustine must not be understood as applying to purgatory. All merit is obtained in this life and not beyond this life, that is, not in heaven or hell. Finally, according to St. Augustine also, the merit by which a man is worthy of being helped by intercession in purgatory is acquired in this life. Otherwise he possesses no merit either in heaven or hell by which he deserves to be helped. There, at least, he has respect for purgatory, here on earth he has none at all.

However, if a more obstinate person should wish to maintain that the authorities already cited do not deny purgatory in any way and that souls can be saved by holding to a doctrine of a two-fold judgment or two-fold retribution after death, namely, a temporal retribution, which is purgatory, and an eternal retribution, which is hell, and thus one reaps purgatory, the other hell, and likewise the works of one man follow him to purgatory, the other to hell; if anyone should maintain this, I answer that, by speaking in such a manner, that is, through such a detestable and arbitrary ambiguity, those authorities are destroyed along with purgatory rather than preserved, since the other side of that ambiguity can never be proved. In my judgment, it is unlawful and an exceedingly wicked use of a practice that has been preserved by some up to the present time, namely, that of dividing the simple meaning of Holy Scripture into an ambiguous and doubtful meaning. For it is better to state that this authority says nothing at all about this matter, than, in seeking to understand it in both connections, to give the impression that it is by no means reliable. "A short covering cannot cover both," says Isaiah [Isa. 28:20], and, as the saying goes, "One altar must not be adorned by laying bare another." Therefore, it should be said that the statement, "a man reaps there what he has sown here," refers to the present and the future life. For the word "reap" must be kept free from the distortion and double meaning of our own judgment and retain the same meaning in which it is used in Scripture, namely, as referring to a future and universal judgment. Therefore those authorities do not fight against purgatory at all, nor do they deal with it by the sophistry of double meaning, but they deal with it only in the sense of ignoring it. By the same token they also say, "Here every merit, there none." Moreover, how great an effort would it have been for me also to say that merit has a double meaning, namely, that after death no merit achieved in this world is valid, but only the merit obtained in that circumstance, and that Augustine speaks of the first! But I had no desire to do so.

What, moreover, do they say about that passage in Ecclesiastes: "Wherever the tree falls either to the north or to the south, . . . there it will lie" [Eccles. 11:3], if indeed they understand the word "fall" to mean death? Therefore, if by north is meant hell and by south is meant heaven, in which direction do those who enter purgatory fall? "To the south," they say, but they speak ambiguously. But what do they say about the words, "There it will lie?" Do they mean, "There it will remain?" Will they, therefore, never leave purgatory? In this respect the "remaining" is also ambiguous; namely, is it temporal or eternal?

It is evident, therefore, that this authority is directly opposed to purgatory, indeed by his ambiguity it makes a hell out of purgatory. Therefore, the matter cannot be solved except by saying (as I have already said) that that passage has nothing more to say about purgatory than the phrase: "The book of the genealogy of Jesus Christ" [Matt. 1:1].

19

Nor does it seem proved that souls in purgatory, at least not all of them, are certain and assured of their own salvation, even if we ourselves may be entirely certain of it.

We ourselves, because we believe that no man goes to purgatory unless he belongs to the number of those who must be saved, are certain about the salvation of those in purgatory just as we are certain about the salvation of the elect. Although I do not object too much if anyone should assert that they are certain of their salvation, I myself do not say that all are certain. But since every matter concerning the souls in purgatory is most obscure, I support this thesis by persuasion rather than by proof.

1. My thesis holds true, first, according to what has been said above, if the punishment of purgatory consists of trembling and dread of condemnation and hell, and every trembling causes the soul to be distressed, uncertain, in need of counsel and help, and that so much more when that trembling and dread is most violent and unexpected. Moreover, it is the strongest and most unexpected trembling for every soul, as I have said before and as Christ says, "That day will come upon you suddenly like a snare" [Luke 21:34]. The Apostle says, "The day of the Lord will come like a thief in the night" [I Thess. 5:2; II Pet. 3:10].

Because of their confusion they probably do not know whether they are damned or saved; indeed they may seem to be already on the way to condemnation and descending to the pit, and, to be sure, even now at the gates of hell, just as Hezekiah says [Isa. 38:10-20]. But I Sam. 2[:6] also says, "The Lord brings down to hell and raises up." Therefore they feel only that their condemnation has just begun, except that they feel that the gate of hell is not yet closed behind them. And they do not give up that longing and desire for help although it is never apparent to them. That's what those who have experienced it say. To explain: If anyone should come unexpectedly to the judgment of death, if for example, he should fall into the hands of highwaymen who, while they threaten in every respect to kill him, even though they have decided only to frighten rather than kill him, then these are certain that he will prevail. The man himself sees nothing except the very presence of death and by that very fact already dies. The only hope he has is the fact that he is not yet dead and can be saved from death, although he does not know from what quarter that help will come (for he sees that they could but do not want to kill him).

Therefore his condition differs very little from death itself. Such seems to be the case in the dread of eternal death, for men feel that they are threatened in every respect with nothing else than eternal death. So the church sings in their behalf, "Deliver their souls from the gate of hell," and "Free them from the lion's mouth, lest hell engulf them." They have only that remnant of knowledge which tells them that God can redeem them, but it seems to them he does not want to. Thereupon the condemned immediately add to this evil of doubt that of blasphemy, but, sustained by the Spirit, they add only their complaint and indescribable groaning [Rom. 8:26]. For here the Spirit moves over the waters where darkness is upon the face of the deep [Gen. 1:2]. But concerning this I have spoken more fully on a previous occasion.

2. Records of many examples claim that some souls have confessed this uncertainty of their position, for they have appeared, so to speak, going to the judgment to which they have been called, as St. Vincent and others testify.[27] On the other hand, many examples are recorded in which they have confessed their certainty. To this I respond: First, I have said that not all are certain. Secondly, perhaps it is better, according to the aforesaid, to say that they have not actually been certain, but that, because of their great desire for help, they are, so to speak, certain; and as though they were certain, they have asked to be helped quickly. So they rather imagine they are certain and timidly presume that they are certain as if they know for sure. It is as the gospel says, that the demons knew Jesus was the Christ, that is, they strongly imagined it, as the gloss[28] says. It is natural in every distress and anxiety to imagine very strongly that we may still be restored, although it may be more of a desire for restoration than the hope or knowledge of it, just as in the case of the demons there was more the desire to know than to have knowledge itself. For the actual knowledge of salvation does not make us anxious or cause us to tremble but makes us confident and enables us to bear all things with the greatest courage.

At this point one might ask: "Why is it, therefore, with regard

---

[27] The "Vita Vincentii Ferrerii," *Acta Sanctorum*, April, I (Paris and Rome, 1866–), 476-510.

[28] Cf. the *"glossa ordinaria"* of Walafrid Strabo (d. 849) on Mark 1:34. In this instance a "gloss" is a marginal note employed for explanation of biblical passages.

to a particular judgment, and Innocent testified to this,[29] that at death the reputation of a man, no matter who he is, is tested, for it seems that by means of this a man is made certain concerning his condition?" I answer that it does not follow that he is made certain even if special judgment is passed. It can happen that a dead man is judged, indeed may be accused, nevertheless the opinion concerning him may be deferred and not revealed to him. In the meantime, however, while conscience accuses, devils wheedle, and the wrath of God threatens, the wretched soul does nothing but tremble with horror at the judgment which may come at any moment, just as it trembles at the prospect of physical death. Deuteronomy 28 [:65-67] threatens, "The Lord will give you a trembling heart . . . and your life shall hang in doubt before you. . . . In the morning you shall say, 'Would that it were evening' and at evening you shall say, 'Would that it were morning.'" So there also, eternal death shall strike with a similar anxiety and torture the soul with a terrible horror. This interpretation is not far from the truth inasmuch as Christ also says in Matt. 5 [:21-26] that the Lord distinguishes between those guilty of judgment, of council, and of hell, that is, between the accused, the convicted, and the condemned.

But certain authors, distinguished more by knowledge than reputation, dare to say that some souls, on account of the lukewarmness of their life [Rev. 3:16], will be snatched away by death and thus be cast out by God so that until the end of the world they will not know whether they are condemned or saved. If one accepts the story concerning the monk who was about to die and because of the sin of fornication was condemned, having already blasphemed against God, but was then restored to health, then it is evident enough that the judgment and accusation of hell can afflict the soul, even though the final verdict has not been pronounced. This is borne out by a story in one of St. Gregory's [Gregory I, d. 604] sermons concerning a young man whom a dragon wanted to swallow up in death.

In positing this as most likely true concerning the whole matter of the punishments of purgatory, I am moved to do so, first of

---

[29] Innocent IV, *Apparatus in quinque libros decretalium,* ad. C.V. tit. 38, cap. 14, as cited in *MA*[3] 1, 496.

all, because of the nature of dread and anxiety, then because Scripture attributes this punishment to the damned, and, finally, because the whole church says that the punishments of hell and of purgatory are the same. Therefore I believe that this opinion of ours is sufficiently rooted in the Scriptures. Indeed, the trumpeters of indulgences seem to imagine that the punishments of souls are, as it were, inflicted externally and are entirely external, not born from within the conscience, as if God only removed the punishments from souls, and not souls from punishments. As it is written, "He relieved his shoulder of the burden" [Ps. 81:6]. It does not say, "He removed the burden from his shoulder."

And again the Scripture says, "When you walk through fire, the flame shall not harm you" [Cf. Isa. 43:2]. In what manner shall it not do any harm except that God gives courage to the heart, so that the soul does not fear the fire. This does not mean, however, that there is no fire through which man's soul must pass. Therefore freeing the shoulder from burden does not take place except by healing the fear of the soul and by comforting the soul. No punishment is overcome by fear but by love and disdain. Indulgences do not remove fear but increase it as much as they can while giving the impression that they remove punishments like some dispicable thing. However, God has purposed to have children who are fearless, untroubled, and generous forever and perfectly—children who shall fear absolutely nothing, but who through trust in his grace shall overcome and despise everything and make light of punishments and death. He hates the cowards who are confounded by a fear of all things, even by the sound of a fluttering leaf.

Another objection must be made at this point: "If souls bear punishments willingly, why do we pray for them?" I answer: Unless they bore them willingly, they would certainly be condemned. But why shouldn't they desire prayers said for them, since the Apostle also wanted prayers to be offered for him, that he might be freed from the unbelievers and that a door might be opened to him for the Word [Col. 4:3]. Yet Paul was one who with complete confidence gloried in the fact that he himself despised death. Even if souls would not desire prayers, nevertheless it is up to us to pity them in their fear and to help them with our prayer, just as we would for any others who are suffering. We should do this without making any distinctions, no matter how courageously they suffer. Finally, since souls do not grieve so much over present punishments as over their dread of impending and anticipated destruction, it is not strange if they should desire intercession in order that they might persevere and not falter in faith, since they are uncertain (as I have said) concerning their condition and do not fear so much the punishments of hell as the hatred of God, which is hell, just as Scripture says, "In death there is no remembrance of thee, in hell who can give thee praise" [Cf. Ps. 6:5]. It is evident, therefore, that they suffer, not because of the fear of punishment, but because of their love for righteousness, as I said above, for they are more afraid that they shall not praise and love God (which would actually happen in hell) than that they shall suffer. The whole church does right when it aids as much as it can this most holy and anxious desire of theirs, especially since God also wishes them to be helped through the church. We have finally come to the end of this vague and questionable disputation concerning the punishments of souls. If there are any who can produce better arguments concerning these matters, I shall not be jealous of them. I insist only that the one who does so should base his arguments on better examples of Scripture without veiling himself in the smoky opinions of men.

20

Therefore the pope, when he uses the words "plenary remission of all penalties," does not actually mean "all penalties," but only those imposed by himself.

I defend this thesis, but I do not yet assert it with finality. My reasons are these:

1. The first rests upon what was said in the fifth thesis, that only canonical punishment is remitted through the power of the keys. Therefore this thesis is a corollary of that one; to deny the one is to deny the other.

2. The second reason is drawn from that statement of the pope himself in which he says, "Concerning the imposed penances, we

145

relax them with mercy." Therefore he does not relax those which are not imposed by himself or by canon law. I do not think that we must be concerned here about the arbitrary statement of certain scholars who say that when the pope does not add this clause concerning imposed penances, then one is to understand that he means simply the remission of all punishment. I might say that even if it is not added, it is understood that it should be added as a necessary clause and one that concerns the very essence of the statement. Otherwise my opponents should prove what they say by some text.

3. I come to the usual argument, which is the strongest of all, when I ask by what authorities they prove that punishments other than the canonical are waived through the power of the keys. In answer they point out to me Antoninus, Peter de Palude, Augustinus de Ancona, Capreolus. Finally, Angelus de Clavassio cites his predecessor, Francisco de Mayronis,[30] who carried the sale of indulgences so far that he dared to pronounce them meritorious, if it may please Christ. Indeed it is as if those men were of such importance and authority that whatever they think must be immediately counted among the articles of faith. Rather they ought to be reproached for having brought forth these claims to our shame and harm, claims which they have invented in accordance with their pious desire, paying absolutely no attention to that faithful admonition of the Apostle, "Test everything; hold fast what is good" [I Thess. 5:21]. They are far more foolish than the Pythagoreans who assert only those things which Pythagoras has said. These, on the other hand, assert those things which the Pythagoreans doubted. But let us come to the source and fountains of these rivulets, that is SS. Thomas

---

[30] Antoninus (1389-1459) was archbishop of Florence and a Dominican scholar whose *Summary of Moral Theology* Luther has in mind; Peter de Palude (1275?-1342) was a teacher at Paris and a well-versed theologian to whose commentary on Peter Lombard's *Sentences* Luther refers; Augustine of Ancona (d. 1328) was an Augustinian Eremite whose *Summary of the Power of the Church* Luther knew; John Capreolus (d. 1444) was a Dominican who was considered the most able student of Thomas Aquinas in the fifteenth century. Francisco de Mayronis (1280?-1327) is considered one of the most distinguished disciples of Duns Scotus. Angelus de Clavassio (d. 1495) whose *Summary of Questions of Conscience (Summa casuum conscientiae)* went through thirty editions between 1476 and 1520, was superficial in his treatment of matters relating to indulgences, and his book became the object of Luther's scorn.

and Bonaventura.[31] For my opponents have received some of their ideas from them and they have added some of their own. Therefore these men are holy and carry much weight.

However, since they state these things as their opinions rather than maintain them as certain—for even St. Bonaventura confesses that the matter is most doubtful and entirely uncertain—is it not also clear that nothing can be proved from them? See for yourself whether they cite any [canonical] text or Scripture! It is no wonder that they themselves assert nothing ás certain. For since this matter would be an article of faith if it had been settled, therefore it is not up to the teachers to define it, for it must be supported also by the decision of a general council. Nor does the pope have the power heedlessly to decide on matters of faith; only indulgence preachers do. These are permitted to do whatever they wish. They all, however, have a single reason for their opinion, as Panormitanus also points out in book five of *Concerning Penance and Remission,* in the chapter entitled *Quod autem,* namely this: If indulgences are said to remit only canonical punishments, this makes indulgences of too little value.[32] Therefore in order that indulgences might not be esteemed too lightly, they would rather invent something they know nothing about, since souls would not be endangered in any way if indulgences were worthless, to say nothing of the fact that they are. But it would be a most terrible thing to preach to souls about fictitious things and illusions, even if indulgences were found to be most useful. No consideration is given to the salvation of souls but only to ourselves, and in order that we may not appear as inadequate teachers, we work harder for the glorification of our own words, even though this is superfluous, than we do for the faith of the simple folk and those committed to our care, which is the only thing that is necessary. But before I answer SS. Thomas and Bonaventura, it seems worthwhile to enumerate opinions concerning in-

---

[31] St. Thomas Aquinas (1225-1274), a Dominican, was the greatest of the scholastic theologians. St. Bonaventura (1221-1274), a general of the Franciscans, was a respected scholastic theologian contemporary with St. Thomas.

[32] Nicholas of Tudesco, archbishop of Palermo (Panormitanus) was a learned Benedictine scholar. Luther refers to his gloss in *Decretalium D. Gregorii Papae IX* v. tit. XXXVIII, cap. 4. *Corpus Iuris Canonici,* II, col. 885.

dulgences lest I appear to be the first or only person to have expressed doubts about them.

The gloss to the chapter beginning with the words *Quod autem,* in book five of *Concerning Penance and Remission,* which deals with the declaration concerning the efficacy and power of indulgences, begins with these words: "The efficacy of such remissions is an old debatable question and one which is still rather doubtful."

Some say indulgences are of use in the God-relationship but not in the church-relationship. For if anyone dies without mortal sin, and without having done penance, he feels the punishments of purgatory less in proportion to the measure of the remission granted him. Yet the church does not because of this relax the satisfaction for the living. This opinion is condemned by Panormitanus in the same place,[33] and I agree with him.

Others say indulgences are useful with regard to the penance which is imposed here over and beyond what is necessary for the sake of caution, that is, they are enjoined only with regard to those punishments which the pope has imposed, not according to the measure of the sin, but out of caution and to a greater extent than the sin deserves. This opinion is to be condemned more than the former.

Still others say indulgences are useful in relation to God and the church, but the one who grants the remission burdens himself with making satisfaction for the recipient. This also is absurd.

Others say indulgences are useful with regard to the remission of a penance which has been omitted through neglect. Panormitanus, in condemning this opinion, says that this rewards negligence. But in my judgment this is not altogether false, since actually all punishments are remitted, even those which have been omitted through neglect, provided one is displeased with one's negligence. Even those punishments are remitted which have not been omitted through neglect and which must still be completed.

Others say that indulgences are valuable for relaxing imposed penances, provided the priest who has imposed the penance permits the one who confesses to exchange the penance for the remissions.

---

[33] *Ibid.*

This is the good and true meaning of the matter, except that it restricts the power of him who confers indulgences. It is true that indulgences relax imposed penances; but the consent of the one who has imposed them is not required.

The sixth interpretation of indulgences, which Panormitanus introduces beyond those five established in the aforesaid gloss, is to the effect that they are useful, as the words indicate, both with respect to God and with respect to the penance which is imposed here, and he says this interpretation is held by Godfrey, Hostiensis, and Johannes Andreæ.[34] I myself also hold this as it stands and is conveyed by the words. But I do not follow them in their understanding of all words, especially that phrase "with respect to God." If these words mean that even punishments imposed by God are remitted, either here or in purgatory, beyond the penances imposed by the church or canon law, I do not believe it is true, except in a qualified sense, since the punishments of purgatory are remitted through contrition alone, without the power of the keys. So if anyone shall have become perfectly contrite, I believe that, as far as God is concerned, he has been absolved from purgatory.

As far as punishments for deeds done in this life are concerned, however, I say that there is no authority for this, as I have pointed out sufficiently in Thesis 5. For that punishment cannot be identified which is believed to be remitted as far as God is concerned. So I might say that the phrase "with respect to God" should be understood to refer, not to the punishments imposed by God, but to those imposed by the church. The meaning should be that remission of penances imposed by the church pertains as much to God as to the church, because God approves this remission of his church according to that passage, "Whatever you loose on earth shall be loosed in heaven" [Matt. 16:19]. It does not say, "Whatever you shall loose on earth, something else shall be loosed in heaven," but, "That very same thing which you loose I shall consider as loosed." For by this God wishes men to be subject to the priest,

---

[34] Godfrey of Trani was a thirteenth-century canonist at the Roman Curia. Henry of Segusio also served in the Curia and became cardinal and archbishop of Ostia (thus called Hostiensis). Johannes Andreæ was a canonist who taught at the universities of Bologna and Padua

something which might not happen unless we knew that God approves the deeds of the priest. You see, therefore, that all these interpretations are based on mere opinions.

Again, that which Angelus[35] adduces from his Francisco de Mayronis, that indulgences are also valuable for the increase of grace and glory, does not take into account that indulgences are not good works but remissions of good works for the sake of another lesser work. For even if a good work, for which purpose indulgences are granted, may be meritorious, nevertheless indulgences are not therefore meritorious, since a work done by itself would be no less meritorious and perhaps more. Indeed indulgences taken by themselves are rather demeritorious because they are remissions of good works. Therefore since in every matter that is doubtful it is permissible for anyone to dispute and oppose it, I say that I differ from SS. Thomas and Bonaventura in this respect until they give better proof for their own claims and disprove mine. I see nothing but opinions adduced to prove their points, not even one canon, while I, on the other hand, have produced many passages of Scripture in Thesis 5 above to support my position. Now, in order that I too may not speak without proofs from canon law, consider what follows.

4. In the chapter beginning with the words, *Cum ex eo,* in book five of *Concerning Penance and Remission,* there is the statement, "Penitential satisfaction is weakened by indulgences."[36] Though the pope may make this statement out of grief rather than out of grace, nevertheless the teachers of canon law interpret it as it stands. Therefore if penitential satisfaction is weakened, it is evident that only canonical punishment is remitted, since penitential satisfaction is nothing more than that third part of ecclesiastical and sacramental penance. For the church has nothing to do with evangelical satisfaction, as I have indicated previously.

But if anyone should disagree with me when I say that the pope does not deny that other punishments also are weakened, but merely affirms it and does not speak exclusively of that when he says, "Penitential satisfaction is weakened," I answer: Prove then,

---

[35] Angelus de Clavassio.
[36] *Decretalium D. Gregorii Papae IX* Lib v. tit. XXXVIII, cap. 14. *Corpus Iuris Canonici,* II, cols. 888-889.

that he also relaxes other punishments and that he does not speak exclusively of that. Since you do not do so, I prove that he does speak exclusively of that by referring to the chapter beginning *Cum ex eo*, cited above, where he says that hucksters of alms are permitted to place before the people nothing except that which is contained in their letters.[37] But nothing is contained in any apostolic document except remissions of sacramental satisfaction. As the pope himself says: "Penitential satisfaction is weakened by indiscreet and unnecessary indulgences." Indeed by this word the pope places an even more severe restriction on indulgences, for if only unnecessary indulgences weaken sacramental satisfaction, then moderate and lawful indulgences do not weaken that penitential satisfaction. Much less do they weaken any other punishments. But these things are no affair of mine or of my doing; the teachers of canon law will see to this.

21

Thus those indulgence preachers are in error who say that a man is absolved from every penalty and saved by papal indulgences.

I assert this thesis absolutely and prove it.

At least the third punishment remains, that is, the evangelical punishment. The fifth also remains, namely death and sickness, and that which is considered by many to be the greatest of all punishments—the dread of death, trembling of conscience, weakness of faith, timidity of spirit. To compare these punishments with those remitted through indulgences would be the same as comparing an object with its shadow. But it is not the intention of the pope that they should chatter so lightly and smugly, as is evident from the chapter beginning *Cum ex eo*.[38]

If, however, they should say, "We do not say that these punishments are removed by means of indulgences," I answer, Why do you not explain to the people what you mean by the punishments which you remit? Instead, you shout that all punishments are remitted be-

---

[37] *Ibid.*
[38] *Ibid.*

fore God and the church, no matter what punishments a man should pay for his sins. How shall the people know thereby what you are talking about when you speak so vaguely and with such sweeping statements?

22

As a matter of fact, the pope remits to souls in purgatory no penalty which, according to canon law, they should have paid in this life.

I shall defend this thesis at no greater length than the eighth, from which it follows as a corollary, for the penitential canons do not apply to the other life. Every temporal punishment is changed into the punishment of death. Indeed, because of the punishment of death every punishment is removed and must be removed. For further proof of this, consider the Roman church as it was at the time of St. Gregory, when it had no jurisdiction over other churches, at least not over the Greek church. It is evident that canonical punishments were not binding upon the Greeks, just as they are not binding now for Christians who are not subject to the pope, as in the case of the Turks, Tartars, and Livonians. For these people, therefore, indulgences are not necessary, but only for those who come under the authority of the Roman church. If, therefore, they are not binding upon those who are living, much less are they binding upon the dead, who are not under the jurisdiction of any church.

23

If remission of all penalties whatsoever could be granted to anyone at all, certainly it would be granted only to the most perfect, that is, to very few.

I interpret this to mean all kinds of punishment and declare the same. Undoubtedly enough has been said of the fact that remission of penitential satisfaction can be given to anyone. Indeed, I amend this thesis to read that the remission of all punishments can be granted absolutely to no one, whether he be perfect or imperfect. I prove this in the following way: Even though God should not impose scourges, or the fourth type of punishment, upon the most perfect, at least not for everybody and for all time, nevertheless there still remains the third type, the evangelical punishment, as well as the fourth, namely death and those punishments which are related to death and lead to death. Even if God could make all men perfect by grace, perhaps without punishments, nevertheless he has not decided to do it, but rather has decided that all men should conform to the image of his Son, that is to the cross [Cf. Rom. 8:29]. Why waste so many words? However highly one might extol the remission of punishments, what, I ask, is accomplished for that one who faces death and the fear of death and judgment? If every other remission is preached to a person and it is conceded that punishment is not remitted, I doubt whether this will be any consolation to him. Therefore keep in mind the dread of death and hell, and whether you want to or not, you will care nothing about remissions of other punishments. And so indulgences which do not take away the fear of death are not minimized through my effort but necessarily through what they are.

24

For this reason most people are necessarily deceived by that indiscriminate and high-sounding promise of release from penalty.

I declare this also and know that it actually happens. For I myself have heard that many understand it in no other way than that they fly to heaven by means of indulgences without any punishment at all. It is no wonder, when preachers of indulgences write, teach, and shout so as to give the impression that if one has obtained indulgences and dies before he falls back into sin, he will straightaway fly to heaven. They say all these things as if there were no sins except actual sins, and as if the tinder [of original sin] which is left is not an impurity, not a hindrance, not a means which would delay entrance to the kingdom of heaven. Unless this [original sin] is healed, it is impossible to enter heaven, even if there is no actual sin present, "For nothing unclean shall enter it" [Rev. 21:27]. Wherefore the very dread of death, since it is an imperfection of the tinder and a sin, even by itself prevents one from entering the kingdom, for he who dies unwillingly obeys God's summons reluctantly. Insofar as he dies reluctantly he does not, in that case, do the will of God.

His sin is therefore as great as his disobedience to the will of God. So he is a very uncommon individual who, after he has obtained all indulgences, does not also sin in death. Those who desire to be released and beg for death are an exception. In order that I may not be entirely at variance with them, I say that if anyone is perfectly contrite, that is, if he hates himself and his life and loves death to the highest degree, he shall immediately go to heaven after his punishments have been remitted. See for yourself how many of these there are.

25

That power which the pope has in general over purgatory corresponds to the power which any bishop or curate has in a particular way in his own diocese or parish.

This is that blasphemy which has made me worthy of a thousand deaths in the judgment of the indulgence hucksters, not to say "Shylocks." But before I prove this thesis I shall say a little bit about my argument. First of all I repeat that I am disputing here not with regard to the meaning which I intend by these words (for I firmly assert this, since the whole church maintains it) but with regard to the words themselves.

So I ask my adversaries to bear the grief with which I am afflicted when I hear that these things, which have never been written or established, are preached in the church of Christ. For we read that at one time it seemed most dangerous to the holy fathers to teach anything beyond the heavenly rule, as Hilary says;[39] and the holy Spiridion,[40] bishop of Cyprus, observed this discipline so

---

[39] Hilary of Arles (401?-450?) was an ascetic bishop who became involved in a dispute with Pope Leo I about luxurious living.

[40] Spiridion was an archbishop of Tramathus on Cyprus in the fourth century. He defended the Apostolic faith against the Arians at the Council of Nicaea (325).

strictly that he interrupted a person who only used a Greek word ambiguously, saying "Take up your couch and walk" instead of "Take up your pallet or your bed and walk," finding fault with the word he used even though it did not change the meaning at all.[41] I think that in the interest of pure justice they owe me forbearance for my grief since, without any question or warning, we are compelled to bear their presumptions which they take a great delight in preaching, and which we suffer by listening to them.

I do not say these things or act in this way because I am so impudent and arrogant as to think that I must be numbered among the learned ones of the holy church, much less among those whose province it is to decide upon these things or to condemn them. Would that I might once deserve to be accounted the most insignificant member of the church. I do this rather for the following reasons: Although there are in the church men who are most learned as well as most holy, nevertheless it is the tragedy of our age that even such great men are not able to help the church.

An example of what learning and godly zeal could do today has been adequately proved by the unfortunate fate of those most learned and holy men who, under Julius II, desired to reform the church by calling a general council for that purpose.[42] There have been, to my knowledge, a few good and learned pontiffs but the example of these is overshadowed by that of the many. "For it is a most evil time," as the prophet Amos says, "therefore he who is prudent will keep silent in such a time" [Amos 5:13].

Finally, we now have a very good pope, Leo X, whose integrity and learning are a delight to all upright persons. But what can this man who is so worthy of our respect do amidst such confusing circumstances? He is worthy of having become pope in better times, or of having better times during his pontificate. In our day we are only worthy of popes like Julius II, Alexander VI, or some other

---

[41] The Latin *cubile* usually means couch or bed, *grabatum* a low couch, and *lectum* a couch of leaves. Virgil in *Aeneid* iii, 324 speaks of *cubile* as a marriage bed.

[42] This reference is evidently to the scandalous Council of Pisa which was called in 1511 by a few French and Spanish cardinals to condemn Pope Julius II; but the cardinals refused. Luther here seems to refer to the Fifth Lateran Council (1512-1517) dominated by Julius II and Leo X.

tyrannous Mezentians[43] as described by the poets. For today even Rome itself laughs at the good popes, indeed Rome most of all. In what part of the Christian world do they ridicule the popes more freely than in that veritable Babylon, Rome? But enough of that. Since the church has the most learned people in positions of authority, except for countless private persons, I should keep quiet if, according to their standard, I should like to be considered wise. But it is better for the truth to be spoken by fools, children, and drunkards than to be silenced completely, so that the faith of the learned and wise might become more lively when they hear that we, the ignorant mob, finally cry out against the overwhelming indignity of the matter, just as Christ says, "If these were silent, the very stones would cry out" [Luke 19:40].

With this preface I come to the thesis and will consider it, first, according to the meaning and, secondly, according to the words or the opinion of others. Therefore in this thesis I say nothing concerning the power of jurisdiction which I shall deny in the thesis immediately following and which I have denied in the same manner in Theses 22 and 8 above. For they have taken this authority from the words previously mentioned, about which authority I say, as I have said before, that the church may decide upon the other part of that question and I will gladly acquiesce. In the meantime, may the insolent exponents of their dreams desist.

I doubt and dispute whether the popes have the power of jurisdiction over purgatory. As much as I have read and perceive up to this moment, I hold fast to the negative position. I am prepared, however, to maintain the affirmative after the church has decided upon it. Meanwhile I speak here concerning power of force, not of rights—the power of working, not of commanding— so that the meaning is this: The pope has absolutely no authority over purgatory, nor does any other bishop If, however, he does

---

[43] The reference here is to Mezentius, king of Caere in Etruria, whose aid was invoked by Turnus against the invading Aeneas. According to the earlier story, told in Cato's *Origines*, Turnus and Aeneas alike fell in the subsequent conflict, and Mezentius was later killed or forced to submit in single combat with Acanius. Virgil in *Aeneid* (vii-x) develops Mezentius into a full-blooded, atheistic tyrant, killed by Aeneas after the death, in his defense, of his attractive son Lausus.

have some authority, he certainly has only the same kind in which his subordinates also share.

Moreover, this is an authority by which the pope and any Christian who so wishes can intercede, pray for, fast, etc. on behalf of departed souls—the pope in a general way, the bishops in a particular way, and the Christian in an individual way. Therefore it is evident that the thesis is absolutely true. For just as the pope, at one time and with the whole church, may intercede for souls (as is done on All Souls' Day), so every bishop who wishes may do it with his own diocese (as is done on "Common Days"),[44] also the curate in his own parish (as is done at funerals and anniversaries), and any Christian who wishes in his own private devotion. Either one denies that such aid is an intercession or else concedes that each and every prelate, along with his subordinates, can intercede for souls. I think that these things are not nearly as doubtful as those bold statements of my opponents concerning the jurisdiction of the church over purgatory.

26

The pope does very well when he grants remission to souls in purgatory, not by the power of the keys, which he does not have, but by way of intercession for them.

I do not believe it is necessary again to declare publicly that which I here debate or maintain. However, since in our time the inquisitors of heretical depravity are so zealous that they attempt by force to drive the most orthodox Christians to heresy, it would be best to give an explanation for every single syllable. It is not very clear to me what else Giovanni Pico della Mirandola, Lorenzo Valla, Peter of Ravenna, John of Wesel, and very recently Johann Reuchlin and Jacques Lefèvre d'Etaples[45] did to be compelled

---

[44] The days in the week following Michaelmas Day (Sept. 29).

[45] Pico della Mirandola (1463-1494) and Lorenzo Valla (1405-1457), Italian humanists; Peter of Ravenna (1448-1518), an Italian jurist who late in life taught at Greifswald and Wittenberg; John Ruchrath of Oberwesel, or Wesel (1410?-1481), an Erfurt theologian and preacher in Mainz and Worms; Johann Reuchlin (1455-1522), noted German lawyer, statesmen, and humanist; and Jacques Lefèvre d'Etaples (Faber Stapulensis, 1455-1536), a French humanist. All these were at one time or another tried or threatened by the Inquisition.

to judge badly against their will, unless it is that they failed to explain every single syllable (as I have said). So great is the tyranny of young zealots and effeminate healers in the church today! Therefore I declare once again that I am about to do two things in this thesis, first, to discuss the power of the keys over purgatory and prove that it has no such power, until someone who affirms it shall prove that it does, and second, to inquire into that method and manner of intercession for the souls of the dead.

The first I prove in this manner:

1. According to that generally accepted reasoning of Henry of Segusio, namely, if the keys themselves should extend to purgatory, they could empty purgatory. Therefore the pope would be cruel if he did not empty purgatory.

They resolve this argument thus: The pope can, but he must not, empty it unless there is a justifiable and reasonable cause for doing so, lest he act rashly against divine justice. I hardly think that they would advance this cold and careless solution unless they do not care what they say, or unless they think that they are talking to sea calves who are in deepest sleep. So it happens that from one given absurdity many others follow. As the saying goes, "One lie requires seven lies to make it appear true."[46]

Therefore this argument could hardly be supported more strongly than by such refutation. We now ask, what will be the name of this reasonable cause? It is well known that indulgences are granted either for participating in the war against the infidels or for building churches or for some other common need of this life. But none of these reasons is so great that love is not incomparably greater, more righteous, and more reasonable. Therefore, if divine justice is not offended when, for the sake of the bodies of the faithful and the protection of their goods, or for the benefit of inanimate buildings, or the briefest need of this corruptible life, as many sins are remitted as one should desire (even if one includes all people in that number so that purgatory would be evacuated), how much less is divine justice offended if, for the sake of holy love,

---

[46] A German proverb having its origin in law court procedure according to which the testimony of seven persons in favor of the witness could be superseded through the testimony of seven other persons. Cf. Wander, *Sprichwörterlexikon*, III, 255. MA³ 1, 502.

all men are redeemed. Probably, however, divine justice is so unfair or gloomy that it is more favorably inclined to a love for the property and purse of the living than it is to souls that give evidence of such needs.

Especially is this so since it is of such great importance to give aid to souls, so that the faithful should prefer to serve the Turks and be killed in body than to lose their souls. Therefore if the pope for a lesser purpose would redeem an infinite number of souls, even for the same reason all souls, why would he not also redeem men for the sake of that which is greatest, that is, for the sake of love? Nevertheless, at this point I might advise those who have their backs to the wall to say that there can be no reasonable cause so that they may safely slip out from under this objection. Even if the pope had the power of jurisdiction over purgatory as far as he himself is concerned, he does not have it as far as the reason for such action is concerned, for such a reason does not exist.

2. The very manner in which the pope speaks about imposed penances proves the same thing.. Moreover it is evident that he gives only as much as he declares, and that he gives in the manner in which he declares, therefore just as a bishop remits forty days, a cardinal one hundred days of the imposed penances, so the pope remits completely all the days of the penances which have been imposed. Yet no power of the keys has imposed the punishments of purgatory.

In this matter a pretty dreamer has conjured up the following: When the pope says, "We grant indulgences for all sins with respect to imposed penance," it is understood to refer to a punishment imposed by the priest. However, when he says, "We grant indulgences for all sins for which they have been truly sorry and which they have confessed," then those which have been forgotten or which they do not know about are not remitted. But when he says, "We grant remission of all sins," then the soul flies to heaven at death. Thus the pope has the power to save whomever he wishes. What madness! Behold how confidently this boaster makes this claim, as if he were proclaiming an oracle! If I should say to him, I beseech you, how shall I prove this, if I must give a reason for this belief [Cf. I Pet. 3:15], perhaps he would invent other new lies, by means of which he would resolve these first big lies with even greater ones. Oh unhappy Christians who are compelled to listen to all these things that these weak-minded men are permitted to babble at length, as if we did not have the Scripture itself which Christ has commanded us to teach the people, and whom we should give the measure of wheat instead of jars of burrs and thistles!

Among other strange tales, which this most persuasive writer invents here, is the fact that he dares to try to persuade us that the pope has the power of remitting or not remitting sins which we do not know about or which have been forgotten, as if the whole church did not know that after the pope has done all his pardoning it still remains for all the faithful to say: "Who can discern his errors? Clear thou me from hidden faults, O Lord" [Ps. 19:12]. The whole church knows that along with Job we must be afraid of our good works, lest they be considered by God as terrible sins [Cf. Job 9:28]. But the holder of the keys of the church does not know or determine whether good works are evil or not before God; much less does he remit them. Secondly, this dream of his elaborates on that most tedious and useless art of confessing, rather of leading souls to despair and destruction, in which we are taught even to count the sand, that is, to examine, gather together, and weigh every single sin in order to make us truly repentant. But if we do this we shall revive the lusts or hateful memories of the past, and while we confess past sins, we sin anew. Even if the best kind of repentance results, it would surely be only forced, wretched, and insincere, brought forth artificially out of fear of punishment. Out of such fear we are taught to feel sorrow for sins, that is, we are taught to attempt the impossible or make matters worse.

True sorrow must spring from the goodness and mercies of God, especially from the wounds of Christ, so that man comes first of all to a sense of his own ingratitude in view of divine goodness and thereupon to hatred of himself and love of the kindness of God. Then tears will flow and he will hate himself from the very depth of his heart, yet without despair. Then he will hate sin, not because of the punishment but because of his regard for the goodness of God; and when he has perceived this he will be preserved from despair and will despise himself most ardently, yet joyfully. Then, when he has true sorrow for one single sin, he will at the same time have true sorrow for all sins. Thus the Apostle says in Rom. 2 [:4], "Do you not know that God's kindness is meant to lead you to repentance?" Oh St. Paul, how many there are who do not know that, even those who teach others! So we read in the book of Numbers [21:9], that the children of Israel were not freed from their fiery serpents through the sight and the dread of them, but rather by turning their eyes from them to the bronze serpent, that is to Christ. Likewise also they were terrified when they saw the Egyptians; but after they had turned their backs to them and crossed the sea they were saved [Exod. 14:10, 22]. So our sins must be borne by the wounded Christ rather than in our own conscience. For in Christ our sins are dead, but in us they live. Otherwise, if the torture chamber of those sins were to be preserved, it might happen that a person suddenly snatched away by death could not be saved because he has no time to recollect his sins. But my opponents have an answer for this!

Therefore it can be said in answer to that contriver of falsehood: In every remission of the pope, especially in that one which is made in public and before the entire church (as is the case in indulgences), that phrase, "regarding imposed penances," should be understood to include sins that are either forgotten or not known, for these do not belong to the jurisdiction of the church.

Moreover, that sea of words (it seems to me) of the indulgence preachers has stemmed from a certain neglect to examine the origin of indulgences. For at that time when canonical penances were considered very important, four days was considered a remission of great length. Later they began to grant a hundred days, then a thousand days, finally many thousands of days, then years, then hundreds and thousands of years. So little by little a greater and greater generosity developed with respect to indulgences. After this one-seventh of all sins began to be remitted, then one-third, lately one-half, and thus it has come to plenary remission of all sins, as one can well see even yet in the main churches[47] of the city

---

[47] Latin is *stationibus*. The reference is to the seven titular churches of Rome.

of Rome. But if the imposed penance is understood with reference to the first stages, it must certainly also be understood with reference to plenary remission.

3. Once again the manner in which the pope speaks supports this thesis when he says he grants remission "by means of intercession," for the means of intercession must be separated from the means of authority of jurisdiction. If we shall believe the pope himself (as we should) more than any of those preachers or ourselves, it is clear that no authority, but only intercession is of any avail for those in purgatory. At any rate it is safer for me to agree with the pope than with them. The pope does not arrogate to himself authority but claims for himself the right of intercession. I am surprised by the confidence with which the indulgence preachers, contrary to the expressed prohibition of the chapter beginning *Cum ex eo,*[48] dare to proclaim more than is contained in the papal documents, since only the means of intercession is contained there. If it is their understanding that the pope does not have any power of jurisdiction over purgatory, although he does have the power of the keys for applying intercessory prayers for those in purgatory, I say here and now that no one denies this. The power of applying either intercession, satisfaction, or the praises of God is absolutely in the jurisdiction of the supreme pontiff. Whether or not that power thus belongs to the pope alone, so that not even other bishops possess it, as I have said in the preceding thesis, or what is involved in that method of application which I do not yet understand, I shall discuss in the second part of this thesis. Meanwhile we shall pursue the discussion of this first part further.

4. By far the strongest reason is that Christ states, not in ambiguous, but in clear, open, and concise words: "Whatever you bind on earth shall be bound in heaven, and whatever you loose on earth shall be loosed in heaven" [Matt. 16:19]. He has not added the words "on earth" in vain. Otherwise, if he had not wished to restrict the power of the keys, it would have been sufficient to say, "Whatever you loose shall be loosed." Therefore either Christ was a babbler who used too many words, or else the power of the keys applies only upon earth. But here, oh gracious God,

---

[48] *Op. cit.*

how manifest is the superstition of certain people, who without the knowledge and will of the pope wish by means of these words to give him authority, where he appropriates for himself only intercession. And when they realized that these words of Christ strongly opposed them and exposed their error, they did not thereby cease to defend their error and make their opinion conform to the clear words of Christ. On the contrary they make his words conform to their perverted meaning and twist them, saying, "That term 'upon earth' can be construed in two different ways, in one way as pertaining to the one who looses, in another way as pertaining to that which must be loosed." According to the first way, Christ must be understood as having said, "Whatever Peter shall have loosed while he was on earth, shall be loosed also in heaven." Perhaps they also wish that if he should loose the devil (provided he were loosed on earth) the latter would be loosed in heaven. For he who says "whatever" and adds nothing to limit it certainly shows that everything may be loosed.

I do not know with what words I should label this rude and insolent superstition—this brazenness. The author here is worthy of the displeasure and eloquence of a Jerome, so that such a presumptuous violence and corruption of the sacred words of Christ would be avenged. Grammar itself could have taught them that this meaning of theirs could not be maintained according to these words (but they follow a new dialectic rather than correct grammar). It seems as though they knew all along that Christ was afraid that some day some such Peter or pope would arise who even though dead would desire to bind and loose. Thus it would become necessary for him to anticipate such an extraordinary ambition and tyranny of dead popes and to prevent them from binding and loosing except while they were alive and upon earth. (To ridicule in a fitting manner such worthy interpreters of Scripture), perhaps Christ had reason to fear—and not without reason—that some day a dead pope might bind something which his living successor might loose. Then great confusion would arise in heaven and the troubled Christ would not know which of these two works he should approve, since he had rashly permitted the same work to both of them and did not add the words "on earth" in order to restrain the dead pope.

If they do not understand this in such a manner, why do they get so excited? Why do they try so hard to show that the phrase "on earth" pertains to the one who does the loosing? Behold, indeed, this little golden work of a golden teacher![49] It is a work most worthy of golden letters, and lest there be something about it which is not golden, it must be handed down by golden disciples, namely, by those about whom it is said, "The idols of the nations are silver and gold. . . . They have eyes, but they see not, etc." [Ps. 135:15-16]. These people proceed in a straight path against Christ. Christ has added the phrase "on earth" in order that the pope, who cannot be anywhere except on earth, might not presume to bind and loose that which is not on earth. It is as though Christ purposely wanted to anticipate the detestable flatterers of our day and to restrain them when they proceed to hand over to the pope the kingdom of the dead against his will and despite his objection. St. Jerome, because of his zeal, would have called these individuals "theologians," that is, people through whom God speaks but actually that god who, according to Virgil, inspires his soothsayers to great frenzy.[50] Nevertheless we shall discuss this matter in opposition to them.

First, if, according to this understanding the keys loose the dead, they also bind them, since the phrase "on earth" is added in both cases when it reads, "Whatever you bind on earth." Therefore we must discriminate here also with the same diligence and discernment and interpret the phrase "on earth" with a two-fold meaning, in one sense as pertaining to the one who does the binding, in the second sense as pertaining to that which must be bound. Thus they should conclude that the pope can bind beneath the earth, in purgatory. But we should take care (in the manner of good physicians, of course) that he does this while he is alive and on earth, for if he is dead he cannot bind. But if the first part of the words of Christ does not suffer such an unbearable and violent mockery as this, as they themselves maintain, although they are

---

[49] Refers to the best known book of Hostiensis (Henry of Segusio; d. 1271), entitled *Summa super titulis Decretalium*, also known as the *Summa aurea*, or *Golden Summary*. The author was an Italian canonist who taught at Bologna and Paris and later was made chaplain to the pope. See above, p. 149, n. 34.
[50] Cf. *Aeneid* vi, l. 12.

badly lacking in judgment, with what impudence will they dare to attribute that force to the second part, since this has been composed in a similar vein throughout? Or, perhaps, they should be permitted, according to their custom, to call everything one and the same and to speak ambiguously and deceitfully however and wherever they please. They may say that the term "on earth" pertains in the first part of Christ's words to that which must be bound, but in the second part to the one who does the loosing, for they have dragged even more monstrous things into the Holy Scripture, according to their praiseworthy custom.

Therefore, since everyone denies that the keys have power to bind in purgatory, it must also be denied that they have power to loose, for both of these are equal powers and have been given equally by Christ to his church. This is the opinion of certain ones who are not the worst jurists. My opponents may judge whether they are saner than the others.

Second, this opinion is also refuted by their own antithesis, "in heaven"—"on earth." For just as the term "in heaven" refers undoubtedly to what must be loosed in heaven, so the term "on earth" must refer to what must be loosed on earth. And again, just as the term "in heaven" refers to what is bound, so the term "on earth" must refer to what is bound. Hence Christ purposely has not said, "I shall loose in heaven," but rather, "it shall be loosed in heaven," so that, if anyone by the first word, "Whatever you shall loose upon earth," should try to deduce from it a false interpretation, he would be prevented from doing so by the conclusion. And one would not be permitted to apply this word to him who does the loosing, for the premise "what is loosed in heaven" must certainly be understood to refer to the conclusion "what is loosed upon earth," and not to the one who does the loosing. Likewise what is bound in heaven must be understood to refer not to the one who does the binding, but to what is bound on earth, or at least to both.

Third, if the power of the keys extends to purgatory, why do they go to all this futile trouble? Why do they not omit the word "intercession"? Why do they not persuade the pope to say that he looses and binds by means of his power and authority rather than by mediation of intercession? Surely whatever he shall loose (only let him be careful that he is not dead!) shall be loosed. Why does he annoy us with the word "intercession," which no one understands as "power," but everyone as "mediation?"

Rather we should do even more and ask the pope to do away with purgatory and remove it from the realm of nature. For if the keys of the church extend so far, even with regard to that which must be loosed, then the whole of purgatory is under the pope's authority. I prove this in the following manner: The pope should give plenary remission to all those who are in purgatory; secondly, in a similar manner he should give that same remission to all those Christians who are about to die. Then it would be certain that no one shall remain in purgatory, no one shall enter it, but everybody shall fly to heaven and purgatory shall end. Moreover he is in duty bound to grant plenary remission; and there is a most just reason why he should, namely, love, which must be sought through all things, above all things, and in all things. Nor do we need to fear that divine justice will be offended by love, for it is toward that end that righteousness actually impels us. But if this is done, we shall lay aside the whole "Office of the Dead," which today is burdensome and neglected enough, and change it into a festival service.

Fourth and last, if the punishment of purgatory is a corrective and punitive one, as I mentioned in Thesis 5, then it is certain that it cannot be loosed by the power of the keys. The exhaustive classification of punishments makes it sufficiently clear in my opinion that no other punishment exists.

Therefore the first part of this thesis is clear, and thereby the whole thesis has, in all probability, confirmed the fact that the pope's intercession and not his power of jurisdiction affects purgatory.

It was not my intention that the second part of my thesis, namely, that which deals with the method of intercession, should be investigated. And it is not necessary for the sake of my arguments to know what that method is or what its nature is. Nevertheless I shall express myself in that matter, which I could justifiably overlook, in order that I may not appear to dodge the issue. Without prejudice to my position in any way, I declare that it is not for me to decide what that method of intercession should be; it is a matter for the pope or even perhaps for a church council to decide. It is my intention only to inquire, discuss, and, by citing reasons, to indicate what I understand that method to be or what I do not yet understand it to be.

Intercession is applied to souls in a two-fold manner: first, by the act of intercession itself and by means of the current burial service which takes place when the priest prays with the people, fasts, sacrifices, and does other designated works for designated souls. Undoubtedly this kind of intercession has much in its favor and, as St. Augustine points out, it redeems souls according to their desert and God's good pleasure.[51] As I said in the preceding thesis in regard to this matter, a bishop has as much power in a particular way as the pope has in a general way, namely, not that of jurisdiction, but of making intercession in regard to purgatory. The method is not considered here, as is evident.

In the second place, intercession is made without a public service, but purely by official announcement, either in writing or orally. And this is done from two treasuries.

The first treasury is that of the church triumphant, which is the merit of Christ and his saints, who have achieved more merit than is necessary for salvation. This treasury has been left to the church to reward and balance out merits here, as my opponents maintain.

The other is the treasury of the church militant. Such merits are the good works of living Christians which the pope has authority to apply either for the satisfaction of those who do penances, or for intercession on behalf of the dead, or for the praise and glory of God. On a former occasion I have both taught and written that the pope in three different ways has authority over the merits of the church militant: first, to offer these merits to God for the satisfaction of others; second, to use them for intercession of souls; third, for the praise of God. If this is true, I firmly believe that the bishops have this same spiritual power in their dioceses. If I am wrong, let him who can correct me. Otherwise how could those brotherhoods exist without erring in which higher and lower pre-

---

[51] *City of God.* Migne 41, 149ff.

lates impart to each other their endeavors and good works? The same question applies to monasteries, orders, hospitals, and parishes. All of this only makes sense if in this way the work of one makes satisfaction for the sins of another, intercedes for him before God, and glorifies God.

Therefore I say the following:

Even though I do not understand at all how those merits of the church militant may come under the authority of the pope, I shall meanwhile believe it out of respect until someone cuts the Gordian knot. However, I do not understand it for the following reasons.

First, if the pope presents the works of the living as sacrifices for the living, I do not see how that can be remission out of grace and not true and just satisfaction and payment up to the very last penny. Although he for whom remission is made does nothing, others work and make satisfaction for him. Then that will happen which all constantly deny, namely, that he who grants remission burdens himself to make satisfaction for another. Actually, then, the pope does not remit sins but makes satisfaction through the good works of his subordinates.

The second reason is that the power of the keys of the church would do absolutely nothing more than what has already actually been done in the church, even without the power of the keys. According to the law of love each one is constrained to pray for the other. The Apostle says, "Bear one another's burdens, and so fulfil the law of Christ" [Gal. 6:2].

The third reason is that the term "indulgence" contradicts the meaning of the term itself, for the term should mean "to grant," that is, "to remit," so that a person does not need to do what he should do. This does not mean to impose something upon another, however, or to declare that it has been so imposed. The indulgence certainly wipes out the debt, but it does not pay the debt through someone else. Therefore it seems to me that the power of the keys alone, without the treasury of the church militant, suffices for indulgences, especially since only the canonical, not the evangelical, satisfaction is remitted. Otherwise one must say again what I have said previously concerning the remission of guilt, that is, that the pope also remits punishments by means of this treasury, that is, he declares that something happens which takes place without the treasury, namely that the church makes satisfaction for the one to whom the punishment is remitted. As St. Augustine says, no one will be raised up except the one whom the unity of the church raises up, which he says is symbolized in the case of the widow.[52] But it still holds true, as indicated in the first and second reason, that it is a satisfaction rather than a remission, whether it is declared or granted.

Fourth, this treasury of the church militant produces the grace of the Spirit rather than the remission of punishment. It appears to be treated in a very cheap manner when it is applied to the remission of punishments. For remission of punishments is the cheapest gift the church grants, which, it seems, is given even to the wicked and, it seems, already by the power of the keys.

In the second place I say the following:

I do not know how it happens or what takes place when the pope applies the treasury of the church to the intercession for the dead. My reasons are these:

First, because the pope does not seem to do anything more than what has already actually been done. For the church as a whole actually prays and intercedes for the dead; unless the thought here is that he does it by way of explanation. I do not see how this is any different from what is said concerning the mass, that is, that the mass is more profitable if it is applied by the priest for the benefit of one person than if it is celebrated for all without application to any one particular member. I confess that I believe this is true. But the pope as the highest and general priest of all priests certainly can do nothing more than apply it generally; indeed he is under obligation to do this, even without letters of indulgences.

Second, since only canonical punishments are remitted through indulgences, I certainly cannot understand what it is that is remitted for souls in purgatory since the canon laws do not bind them. Finally, at death they are freed from canonical punishments, for every priest is a pope in the hour of death. By the same token no soul suffers in purgatory because of crimes and mortal sins,

---

[52] *Exposition of Psalm 145.* Migne 37, 1897.

but only because of venial sins, as stated in distinction 25, in the chapter beginning with the word *Qualis*.[53] The canons, moreover, are imposed for venial sins; not for secret mortal sins, but only for acknowledged crimes, as I have indicated previously. Therefore, let him who can say how indulgences, that is, remissions of the canons, help people, when the pope only bestows indulgences, indeed, when indulgences are granted out of superfluous caution (as also the dead are usually absolved in the year of the church), and how the pope includes the application of the merits of the church with indulgences. Then certainly indulgences do not become an intercession, but are granted to souls along with intercession, as it were as a second gift, that is, they are declared as given, or are applied.

I say in the third place: Concerning the treasury of the merits of Christ and the saints as applied to the remission of punishments I shall speak later in Thesis 58. You see how obscure and doubtful all these matters are, and therefore how extremely dangerous to teach. I see and say this one thing, that the pope according to the work of Clement, *Concerning Penance and Remission*, the chapter beginning with the word *Abusionibus*,[54] seems to condemn the opinion that souls can be redeemed by indulgences. According to Clement, the pope says, "In asserting that they release souls from purgatory, they lie." Clement's explanation of the word "lie" says, "Because they are reserved for the judgment of God." Distinction 25, the chapter beginning with the word *Qualis*,[55] attests to this, and it seems absolutely right to me. For if souls are redeemed through intercession it does not thereby follow that they immediately fly to heaven. The words "intercede," "redeem," and "free" do not have the same meaning. I am discerning enough to see that indulgences and the intercession of the merits of the church are two entirely different things. One can be given without the other and with the other. The power of the keys alone suffices for indulgences without adding the treasury of merits. This treasury can

---

[53] Cf. p. 136, n. 25.
[54] *Clementis Papae V, Constitutiones* v. tit. IX, cap 2. *Corpus Iuris Canonici*, II, cols. 1190-1191.
[55] Cf. p. 136, n. 25.

either be added to the power of the keys or applied by itself. The treasury taken by itself can effect participation in good works of the church, as I have said before. If these things are certain and true, it follows that indulgences, insofar as there are such things, are of absolutely no value to people, unless individuals are absolved in the presence of the church, that is, are declared absolved. If they should have any value it would not be because they possess it in their own right but because another gift has been added to them, namely the merits of the church. These merits of the church must, on the other hand, be distinguished from the general application, by which the church through the merits of the saints actually helps people without the application of the pope. One must determine what value these merits of the church have. But the work of inquiring must be left to others who have not yet lost their desire for doing so because of the many doubts that have been raised.

The objections to my arguments are these:

First, it is frequently claimed that a certain professor in Paris[56] maintained in a disputation that the pope has power over purgatory. When the pope learned of this he granted remission to the professor after his death, thereby supporting or, as it were, commending the truth of the man's assertion.

My answer to this is: It makes no difference to me what pleases or displeases the pope. He is a human being just like the rest of us. There have been many popes who have been pleased not only with errors and vices but even with horrible things. I listen to the pope as pope, that is, when he speaks in and according to the canons, or when he makes a decision in accordance with a general council. I do not listen to him, however, when he speaks his own mind. In this way I am not compelled to say with certain people who hardly know the teaching of Christ that the horrible murders committed by Julius II[57] among Christians might have

---

[56] *Clementis Papae V, Constitutiones* v. tit. IX, cap. 2. *Corpus Iuris Canonici*, served as head of the school of his order in Paris. Cf. *CL* 1, 88, footnote to line 37.

[57] Julius II (pope: 1503-1513), the "warrior pope," joined the League of Cambrai against Venice and was attacked for this by many of his contemporaries.

been blessings by which he demonstrated to the flock of Christ that he was a true shepherd.

The second objection to my argument is this: St. Bonaventura in Book 4, chapter 20, says that one must not resist strenuously if anyone should maintain that the pope has power over purgatory.

I answer, first, that the authority of St. Bonaventura is not sufficient in this matter. Second, if the pope has maintained this, one must not oppose it. Third, Bonaventura speaks rightly, because he expresses his opinion by adding the words, "only if that claim is supported by the clear authority of the Scriptures or reasonable proof." So far no clear authority for that claim exists.

At this point the following objection is raised:

First, Sixtus IV is said to have decided that the method of intercession in no way lessens the over-all value of indulgences.[58]

My answer is this: First, if anyone wishes to be obstinate about this, he should say, "Prove what you say, Holy Father, especially since it is not for the pope alone to decide upon new articles of faith, but, according to the laws, to make judgments and decisions about questions of faith. This, however, would be a new article of faith. Therefore that decision would be a matter for a general council much more than the doctrine of the conception of the Holy Virgin would be, especially since the latter constitutes no danger, while determining new articles of faith on the part of the pope could be a grave and great danger for people. Otherwise, since the pope is only human and can err in matters of faith and morals, the faith of the whole church would be constantly in danger if it were necessary to believe as true whatever might occur to the pope to be true.

Second, even if the pope along with a large part of the church should feel thus and so, and even if it were true that he does not err, it is still not a sin, nor is it heresy, to take the opposite position, especially in something which is not necessary for salvation, until

---

[58] In his explanation of the bull of indulgence, *Romani pontificis*, issued 1477 by Sixtus IV (pope: 1471-1484) for the church at Saintes, the commissary for indulgences, Raimund Peraudi, states: "The way of intercession does not detract from the way of authority." Cf. *MA*³ 1, 503 and *CL* 1, 88, footnote to line 24. Cf. also *Proceedings at Augsburg*, p. 262.

the one position has been rejected by a general council and the other approved. But, lest I become too involved, let me state that my position is proved in this one instance, namely, that the Roman church along with the general council at Basel and almost with the whole church feels that the Holy Virgin was conceived without sin. Yet those who hold the opposite opinion should not be considered heretics, since their opinion has not been disproved.

Third, I have not read the decision of Sixtus IV, but I have read another to the effect that indulgences are bestowed for the dead by means of intercession. It does not follow from this, however, that therefore souls for whom the intercession is made fly to heaven.

Fourth, I cannot be the interpreter of a word that is unfamiliar to me, and even less can I be the pope's interpreter. Therefore, until he interprets it himself, I shall continue to have my opinions and defend them out of self-respect in discussing this poorly understood matter. The statement of Sixtus can be understood in a twofold manner. First: "The method of intercession does not lessen the over-all value of indulgences." That means that even if an indulgence should be given, not as an indulgence, but as an intercession, nevertheless, by such approval and intercession of the pope, those for whose benefit the intercession has been made certainly fly to heaven. They go to heaven, not because they have been loosed, but because intercession has been made for them. I myself do not believe this, but my opponents think it is true. Second: "The method of intercession does not lessen the over-all value of indulgences." This means that, when indulgences are applied for the souls of the dead by the method of intercession, they retain their basic nature, that is, they are plenary indulgences and do not lose that essential nature, though they operate not as indulgences but as intercession. I accept this meaning and add to it the thought: If it is true that intercession does not lessen indulgences in any way, it is also true that the application of intercession does not increase the value of indulgences in any way. It follows from this that souls do not go to heaven by indulgences. And even the words themselves confirm this fact, for the statement does not say, "The method of intercession fully redeems souls," but rather, "It does not lessen the over-all value of indulgences." Therefore indulgences, of whatever nature they may be, do only as much as intercession can do and no more.

Another objection to my argument is this:

The form of apostolic absolution reads: "I remit for you the punishments of purgatory, as far as the keys of the holy mother church extend." And the pope's father confessors observe this form, even in Rome.

My first answer to this objection is that these words are irrelevant, for the form mentioned is that for absolving the living and the dying. It is not a form for applying indulgences to those already dead.

Yet in the interests of searching for the truth, I say, second, that since these words are doubtful and posited in an unintelligible manner one cannot err in faith if one holds to an opinion contrary to that which the fathers think should be accepted. Why does the form worry them? Why does the author say, as though he were in doubt, "As far as the keys extend?" That dangling tail makes me suspicious. I am not duty bound to believe firmly that which the pope himself does not dare to pronounce with certainty. Why does he add the words "as far as the keys extend" only here and not elsewhere? Do you not see how vigilant Christ is in his church, that he does not even permit those to err who want to err? If only we would not rush headlong into error by neglecting his warning!

I say in the third place, as I have said previously, that even if the pope, along with his father confessors, should not err here, those who deny the pope's meaning or do not believe it are not thereby heretics, until one or other of these opinions will have been accepted or rejected by the judgment of the general council. Even though they adorn the festival of the Conception of the Virgin Mary with indulgences as a settled matter of faith, they still do not condemn or bind those who do not seek the release which such indulgences bring. No matter how many indulgences may be granted, it is not necessary to accept that form of apostolic absolution as true until the church decides upon it. You see again how necessary it is to have an official and general council. But I am afraid our generation is not worthy enough to be granted such a boon, but only to be mocked by the works of error [II Thess. 2:11] which we have deserved.

27

They preach only human doctrines who say that as soon as the money clinks into the money chest, the soul flies out of purgatory.

They preach a man-made doctrine, that is, vanity and lies, according to that word of Scripture, "Every man is a liar" [Cf. Ps. 116:11], and that statement, "Every man living is superficial" [Cf. Ps. 39:6]. This thesis needs no proof, in my opinion. Nevertheless it is proven by the following conclusion: "Because the intercession of the church for souls in purgatory is efficacious by virtue of the will of God and dependent on the merit of the soul." But even if their opinion were true, that souls are benefited by means of intercession, it does not follow that souls immediately fly from purgatory to heaven.

1. It does not follow, first, because it is not the intercession but the favorable hearing of the intercession and the acceptance of it that frees, since souls are set free not by the prayers of the church but by the work of God.

2. As is evident from the prayers and teachings of all saints, God acts in such a way that he is quick to hear and slow to give in order to test our perseverance. Therefore long lapses of time occur between intercession and the favorable hearing and fulfilment of it.

3. It does not follow that, because the same thing has been taught recently without authority and contrary to the prohibition of church law, nothing is to be taught by indulgence preachers which goes beyond their letters of authorization. Therefore they do not speak the words of God and the church, which are true, but they speak their own thoughts, which are lies.

5.[59] There is no difference between one who knows he speaks

---

[59] WA 1, 584, footnote 37, indicates that all editions read *"Quinto"* and suggests that the fourth point of the original manuscript may have been left unprinted by mistake.

falsehood and one who maintains something as certain which he does not know to be certain. For the one who speaks the truth also lies at times. These men know that those things just stated are uncertain and yet they affirm them with as much certainty as they do the gospel. They cannot prove these words to be certain by any authority of Scripture or by reason.

6. Intercession, then, would be better as a service to another, and then only by chance, than for a man's own benefit, for it is not as profitable for the one who makes intercession as for another on whose behalf it is made. This is a specious claim. For that reason I pass over this, especially since they dare to admit that intercession is not profitable to the one who makes it, but to the soul for whom it is made. I could make a laughing-stock out of these inventions of theirs and ridicule them just as they ridicule the truth by means of them, but I refrain from doing this in order that I may not appear to consider these matters as dogma rather than as a problem for debate.

28

It is certain that when money clinks in the money chest, greed and avarice can be increased; but when the church intercedes, the result is in the hands of God alone.

It is strange that my opponents do not preach the most precious gospel of Christ with as great a desire and loud wailing as they do other things. The fact that they seem to think more of profit than of piety makes me suspicious of this business. Perhaps, however, they may be justifiably excused by the fact that they do not know the gospel of Christ. Therefore, since indulgences possess no piety, no merit, and are not a command of Christ, but only something that is permitted, even though it may be a pious work which redeems people, it certainly appears that profit rather than piety is increased by indulgences. For these indulgences are promoted so extensively and exclusively that the gospel is treated as an inferior thing and is hardly mentioned.

1. My first proof of this thesis is that the intercession of the church does not come under the jurisdiction of the pope. And the

pope does not have the power to say that the intercession is accepted by God, but only that it can be offered. This is so even if their opinion were correct which is to the effect that souls are redeemed through this intercession.

2. According to their interpretation the commonly accepted opinion of St. Augustine[60] would be false, to the effect that intercessions are profitable only to those who deserve to profit from them, for they would be profitable for whomever they should profit only by authority of the pope, not through the merits of people themselves.

3. It is contrary to the nature and meaning of the word "intercession" to say that the pope has power to redeem through intercession. For however excellent a work may be, if it is turned into intercession, it operates not as a work but as intercession. It is much rather the favorable hearing of intercession which redeems. Therefore, either they are talking about intercession by the use of other terminology and thereby are deceiving people even more wickedly, or else they are talking about their own opinion of intercession by the use of accepted terminology. In the latter case their opinion does not prevail, since the meaning and concept of "power" cannot be reconciled with the word "intercession."

4. If their interpretation prevailed there would be no difference between intercession and authority except in the words themselves. Actually they would be one and the same thing since they have the same effect without any other requirement except the will of the pope. Why does not the pope keep quiet about intercession and stop compelling us to understand by intercession something else than power?

Once again I declare, dear reader, that I am speaking about that very same intercession as if there really were such a thing. I have expressed previously the opinion that I doubt and do not understand whether there is or could be that kind of intercession. I repeat this here so that no one may imagine that I am contradicting myself when I appear to accept intercession here and have almost denied it previously.

---

[60] *Enchiridion ad Laurentium,* cap. 110. Migne 40, 283.

29

Who knows whether all souls in purgatory wish to be re-
deemed, since we have exceptions in St. Severinus and St.
Paschal, as related in a legend.

I have not read any credible account concerning these two men.
Yet I have heard it said that they could have been freed by their
own merits if they had wished to be satisfied with achieving lesser
glory. So they endured purgatory rather than impair the glory
of the beatific vision. But in these matters anyone may believe
whatever he wants to, it makes no difference to me. I have not
denied that souls suffer other punishments in purgatory, as I have
said above; but I wanted to show that they would not fly from purgatory to heaven even with these remissions unless they were made
perfectly healthy by grace. Nevertheless it is possible that some out
of very great love of God do not wish to be freed from purgatory.
Thus it is understandable that Paul and Moses could have desired
to be anathematized and eternally separated from God [Cf. Rom.
9:3 and Exod. 32:32]. If they were prompted to do such things
in this life, it does not appear as though we could deny that the
same could also be done by the dead. There is an example in the
sermons of Tauler of a certain virgin who did just that.

30

No one is sure of the integrity of his own contrition, much
less of having received plenary remission.

I say this in the same sense as those who desire to make contrition
necessary for the remission of punishments, and yet do not see how
very uncertain they render everything. The thesis is clear enough.
Everybody accepts the first part and the second part necessarily follows. In my opinion, however, remission of punishments specified
by canon law can be effected with certainty even if a person were
neither worthy nor contrite. It is not contrition, much less the certainty of contrition, that is required for the remission of punishments. Remission itself takes place even if it is granted for imaginary punishments, since it is merely a matter of papal authority.

But, as I have also said previously, if my opponents desire to have punishments other than those for crime remitted, that is to say, for any kind of mortal sins whatever, they make indulgences worthless while magnifying them. Actually indulgences are not indulgences if they are uncertain. Indulgences are indeed uncertain if they depend upon contrition for all mortal sins and not evident crimes only, since no one is sure that he is without mortal sin. Yet he can be sure that he is without crime, that is, without a sin for which he can be accused publicly in the church, as stated above. So I deny that this thesis is true when I speak in my own sense of the term. I have maintained this, however, in order that those who oppose me might see the absurdity of their boastfulness, by means of which they expand indulgences.

31

The man who actually buys indulgences is as rare as he who is really penitent; indeed, he is exceedingly rare.

Again I speak in their sense in order that they may see the presumptuousness, indeed the contradiction, of their unrestrained preaching. When they cry that indulgences are profitable for so many people and yet confess that there are so few who walk the narrow way, they do not even blush or give attention to what they are saying. But this is not surprising. They have not assumed the office of teaching contrition and the narrow way [Matt. 7:14]. Therefore I advance the opinion that, if only a few are contrite, nevertheless many, indeed everybody in the whole church could be set free from the punishments of the canons, as they actually are now, simply by abolishing the canons.

32

Those who believe that they can be certain of their salvation because they have indulgence letters will be eternally damned, together with their teachers.[61]

---

[61] This is one of Luther's most important arguments against indulgences. He was not vehemently opposed to indulgences *per se*, but to the church and teachers who permitted the ignorant masses to believe that the purchase of indulgences made them sure of salvation and free from guilt before God, instead of free from punishments imposed by the church.

I maintain this thesis and prove it in the following way:

Jeremiah 17 [:5] says: "Cursed is the man who trusts in man and makes flesh his arm." We have no other hope of salvation except in Jesus Christ alone, "nor is there any other name given under heaven, by which we must be saved" [Acts 4:12; cf. Acts 15:11]. May the hope that is based upon dead letters and on the name of indulgences and intercessions perish!

Secondly, as I have said, letters and indulgences do not confer salvation, but only take away punishments, that is, canonical punishments, and not even all of these. Oh that the earth and all its fulness would cry out and weep with me over the manner in which Christian people are seduced who have no other understanding of indulgences except that they are useful for salvation and for the fruits of the spirit! It is no wonder that this is so, since the plain truth of the matter is not made clear to them.

Oh unhappy Christians, who can trust for their salvation neither in their merits nor in their good conscience! They are taught to put their confidence in a signed parchment and sealing wax. Why should I not speak in such a manner? What else, I ask, is conferred by indulgences? Not contrition, not faith, not grace, but only the remission of punishments of the outer man which have been established by the canons.

To digress just a little: I myself have heard that there are many who, after their money was given and their letters purchased, placed their complete confidence in these indulgences. For (as they said) either they heard these things about indulgences or else (I believe this to their credit) they must have understood that the preachers of indulgences taught these things. I am not censuring anyone, for I should not do so since I have not heard the indulgence preachers. As far as I am concerned, they may excuse themselves until they become whiter than snow. Surely these people must be reproved for having wax in their ears that they hear only pernicious things when these preachers tell them salutary things. This occurs when these preachers say, for example, "Above all, brothers, believe in Christ, trust in him and repent, take up your cross, follow Christ, mortify your flesh, learn not to be afraid of punishments and death. Above all else, love one another, serve one another even by neglecting indulgences. Minister first to the needs of the poor and the destitute" [I Pet. 4:8-11]. I say that when they are preaching these and similar pious, religious, and holy matters, the gullible populace, turned aside as it were by a strange miracle, hears entirely different things, namely, things like these: "Oh you senseless and stupid people, almost more like beasts than men, who are not aware of such a great outpouring of grace! See now how heaven is open on all sides! If you do not enter now, when will you ever enter? See how many souls you can redeem! O hard-hearted and indifferent people! For twelve denarii you can release your father from purgatory, and are you so ungrateful that you would not come to the aid of your parent who is in the midst of such great punishment? I myself deserve to be excused at the final judgment, but you stand accused all the more since you have neglected such great salvation [Cf. Heb. 2:3]. I tell you, that if you had only one tunic, in my judgment you should tear it from your body and sell it piece by piece in order that you might obtain such great favors." But then when the point has come to discuss those who speak against the grace given through indulgence, while they gush forth with nothing but benedictions, the crowd stands trembling and is afraid that heaven will crash to the ground and that the earth will open up.

The people hear that punishments far worse than those of hell threaten them, so that it is probably true that when those preachers curse, God blesses by means of their curses, and when they bless, God curses. For how else could it happen that these preachers speak things that are so different from what the people hear? Who can understand it? Where, I ask, do those hobgoblin words come from?[62] I still do not believe all the things which the populace says it has heard here and there. Otherwise I would consider the ideas which they preach heretical, wicked, and blasphemous.

I do not believe it is true that one of them prohibits burials of the dead and the invitation of the priests to be made until those who want funeral rites, masses, and festivals for the dead to be conducted drop more money into the chest. The people make up

---

[62] *CL* 1, 96 omits this question from the text.

these things also. I do not believe that story which is said to have been brought back by a certain person and embellished with lies, namely, that in a certain place thousands of souls (I don't know how many; if I remember correctly, it was either three or five thousand) were redeemed by means of these indulgences. Of these thousands of people only three were condemned; and they were condemned because they withheld indulgence money. No one actually said this, but while the preachers were telling the story of Christ's passion the crowd heard such things, or else they afterwards imagined that they had heard it. I do not believe it is true that these preachers of indulgences indiscriminately grant to coachmen, landlords, and servants indulgences for four, five, or as many souls as they want instead of paying them with money.

I do not believe it when the people say that, after the preachers have poured forth their exhortations with violent bellowing from their pulpits that the people put their money in the chest, they shout, "Deposit, deposit, deposit" (for the people imagine that this is the head and the tail [Isa. 9:14], indeed even the very heart, of the sermon and almost the whole sermon itself). And I do not believe that then, in order that the apostolic preachers may teach the message of indulgences not only with words but also by example, they come down from their pulpits, go first of all to the collection box so that everyone can see, all the while stirring up and provoking the simple and foolish people in the hope of sucking out their very marrow, then deposit their own coin in a magnificent gesture with a resounding ring, wonder whether all the others will let their whole lifesavings flow in, smile at those who do deposit their coins, and become indignant at those who refuse to do so. I myself do not say that they have a corner on the soul-market. I am indignant at the people who because of their ignorance not only interpret such pious efforts as an appearance of greed but as a greed that reaches frenzy. Nevertheless it appears to me that the people who accept from these new spirits either a new interpretation or error perhaps deserve to be pardoned, although they have in former times been accustomed to hearing those things which pertain to love and humility.

But if I wanted to draw up a catalogue of all the monstrosities

I have heard about, a new volume would be necessary. My own opinion is that even if indulgences were enjoined and salutary, nevertheless, because they have now been so terribly abused and reduced to such a scandal, this would be reason enough for abolishing them altogether. If they are permitted to thrive much longer, those who preach them will, because of their love for money, finally become insane. I honestly believe that the indulgence preachers have not said all the things which have been reported about them here and there. But at least they should have set the people right and expressed themselves more clearly, or, better still, they should speak moderately about indulgences in accordance with the wording of the canons.

33

Men must especially be on their guard against those who say that the pope's pardons are that inestimable gift of God by which man is reconciled to him.

I should have called them destructive heretics. For what is more impious and heretical than to say that papal indulgences are a means of grace whereby one is reconciled with God? Yet in order to suppress my displeasure, I wish rather to believe that they have spoken or maintained such things, not out of malice or design, but only out of ignorance and for want of learning and ability. Even in this respect it is presumptuous for men who are so ignorant not to take up the work of a herdsman, rather than take upon themselves the work of teaching the people of Christ.

Let us now listen to that herdsman as he grunts his words. After he has divided indulgences into four principal graces and many other lesser graces, he has this to say in his pamphlet: "The first principal grace," he says, "is the plenary remission of all sins. There is no grace which can be called greater than this. By means of this, one who is a sinner and is deprived of divine grace obtains perfect remission and the grace of God anew." [63] That is what

---

[63] Reference here is to the *Summary Instruction* of Archbishop Albrecht of Mainz, the general commissioner of the indulgence of Leo X, written for the sub-commissioners. Walther Köhler, *Dokumente zum Ablassstreit* (Tübingen, 1934), pp. 104-124.

he says. I ask you, what bilgewater of heresies has ever been spoken so heretically as that? One can see from this how it happens that when the indulgence preachers say they teach the most sacred truths, the people nevertheless take them to mean the most wicked things. Would that we had here someone with the zeal and the eloquence of a St. Jerome! I am ashamed of a presumptuousness so great that this babbler has not hesitated to publish his pamphlet with four outstanding universities in the immediate vicinity, as though the astute minds of the universities were completely turned into stinking mushrooms. It grieves me also that our neighboring heretics, the Picardi,[64] finally have an occasion for justly accusing the Roman church, if they should hear that these things are taught in it.

Moreover, the fact that this insolent author has spoken not out of malice, perhaps, but out of ignorance, may be seen by this statement of his: "Through this (that is, the first grace, plenary remission) man obtains perfect remission." What does he mean when he says, "Through plenary remission one obtains perfect remission and through the grace of God he obtains the grace of God?" Is he dreaming in the throes of a fever or is he laboring under a madness? Note well this heretical opinion! He wishes to say that nothing can be called greater than this first grace, and that man, deprived of grace, obtains it. It is evident that this cannot be understood to be anything but the justifying grace of the Spirit, and he himself would not have understood it otherwise. Else it would not be true that no grace can be called greater. If, however, he should say other things concerning justifying grace he would speak in a most wicked manner, since it is God alone about whom it can be said that nothing is greater. Unlike the archbishop of Mainz, St. Augustine says that among created gifts nothing is greater than love.[65] But here this author, who is capable of such an opinion or error, confuses the grace of God and the grace of the pope in the chaos of a single word.

---

[64] Cf. p. 125, n. 19.
[65] Cf. Migne 38, 793, sermo CXLV, where St. Augustine points out that love is greater than the eyes, hands, feet, stomach, and any other member of the body.

There follow in the same book these words: "Through this remission of sins the punishments which should be endured in purgatory because of the offense against the divine majesty are also fully remitted for him and the said punishments of purgatory are completely canceled." We have heard a Delphic oracle! He who is completely ignorant has absolutely no doubt at all. He makes a positive pronouncement concerning the power of the keys over purgatory. But we have already said enough about these things.

In the same place there follow these words: "Even though, to merit such grace, nothing can be done that is worthy enough to repay it, because the gift and grace of God cannot be appraised, etc. . . ." See how he again calls that which the pope remits the inestimable gift and grace of God. This is the person most capable of teaching the churches, that is, the prostitute of heretics! After he has diligently used these words to garnish this grace for purposes of business and profit, he quickly clothes his Mercury with the garment of Jupiter so that no one may know that he is after money, especially if the person knows no more than he himself. He also permits that grace to be given free to the poor, but only if they have first tried in every way to rake up money from what he calls "good patrons." In this way even mendicant brothers may obtain money without the authority of their superiors. Like Pseudolus,[66] this liar considers the remission of even imaginary punishment far better than salvatory obedience. But since there was no way open for raking in money, in order to obtain (*redimant*) this grace (that is, "buy it anew"; not that they actually sell it, but the great similarity of terms compels them to misuse the words), this liar goes on to say, "The kingdom of heaven ought to be no more open to the rich than to the poor." Once again he wants to open heaven by means of indulgences. But I must restrain my pen so that I do not rave against them the way they deserve it. I have done enough by indicating to the faithful that the corruptness of their sermons assumes such remarkable ignorance and crudeness on their part. Once again, the proverb has proven itself to be true: "The cover fits the dish."

---

[66] Pseudolus, meaning liar, is also the title of a comedy by Plautus (254-184 B.C.).

34

For the graces of indulgences are concerned only with the penalties of sacramental satisfaction established by man.

This is clear enough from the fifth and twentieth theses.

35

They who teach that contrition is not necessary on the part of those who intend to buy souls out of purgatory or to buy confessional privileges preach unchristian doctrine.

I ask you, why do they subject men to the danger of putting off repentance? And what good does it do them to have such things preached, even if they were true, unless it is because they seek money instead of the salvation of souls? Since these doctrines are wicked and false there is all the more reason for rejecting them. To be sure I have admitted previously that punishments can be remitted even to those who are not truly repentant. These teachers deny this. Here again, that which they affirm I believe must be denied. And I have the same conviction concerning letters of confession as I do concerning punishments, that is, that true repentance is not required for either one, neither with regard to their redemption nor their use. They deny this. The same thing is true in the matter of remitting punishments, since the remission belongs to the content of the letter of confession. But in the matter of redeeming souls from punishment I disagree completely and ask them to prove what they say.

Indeed, I believe there is a big difference between redeeming souls and the remission of punishments. In the remissions of punishment one receives good, but in the redemption of souls one does good. Moreover, the wicked man can receive good, but by no means can he do good. And the work of the wicked man cannot be pleasing to God if the man himself is not pleasing to God, as Gen. 4 [:4] says: "The Lord had regard for Abel and his offering." It is contrary to Scripture for anyone to pity another rather than his own soul, and for anyone to pluck out the speck from his brother's eye rather than the beam from his own eye [Matt. 7:3].

And it is altogether contrary to Scripture for a servant of the devil to redeem a child of God and do this even in the name of God himself. It is ridiculous for an enemy to intercede for a friend of the king. What kind of madness is this? To magnify the remission of worthless punishment which is unprofitable for salvation, they play down the importance of sins for which penance alone should be magnified. If this is not heretical, ill-sounding, scandalous, and offensive to pious ears, what other term could be applied to these horrible things? Or are the inquisitors of heretical depravity harassing and wearing down orthodox people and orthodox ideas under these pretexts so that they alone may be permitted to flood the world with heresies without fear of punishment and as they please?

The indulgence sellers say, however, that redemption rests not upon the work of him who does the work of redeeming, but upon the merit of the one to be redeemed. My answer is: Who said this? From what source is it proved? Why, therefore, is not the one who must be redeemed freed by his own merit, without the work of him who does the redeeming? But then the money which they covet from the saving of souls would not increase. Why do we not call upon the Turks and Jews to contribute their money with us also, not, you understand, because of our greed, but for the redemption of souls? The fact that they are unbaptized does not pose any obstacle, for only the contributor of money matters, not at all the soul of him who is lost. The effect of the contribution depends only upon the merit of the soul to be redeemed. I believe that even if a jackass deposited gold, he would also redeem souls. If any qualification is required, surely it is grace, since a Christian who is a sinner displeases God more than any infidel. And braying does not distort the jackass as much as wickedness distorts the Christian.

Secondly, I have said that anyone can grant sinners confessional letters as well as remissions of punishments, but I have not said that they should be exhorted or even permitted to buy such things, as these hucksters teach so wickedly and crudely. I prove my argument in the following manner:

Every doctrine of Christ is an exhortation to penitence and points to the fact that men should turn from the devil, the sooner the better. As Ecclesiasticus says, "Do not delay in turning to the Lord" [Sirach 5:8]. The Lord himself says, "Watch, therefore, for you do not know the day or the hour" [Cf. Matt. 25:13]. The Apostle Paul says, "Let us therefore strive to enter that rest" [Heb. 4:11]. The Apostle Peter says, "Since therefore all these things are to be destroyed, what sort of persons ought you to be in holy and pious behavior, you who hasten toward the coming of the day, etc." [Cf. II Pet. 3:11-12]. The apostles taught these things because they were eager to do so, not for the purpose of collecting money, but for saving souls.

These false teachers, however, with complete self-confidence granted the people deferment in a miserable manner, and, as far as they were concerned, left them in danger of eternal death. I do not know, therefore, whether or not those who have desired to keep people in such anxiety should be excused from the crime of murdering souls. Surely in this case it is not the salvation of the giver which is sought, but rather his gift, even if he perishes. If they were good shepherds of souls and true Christians, they would endeavor with every effort to guide the sinner to the fear of God and a dread of sin, and not discontinue with weeping, praying, admonishing, and rebuking until they had won the soul of a brother. But if a person were to continue to give money and persist in doing evil, these hucksters should throw the money in his face and say with the Apostle, "I seek not what is yours but you" [II Cor. 12:14]. And again they would say, "Your money perish with you" [Acts 8:20]. Whereupon they would shrink back from him with horror. In that respect they would treat him rightly. But this is a far cry from our Mercury[67] who says, "Nay, rather we shall do this: if sinners come to us trusting in capable mediators (by which they mean money), they may be one of us, able to do what we can do, even able to redeem souls, even if this is contrary to Christ and the apostles. And while they immediately perish we shall laugh and rejoice because we are sure of their gift. This is love for the people of Christ and for our brothers. In this manner we take care of their souls so that they may know our newest kind of compassion for them in their sins, that is, no compassion at all."

---

[67] Mercury was a Roman god of commerce.

188

36

Any truly repentant Christian has a right to full remission of penalty and guilt, even without indulgence letters.

Otherwise, those who did not have letters of that type would be in danger. This is a false assumption, since these letters are neither commanded nor recommended, but may be freely accepted or rejected. By the same token those who neglect to purchase them do not thereby sin, nor are they for that reason in danger of losing their salvation. From this it is evident that such people are already following God's commands. In the event that a remission such as this were not granted a man, it would nevertheless be due to him, as the pope says. But at this point there are those who interpose a very subtle objection, saying, this would be true if the canons were punishments imposed only by the pope; but the canons are declarations of the punishments inflicted by God. It behooves those to speak thus who have undertaken to persecute the truth once and for all with a perpetual hatred.

First, they declare, as if by an oracle, that God requires a punishment which makes satisfaction for sins, namely, punishment other than the evangelical cross, that is, fasts, labors, vigils, and other than the punishment of chastisement. They do not understand these as among evangelical punishments, for they cannot deny that such punishments are remitted by God alone.

Second, they add to this monstrosity an even greater one, namely, that the canons only declare punishment which is imposed by God. Therefore the pope uses only declarative power; he never imposes or removes punishment. Otherwise, contrary to the word of Christ, these indulgence sellers would teach us something like this: "Whatsoever I shall bind, you shall loose."

37

Any true Christian, whether living or dead, participates in all the blessings of Christ and the church; and this is granted him by God, even without indulgence letters.

It is impossible for one to be a Christian unless he possesses Christ.

If he possesses Christ, he possesses at the same time all the benefits of Christ. For the holy Apostle says in Rom. 13 [:14], "Put on the Lord Jesus Christ." And in Rom. 8 [:32] he says, "Will he not also give us all things with him?" And in I Cor. 3 [:21-22] he says, "All things are yours, whether Cephas or Paul, or life or death." And in I Cor. 12 [Cf. :27] he says, "You are not your own, but individually members of the body." And in other places, where he describes the church as one body, one bread, we are altogether in Christ, members one of another [Cf. I Cor. 10:17]. And in the Song of Solomon we read, "My beloved is mine and I am his" [Song of Sol. 2:16]. By faith in Christ, a Christian is made one spirit and one body with Christ. "For the two shall be one flesh" [Gen. 2:24]. "This is a great mystery, and I take it to mean Christ and the church" [Eph. 5:31-32].

Therefore, since the spirit of Christ dwells within Christians, by means of which brothers become co-heirs, one body, and citizens of Christ, how is it possible for us not to be participants in all the benefits of Christ? Christ himself has all that belongs to him from the same Spirit. So it happens through the inestimable riches of the mercies of God the Father, that a Christian can be glorified with Christ and can with confidence claim all things in Christ. Righteousness, strength, patience, humility, even all the merits of Christ are his through the unity of the Spirit by faith in him. All his sins are no longer his; but through that same unity with Christ everything is swallowed up in him. And this is the confidence that Christians have and our real joy of conscience, that by means of faith our sins become no longer ours but Christ's upon whom God placed the sins of all of us. He took upon himself our sins [Cf. Isa. 53:12]. Christ himself is "the Lamb of God who takes away the sins of the world" [John 1:29]. All the righteousness of Christ becomes ours. He places his hand upon us and all is well with us [Cf. Mark 5:23]. He spreads his cloak and covers us [Cf. Ruth 3:9], blessed Savior throughout all ages, Amen.[68]

Indeed, this most pleasant participation in the benefits of Christ

---

[68] This paragraph gives an excellent idea of Luther's conception of the atonement and justification by faith.

and joyful change of life do not take place except by faith. Moreover, no man gives this or takes it way. Since this is so, I think it is sufficiently clear that this participation is not granted by the power of the keys or by the benefit of letters of indulgence. Rather it is granted by God alone before and without these indulgences. Just as remission is granted by God before the remission of the church, absolution before the absolution of the church, so also is participation in the benefits of Christ granted before participation in the benefits which the pope confers.

What, therefore, does the pope impart by granting his participation? My answer is: They should say, as I have said in Thesis 6 about remission, that he grants permission only in a declarative way. I confess that I do not understand how they could say it otherwise. I shall give my interpretation in the thesis which follows.

38

Nevertheless, papal remission and blessing are by no means to be disregarded, for they are, as I have said [Thesis 6], the proclamation of the divine remission.

The declaration which is made in the form of public letters of indulgences is not necessary, for the declaration which is made in private confession is sufficient. But this public declaration should not be despised for by means of it the declaration which is made privately is made known also to the church and is approved. I think it must be understood in this manner. Whoever has some better explanation to offer should say so. I do not see what else public dispensation may accomplish. Although I believe that this thesis has been accepted by everybody, nevertheless I have said in Thesis 6 above that I do not like to say that the pope does nothing more than declare or approve the divine remission or granting of Christ's benefits, first, because this is the same as declaring that the keys of the church are virtually worthless. In fact, in a manner of speaking, it makes the word of Christ of no effect when he says, "Whatsoever etc." [Matt. 16:19]. To speak of it as a "declaration" is too modest a statement. Second, I do not like to speak in this manner, for then the one to whom the declaration is made would be uncertain about everything, even though his remission and reconciliation would be confirmed publicly before others and openly before the church.

Here I wish to maintain about participation in the blessings of the church that which I have maintained previously about the remission of guilt, until I have been taught something better.

I believe that just as a man who has sinned trusts with the greatest difficulty in the mercy of God, so the sin which lies heavily upon him as a burden forces him to despair and he is prone to think much more about the wrath than the mercy of God. On the other hand, before he has sinned he is prone to think much more about mercy than wrath. Man does everything the wrong way. He is afraid when he should not be afraid but hopeful, that is, after he has sinned. Before he has sinned he is confident, when he should not be confident but be afraid.

An example of this human perversity has been adequately pointed out in the resurrection of Christ, where Christ needed to give many proofs in order to establish himself again in the hearts of the disciples. The first announcement of his resurrection was made to women, and the disciples looked upon it as an absurdity. Just so the first stage of trust appears effeminate to the sinner and as something which he should consider entirely, or at least almost, incredible. By the same token it is much more difficult for him to believe that he is a participant in the benefits of Christ, that is, indescribable benefits, and "partaker in the divine nature" [II Pet. 1:4], as St. Peter says. The magnitude of these benefits even produces a distrust, which is nourished by the fact that he not only has such great evils remitted, but such great benefits conferred upon him, such as being made a child of God, an heir of the kingdom, a brother of Christ, a companion of the angels, a lord of the world. I ask you, how can one believe that these things are true, when by the gnawing of his sin, indeed overwhelmed by the burden of it, he feels that he is being carried away to hell? In this respect, therefore, the judgment of the keys is necessary, so that a man may not believe in himself, but rather trust in the judgment of the keys of the church, that is, of the priest. And it makes no difference to me if the one who bears the keys is unlearned or flippant. He may believe, not on account of the priest or his authority, but on account of the word of him who said and did not lie, "Whatsoever thou shalt loose etc." [Matt. 16:19]. For those who believe in that word, the authority of the keys cannot err. The keys err only for those who do not believe that the absolution of the priest is valid.

Suppose, by some impossible or accidental circumstances, that someone were not sufficiently contrite or else did not think he was, and yet believed with absolute confidence that he was absolved by the one who does the pardoning. I personally believe this is possible. That man's very faith causes him to be truly pardoned, for he believes in him who said, "Whatsoever etc." [Matt. 16:19]. Moreover, faith in Christ always justifies, even if an inept, irresponsible, and inexperienced priest baptizes you. Furthermore, even if you do not think you are contrite enough (for you cannot and ought not trust yourself), nevertheless, if you believe in him who said, "He who believes and is baptized will be saved" [Mark 16:16], I tell you, faith in that word of Christ makes you truly baptized, whatever feeling you may have about your contrition.

So faith is necessary everywhere. You receive as much as you believe. And this is what I understand it to mean when our teachers say that the sacraments are efficacious signs of grace, not because of the mere fact that the sacrament is performed but because it is believed, as St. Augustine contends[69] and as I have said previously. So also here. Absolution is efficacious, not by the mere fact that it takes place, no matter who finally does it and whether he errs or does not err, but because it is believed. And no reservation of certain cases [by the pope] can hinder this faith from receiving absolution, unless the faith itself should be manifestly undeserving or despise the absolution. So I say that when a man is in sin he is so vexed and disturbed by his conscience that in his own opinion he believes that he is participating in everything that is evil. Such a man is certainly close to justification and has the beginning of grace. Therefore he ought to flee for refuge to the consolation of the keys in order to be quieted by the authority of the priest, obtain peace,

---

[69] Cf. Tract 80, 3, concerning the Gospel according to St. John, in Migne 35, 1840: "From whence does water have such great power that it cleanses the body and purifies the heart except from the word, not because it is spoken but because it is believed?" Cf. also Augsburg Confession, Article XIII.

and attain the confidence that he is participating in all the benefits of Christ and the church. But if anyone shall not believe that this man participates in the benefits of Christ and the church through this work of absolution by the priest or should have doubts about it, he is led astray not by an error of the keys but by the error of his own faithlessness, inflicts upon his soul great condemnation, and does to God and his Word both an injustice and the greatest irreverence. So it is much better for him not to go to the absolution at all, if he does not believe that he is absolved, than it is to go without faith. For if he goes without faith he approaches half-heartedly and thereby receives "judgment upon himself" [I Cor. 11:29], as he would if he were to receive baptism or the sacrament of the bread half-heartedly. Therefore contrition is not as necessary as faith. In this respect faith in absolution receives incomparably more benefit than does zeal in penitence.

In neglecting this faith most of us only strive toward nurturing contrition. We teach men to trust in the remission of sins in proportion to their feeling of penitence. This means they are taught never to trust in the remission of sins but to strive for despair. According to the prophet we ought to place our hope in Christ's word, not in our penitence. The Psalmist did not say, "Remember my contrition to thy servant, in which thou hast made me hope," but "Remember thy word . . . in which thou hast made me hope" [Ps. 119:49]. Again he says, "In thy word [certainly not in our own work] have I placed great hope" [Cf. Ps. 119:81]. In another psalm he says, "My soul is sustained by his word," etc. [Cf. Ps. 130:5]. And according to the Hebrew he says in Psalm 51 [:4], "Against thee, only, have I sinned, . . . wherefore thou wilt justify me by thy word." Therefore it is neither the sacrament nor the priest, but faith in the word of Christ spoken through the priest and his office which justifies you. What difference does it make to you, if the Lord should speak through an ass, either male or female, as long as you hear that word by which you may hope and believe?

I would interpret what our scholastic teachers[70] say, namely that the sacraments of the church are given to us to be used, as the

---

[70] E.g. Thomas Aquinas, *Summa Theologica* iii. ques. 61, art. 1.

inestimable gifts of God by means of which we have an opportunity to believe and be justified. Formerly, in the time of Saul, the word of the Lord was considered precious [I Sam. 3:1]. Now his word comes to you even through most irresponsible, wretched, and unlearned men. Pay attention to the word and dismiss the outward appearance of the person. Whether the person errs or does not err, you shall not err if you believe God's word. If I err at this point and sound foolish, let him who understands put me straight again.

It will follow from these things which I have said that the three truths of Jean Gerson,[71] which for some time now have gotten into all books and ears, must be understood prudently. Take, for example, this statement of his, that a man should not trust himself as being in a state of salvation because he can say that he is sorry for his sins; rather he should direct his attention to whether or not he longs for the sacrament of absolution so much that when he has received it he believes he is absolved. This is what he means by receiving the sacrament with longing, that is, by faith in the word which one actually hears or desires to hear. Take care, therefore, that you do not in any manner trust in your own contrition but completely and alone in the word of your kindest and most faithful Savior, Jesus Christ! Your heart may deceive you, but he will not deceive you, whether you have him or only desire him. If these words are not understood intelligently (and may the Lord God grant that, in the words of the prophet Micah, I may be a man who is without the Spirit and rather speaks lies [Mic. 2:11]), then I am afraid many souls will be lost because of those most unlearned men who babble about works and contrition. They are blunderers, first, because they do not teach faith in the word but rather contrition, and even this superficially. Secondly, because they are so quick to dole out absolutions and to grant participation in the blessings of the church in the same manner, as though everybody everywhere has that faith. And they do not inquire whom they absolve or why.

Therefore it is not as necessary to ask when a person is absolved, "Are you sorry?" as it is to ask, "Do you believe that you can be absolved by me?" In the same manner Christ asked the

---

[71] Cf. p. 262, n. 8.

blind men, "Do you believe that I am able to do this for you?" [Matt. 9:28]. "All things are possible to him who believes" [Mark 9:23]. The sure proof of this faith is seen especially in the case of those who are disturbed by a trembling conscience and feel that they cannot trust in themselves. But for those who do not feel such wretchedness, I do not know whether the keys are their comforters or not, since only those who are sorry deserve to be comforted. And the only one who should be urged to have faith that his sins are remitted is the one who trembles in the fear that his sins might be retained.

To bring this thesis to a close, I say that I do not believe this opinion of mine lessens the power of the keys, of which I have been accused, but rather restores it from a false honor and tyrannical reverence to a place of worthy and loving esteem. It is no wonder if the keys are held in contempt when they are offered to those who receive them with hollow respect, i.e., with intimidation; yet anyone who knows of their most salutary benefit would be a stone or blockhead if he were not to embrace and kiss them with tears of joy. Why, therefore, do we exalt the pope because of the keys and at the same time think of him as a power-hungry individual? The keys are not his but mine, given to me for my salvation, my consolation, bestowed to grant peace and rest. With respect to the keys, the pope is my servant and minister. As pope he does not need the keys, but I do. These flatterers turn everything over to the popes, thereby extolling, not our need of consolation, but their own power. By so doing, they terrify us by the same power with which we should be consoled. Today everything is completely topsy-turvy, and yet we do not think that these are unhappy times when the best things are so abused as to be turned into the worst things for us. So, as it stands, I do not maintain this thesis in its entirety, but deny a large part of it.

39

It is very difficult, even for the most learned theologians, at one and the same time to commend to the people the bounty of indulgences and the need of true contrition.

The reason for this thesis is found in the following thesis.

40

A Christian who is truly contrite seeks and loves to pay penalties for his sins; the bounty of indulgences, however, relaxes penalties and causes men to hate them—at least it furnishes occasion for hating them.

Look at a true penitent and you will see that he seeks revenge upon himself so ardently for his offense against God that he compels you to have mercy upon him. In fact it is even necessary to dissuade him, lest he destroy himself, as we have often read and seen it happen. St. Jerome writes that such a thing happened to his Paula and even to himself.[72] No punishment is enough for such individuals, so with the prodigal son they invoke heaven and earth and even God himself against themselves. David did this when he said, "Let thy sword, I beseech you, be turned against me and against my father's house" [Cf. II Sam. 24:17].

Therefore I believe that I have spoken correctly when I say that canonical penances are imposed only upon those who are sluggards and do not wish to do better or to test the sincerity of their contrition. One can see how difficult it is even for the learned to take a middle course between hatred and love of punishments; to teach people to hate them and yet do it in such a manner that the people are persuaded to love them. But since nothing is difficult for the unlearned, there is nothing to prevent this from being easy also. But the gospel teaches us not to escape the punishments or to relax them but to seek and love them, for it teaches the spirit of freedom and the fear of God to the point of showing contempt for all punishments. But it is far more lucrative and profitable to the moneybags of the indulgence treasurers for people to fear punishments and drink in the spirit of the world and of fear in the letter of the law and in servitude. At the same time the people hear that some canonical punishments are such horrible things that they can be avoided only with great zeal, expense, pomp, and ceremonies.

---

[72] Cf. Migne 22, 891, epist. 108, cited in *CL* 1, 108. Paula was a wealthy friend of St. Jerome who lived near him in Bethlehem from A.D. 386 on.

They are taught these matters with more zeal than they are taught to love the gospel.

The following question is raised:

"What do you say, then, about those who make pilgrimages to Rome, Jerusalem, St. James,[73] Aachen, Trier, and many other regions and places to obtain indulgences? Also what do you say about indulgences bestowed at the dedications of churches?"

My answer is:

Those who make pilgrimages do so for many reasons, very seldom for legitimate ones.

The first reason for making pilgrimages is the most common of all, namely, the curiosity to see and hear strange and unknown things. This levity proceeds from a loathing for and boredom with the worship services, which have been neglected in the pilgrims' own church. Otherwise one would find incomparably better indulgences at home than in all the other places put together. Furthermore, he would be closer to Christ and the saints if he were not so foolish as to prefer sticks and stones to the poor and his neighbors whom he should serve out of love. And he would be closer to Christ also if he were to provide for his own family.

The second reason for making pilgrimages is bearable, namely, for the sake of indulgences. Since indulgences are voluntary, have not been commanded, and therefore have no merit, surely those who make pilgrimages only for the sake of indulgences merit nothing at all. Moreover, those people are to be justifiably ridiculed who neglect Christ and neighbor at home, in order to spend ten times as much money away from home without having any results and merit to show for it. Therefore he who would remain at home and consider that passage of Scripture, "Love covers a multitude of sins" [I Pet. 4:8], as well as that other passage, "Whatever is left over, give as alms, and behold everything is clean for you" [Cf. Luke 11:41], would be doing far better—indeed, he would be doing the only right thing—than if he were to bring home all the indulgences from Jerusalem and Rome. But there is no pleasure in being so wise, so we shall surrender "our hearts to impurity" [Cf. Rom. 1:24].

---

[73] St. James of Compostella in Spain.

The third reason for making pilgrimages is a longing for affliction and labor for one's sin, which, I believe, rarely occurs, at least by itself. To satisfy that desire, a man could torture himself and labor at home, if it were labor only that he sought. Yet if he does this, it is not evil but good.

The fourth reason is an honest one, namely, if a man is motivated by a singular devotion for the honor of the saints, the glory of God, and his own edification, just as St. Lucia made a pilgrimage to St. Agatha[74] and some of the holy fathers made a pilgrimage to Rome. The result proved that they did not do this out of curiosity.

Accordingly, in such cases as these, I am glad that the vows made to go on such pilgrimages are commuted to other works. Would that they were commuted gratis!

41

Papal indulgences must be preached with caution, lest people erroneously think that they are preferable to other good works of love.

I would say this to people: Look, brothers, you ought to know that there are three types of good works which can be done by expending money. The first and foremost consists of giving to the poor or lending to a neighbor who is in need and in general of coming to the aid of anyone who suffers, whatever may be his need. This work ought to be done with such earnestness that even the building of churches must be interrupted and the taking of offerings for the purchase of holy vessels and for the decoration of churches be discontinued. After this has been done and there is no longer anyone who is in need, then should follow the second type, namely, contributing to the building of our churches and hospitals in our country, then to buildings of public service. However, after this has been done, then, finally, if you so desire, you may give, in the third place, for the purchase of indulgences. The first type of good work has been commanded by Christ; there is no divine command for the last type.

---

[74] Both became martyrs during the persecution of the Roman Emperor Decius in Sicily *ca.* A.D. 250.

If you should say, "With that type of preaching very little money would be collected through indulgences," I answer, I believe that. But what is so strange about that, since popes by means of indulgences do not seek money but the salvation of souls, as is evident in those indulgences which they bestow at the consecration of churches and altars? So they do not wish, through their indulgences, to hinder the better things, but rather to promote charity.

I say very frankly that whoever teaches people otherwise and reverses this order is not a teacher but a seducer of people, unless people, because of their sins, at times do not deserve to hear the truth rightly preached.

42

Christians are to be taught that the pope does not intend that the buying of indulgences should in any way be compared with works of mercy.

As I have said I understand the pope as a public person, that is, as he speaks to us through the canons. And there are no canons which preach that the value of indulgences is to be compared to works of mercy.

The thesis, moreover, is clear. A command of God has infinitely more value than that which is permitted to exist by man's word and is in no way commanded by God. The command of God has merit. What man decrees has none.

The objection is made here: "But indulgences are sold for a godly work, for example, for a contribution to a building or for the ransom of captives. Therefore they are meritorious."

My answer is: I am not speaking about the work, but about the indulgences. Such a work as that could have been done without indulgences, for it is not necessarily bound up with indulgences. Moreover, indulgences which are bestowed without good works confer nothing; they only detract. The work, however, without indulgences does confer something. In the former case we receive benefits for ourselves, in the latter we give them. The former serves the flesh, the latter serves the spirit. Briefly the former satisfies our nature, the latter satisfies the grace of God. Therefore indulgences in themselves are not comparable to a work of mercy.

Likewise a work without indulgences is purer than one with indulgences. Indulgences are somewhat of an imperfection of the work, for the work receives its own reward, indeed much more than its own reward. Therefore people would act in a holier manner if they simply made a contribution for a good work and not for the sake of indulgences. It is not that indulgences in themselves are evil and harmful, but that the perverted abuse of indulgences is harmful, since people would not do such a work of mercy if no indulgences were granted for it. So in this type of work the indulgence becomes the end pursued—indeed a man who looks out for his own interests becomes that end. Man ought rather to do a work of mercy freely and for the sake of God. And he ought to accept only those indulgences which are given to him freely, and not as the result of a financial contribution that he has made. Thus a man should not buy indulgences and the church should not sell them. For both it must be a free gift or it will become a clear case of simony[75] and a foul transaction. But who explains these things to the people when the indulgence sellers say, "Contribute freely, and I will give the indulgence freely?"

At the same time one must fear that by such a perversion of the order of indulgences and works a great idolatry may be perpetrated in the church. If the public is taught to contribute money in order to escape punishment (which I hope does not happen, even though many people probably understand it in this way), then it is evident that they are not contributing for God's sake, and the fear of punishments, or the punishment itself, is their idol to which they sacrifice. But if such a thing should happen, then such an evil would arise in the church as at one time arose among the pagan Romans when they sacrificed to Febris[76] and other little and

---

[75] In the Middle Ages simony became a technical term referring to the practice of securing ecclesiastical office or preferment with money. The term is derived from Simon, the Magician, who offered the apostles money for the gift of the Holy Spirit (Acts 8:9-24). Gregory VII (pope: 1073-1085) defined as simony acceptance of a clerical appointment from the hands of a layman.

[76] Febris was a goddess to whom three temples were erected in Rome. Remedies which had been helpful in cases of fever were placed in these temples.

harmful deities so that no harm could come to them. So we must be ever watchful for the sake of the people and scarcely entrust such doubtful and dangerous matters to the most learned scholars.

43

Christians are to be taught that he who gives to the poor or lends to the needy does a better deed than he who buys indulgences.

I state this thesis for the benefit of the ignorant, for it is clear enough from what was said previously. I am not the first or the only one, however, who holds this thesis along with the two which precede it and the two which follow, for everybody, including the whole church, accepts them, except that the people alone never get to hear these things. Perhaps there is a fear that such a clear and basic truth might be understood too readily. Even when St. Bonaventura and all the others discussed this matter among themselves, and the objection was raised, "Then the other good works must be omitted," they answer unanimously, "Not at all, for the other good works are more valuable with respect to obtaining the essential reward." [77] Therefore my thesis holds, since those who say this nevertheless assert that indulgences are a treasury of the merits of Christ and the church.

44

Because love grows by works of love, man thereby becomes better. Man does not, however, become better by means of indulgences but is merely freed from penalties.

This is self-evident. Only remission of punishment is granted by indulgences, and these indulgences have no more usefulness, as everyone recognizes, than to take away punishments. But the taking away of punishment does not make one good or better in the exercise of love.

---

[77] Luther's free rendering of Bonaventura's comment on Peter Lombard's *Sententiarum* iv. dist. XX, cap. 2, ques. 6. Cited in *CL* 1, 111.

45

Christians are to be taught that he who sees a needy man and passes him by, yet gives his money for indulgences, does not buy papal indulgences but God's wrath.

By doing this a man reverses the order mentioned previously and acts contrary to that passage in John: "If anyone sees his brother in need yet closes his heart against him, how does God's love abide in him?" [I John 3:17]. Our sophists, however, interpret this need that the Scripture mentions as one of extreme necessity, that is, when there is no opportunity given for showing love, or very little opportunity. Yet if these sophists themselves were in superficial need rather than in extreme need, they would want to be helped But they want to help others only after the latter have already given up the spirit. What wonderful theologians and Christians they are, who do not do for others that which they want done for themselves [Matt. 7:12].

46 [78]

Christians are to be taught that the buying of indulgences is a matter of free choice, not commanded.

I have said repeatedly that indulgences belong to the list of those things which are permissible, not, however, to those which are profitable. They are permitted in the same manner as the certificate of divorce [Deut. 24:1-4] and the offering for jealousy [Num. 5:15] were permitted in the Old Testament. By the same token disputes and law suits for the sake of the weak are permitted in the New Testament, "because of your hardness of heart" [Matt. 19:8], as Christ says. Whoever purchases indulgences, however, will be tolerated rather than commended, as the gloss says, Book V, *Concerning Penance and Remission*, in the chapter beginning *Quod autem*. [79] Many others would do better to make satisfaction rather

---

[78] Theses 46 and 47 are given in inverse order in the *Explanations* from that in the *Ninety-five Theses* of 1517.
[79] Cf. Thesis 20.

than purchase indulgences, since only criminals need to purchase indulgences.

47

Christians are to be taught that, unless they have more than they need, they must reserve enough for their family needs and by no means squander it on indulgences.

The Apostle says: "If anyone does not provide for his relatives, and especially for his family, he has disowned the faith and is worse than an unbeliever" [I Tim. 5:8]. But there are many who have neither bread nor proper clothing and yet, led astray by the din and noise of the preachers of indulgences, rob themselves and bring about their own poverty in order to increase the wealth of the indulgence sellers.

48

Christians are to be taught that the pope, in granting indulgences, needs and thus desires their devout prayer more than their money.

Our masters, the courtiers and accomplices of the Roman Curia, might laugh at this thesis. Nevertheless it is true that before anything else the pope should desire prayer from his subjects, as the Apostle Paul often did from his fellow-Christians. This is a far more just reason for granting indulgences than the building of a thousand basilicas, in that the pope, who is besieged rather than surrounded by so many monstrosities of devils and godless men, cannot err without bringing great harm upon the whole church. Especially should prayers be offered for him if he were to lend a willing ear to the pestilent voice of his sirens who say, "It is not presumed that one of such distinguished prominence should err," as well as, "All positive laws are to be found in the shrine of his heart." As a matter of fact it is presumed by people that the pope does not err, but it is questionable whether or not that is a good presumption. And indeed, all his laws are to be found in the shrine of his heart; but it is questionable whether or not his heart is good, for that must be nourished by prayer. St. Bernard has written about this matter in a most attractive way to Pope Eugenius in his work, *Consideration.*[80]

49

Christians are to be taught that papal indulgences are use-ful only if they do not put their trust in them, but very harmful if they lose their fear of God because of them.

Consider the danger of indulgences. They are preached to people directly contrary to the truth of the cross and the fear of God. Through indulgences people are granted freedom from punish-ments and then assurance of remissions of sins. There is every indication that indulgences, which are preached so boastfully, are not from God, for the people run after them eagerly, accept them, and even look upon them as that holy gospel of God, so that the truth of Scripture is proved which states, "For that which comes from God, the world despises; another comes in his name and the world receives him" [Cf. John 5:43]. Those who teach such fables are the cause of this error. They preach indulgences more zealously and with more pomp than they do the gospel. And the error is due also to the fact that they preach to all people those things which are only for the few. I have made it clear enough previously that pardons are relaxations, liberties, permissions, and clemencies, and they are true indulgences, if we accept the strict meaning of the term, that is, they are permissions given out of softness of heart to delicate, cold, hard Christians, that is, rather to Gibeonites, the water-carriers [Josh. 9:21, 27], and slaves, than to the leaders and children of Israel.

My proof for this thesis is this:

Even the one who does works of love fervently cannot put his trust in those works or feel sure of his salvation because he does them. Even the most holy Job feared all his works [Job 9:28], and Scripture states, "Blessed is the man who fears the Lord" [Ps. 112:1] and "Blessed is the man who fears the Lord always" [Prov. 28:14]. How much the more should we accept in fear in-

---

[80] St. Bernard was a great preacher during the crusades of the twelfth century. He heartily approved the election of Eugenius III as pope in 1145. *Considera-tion* was St. Bernard's last work, written about 1148 at the pope's request and for his edification and guidance.

dulgences, which are of incomparably less value than such works, and place less than the least possible confidence, that is, none at all, in them! A saint is afraid that he might work less or suffer less than he should. Where does that put the sinner who has his sin remitted when he does less than he could do? And as far as I understand these prattlers of ours and these corruptors of minds, they are making indulgences a racket among us and a work of error [II Thess. 2:11] as they stalk around in darkness [Ps. 91:6]. At the same time they persuade all men to trust in these indulgences, whereas they only apply to a few people, to those who are cold and weak, as I have said. Look how they are prompted afterwards by the Holy Spirit through their own witness to call the business of St. Peter the business of the Holy Spirit, as though they were to confess that they themselves are the merchants and that they conduct simoniac market days.[81]

However, when I said, "indulgences are useful," I had in mind that they are useful "not for all men, but for old persons and snoring [workrighteous] laborers," because it is better for them to have the punishments remitted than to bear them unwillingly. Nevertheless, when the choice has been given them to purchase indulgences, in order to avoid a greater evil they should not rejoice as persons who feel secure or put their trust in that fact; rather, they should grieve and fear since they are the kind who, because of the possibility of a greater evil, need to be left to a lesser one. This should be clear to them when they see that even those who have made the greatest progress in goodness are afraid. For this reason I have said that indulgences are most harmful if people rejoice over such liberty without fear of God.

50

Christians are to be taught that if the pope knew the exactions of the indulgence preachers, he would rather that the basilica of St. Peter were burned to ashes than built up with the skin, flesh, and bones of his sheep.

---

[81] That is, days for buying and selling divine privileges. Cf. also p. 201, n. 75.

After our "mighty hunters" have imposed a fixed sum of money upon every Christian according to his economic status, they even teach wives to go out and beg, and that against the will of the husbands. Mendicant friars are taught to scrape money together anywhere, even against the will of their superiors. This goes on until there is no one who has a penny left in his pocket which he might contribute to this cause. Matters were carried so far, it is said, that people were exhorted even to sell their clothes or borrow anywhere.

In my opinion indulgences are the most worthless of all possessions of the church and ought to be granted only to its most worthless members. Furthermore, they are neither meritorious nor useful but, what is worse, extremely harmful if they who receive them have no sense of fear. Therefore I feel that such teaching deserves to be cursed and is contrary to the commands of God. For a wife should live under the authority of her husband and do nothing contrary to his will, even if it were meritorious to do so. Even less should she go begging for indulgences she probably does not need. Also, those in religious orders should serve in obedience, even if they otherwise could in some manner attain the martyr's crown. The pope never intends anything different, although his false interpreters do. Let someone else give vent to his anger; I shall exercise self-restraint. One thing I want to say: Learn at least, dear reader, whether they do not by their pestilential preaching make people believe that salvation and the true grace of God depend upon indulgences. Otherwise why would they commend these indulgences so zealously as to make meritorious works and the commands of God useless? Yet until now they are not considered heretics, so they may take pride in being the persecutors of heretics.

Has it been the pope's desire that men who are committed to his care be stripped to the very skin for the sake of sticks and stones? Or has it been his desire that by the pestilential doctrines of these "thieves and robbers," as Christ calls them [John 10:1], they should be slaughtered and destroyed? It was better to have him as emperor who said, "A good shepherd shears but does not skin his sheep." [82] The indulgence sellers not only skin the people, but devour them in body and soul. "Their throat is an open sepulchre, they flatter with their tongues, etc." [Ps. 5:9].

51

Christians are to be taught that the pope would and should wish to give of his own money, even though he had to sell the basilica of St. Peter, to many of those from whom certain hawkers of indulgences cajole money.

St. Ambrose melted down the sacred vessels to redeem the captives,[83] and St. Paulinus of Nola[84] handed himself over as a captive for the sake of his own. It is for such a purpose that the church has its gold[85] as the decretals, which have taken this from that same Ambrose, show. And now, dear God, how many there are who carry firewood, even leaves, to the forest and little drops of water to the sea, that is, their pennies to that purse, whose gain, to use the word of Jerome, is the religion of the whole world.

52

It is vain to trust in salvation by indulgence letters, even though the indulgence commissary, or even the pope, were to offer his soul as security.

They dare to expound this monstrous doctrine without shame in order to take away from men the fear of God and through indulgences hand them over to the wrath of God, contrary to the word of that wise one who said, "Do not be without fear concerning the

---

[82] Caesar Tiberius (A.D. 14-37), quoted by Suetonius in his *Life of Tiberius* (*Vita Tiberii*), chap. 32.

[83] Cf. *De officiis ministrorum* ii. 28. Migne 16, 148-150.

[84] St. Paulinus (354?-431) was a personal acquaintance of St. Ambrose (340-395), bishop of Milan. After the death of his only child, who died in infancy, he and his wife Therasia entered monastic life. He became bishop of Nola about 409 and held that office until his death in 431. His feast day is June 22.

[85] When Paulinus made the decision for the ascetic life he turned over his enormous wealth to the church.

propitiation for sin" [Sirach 5:5], and of the Psalmist, "Who understands his faults?" [Ps. 19:12]. But the preachers of indulgences
say, "We do not take away the fear of God." If security through
indulgences is compatible with the fear of God, then you do not
take it away; but the people do, when they receive letters of indulgence which have been extolled with such a noisy taking of
oaths. If a person is afraid that the letters of indulgence might not
be sufficient before God, how can this glorious promise of security
be true? But if a person is confident that they are sufficient, how
can he be afraid? May every single sermon be forever damned
which persuades a person to find security and trust in or through
anything whatever except the pure mercy of God, which is Christ.
All the saints not only fear but cry out in despair, "Do not enter
into judgment with thy servant, O Lord" [Ps. 143:2]. And by
those letters of indulgence you give them a sense of security and
lead them to God's judgment. In answer to such unrestrained whirl-
pools of falsehood some have concocted a story which I believe
is not completely devoid of truth. A certain dead person arrived at
hell with his letters of indulgences and pleaded for freedom by
virtue of those letters. The devil came to meet him and, while he
was reading the letters before the heat of the fire, it devoured the
wax and the parchment in his hands, and he dragged the man along
with him to the depths of hell.

53

*They are enemies of Christ and the pope who forbid alto-
gether the preaching of the Word of God in some churches
in order that indulgences may be preached in others.*

It is the duty and intention of the pope to desire the Word of
God to be preached above everything else, always, and everywhere, as he knows he has been commanded by Christ to do. How
can we believe, therefore, that he opposes Christ himself? And
yet our preachers dare to believe this as well as everything else.

54

Injury is done the Word of God when, in the same sermon,

an equal or larger amount of time is devoted to indulgences than to the Word.

This is clear enough from the dignity the Word of God possesses, and the necessity for preaching that Word, while the preaching of indulgences is neither necessary nor of much value.

55

It is certainly the pope's sentiment that if indulgences, which are a very insignificant thing, are celebrated with one bell, one procession, and one ceremony, then the gospel, which is the very greatest thing, should be preached with a hundred bells, a hundred processions, a hundred ceremonies.

Nothing in the church must be treated with greater care than the holy gospel, since the church has nothing which is more precious and salutary. Therefore it is the only single work which Christ enjoined upon his disciples at so many different times. And Paul says that he was not sent to baptize but to preach the gospel [I Cor. 1:17]. Christ commanded that the sacrament of the Eucharist should be celebrated only in remembrance of him, and Paul says in I Cor. 11 [:26], "As often as you eat this bread and drink the cup, you proclaim the Lord's death." It is better to omit the sacrament than not to proclaim the gospel. The church has decided that the mass must not be celebrated without the reading of the gospel. Therefore God has placed greater importance on the gospel than on the mass, for without the gospel man does not live in the Spirit, but he does without the mass. "For man shall live by every word that proceeds from the mouth of God" [Cf. Matt. 4:4], as the Lord himself teaches at greater length in the sixth chapter of John. The mass then renews those who are already a part of the body of Christ, but the gospel, the sword of the Spirit, devours the flesh, divides the kingdom of the devil, takes away the possessions of the strong and increases the body of the church. The mass helps only those who have life; the gospel, on the other hand, helps everybody. Hence, in the early church, the demoniacs and catechumens[86] were permitted to remain until after the reading of the gospel and only then were dismissed by those who were permitted to eat and drink of the body of Christ in the mass. Even now church law permits those who have been excommunicated to remain at the mass until after the reading of the gospel. As John preceded Christ, so the gospel precedes the mass. The gospel prostrates and humbles, whereas the mass conveys grace to those who are humbled. Therefore it would be better if they forbade the mass [rather than silence the gospel].

But what a beautiful spectacle do you think that would be for the devils to watch, if at some time these wasters of indulgences, who especially need indulgences themselves (for example, simoniacs,[87] and those who according to the canons have fallen from grace), were to bestow them upon those who do not need indulgences at all?

56

The treasures of the church, out of which the pope distributes indulgences, are not sufficiently discussed or known among Christians.

This is the second time that I have deserved death. After I have maintained many things which have been so evident for a long time that no protest was necessary, I now must discuss them once more. So in this discussion I must deal with the most recent protest. Therefore I shall discuss here these unfamiliar matters and seek to find the truth, to which the reader, the listener, or the inquisitor of heretical depravity may be my witness.

57

That indulgences are not temporal treasures is certainly

---

[86] Luther refers to the division of the mass into the *missa catechumenorum* and *missa fidelium* which evolved in the course of the second and third centuries of the Christian era. "Catechumens" is the name given those who were being instructed in preparation for baptism, not, as is the custom in many churches today, for confirmation.

[87] Cf. p. 206, n. 81.

*clear, for many indulgence sellers do not distribute them
freely but only gather them.*

Experience makes this quite clear.

58

*Nor are they the merits of Christ and the saints, for, even
without the pope, the latter always work grace for the inner
man, and the cross, death, and hell for the outer man.*

The substance of this thesis is very deeply rooted in and close to
the heart of almost all teachers. Therefore I must test it very extensively and firmly, and I do so with confidence.

1. First of all concerning the merits of the saints.

They say that the saints during this life have contributed many
more good works than were required for salvation, that is, works
of supererogation, which have not yet been rewarded, but have
been deposited in the treasury of the church, by means of which,
through indulgences, some fitting compensation takes place, etc.
Thus they are of the opinion that the saints had done enough for
us. I argue against this.

First, indulgences then are not indulgences, as I shall prove,
since they are not free remissions but applications of some other
satisfaction, and they possess all the benefits which I have demonstrated above with regard to the treasury of the church militant.
That means, then, that nothing is accomplished by the authority
of the keys except a certain transference of works, but that nothing
is pardoned. This is contrary to that word of Christ, "Whatsoever
you shall loose" [Matt. 16:19]. Likewise, the same thing is accomplished then by the keys which has already taken place, for if there
are in the church works of the saints which could be applied to the
salvation of others, surely the Holy Spirit will not permit them to lie
idle but will actually use them to aid those who can be helped.

Second, no works of the saints are left unrewarded, for, according to everybody, God rewards a man more than he deserves.
As St. Paul says, "The sufferings of this present time are not worth
comparing with the glory that is to be" [Rom. 8:18].

Third, no saint has adequately fulfilled God's commandments in this life. Consequently the saints have done absolutely nothing which is superabundant. Therefore they have left nothing to be allocated through indulgences. I believe that the inference is clear enough. But I shall prove the major premise so that there is no doubt about it, but that it must be believed in such a way that the opposite view would be considered heretical.

I prove this argument first by that saying of Christ, "When you have done all that is commanded, say 'We are unworthy servants'" [Luke 17:10]. But the term "unworthy servant" is understood to refer to one who has done less and not more than he should, unless perhaps we should follow the dreams of certain absurd individuals who chatter that by his words Christ wanted this to be said for the sake of humility, not for the sake of truth, thereby making Christ a liar, so that they might appear truthful. I prove this argument secondly by that passage in Matt. 25 [:9] which says that the wise maidens had no desire to share their oil for fear that there would not be enough also for themselves. Third, Paul says, I Cor. 3 [:8], "Each shall receive his wages according to his labor." He does not say, "according to another's labor." Fourth, I adduce Galatians 6, "Everyone must answer for himself" [Cf. Gal. 6:4-5], as well as the saying, "So that each one may receive . . . according as he has done in the body" [II Cor. 5:10]. Fifth, every saint is obligated to love God as much as he can, indeed more than he can, but no one has or can do that. Sixth, the saints, in their most perfect work, that is, through death, martyrdom, and suffering, do no more than is required. Indeed they do what is required and scarcely that. Therefore they have done much less than they should in other works. Seventh, although I have produced so many reasons, they, on the other hand, to support their position, have not produced one, but only a recital of the circumstances, speaking without proof from the Scriptures, the teachers of the church, and sound reasons. For that reason we can, indeed we must, completely ignore their opinion. The following may serve as my proof.

Now I shall prove my argument with the authority of the holy fathers. I will do this first by quoting that well-known saying of St. Augustine: "All saints need to pray, 'Forgive us our debts,' even though they have done good deeds, for Christ made no exceptions when he taught us to pray."[88] But surely those who confess their debts have stored up no superabundant merits. Second, according to Psalm 32 [:2], "Blessed is the man to whom the Lord imputes no iniquity." And further on in the same psalm one reads, "Therefore let everyone who is godly offer prayer to thee" [Ps. 32:6]. St. Jerome, reflecting upon this in his *Dialogue Against the Pelagians,* says in excellent fashion, "How can he be a saint if he prays for his own ungodliness?" He says again, "If he is ungodly, he is not a saint, etc."[89] Therefore the saints, through prayer and the confession of their ungodliness, deserve to have no sin of theirs charged against them. Third, St. Augustine says in Book I of his *Retractations,* "All the commandments shall be fulfilled when that which is not fulfilled is forgiven."[90] There he deals with the question whether or not the saints have completely fulfilled the commandments, and he denies that they have when he says that this takes place by God's forgiveness rather than by man's fulfilment. Fourth, the same writer says in the ninth book of his *Confessions,* "Woe to the life of men, however praiseworthy it may be, if it should be judged without compassion."[91] See how even the saints need compassion throughout their lives. To this Job adds, "Even though I am innocent, I shall appeal for mercy to my accuser" [Job 9:15]. How, therefore, can these saints have superabundant merits for others, when they have not sufficient for themselves? Fifth, St. Augustine in his second book of *Against Julian*[92] lists ten of the ancient church fathers who were of this same opinion, namely, Hilarius, Cyprian, Gregory Nazianzen, John Chrysostom, Ambrose, Irenaeus, Olympius, Rheticius, and Innocent [I],[93] and he draws his support from their authority, proving that no saint is without sin in this life, according to that

---

[88] *Concerning Nature and Grace.* Migne 40, 266ff.

[89] Migne 23, 538: "If he is a saint, how can he pray for his ungodliness? If he has ungodliness, why is he called a saint?"

[90] Migne 32, 615.

[91] Migne 32, 659-868; cf. 778.

[92] Migne 44, 671-874.

[93] Actually only 9 are listed here.

saying in I John 1 [:8]: "If we say we have no sin, etc." St. Augustine says the same thing in his work *Concerning Nature and Grace*.[94]

From these and from many other references which would take too long to enumerate, I conclude that the saints have no super-abundant merits which would help those of us who are lazy. Speaking boldly, I declare that I have no doubt about those things I have just now said, rather I am prepared to endure death by fire for them, and I maintain that everyone who holds the contrary is a heretic.

Nevertheless, if I were to admit the impossible, that is, that the saints have actually stored up surplus merits, I am not sure whether the church would be doing such a worthy work when it expends such precious merits so cheaply, that is, for the remission of punishments. For the remission of punishment is the cheapest gift the church possesses and deserves to be presented to the most worthless people, as I already said so often. However, the punishments of the martyrs and saints should be instead an example for us in bearing punishments. For we pray in this manner: "As we observe the feasts of the martyrs, let us imitate their courage in suffering." Likewise, Mother Church does not appear to act piously when she remits punishments, but only when she chastises and coerces her children, as in the case of excommunications and other severe censures, which punishments she does not remit at all, but rather inflicts, especially when she has been most anxious about her children. But if she does remit the punishments, she does so as if out of despair, because she is afraid that something worse will happen. Therefore since remissions of punishments are such a cheap gift and the power of the keys alone is sufficient for that, it would certainly appear that not the slightest disrespect is done to such noble efforts of the saints if remissions were bestowed upon those who are snoring. St. Augustine said this much better in his sermon, *Concerning Martyrdom*, in these words: "The festivals of the martyrs are not remissions but exhortations to martyrdom, so that we should not hesitate to imitate that which we like to celebrate."[95]

Therefore this part of the thesis has been proved, that is, that

---

[94] Written A.D. 415 against the Pelagians. Cf. p. 9 n. 1, and p. 214 n. 88.
[95] *Sermo* 123, chap. 2. Migne 38, 684-685.

the merits of the saints cannot act as a treasury for us since the saints themselves considered them deficient; unless someone should think that they are a treasure for us, not because they are surplus merits, but because the church is a communion of saints in which each one works for the other, as members one of another. But the saints did this during their lifetime, and if they were to do it now, it would be accomplished by intercession rather than by the power of the keys.

But at this point I hear at a distance the clever argument of certain individuals. "It is true," they say, "that the saints were not without sin in this life, but they were only venial sins, and in spite of that the saints were able to do more than was required for salvation." It is difficult to deal with such exceedingly stupid people in this matter. Nevertheless let me say it briefly: Their venial sin is that they do less than they should, not, however, that which my opponents alone imagine as a venial sin, namely, a laugh, a frivolous word, or a thought. This is, to be sure, a venial sin, but it is a big venial sin. But even a good work which has been done in the best manner is a venial sin, as cited above from the words of St. Augustine: "The commandments are fulfilled when what is not fulfilled is forgiven."[96] And this happens in every good work, for according to the Lord's Prayer we must always seek forgiveness. But these things require another disputation which will be dealt with elsewhere. Hence St. Bonaventura, who was a holy man, was absolutely wrong when he maintained that a man can exist without venial sin.

2. Concerning the second part of my argument, namely, the merit of Christ:

I argue that this is not the treasury of indulgences; but that it is the treasury of the church only a heretic would deny. For Christ is the Ransom and Redeemer of the world, and thereby most truly and solely the only treasury of the church. But that he is the treasury of indulgences I deny until I shall be taught differently. My reasons for denying this are these:

First, because, as I have often said, this cannot be proved by any Scripture passages, nor can it be demonstrated by reason. Fur-

---

[96] Cf. p. 214, n. 90.

thermore, those who hold this opinion do not prove it but simply state it, as everybody knows. Moreover, I have said before that to make any assertion in the church without a reason or authority to support it is to expose the church to ridicule by its enemies and by heretics, since according to the Apostle Peter we are bound to give a reason for the faith and hope that is in us [I Pet. 3:15]. And Paul says that a bishop should be able by sound doctrine to confute those who contradict that doctrine [Titus 1:9]. But there is no such authority here, so that if today the Roman church should settle upon the affirmative side,[97] nevertheless the same danger remains because we can give no other reason except that it pleased the pope and the Roman church to do so. But what good would that reason be if we were pressed by those who do not believe in the Roman church, such as the heretics or the Picards? These people will not ask whether it is the will of the pope or the Roman church, but whether there is an authority or a plausible reason for it. And certainly that is my sole purpose in this whole matter.

Second, all the arguments which are adduced to prove the treasury of the church militant and the merits of the saints have more weight here. First, that indulgences are not really indulgences but rather transfers of the works of some to others, and constitute a true and legitimate satisfaction, since what we do, we do through another. But, as the canon says in book five of *Concerning Penance and Remission (Cum ex eo)*,[98] penitential satisfaction is weakened by indulgences. The canon does not say, "it is transferred," but, "it is weakened." My second argument also has more weight here, namely, that the keys of the church accomplish nothing and actually are rendered worthless since they do not loose but transfer to someone else that which is bound. But it is wicked to say that the keys do not loose. If they do loose they remove completely that which is loosed. My third argument is that the merits of Christ actually accomplish the same thing without the keys, for surely they will not lie idle! The fourth argument is that there would develop an extraordinary disrespect for the merits of Christ if they were to be used

---

[97] That is, the opinion that the merits of Christ become a part of the treasury of indulgences.

[98] *Op. cit.*

only for the remission of punishment, since he himself, by his merits, has become an example to all martyrs. Therefore it would be contrary to the nature of Christ's merits that these merits should serve the sluggards while at the same time stimulating the zealous. As I have already pointed out, the remission of punishment is very cheap.

Third, let them give me an answer to the following contradiction: St. Thomas and St. Bonaventura and their followers say continually and unanimously that good works are better than indulgences, as I have said often enough previously. Granted that this is true. Likewise the merits of Christ are applied and administered through indulgences. Granted also that this is true, for all teachers continually maintain this opinion. Likewise, the merits of Christ are far better than our own good works, indeed they alone are good. Granted that this also is true.

Here I conclude with this inference. Unhappy is he who does not put aside his good works and seek the works of Christ alone, that is, indulgences, since it would be the greatest blasphemy of all for one to prefer his own good works over the works of Christ. Therefore either the works of Christ are not the treasury of indulgences or else that person is a most arrogant and wretched individual who does not disregard all the commandments, even the divine commandments, and only purchases indulgences, that is, the merits of Christ. In opposing this view, St. Thomas and St. Bonaventura say indulgences are not commanded and are less important than good works. Therefore indulgences are not the works of Christ, yet at the same time and in a certain sense they are the works of Christ.

But perhaps, since my opponents are so ingenious, they will answer by Aristotelian distinctions in these words: "It is true that the merits of Christ, taken simply, by themselves, are better than our works, but as such they are not indulgences, or rather they are not applied to indulgences in such a manner. They are received, however, just as they are in themselves, as satisfactions for punishments, and in this manner will they also be applied." I reply, Prove what you are saying. What if I do not care to believe your scant statement? I am commanded to "test the spirits to see whether they are of God" [I John 4:1].

Then, where does that put the statement which was made above, namely, that the merits of the saints are dispensed through indulgences not because they were rewarded, but because the saints had done some good works which they were not required to do? Are such merits, therefore, of so little value as to receive no other reward than that of satisfactions for others who are lazy? If so, I contend that the works of supererogation are the most noble and perfect of all. Do you agree? Yes. And do you mean that merits are not given as a reward to the martyrs and saints, but are granted to snoring sluggards? And is it true that the saints shall be rewarded according to their lesser works and merits while the more perfect works shall be left to others? I ask you, who is so insane as to believe that? Therefore St. Catherine[99] received nothing for her martyrdom and virginity, but left that for the church. Is her reward for prayer, vigils, and other good works sufficient? But if you should say that the saints were rewarded for their good works and at the same time left their superabundant merits to the church, what becomes of that statement which was made previously, that there are certain merits which have not yet been rewarded? Do you not see what it means to speak without authority and to prophesy in the dark?

But if it is wicked to say that the works of supererogation or those which the saints did over and above what they were required to do are of such little value and are not given to them as a reward, how much more wicked is it to make of such little value the works of Christ, all of which are in excess of what was necessary! Therefore to magnify indulgences in such a manner and at the same time to depreciate them by our own works is blasphemy against Christ and his saints in their merits, unless it is done by error and not intentionally.

---

[99] St. Catherine, one of the most honored saints of the Eastern and Western churches, whose name is linked with many legendary accretions on account of the martyrdom she presumably met at the hands of Maximinus or Maxentius during the Diocletian persecutions (284-305).

Fourth, I take up again the argument which the gloss to the work "Concerning Penance and Remission" *(Quod autem)*[100] raises, namely, "If indulgences are remissions of all punishments, then man no longer needs to fast or do good deeds." We must not conclude from this that remission is uncertain, but rather that the keys of the church are blasphemed, even though almost all the scholastic teachers support this opinion of Gregory. The quotation, "Man does not know whether or not he deserves [God's] love,"[101] by which he proves his position, refers to a future event, for he who believes now does not know whether or not he will continue in faith. Hence in the same ninth chapter of Ecclesiastes it is immediately added that man does not know whether he deserves love or hate [Eccles. 9:2], but all things are kept uncertain up to the future, for he had said previously, "The righteous and their deeds are in the hand of God," etc. [Eccles. 9:1]. But if these passages make the remission of guilt uncertain, how much more uncertain do they make the remission of guilt. For if guilt remains, punishment also must remain. The gloss also states that it is speaking of remission in which the sin is completely erased through contrition, especially through faith in the keys.

What are indulgences then? An uncertain gift? Far be it, far be it that such a wicked illusion should stem from the church of Christ, indeed from the keys. Actually, then, as some say, indulgences would be a wicked deception of the faithful. Such an error arises when we seek to be justified through our own works and righteousness rather than through faith. At best the church teaches only about contrition. It teaches nothing about faith in the keys which should be taught most of all. But I spoke of these things at great length above. So either indulgences are not the treasury of the merits of the saints, or it must necessarily follow that one who has obtained indulgences must desist from doing good works for sins, as the gloss referred to maintains.

The explanation offered by this gloss is wickedness against Christ, for, if by indulgences the merits of Christ are granted to me

---

[100] *Op. cit.*
[101] *MA³* attributes this quotation to Eccles. 9:1.

and I am still in doubt whether my sins are remitted, then I must still work for the remission of those sins. It follows from this, that I doubt whether the merits of Christ which have been applied through indulgences and given to me are sufficient for the remission of sins. What could be more detestable than such a doubt? Moreover, if I do not doubt this but believe that they are sufficient, I should act in a most wicked manner if I should consider my own works better than indulgences, that is, the works of Christ which have been granted to me. For if I could obtain one, single work, just one-millionth part of the smallest work of Christ, I would be sure of eternal salvation. Therefore let us stop doing our own works for our sins and only purchase indulgences, for through indulgences we obtain not only one work but all the merits of Christ, and not only his but those of all the saints. Therefore, since the merits of Christ cannot be compared to ours in any way as far as excellence is concerned, either they are not the treasury of indulgences or else indulgences must be preferred to all the works of all commands of God; otherwise the greatest disrespect and blasphemy would be done to the merits of Christ. So watch how they add to this treasury the merits of the saints as well as the merits of the church militant, as if the merits of Christ alone were not enough.

But you ask, "Did not St. Thomas err also along with others? Does not the pope err along with the whole church, which is of the same opinion? Or are you the only one and the first one to have the right opinion?"

My first answer is, I am not the only one: the truth is on my side, as are many others, namely, those who have doubted and still doubt the validity of indulgences. They do not sin because of this doubt. Since remissions are only for punishments, a person will be saved whether or not he believes in them and whether he obtains them or not.

Second, the pope is on my side, for although he grants indulgences, nevertheless he nowhere says that they are taken from the treasury of the merits of Christ and the church. He explains his position in book five, *Concerning Penance and Remission,* in the chapter beginning with the words *Cum ex eo,*[102] where he says that

---

[102] *Op. cit.* Cf. also Thesis 20.

indulgences are an enervation of penitential satisfactions. But the enervation does not refer to the allotment of the merits of Christ, only to the removal of punishments.

Third, the whole church is on my side, for the church is of one mind with the pope and holds to the same opinion as the pope. I have already said what the pope says about it.

Fourth, even if St. Thomas, St. Bonaventura, and Alexander of Hales are distinguished men along with their disciples Antoninus, Peter of Palude, Augustine of Ancona,[103] besides the canonists who agree with them, nevertheless it is only right to give preference to the truth first, and then to the authority of the pope and the church. Furthermore, it is not surprising that such great men have erred in this respect. For, I ask you, in what great respects did not the scholastics contend that even St. Thomas had erred!

What is more, for more than 300 years now, many universities, and many of the sharpest minds in them, have labored with persistent industry to comprehend Aristotle alone. Yet they not only do not understand Aristotle after all this effort but even disseminate error and a false understanding of him throughout almost the whole church. And even if they should understand him, they would have attained no extraordinary wisdom thereby, particularly not from the Aristotelian books with which they are most familiar. According to his own testimony in the fourth chapter of book twenty by Aulus Gellius,[104] and according to the testimony of Gregory Nazianzen in his *Sermon Against the Arians*, Aristotle is discovered to be nothing more than a mere sophist and a bandier of words.

Here I appear to be bold, brazen, and presumptuous. If I only had time and leisure to account for this boldness of mine and instil confidence in my words, perhaps I could show that this opinion of mine is not so unfounded. I would not harmonize Aristotle with

---

[103] For identification, cf. Thesis, 20, p. 146, n. 30.

[104] Aulus Gellius, a grammarian of the second century A.D., in his *Noctes Atticae* prepared a digest of conversations with contemporaries concerning writings of great literary men, including Aristotle. Aristotle's testimony concerning himself is not to be found in the source to which Luther refers. Cf. *MA*² 1, 511 and *CL* 1, 126. The *Sermon Against the Arians* is in Migne, *Patrologiae, Series Graeca*, 36, cols. 213-238.

Plato and others, which Giovanni Pico della Mirandola attempted, but paint Aristotle in his own colors as he deserves to be painted. He is by profession a master craftsman of words, according to Gregory Nazianzen, and a mocker of brilliant men. Therefore if God permitted such a great cloud and darkness to prevail for so long a time in such outstanding minds, how can we be so confident in our own works instead of looking upon all our efforts with suspicion, as Christians should, in order that Christ alone may become our light, righteousness, truth, wisdom, and our total possession.

The holy fathers of the church saw how the unlearned and those who did not know Christ held Aristotle in such esteem as an authority, and since they were of such meek disposition, they permitted themselves to follow in pious simplicity, and since they had fallen into error they became to others a cause for so many confusing opinions, doubts, and errors which we see reflected today in the scholastic teachers. We who have forsaken Christ have deserved to be abandoned by him and given over, even through his saints, to the risk of error and endless labor, as Ezekiel says, chapter 14 [:9], "If the prophet be deceived and speak a word, I, the Lord, have deceived that prophet." And in the same chapter we read: "If anyone comes to the prophet asking me through him, I, the Lord, will answer him myself because of the multitude of his idols" [Cf. Ezek. 14:4]. Therefore everything must be read and accepted with fear and judgment, even that which is handed down by great and holy men, according to the Apostle who says, "Test everything; hold fast what is good" [I Thess. 5:21]. And John says, "Test the spirits to see whether they are of God" [I John 4:1].

Those who have neglected such advice and entrusted themselves to men as those do, for example, who say, "I prefer to err with great men rather than be considered right with you," deserve to be despised and left to their own counsel. For why should not he who despises the counsel of the Spirit be rightfully despised by the spirit of the counsel? The same thing has happened in the matter of indulgences. When the holy teachers of the church saw how the people extolled so highly these indulgences (as the people always are accustomed to be as foolish in their judgment as Paris and

Midas), and would not believe that they were so worthless, they even began to devise a respectable and extravagant basis for them since no other occurred to them—in fact there never was one.

Therefore let us return to the matter at hand and examine the merit of Christ and then show that it is not the treasury of indulgences.

My fifth argument is the basis for this statement: No one receives the grace of contrition without receiving at the same time the merits of Christ. Therefore a person possesses the treasury of the merits of Christ before he receives indulgences. If he did not possess these merits, indulgences would be of no value to him, according to the opinion of our teachers (for they think so highly of the remission of punishments). A man returns to the grace of God by means of contrition, just as in the parable of Christ the prodigal son returns to his father who says to him, "Everything I have is yours" [Cf. Luke 15:11-32]. And Isa. 9 [:6] says, "To us a child is born, to us a son is given." In Rom. 8 [:32] we read, "Will he not also give us all things with him?"

Sixth, otherwise those who are the worst people in the church would be much happier. For I have said that indulgences are profitable only for criminals, and the treasury of the merits of Christ should be given to them! But it should not be given to children, young women, and the innocent, to whom it especially belongs, indeed, who alone possess it. But that argument counts for little for those who believe that all punishments are removed and that indulgences cannot be conferred upon sinners without contrition, which I do not believe.

Lastly, this thesis bears its own proof, that is, that the merits of Christ and his saints perform a two-fold work without the pope, to wit, a work characteristic of them, and a work alien to them. Works characteristic of them are grace, righteousness, truth, patience, and gentleness in the spirit of a man who has been predestined. For the righteousness of Christ and his merit justifies and remits sins, as John says, "Behold, the Lamb of God, who takes away the sin of the world" [John 1:29]. And Isaiah says, chapter 43 [:24-25], "You have wearied me with your iniquities and burdened me with your sins. I, I am He who blots out your transgressions. . . , and I will not remember your sins." He blots them out by the merit of his suffering. In that sense I might concede that the merits of Christ are so to speak a treasury, not of the church, but of God the Father, for through his efficacious intercession before God Christ obtained for us remission of guilt. So it is stated in a figurative manner in Job: "I will show favor to him" [Cf. Job 42:8]. And the Apostle says in Heb. 12 [:24] that the blood of Christ cries out better than the blood of Abel, for the blood of Abel demands revenge and wrath, but the blood of Christ cries out for compassion and pleads for us. The merits of Christ perform an alien work, for that is what Isaiah calls it in chapter 28 [:21], in that they effect the cross, labor, all kinds of punishment, finally death and hell in the flesh, to the end that the body of sin is destroyed [Rom. 6:6], our members which are upon earth are mortified [Col. 3:5], and sinners are turned into hell. For whoever is baptized in Christ and is renewed shall be prepared for punishments, crosses, and deaths, to the end that "he shall be accounted as a sheep for the slaughter and shall be slain all the day long" [Ps. 44:22]. And as one reads in another psalm, "For I am ready to fall," whether it is appointed for me or not, "and my pain is ever with me" [Ps. 38:17]. Just so must we be conformed to the image of the Son of God [Rom. 8:29], so that whoever does not take up his own cross and follow him, is not worthy of him [Matt. 10:38], even if he were filled with all kinds of indulgences.

From this you can now see how, ever since the scholastic theology—the deceiving theology (for that is the meaning of the word in Greek)—began, the theology of the cross has been abrogated, and everything has been completely turned up-side-down. A theologian of the cross (that is, one who speaks of the crucified and hidden God), teaches that punishments, crosses, and death are the most precious treasury of all and the most sacred relics which the Lord of this theology himself has consecrated and blessed, not alone by the touch of his most holy flesh but also by the embrace of his exceedingly holy and divine will, and he has left these relics here to be kissed, sought after, and embraced. Indeed fortunate and blessed is he who is considered by God to be so worthy that these treasures

225

of the relics of Christ should be given to him; rather, who understands that they are given to him. For to whom are they not offered? As St. James says, "Count it all joy, my brethren, when you meet various trials" [Jas. 1:2]. For not all have this grace and glory to receive these treasures, but only the most elect of the children of God.

Many make pilgrimages to Rome and to other holy places to see the robe of Christ, the bones of the martyrs, and the places and remains of the saints, which we certainly do not condemn. But we lament the fact that we do not at the same time recognize the true relics, namely, the sufferings and crosses which have sanctified the bones and relics of the martyrs and made them worthy of such great veneration. And by not recognizing these true relics we not only do not receive them when they are offered at home, but even reject them with all our might and chase from place to place, while with the greatest thirst and constant tears we should beg God that such precious relics of Christ, which are the most sacred of all, be given to us, as it were, a gift for the elect children of God. Thus Psalm 15 [Ps. 16] in the Hebrew bears the title *Miktam,* which might be interpreted, so to speak, as an excellent golden little present. Yet the psalmist sings only of the suffering of Christ. And the Psalm entitled "A Testimony of Asaph" [e.g., Ps. 80] learned ones prefer to interpret more as an amusement of Asaph or as a delightful gift of Asaph, and yet there too a hymn of the cross is sounded.

Yet, so holy are these relics and so precious these treasures, that while others could be preserved on earth or most honorably in vessels of gold, silver, precious stones, and silk, these can only be preserved in heavenly, living, rational, immortal, pure, and holy vessels, that is, in the hearts of the faithful which are incomparably more precious than every piece of gold and every precious stone. But nowadays the common people lack the faith by which they might cultivate reverence for relics of this kind to the point where even some popes have become authors and leaders not only in condemning these relics, but even persecuting those who seek them. So much is this so that they wanted to devour the Turks and after this

226

banish the Christians themselves to a condemnation worse than that of hell rather than remit one penny of their indulgence tax, to say nothing of upholding the wrong done to their name and body.

Yet in the meantime they have opened the floodgates of heaven and flooded the treasury of indulgences and the merits of Christ so that by this deluge almost the whole Christian world is ruined, unless my faith deceives me. A theologian of glory does not recognize, along with the Apostle, the crucified and hidden God alone [I Cor. 2:2]. He sees and speaks of God's glorious manifestation among the heathen, how his invisible nature can be known from the things which are visible [Cf. Rom. 1:20] and how he is present and powerful in all things everywhere. This theologian of glory, however, learns from Aristotle that the object of the will is the good and the good is worthy to be loved, while the evil, on the other hand, is worthy of hate. He learns that God is the highest good and exceedingly lovable. Disagreeing with the theologian of the cross, he defines the treasury of Christ as the removing and remitting of punishments, things which are most evil and worthy of hate. In opposition to this the theologian of the cross defines the treasury of Christ as impositions and obligations of punishments, things which are best and most worthy of love. Yet the theologian of glory still receives money for his treasury, while the theologian of the cross, on the other hand, offers the merits of Christ freely. Yet people do not consider the theologian of the cross worthy of consideration, but finally even persecute him.

But who will be the judge of these two, in order that we may know which one to listen to? Behold, Isaiah says, chapter 66 [:4], "I will choose what they ridicule." And I Cor. 1 [:27] states, "God chose what is weak in the world to shame the strong, etc." But if one should accept this judgment as true, there is nothing for us to do, if we wish to speak the truth, but confess that the treasures of indulgences are the greatest harm that can be done, if they are understood in such a manner as to be proclaimed universally as the remission of all punishments and not only those of the canons; for there is no harm that is greater than that of taking away from men the image of the Son of God and robbing them of those inestimable treasures, in which St. Agnes[105] took pride, with a joyful and blessed boasting, referring to them as beautiful, glittering stones and jewels, precious necklaces, etc.

59

St. Laurence said that the poor of the church were the treasures of the church, but he spoke according to the usage of the word in his own time.

This is clear enough to those who have read the legend of St. Laurence. But today the word "treasure" has a different meaning so that men no longer speak of the poor as the treasures of the church. With this word we refer to the patrimony of Christ and St. Peter, chaff without grain, as it were, which Constantine has given to the church.[106] Therefore in Ps. 2 [:8], where God says, referring to Christ, "Ask of me and I will make the nations your heritage, and the ends of the earth your possession," one must understand it to mean cities and lands extending from the rising to the setting of the sun. If anyone today should speak in a different way about matters of the church and spiritual things, he would appear to us as one who speaks in a foreign tongue, even when St. Laurence, though not exclusively, referred to the possessions of the church as wealth.

60

Without want of consideration we say that the keys of the church, given by the merits of Christ, are that treasure;

If the merit of Christ were also called the treasure of indulgences, that is to say, the power of the keys, the meaning would be clear.

---

[105] Held in high esteem as representing youthful chastity and innocence in Roman and Eastern Orthodox churches, St. Agnes was put to death *circa* 304.

[106] The patrimony of Christ and St. Peter refers to the Papal States as hereditary territories initially acquired by the pope through Constantine's Edict of Milan in 321 and greatly expanded thereafter. In the late Middle Ages the *Donation of Constantine*, a spurious document having its origin in the eighth century, was employed to defend the legal rights of the pope as a temporal sovereign. Upon its incorporation into canon law certain interpolations were made into the *Donation* by Paucapalea referred to as *palea* (chaff). Hence Luther's play on words in the phrase, "chaff without grain."

For no one doubts that everything which has been given to the church has been given by the merit of Christ.

61

For it is clear that the pope's power is of itself sufficient for the remission of penalties and cases reserved by himself.

1. This thesis is proved by that expression of the pope who in binding and loosing is never mindful of the merits of Christ, but says only that he does so "out of the fulness of his power, with sure knowledge, and on his own initiative."[107]

2. This thesis is proved, secondly, from the opinion common to all who hold that indulgences are granted on the strength of that word, where Christ says, "Whatsoever thou shalt loose, etc." [Matt. 16:19]. This word, they feel, would have no force unless it gave the power of granting indulgences to the pope. They are of the opinion that power alone is sufficient, but prove this treasury of indulgences without any authority, considering these words of Christ, as it were, sufficient. These words, however, speak only of power, not the application of merits.

3. If the above is true, then the distribution of the merits of Christ must be understood to apply to other occasions for binding and loosing as well; for example, when the pope in his priestly capacity excommunicates and absolves, ordains and unfrocks, issues decrees and annuls, commands and prohibits, grants dispensations, changes, or interprets. For all these matters are handled on the strength of that word, "Whatsoever" [Matt. 16:19]. Therefore if a distribution of the merits of Christ is not necessary in those cases, but the power of the keys alone is sufficient, how much more is that true for the remission of canonical punishments, since such a remission is nothing more than an absolution from punishments. Indeed, if a distribution of the merits of Christ is made anywhere, especially should it be made in the absolution of one who has been excommunicated. In that case the sinner is reconciled to the church and is declared once more a participant in the benefits of Christ

---

[107] Luther employs these phrases which were frequently used in papal decrees.

and the church. Therefore there is no reason why the words "What-soever thou shalt loose" [Matt. 16:19] should include the treasury of Christ for indulgences and not also for other relaxations, since the same authority, the same word, and the same meaning are applied in these cases.

4. If loosing through the power of the keys by granting indulgences brings about an unfolding and pouring forth of the treasury of the church, then, on the other side, binding through the power of the keys should bring about a gathering and shutting up of that same treasury. For they are opposite powers and opposite effects. But nowhere and never is it customary to gather or shut up this treasury, and yet, if there is a loosing and pouring forth then there must also be a shutting up, for both powers are given to the church and they are not given in vain or without purpose. Therefore, just as binding is understood as making one debtor without withholding from the treasury, that is, without actually taking anything away from him, so loosing must be understood as making one free, without actually spending from the treasury.

62

The true treasure of the church is the most holy gospel of the glory and grace of God.

The gospel of God is something which is not very well known to a large part of the church. Therefore I must speak of it at greater length. Christ has left nothing to the world except the gospel. Also he has handed down to those who have been called to be his servants nothing else than *minae*,[108] talents,[109] riches, and *denarii*,[110] in order to show by these terms which speak of temporal treasures that the gospel is the true treasure. And Paul says that he himself lays up treasures for his children [II Cor. 12:14]. Christ speaks of the gospel as a treasure which is hidden in a field [Matt. 13:44]. And because it is hidden, it is at the same time also neglected.

---

[108] Greek sum of money, equivalent in weight to a hundred Attic drachmas.
[109] Probably the Attic talent that contains 60 *minae*.
[110] A Roman silver coin.

Moreover, according to the Apostle in Rom. 1 [:3-6], the gospel is a preaching of the incarnate Son of God, given to us without any merit on our part for salvation and peace. It is a word of salvation, a word of grace, a word of comfort, a word of joy, a voice of the bridegroom and the bride, a good word, a word of peace. Isaiah says, chapter 52 [:7], "How beautiful . . . are the feet of those who bring good tidings, who publish peace, who preach good tidings." But the law is a word of destruction, a word of wrath, a word of sadness, a word of grief, a voice of the judge and the defendant, a word of restlessness, a word of curse. For according to the Apostle, "The law is the power of sin" [Cf. I Cor. 15:56], and "the law brings wrath" [Rom. 4:15]; it is a law of death [Rom. 7:5, 13]. Through the law we have nothing except an evil conscience, a restless heart, a troubled breast because of our sins, which the law points out but does not take away. And we ourselves cannot take it away. Therefore for those of us who are held captive, who are overwhelmed by sadness and in dire despair, the light of the gospel comes and says, "Fear not" [Isa. 35:4], "comfort, comfort my people" [Isa. 40:1], "encourage the fainthearted" [I Thess. 5:14], "behold your God" [Isa. 40:9], "behold the Lamb of God, who takes away the sin of the world" [John 1:29]. Behold that one who alone fulfils the law for you, whom God has made to be your righteousness, sanctification, wisdom, and redemption, for all those who believe in him [I Cor. 1:30]. When the sinful conscience hears this sweetest messenger, it comes to life again, shouts for joy while leaping about full of confidence, and no longer fears death, the types of punishments associated with death, or hell. Therefore those who are still afraid of punishments have not yet heard Christ or the voice of the gospel, but only the voice of Moses.

Therefore the true glory of God springs from this gospel. At the same time we are taught that the law is fulfilled not by our works but by the grace of God who pities us in Christ and that it shall be fulfilled not through works but through faith, not by anything we offer God, but by all we receive from Christ and partake of in him. "From his fulness have we all received" [John 1:16], and we are partakers of his merits. I have spoken of this more extensively on other occasions.

63

But this treasure is naturally most odious, for it makes the first to be last [Matt. 20:16].

The gospel destroys those things which exist, it confounds the strong, it confounds the wise and reduces them to nothingness, to weakness, to foolishness, because it teaches humility and a cross. Thus Ps. 9 [:5] says, "Thou hast rebuked the nations, thou hast destroyed the wicked; thou has blotted out their name for ever and ever." Yet all those whose pleasure is in earthly things and in their own doing shrink back before this rule of the cross, complaining, "This is a hard saying" [John 6:60]. Therefore it is not surprising that this saying of Christ is most odious to those who desire to be something, who want to be wise and mighty in their own eyes and before men, and who consider themselves to be "the first."

64

On the other hand, the treasure of indulgences is naturally most acceptable, for it makes the last to be first.

The treasure of indulgences teaches people to tremble before punishments, indeed makes them free from punishment which is due only to the righteous. For no one needs indulgences except one who is a slave of punishments, that is, one who does not look upon them with disdain and in proud contempt despises them, but is burdened by them and flees before them as a child flees from the shades of night and darkness. Yet they are permitted to go free while the righteous are subjected to various types of punishments.

65

Therefore the treasures of the gospel are nets with which one formerly fished for men of wealth.

The Apostle said, "I seek not what is yours but you" [II Cor. 12:14]. And Christ said, "I will make you fishers of men" [Matt. 4:19]. This sweet word directs as it attracts the will; indeed, it makes a man surrender his will to Christ. Hence St. Peter, portrayed as a fisherman in the city [of Rome], says,

> For my ship I steer the church, all the regions of the world are my sea, the Scripture is my net, man is the fish.[111]

66

The treasures of indulgences are nets with which one now fishes for the wealth of men.

I believe this is clear from what has been said, for man does not become better through the remissions of punishments, nor is he drawn to God more because of them. Only the word of Christ can do that. Remissions of punishments are words of a man who grants exemption and release rather than of one who "catches" and binds. But if they "catch" anything, surely it is nothing except money, for they do not catch souls.[112] It is not that I condemn this business of contributing money. Indeed, in my judgment, God's providence seems to watch over this business to the extent that, at least in this life, he will reward it with some money so that nothing will lack its reward, even though it is the most insignificant among the gifts and offices of the church and not worthy to be crowned with reward in the future life. However, in former times releases were granted free of charge.

67

The indulgences which the demagogues acclaim as the greatest graces are actually understood to be such only insofar as they promote gain.

The brazen ignorance of the indulgence merchants dares to call that which is of least value the greatest; and judgment in these matters, as well as the ability to understand indulgences properly, is left to the people. As a consequence the people mistakenly believe that the grace of God is bestowed when they purchase indulgences. The merchants themselves do not explain indulgences in order that

---

[111] According to *CL* 1, 133, this may be a reference to Luther's visit to Rome in the winter of 1510-1511.

[112] Cf. Luke 5:10: "Do not be afraid; henceforth you will be catching men."

they may not be forced to contradict themselves or be discovered to be liars because they have called that which is the least value the greatest.

68

They are neverthless in truth the most insignificant graces when compared with the grace of God and the piety of the cross.

As a matter of fact, compared to the grace of God they are null and void since they work just the opposite of the grace of God. Nevertheless, put up with them for the sake of the sluggards and the indolent, as I have already indicated.

69

Bishops and curates are bound to admit the commissaries of papal indulgences with all reverence.

This is so because one must yield in reverence to the papal authority in everything. "He who resists the authorities resists what God has appointed, and those who resist will incur judgment" [Rom. 13:2]. And the Lord himself said, "He who rejects you rejects me" [Luke 10:16]. Therefore one must yield to authority in small matters no less than in great ones. Thus it develops that even if the pope should hand down unfair judgments, they must be respected, as the Emperor Charles[113] said, "Whatever has been imposed, however difficult it may be, must be carried out." And we have seen by experience that this has taken place in the church, which is surely hard pressed today with infinite burdens and yet bears them quietly in a godly and humble manner.

Nevertheless this statement must not be understood in such a way that a person develops a false conscience, that is, as if these unfair judgments should be respected because they must be acknowledged as fair by those who are required to respect them. The pope himself decreed that some should be bound by the church, who nevertheless are not bound in the sight of God, and he com-

---

[113] I.e., Charles the Great, or Charlemagne.

pels them to endure this binding. Yet such a binding does not harm them since it is only a punishment and should be respected. But it should not result in scruples of conscience. By the same token we must respect God in every other act of violence, in the secular realm as well, and not with contempt arrogantly resist it. In the same manner must we bear burdens, not because they were imposed fairly and must be accepted, but as a scourge that has been inflicted by God and which must be borne humbly. Therefore unfair decrees and burdens must be respected, not because of that word, "Whatsoever thou shalt bind" [Matt. 16:19], but because of that general command, "Make friends with your adversary while you are on the way with him" [Matt. 5:25], and that passage, "If anyone strikes you on the right cheek, turn to him the left also" [Matt. 5:39], and in Rom. 12 [:19], "Never avenge yourselves, etc." If this were only advice (since even many theologians appear to err), then by this same freedom it should be just as permissible to resist the pope when he inflicts his burdens and unfair decrees, as it is to resist the Turk or other adversaries. But one must not resist anyone, even if one does not approve his action, so that one does not act against one's conscience. But this matter, which is very essential, demands more time and another work.

70

But they are much more bound to strain their eyes and ears lest these men preach their own dreams instead of what the pope has commissioned.

It is a well established rule of the jurists that the pope, in all the concessions which he makes, handles them in such a manner that he does injury to no other person unless he expressly mentions it and does so out of the fulness of his power, as the custom and manner of speaking of the Roman Curia shows. Therefore it is most certain that when a person bestows indulgences his desire is that they be considered nothing more than indulgences and that they have no value other than that which they have by their own nature. However, the pope does permit them to have as much value as they are worth and is satisfied to grant it. But nowhere does he declare what value they do have. This is the commission of the pope himself. But our preachers of indulgences go further and not only boast from their pulpits that they are popes, though others consider them more correctly "little poplar seeds,"[114] but join to the name of pope also the office of pope as well as that of the church. Then they make us believe that they are, as it were, from heaven, and declare confidently what indulgences are, as a matter of fact, far more than they really are or ever could be, which they say can be proved from their very latest book.[115] Therefore the bishops are obligated to prevent these fancies of theirs, lest they permit the wolves to enter the sheepfold of Christ, as it is expressly commanded in book five, *Concerning Penance and Remission* (*Cum ex eo*),[116] and as Clement commands in the same book, in the chapter entitled *Abusionibus*.[117] So the bishops should permit these indulgence preachers to present nothing to the people except that which is contained in their letters of authorization.

71

Let him who speaks against the truth concerning papal indulgences be anathema and accursed;

For although the bestowing of indulgences is a small matter compared to the grace of God and in contrast to the loud bellowing of those who preach them, nevertheless he who would raise his voice against it acts arrogantly against [papal] authority. Therefore he deserves to be cursed, since ecclesiastical obedience to the pope is so much more admirable when he gives up his own feeling in lesser things and humbles himself. But whatever may be the truth concerning indulgences enough has been discussed up to this point and still awaits the decision of the church. Whatever may be the final decision about them it is evident that indulgences are only relaxations of temporal punishments. The relaxation of punishments,

---

[114] A play on the words *papae* (popes) and *pappi* (little seeds floating through the air like flakes).

[115] The *Summary Instruction* of the archbishop of Mainz.

[116] *Op. cit.*

[117] *Op. cit.*

however, as I have said, is the cheaper gift the church can give, especially if it is given to those whose guilt is remitted. But next to the holy gospel, the remission of guilt is the greatest gift of all, for which my opponents care very little and of which they know nothing.

72

But let him who guards against the lust and license of the indulgence preachers be blessed;

For such is today the condition of the widow of Christ,[118] the holy church, that everything is permitted to everybody and especially to the scholastic theologians, among whom it is possible to find those who even condemn true opinions for no other reason than that they do not flow forth from their own spring. Yet they are permitted to maintain that God commits sin, that God is the cause of evil and of guilt, and many other things do they maintain. But if a poet or orator (as they are called) or a scholar of Greek, Latin, or Hebrew were to say this, he would be considered the most wicked of all heretics. But they do much more harm. If a Christian should supply weapons to the Turks or waylay pilgrims who journey to Rome, or should forge papal documents, it is such a great crime that authority has never been given to anyone to grant remission for an outrage of that kind even if the fullest authority of the highest plenary indulgence should be granted. But the papal chair reserves that for itself. So holy did the church at one time consider these things that when the commandments of God were first observed, the church wanted to punish even the smallest violations with the greatest severity. For there was not yet in the church that Lerna[119] and that infernal abyss of simony,[120] lusts,

---

[118] Rev. 21:2 and 9 describe the church as the bride of Christ. With this metaphor as background in his thinking Luther describes the church when separated from Christ as a widow. /

[119] Reference is to that polycephalous monster that lived in a forest and marsh near Argos, called Lerna. This forest and the stream of the same name which flowed through it was the haunt of the Lernaean Hydra, which Hercules slew with the help of Iolaus. He then drained the marsh.

[120] Cf. p. 206, n. 81.

pageantry, murders, and all the rest of the abominations.

But if these violations are punished so severely, then with what severity do we feel they should be punished who offer weapons, not to the Turks, but to demons, and supply them, not with any kind of weapons but our own, that is the Word of God, while they contaminate that Word with their fancies and, as Isaiah used to say, melt it down into an idol by their spirit [Cf. Isa. 40:19], so that it is no longer an instrument by which the soul is attracted to God but rather seduced into false opinions? Yet this offense is so generally permitted that one would be considered the most wicked of all men who would not consider it as a virtue and a merit above all merits, no matter who should do it. St. Jerome also complained that the Scripture is open to all, not for learning, but for tearing to pieces.[121] Therefore if those who hinder people from going to Rome sin so greatly, what about those who prevent them from going to heaven, not only by their contemptible doctrines but also by their most corrupt practices? And where are they going who do not violate papal documents but the divine Scriptures? They "have taken away the key of knowledge; they do not enter themselves and they hinder those who are entering" [Cf. Luke 11:52]. Are these abominations not considerably greater and worse than those which are read on Maundy Thursday and reserved for that day?[122] But they deserve to be read only in heaven and shall never be remitted.

Therefore they are worthy of blessing who strive to purify the Holy Scriptures and lead them out of the darkness of scholastic opinions and human reasoning into the proper light. In these words we have almost made ourselves Pelagians in doctrine and Donatists in our method. But more about this elsewhere.

---

[121] Migne 22, 544, epist. LIII: "Only the art of interpreting the Scriptures is claimed by all and sundry: the talkative old woman and the feeble old man, the verbose sophist. In short, all presume to do this. They teach before they learn and so tear the Scriptures to pieces."

[122] The bull, *In Coena Domini*, issued by Urban V in 1363, was read in each year on Maundy Thursday, the day of the institution of the Lord's Supper. Among other matters the bull anathematized all those who by robbery prevented the movement of victuals to Rome by land and sea and those who might attempt by robbery to prevent aluminum being transported to Rome from the papal mines at Tolfa. Cf. MA⁹ 1, 514.

73

Just as the pope justly thunders against those who by any means whatsoever contrive harm to the sale of indulgences.

I say again what I have said before (whatever may be the personal intention of the pope) that one must give in humbly to the authority of the keys, be kindly disposed to it and not struggle rashly against it. The keys are the power of God which, whether it is rightly or wrongly used, should be respected as any other work of God—even more so.

74

But much more does he intend to thunder against those who use indulgences as a pretext to contrive harm to holy love and truth.

However much this power of the keys must be honored, we must not be so dastardly as not to reprove its abuse or resist it. In the same way all the saints have supported and honored the secular power, which the Apostle also calls God's power [Rom. 13:1-7], even in the midst of punishments and tortures which that authority placed upon them; nevertheless they deprecated its abuse constantly. And the early Christians did not support this authority because the rulers had used the power rightly by persecuting them, but left them to the consciousness of an evil deed, and through their death bore the witness and confession of their innocence, as St. Peter says, "Let none of you suffer as a thief, etc." [I Pet. 4:15]. So if the church or the pope should deprive anyone of the communion of the faithful without cause, one must support that decision and not condemn authority, but one must not respect it to the point where he approves it as though it were a good deed, but rather he must die in the state of excommunication. For he has been excommunicated only through a misuse of the keys; and if he were to approve this error because of a desire to be absolved, his error would be even worse. He should honor and bear the power of the keys but he should not approve the error.

Those who preach indulgences in such a manner that they

want them to appear as favors of God must be excommunicated, for their practice is contrary to truth and love, in which such grace alone consists. And it would be far better to have no indulgences than to propagate such notions among the people, for we can be Christians without indulgences but we would become nothing but heretics with such ideas. It is certain, however, that the pope either believes or should desire that there should be first of all mutual love and compassion among the people and that the other commands of God should blossom forth in that atmosphere, and so he grants indulgences. But he is deceived, for love, compassion, and faith are almost completely gone and have not merely cooled off among us. If he knew this he would have indulgences eliminated in order that the people might first of all return to mutual love. So I call upon the Lord Jesus as my witness that the people for the most part (some think completely) do not know that works of love are better than indulgences. On the contrary, they believe that they can do nothing better than purchase indulgences. And the people have no faithful teacher to correct this heretical and destructive opinion, but only indulgence-promoters strongly urging them on with their high-sounding fanfare.

75

To consider papal indulgences so great that they could absolve a man even if he had done the impossible and had violated the mother of God is madness.

I am forced to call them foolish who hold such opinions, and we should beg pardon from the holy virgin because we are compelled to say and think such things, yet there is no way open to escape the necessity of saying them. I do not know what diabolical work has caused the people to spread this rumor about papal indulgences everywhere or whether it has really been said by the people or only understood as such by them. Indeed, even if it were maintained by many men and by men of distinction that it has been preached in many places, nevertheless I myself should be surprised at it rather than believe it and consider that they must have heard falsely. Therefore in this thesis I do not wish to censure anyone who harangues the people, but only to warn the people who have begun to hold as opinions what, perhaps, no one has actually said. Whether they themselves have said it or not does not concern me until I am more convinced. Nevertheless, wherever that most wretched opinion may have originated, it must be hated and condemned. Still it would not be surprising that such an opinion is held by the people, since they hear how great and terrible sins are considered to be of the slightest consequence in the interest of magnifying the favors bestowed by indulgences.

True and evangelical preaching is to magnify the sins as much as possible that man may develop fear of God and come to repentance. Finally, what is the benefit of sounding off with so many exaggerations, in the interests of that most worthless remission of punishments, in order to extol indulgences, while hardly mumbling in the interests of that most salutary wisdom of the cross? Yet why would this not be harmful to the simple people who are used to evaluating the Word of God only in proportion to the gestures and pomp which are used in preaching it? While the gospel is expounded with no enthusiasm at all, indulgences are expounded with the greatest pomp. This is done that the people may expect nothing from the gospel and everything from indulgences.

When they dare to shout that murder, robbery, lust of every sort, blasphemies against the virgin Mary and God are insignificant things which may be remitted by these indulgences, is it still surprising that they do not also shout that those lesser things reserved in the bull, *In Coena Domini*,[123] are remitted? "The pope does not remit them." Therefore watch carefully whether or not he remits, or at least remits with great difficulty, those things which are far more serious than these.

76

We say on the contrary that papal indulgences cannot remove the very least of venial sins as far as guilt is concerned.

---

[123] *Ibid.*

I would not have made this understatement if it were not that I wanted to make the opinion expressed in the preceding thesis detestable. It is evident, however, that only God can remit guilt. Therefore those great sins are not remitted by authorities of the church but are only declared by them as remitted and the punishment for them is remitted. I say this according to their interpretation. My own opinion, however, has been made clear enough above. But here I should have said more about venial sin because it is valued so lightly today that it is hardly considered a sin at all. And I am afraid that many will come to great destruction who snore so securely in their sins and do not see that they have committed really big ones. I must confess that as long as I read the scholastic teachers I never really understood what or how great an offense a venial sin was. Whether or not they themselves understand it I do not know. I say this briefly, however: One who does not constantly fear and act as if he were filled with mortal sins, will hardly be saved at all, for the Scripture says, "Enter not into judgment with thy servant, O Lord" [Ps. 143:2]. Not only venial sins, as they generally call them today, but even good works cannot endure the judgment of God, for both of them need the forgiving compassion of God. The Scripture does not say, "Enter not into judgment with your enemy," but "with your son who serves you." Therefore fear should teach us to groan for the compassion of God and to put our confidence in that. When that is lacking, we begin to place our confidence in our own conscience rather than in the mercy of God, until we are no longer conscious of any great sin which we might have committed. Such individuals will meet a horrible judgment.

77

To say that even St. Peter, if he were now pope, could not grant greater graces is blasphemy against St. Peter and the pope.

78

We say on the contrary that even the present pope, or any

pope whatsoever, has greater graces at his disposal, that is, the gospel, spiritual powers, gifts of healing, etc., as it is written in I Cor. 12 [:28].

For all those in the church who possess these gifts come under the authority and obedience of the pope, and he can send them wherever he wants to, even if he himself personally should not possess these gifts. So I should not say that the bull, *In Coena Domini*,[124] with the cases reserved to it, has not yet been repealed. The pope would be more merciful if he would give all these authorized pardons freely to all Christians who need them, and if, by removing canonical burdens, he would restore freedom to Christian people and destroy the tyranny of those holding offices and guilty of simony. But perhaps he has no power to do these things, "for the enemy has prevailed" and "the princess among the cities has become a vassal" [Lam. 1:1]. "The right hand of the Lord does valiantly" [Ps. 118:16], if we should be worthy of obtaining such freedom.

79

To say that the cross emblazoned with the papal coat of arms, and set up by the indulgence preachers, is equal in worth to the cross of Christ is blasphemy.

Who does not see how brazen these men are? What else would they not dare to do, who dare to do such things? Must the souls who are redeemed by the blood of Christ be entrusted to these men? The cross of Christ gives life to the whole world by the destruction of sin. That cross, on the other hand, which is equipped with the papal coat of arms, grants the remission of certain punishments. Are therefore eternal and temporal punishments to be considered of equal value? But why should I pursue all the monstrosities which follow from such preaching, the spreading abroad of which not even heaven itself can endure?

80

The bishops, curates, and theologians who permit such talk

---

[124] *Ibid.*

to be spread among the people will have to answer for this.

One is afraid of the power of the church and therefore afraid that errors and offenses committed today against the Roman chair will be punished by a two-edged sword. But why must one be thus silenced? "Do not fear those who kill the body but cannot kill the soul" [Matt. 10:28]. "Every one who acknowledges me before men, I also will acknowledge before my Father" [Matt. 10:32]. Therefore I am anxious to know who first invented the explanation[125] that the two swords mean, on the one hand, the spiritual—not spiritual however in the sense that the Apostle speaks of it, namely "the sword of the Spirit, which is the word of God" [Eph. 6:17]—and, on the other hand, the temporal. This interpretation is used in order to make the pope appear as a man who is armed with a twofold power, not as a loving father to us but, as it were, a great tyrant, in whom we see nothing but power.

And that is the truest explanation of the decrees of the fathers which so strongly forbid the bearing of arms to clerics.[126] One can see now that an angry God, observing that we choose to interpret this sword as one of iron rather than one of the Spirit and the gospel, treats us most justly when he grants the sword which we desire and takes away that which we do not desire. Because of this there never have been in the world more cruel devastations of war than those among Christians, and the holy Scriptures have hardly been more neglected than among Christians. Lo, you have the sword which you have desired. Indeed, this explanation is one which is worthy of hell. Yet we are stones and do not recognize the wrath of God. Why, I ask, does not that shrewd mind which is so worthy of love use its cleverness also to interpret the two keys in the same manner: one supplying the riches of the world and the other the riches of heaven? Indeed, the meaning of the second key is clear enough, for, as the indulgence demagogues say, this key continually opens heaven and lets the riches of Christ flow down. But one can-

---

[125] Peter Damiani (1007-1072).

[126] *Decretalium D. Gregorii Papae IX* iii. tit. I, cap. 2. *Corpus Iuris Canonici*, II, col. 449.

not see so clearly the meaning of the first key, for he knows how greedy the spendthrift is who controls the wealth of the church. For it is not profitable for the church and the patrimony of Christ that the riches of the world be dissipated with as great a liberality as the riches of heaven. Therefore the first key is the key of knowledge; and if there should be added to it, "The first sword is the sword of knowledge," one would speak apostolically. "For all this his [God's] anger is not turned away and his hand is stretched out still" [Isa. 9:21]. His hand is extended because it is a surprisingly difficult matter to enter into the thought of the Holy Scriptures, in which Scriptures we have been instructed, according to the Apostle, "to destroy arguments and every proud obstacle to the knowledge of God" [II Cor. 10:5].

A shorter way out of this difficulty appeals to us and that is not by getting rid of the heresies and errors but by burning the heretics and those who are in error. In this respect we are led by the advice of Cato rather than by that of Scipio over the question of the destruction of Carthage.[127] By so doing we act contrary to the will of the Spirit, who writes that the Jebusites and Canaanites should remain in the land of promise in order that the children of Israel might learn to fight and develop the habit of fighting [Judg. 3:1-6]. But if St. Jerome does not deceive me, I think that this passage of Scripture speaks figuratively about wars with heretics.[128]

Surely, however, the Apostle is worthy of trust when he says, "There must be heresies" [I Cor. 11:19]. But we answer, Not at all; the heretics must be burned and thus the root must be torn out with the fruit, indeed the tares along with the wheat [Cf. Matt. 13:28-29]. What do we say to this? We can only say to the Lord with tears, "Righteous art thou, O Lord, and right are thy judgments" [Ps. 119:137]. For what else do we deserve? Therefore I mention these things, in order that the Picards,[129] our neighbors, heretics, an

---

[127] Cato advocated the annihilation of Carthage, Scipio Africanus favored its continued existence once its hostile government had been eliminated.

[128] Migne 22, 546, epist. LIII: "As many princes of the people are named in the book of Judges as there are parables."

[129] Cf. p. 125, n. 19.

unhappy people who rejoice in the stench of Rome as the Pharisee rejoiced over the publican [Luke 18:11] instead of showing mercy to him—I say, I mention these things in order that the Picards might not believe that we do not know our vices and imperfections and in order that they might not pride themselves unduly over our wretchedness if we should appear to keep silence about these matters and approve them.

We know our condition and we grieve over it, but we do not flee like the heretics and pass by the one who is half dead [Luke 10:30] as though we were afraid of being stained by the sins of others. Because of this foolish fear these heretics are so afraid that they are not ashamed to boast that they flee[130] in order that they themselves may not be polluted. So great is their love. But, however wretchedly the church operates, we stand by it ever so faithfully and hasten to its aid with tears, prayers, admonitions, and supplications. For love commands us thus "to bear one another's burdens" [Gal. 6:2], not as the love of heretics does, which seeks only to take advantage of another in order that it may be supported and endure nothing harmful from the sins of others. But if Christ and his saints had wanted to do that, who would have been saved?

81

This unbridled preaching of indulgences makes it difficult even for learned men to rescue the reverence which is due the pope from slander or from the shrewd questions of the laity,

Even if my friends have been calling me a heretic, an irreverent person, and a blasphemer for a long time because I do not interpret the church of Christ and the Holy Scriptures in a Catholic sense, nevertheless, relying upon my conscience, I believe that they deceive themselves, but that I cherish the church of Christ and its honor. However, "It is the Lord who judges me although I am not aware of anything against myself" [Cf. I Cor. 4:4]. Therefore I am forced to maintain all these propositions because I saw that some

---

[130] CL 1, 143 reads *surgere* (to arise) instead of *fugere* (to flee).

were infected by false ideas, others made fun of them in the taverns and openly ridiculed the holy priesthood of the church. And all this resulted from the overburdening shamelessness of the indulgence preachers. One should not have stirred up the lay people, by any further occasion, to a hatred of the priesthood, because, even though we have embittered them with our greed and most shameful behavior for many years, they still respect the priesthood (alas, only out of fear of punishment).

82

Such as: "Why does not the pope empty purgatory for the sake of holy love and the dire need of the souls that are there if he redeems an infinite number of souls for the sake of miserable money with which to build a church? The former reasons would be most just; the latter is most trivial."

It is not the pope but the treasurers of the Holy See who provoke this question, for, as I have said previously, nowhere can there be found any decree of the popes concerning this matter. Therefore those who have provoked this question should answer it. I myself would answer all these questions with one word, as far as it can be done to the honor of the pope, namely, that no one informs people of the truth of the matter, and it frequently happens that when they are informed wrongly they yield to wrong ideas.

83

Again, "Why are funeral and anniversary masses for the dead continued and why does he not return or permit the withdrawal of the endowments founded for them, since it is wrong to pray for the redeemed?"

I know that many others like myself have wearied themselves over that question, and although we have considered this question many times, we have troubled ourselves in vain trying to find an answer. We have also said that if souls should fly from purgatory to heaven, then the masses said on their behalf should contribute to the praise

247

of God, which happens when children and infants die. Each one tried to give a different answer to this question, but no one did it satisfactorily. Finally I began to discuss it and to deny that their statements were true in order that I might in this way draw out from those who are more learned than I[131] what answer ought to be given to laymen.

84

Again, "What is this new piety of God and the pope that for a consideration of money they permit a man who is impious and their enemy to buy out of purgatory the pious soul of a friend of God and do not rather, because of the need of that pious and beloved soul, free it for pure love's sake?"

85

Again, "Why are the penitential canons, long since abrogated and dead in actual fact and through disuse, now satisfied by the granting of indulgences as though they were still alive and in force?"

86

Again, "Why does not the pope, whose wealth is today greater than the wealth of the richest Crassus, build this one basilica of St. Peter with his own money rather than with the money of poor believers?"

To this and similar questions I say, it is not for us to judge the will of the pope, but only to endure it, even if it should upon occasion be evil, as I have said previously. Nevertheless, he and the preachers of indulgences must be warned that the people should not be given such an open occasion to say, as the priest Eli once did, that because of his sons "the men treated the offering of the Lord with

---

[131] *CL* 1, 144 reads *doctoribus.* The editors have followed the reading of *WA* 1, 626: *doctioribus.*

contempt" [I Sam. 2:17]. Yet if it was ever the intention of the pope to build the Basilica of St. Peter with all the money scraped together from poor people, rather than the intention of those who abuse his willingness for their own gain, it is not necessary to put down in writing what the people say indiscriminately about that building. God grant that I lie in this matter, for this extortion of money can not go on very long.

87

Again, "What does the pope remit or grant to those who by perfect contrition already have a right to full remission and blessings?"

This question has arisen because many people, even the jurists, say that they do not know what remission of guilt by the keys is, about which I have given my opinion previously.

88

Again, "What greater blessing could come to the church than if the pope were to bestow these remissions and blessings on every believer a hundred times a day, as he now does but once?"

At this point one hears the most surprising things. Some imagine a common treasury which is increased by indulgences. Therefore if a man obtains plenary remission seven times a day, which can happen in Rome, so many more benefits will he receive. These men contradict themselves, for, according to them indulgences are expenditures of the treasury and not receipts. Others, moreover, think that sins are remitted forever by a continuous division, as wood is divided into even more divisible parts. Thus sins are remitted and are always still further remissible, although they become smaller and smaller. I confess that I don't know what I should say about this.

89

"Since the pope seeks the salvation of souls rather than money by his indulgences, why does he suspend the indul-

*gences and pardons previously granted when they have
equal efficacy?"*

This disturbs and displeases me most of all and, I confess, to a great
degree, for this suspending of earlier letters and indulgences is the
only reason that indulgences have become worthless. I cannot deny
that everything which the pope does must be endured, but it grieves
me that I cannot prove that what he does is best. Although, if I
were to discuss the intention of the pope without becoming involved with his mercenary hirelings, I would say, briefly and with
confidence, that one must assume the best about him. The church
needs a reformation which is not the work of one man, namely, the
pope, or of many men, namely the cardinals, both of which the most
recent council[132] has demonstrated, but it is the work of the whole
world, indeed it is the work of God alone. However, only God who
has created time knows the time for this reformation. In the meantime we cannot deny such manifest wrongs. The power of the keys
is abused and enslaved to greed and ambition. The raging abyss
has received added impetus. We cannot stop it. "Our iniquities
testify against us" [Jer. 14:7], and each man's own word is a burden to him [Cf. Gal. 6:5].

90

*To repress these very sharp arguments of the laity by force
alone, and not to resolve them by giving reasons, is to expose
the church and the pope to the ridicule of their enemies
and to make Christians unhappy.*

For while the people are being held in check by fear, a worse evil
develops. How much more appropriate it would be if we were
taught to understand the wrath of God, to pray for the church, and
to endure such trials in the hope of a future reformation, than if
we were to stir up an even worse evil by desiring to compel people
to look upon such manifest evils as virtues. If we did not deserve to
be tormented God would not permit men alone to dominate his

---

[132] The Fifth Lateran Council, whose twelve sessions were held at Rome at
various intervals from 1512-1517.

church. Rather, he would give us shepherds after his own heart [Jer. 3:15], who would give us, instead of indulgences, a measure of wheat in due time [Luke 12:42]. Moreover, even if there still are good shepherds, they cannot administer their office properly; so great is the anger of God's fury.

91

If, therefore, indulgences were preached according to the spirit and intention of the pope, all these doubts would be readily resolved. Indeed, they would not exist.

How so? Namely, if indulgences are only remissions of punishments, which they are, not meritorious and looked upon as inferior to good works, there would not have been any agitation at all to doubt them. Now, because they have been valued too highly, they stir up, to their own disparagement, questions that are unanswerable. For the intention of the pope cannot be anything else than that indulgences are only indulgences.

92

Away then with all those prophets who say to the people of Christ, "Peace, peace," and there is no peace! [Jer. 6:14]

93

Blessed be all those prophets who say to the people of Christ, "Cross, cross," and there is no cross!

94

Christians should be exhorted to be diligent in following Christ, their head, through penalties, death, and hell;

95

And thus be confident of entering into heaven through many tribulations rather than through the false security of peace [Acts 14:22].

Enough has been said previously about cross and punishments. Rarely do you hear a sermon about it today.

TO THE SINCERE AND LEARNED READER

Do not assume that these things were published for you, my learned and sincere reader (but why is this reminder necessary?), as though I were afraid these matters might appear Ciceronian to you. You have other things which you may read according to your own inclination. It was necessary for me to discuss with my equals those things which we have in common, that is, crude and barbarian matters. So it has pleased heaven. And I would not have dared to call upon the name of the pope for these notions of mine if I had not seen how greatly my friends relied upon the pope's power to frighten me and also because it is the official duty of the pope to make himself "a debtor to the wise and to the foolish, to Greeks and to barbarians" [Rom. 1:14]. Farewell.

A.D. 1518

PROCEEDINGS AT AUGSBURG
1518

Translated by Harold J. Grimm

INTRODUCTION

The slow means of communication in the sixteenth century explains the fact that Luther could believe that his *Explanations of the Ninety-five Theses* and accompanying humble letter to Leo X would result in a favorable outcome for his cause while the Roman Curia months before had made decisions which would eventually lead to his excommunication. Already, in June 1518, Leo X had empowered a court consisting of Auditor General Jerome Ghinucci, a jurist, and Master of the Sacred Palace Sylvester Prierias, a theologian, to begin proceedings against Luther. This court, on the basis of Prierias' examination of the *Ninety-five Theses* and his report in his *Dialogue,* cited Luther to Rome. Both the *Dialogue* and the citation reached Cardinal Cajetan, the papal legate attending the Diet of Augsburg, before Luther received them August 7. Luther's reply to Prierias stated that only a general church council could represent the entire Christian church and that only Scripture was an infallible authority, and he asked why it was considered heretical to debate theological questions which had not yet been made official dogmas.

Meanwhile Luther's enemies forged a set of theses on the papal ban which they published under Luther's name, and added a bitter attack on the venality of the Roman Curia. As soon as Luther learned of this, he published his *Sermon on the Ban* (the original preaching of which had suggested the forgery) in order to circulate his true views. The damage had been done, however, for Emperor Maximilian, who had seen a copy of the forgery, wrote a letter to Leo X, urging that immediate action be taken against Luther. This letter and the forgery caused the pope to send Cajetan, on August 23, an official communication commanding him to arrest Luther, to absolve him if he recanted, to use the ban and interdict to deal with him and his supporters if he did not recant. On the same day he wrote Frederick the Wise, requesting him to help arrest this "son of perdition." He also planned with Gabriel della Volta, the general of the Augustinian Eremites, to have the provincial of Saxony arrest Luther over the head of Vicar Staupitz, who still remained friendly to Luther.

Immediately upon receiving the citation to Rome, Luther turned to Frederick the Wise, who was at that time attending the Diet of Augsburg. When Emperor Maximilian sought to have the electors present at the Diet agree to the election of his grandson Charles I of Spain as his successor, Frederick realized that he could use this situation to his advantage. When he and the elector of Trier were not induced to follow the emperor's plans, Leo X became particularly friendly, for he feared that the election of Charles would upset the balance of power in Europe and constitute a threat to his territories in Italy. Frederick accordingly proposed to Cajetan that Luther be given an impartial hearing before a German court. Cajetan countered by offering to give Luther a fair and "fatherly" hearing, to which Frederick then agreed. Cajetan also wrote the pope, requesting a more conciliatory procedure in view of the political circumstances. Leo X agreed to the hearing, but in his breve of September 11 he instructed Cajetan not to enter into a disputation with Luther. To play safe, Frederick took steps to obtain an imperial letter of safe-conduct for Luther.

Luther arrived in Augsburg October 7 but did not appear before Cajetan until he had received the imperial safe-conduct. He approached the cardinal respectfully, and the cardinal received him in a fatherly manner. But in the sessions of the first day it became obvious that Cajetan could not instruct Luther with respect to any possible errors on his part and that Luther would not recant against his conscience. The more Cajetan insisted upon the infallibility of the papacy the more Luther relied upon the authority of Scripture, and the more Cajetan argued that sacramental grace was conferred without faith, the more Luther stressed the importance of his "theology of the cross," although he still believed that his doctrines were in harmony with the church fathers and canon law.

On the second day Staupitz, a notary, and four imperial counselors accompanied Luther when he appeared before Cajetan. Still convinced that his views were not heretical and that a public hearing would clarify all misunderstandings, he asked for such a hearing. The cardinal could not grant this and begged Luther not to be so obstinate. Luther then insisted on preparing a written statement in answer to the objections which Cajetan had raised to his writings, to be submitted to theologians at the universities of Basel, Freiburg, Louvain, or Paris for their opinions.

On the third day Luther, accompanied by two of Frederick the Wise's lawyers, presented this written statement in which he again asserted that the pope could and did err, that a general church council was superior to the pope, that a sacrament without faith on the part of the recipient conveyed no grace, and that the doctrine of justification by faith was supported by many passages of Scripture. Although Cajetan agreed to send the statement to the pope with a refutation, it irritated him so much that he lost his self-control and asked Luther to revoke or never again come into his presence.

On the advice of Staupitz, Luther wrote Cajetan a letter of apology for having spoken disrespectfully during the heat of argument. He promised to refrain from discussing indulgences in the future provided his opponents did likewise, agreed to revoke any doctrines proved to be in error, and announced that he would appeal directly to Leo X. When Staupitz heard a rumor to the effect that Cajetan was planning to arrest Luther and him, he absolved Luther of his monastic vow and left Augsburg without bidding the cardinal farewell. The next day Luther wrote Cajetan another letter, stating that there was no point to his remaining in Augsburg and bidding him farewell. When he received no reply to this letter, his advisors urged him to leave the city. Before leaving, on October 20, he completed his appeal to Leo X "to be better informed."

Upon his return to Wittenberg on October 31, Luther decided to publish the *Proceedings at Augsburg*, better known by the Latin title *Acta Augustana*. Frederick the Wise tried to stop its publication for political reasons, but he was too late. In deference to the elector, the first paragraph of Luther's "Reflections" on the papal breve was blacked out in the copies already printed. This paragraph reflected Luther's belief on the basis of an oral report that Bishop Jerome of Ascoli and Cajetan had falsified the breve. At the time of publication, November 25, 1518, Frederick was carrying on a serious negotiation concerning Luther with Cajetan.

The first printed copy, published by Grünenberg, is included in *WA* 2, 6-26 and translated into English in the following pages. Complete German translations are contained in *St. L.* 15, 448-625 and *MA*³ 1, 58-87. There is a helpful account of the complicated series of events prior to and during the proceedings at Augsburg in Schwiebert, *Luther and His Times*, pp. 338-357.

PROCEEDINGS AT AUGSBURG
1518

Dealings of the Augustinian Friar Martin Luther
with the Lord Apostolic Legate at Augsburg

Forgive me, kind reader, for so often wearying you with my trifles. I do this very reluctantly and again beg you to realize my critical situation. It has pleased heaven that I should become the talk of the people. Nevertheless I confess that without a doubt I should attribute this fact not only to the Lord but also to those people whose ears are so pious that they are offended by the most agreeable and pious truth, even to the extent that they give expression to an insane impiety of heart, mouth, and deed.[1] They have already plagued Johann Reuchlin, for a long time a privy councilor. Now they plague me, an inquiring disputant (as I might call myself), and tolerate neither advice nor debates. We expect that they will in turn eventually plague the dreams and thoughts of all mortals because of their unhappy idleness, for who is safe from the teeth of these beasts which even devour those who desire private advice or public instruction? Good God! Desire for instruction and search for truth is a new and noteworthy crime. And this occurs in the church, the kingdom of truth, in which it is necessary to give account to all who demand it. But of this more at another time.

Now, my reader, what I am doing is this. I see that pamphlets are being published and various rumors are being spread concerning my activities at Augsburg, although I really accomplished nothing more there than the loss of time and money. Probably, however, it was enough of an accomplishment to have heard a new Latin language, namely, that teaching the truth would be the same as confusing the church, indeed, that flattering and denying Christ would

---

[1] Luther here refers to his opponents, particularly the Dominican scholastics. These are the theologians who attacked the humanist Johann Reuchlin for his opposition to the burning of Jewish books.

be equivalent to pacifying and exalting the church of Christ. For I do not see how you could but appear to be a barbarian to the Romans and the Romans barbarians to you if you did not master this kind of eloquence, even if otherwise you surpassed the eloquence of Cicero. Therefore, to avoid extremes, so that the friends of my cause do not excessively elevate it or the enemies excessively lower it, I myself wish to make public the charges against me and my answers to them.

By this testimony I wish to make it known that I excelled in rendering the Roman pontiff exceptional and faithful obedience. In the first place, I, poor and weak though I am, set out on foot on a long journey, thus exposing myself to dangers, and did not take advantage of just and honorable excuses for staying away, which all men would have judged acceptable. In the second place, I appeared before those whom I could have refused to see because they belonged on the side of my enemies. However, it seems to me (were I to follow my nose) that these so-called friends have contrived these evil and troublesome conditions and have arranged all matters so that they would more readily contribute to my destruction and not the search for truth. Nor does it seem as though they expected me to come, but hoped that I would obstinately refuse to come so that they could inflict the punishment without a hearing and secretly triumph over me. The not insignificant proof of this I gathered from the fact that the question of the accusation against me was not raised until after my arrival. And up to the present day my writings are in the house of Caiaphas,[2] where they seek false testimony against me and have not yet found it. So this new custom (as I see it) or new law of the Roman Curia has been initiated, to seize Christ first and then look for a charge against him. Nevertheless, I have been accused of two things, really only one having the appearance of an accusation, that is, my statement concerning the *Extravagante*,[3] as you will presently learn.

---

[2] Luther here compares his hearing before Cajetan with Jesus' trial before Caiaphas.

[3] The papal bull *Unigenitus* (1343) of Clement VI. It was called *Extravagante* because it was not contained in the main compilations of the *Corpus Iuris Canonici*, or body of canon law, but only in an appendix, where it "wandered" outside the canon law. Walther Köhler, *Dokumente zum Ablassstreit* (Tübingen, 1934), pp. 19-21.

For this reason, and also because I did not want to permit the illustrious prince, Elector Frederick, duke of Saxony, etc., to labor in vain in my behalf (for he had kindly provided me with both expense money and letters of introduction and had previously graciously seen to it that my cause would be considered outside the city of Rome), I came to Augsburg. Here I was received by the most reverend lord cardinal legate both graciously and with almost too much respect, for he is a man who is in all respects different from those extremely harsh bloodhounds who track down monks among us. After he had stated that he did not wish to argue with me, but to settle the matter peacefully and in a fatherly fashion, he proposed that I do three things which, he said, had been demanded by the pope: first, that I come to my senses and retract my errors; second, that I promise to abstain from them in the future; and third, that I abstain from doing anything which might disturb the church. Realizing that I could just as well have done these things at Wittenberg without exposing myself to danger and going to so much trouble, and that I did not need to seek this papal admonition in Augsburg, I immediately asked to be instructed in what matters I had been wrong, since I was not conscious of any errors. Then he referred to the *Extravagante* of Clement VI which begins with the word *Unigenitus*, because in Thesis 58[4] I had asserted contrary to it that the merits of Christ did not constitute the treasury of merits of indulgences. Then he demanded that I retract and confidently pursued the matter, sure of victory; for he was certain and secure in assuming that I had not seen the *Extravagante*, probably relying upon the fact that not all editions of the canon law contain it.

In the second place he reproached me for having taught in the explanation of Thesis 7[5] that a person taking the sacrament had to have faith or he would take it to his own damnation, for he wished to have this judged a new and erroneous doctrine. According to him, every person going to the sacrament was uncertain whether or not he would receive grace. By his boldness he made it appear as though I had been defeated, especially since the Italians and others of his

---

[4] This and all other theses referred to in this treatise are contained in the *Ninety-five Theses*.
[5] Cf. p. 98.

companions smiled and, according to their custom, even giggled aloud.

I then answered that I had carefully examined not only this *Extravagante* of Clement, but also the other one of Sixtus IV which emulated and was similar to it[6] (for I had actually read both and had found them characterized by the same verbosity, which destroys one's faith in their trustworthiness, stuffed as they are with ignorance). The *Extravagante* did not impress me as being truthful or authoritative for many reasons, but especially because it distorts the Holy Scriptures and audaciously twists the words (if indeed their customary meaning still should be accepted) into a meaning which they do not have in their context, in fact into a contrary meaning. The Scriptures, which I follow in my Thesis 7, are to be preferred to the bull in every case. Nothing is proven in the bull. Only the teaching of St. Thomas is trotted out and retold.

Then, in contradiction to what I had said, he began to extol the authority of the pope, stating that it is above church councils, Scripture, and the entire church. With the purpose of persuading me to accept this point of view, he called attention to the rejection and dissolution of the Council of Basel[7] and was of the opinion that the Gersonists as well as Gerson[8] should be condemned. Since this was something new to me, I denied that the pope was superior to the council and Scripture and I praised the appeal made by the University of Paris.[9] Then we exchanged words concerning penance and grace in no prearranged order. The second objection caused me much grief, for I should scarcely have feared anything less than that this doctrine would ever be called into question. Thus in no one point did we even remotely come to any agreement, but as one

---

[6] The *Romani pontificis* of 1477. Cf. Walther Köhler, *op. cit.*, pp. 39-40.

[7] In the bull, *Pastor Aeternus*, issued at the Fifth Lateran Council on January 14, 1516, slightly more than two years prior to Luther's appearance before Cajetan, Leo X asserted that the pope alone has authority over all councils "so that he has the complete right and power to call, transfer, and dissolve them. . . ." *Enchiridion Symbolarum et Definitionum*, ed. Henricus Denzinger (Würzburg, 1895), p. 174.

[8] Jean Gerson (1363-1429), chancellor of the University of Paris, was one of the leaders of a group who sought to reform the church through the agency of a church council whose authority would be superior to that of the pope.

[9] The University of Paris had in 1518 objected to the Concordat of Bologna between Leo X and Francis I and had appealed to a church council.

thing led to another, as is usually the case, so a new contradiction arose. When, however, I saw that nothing was accomplished by such a dispute, except that many points were raised and none solved— indeed we already conjured up nothing but papal bulls—and especially since he was representing the pope and did not wish to appear to yield, I asked that I be given time for deliberation.

On the next day, when four counselors of his majesty the emperor were present, I, with a notary and witnesses who had been brought to the meeting, testified formally and personally by reading in the presence of the most reverend legate the following:

"Above all I, brother Martin Luther, Augustinian, declare publicly that I cherish and follow the holy Roman Church in all my words and actions—present, past, and future. If I have said or shall say anything contrary to this, I wish it to be considered as not having been said.

"The most reverend cardinal Cajetan by command of the pope has asserted, proposed, and urged that with respect to the above disputation which I held on indulgences I do these three things: first, to come to my senses and retract my error, second, to pledge not to repeat it in the future, and third, to promise to abstain from all things which might disturb the church. I, who debated and sought the truth could not have done wrong by such inquiry, much less be compelled to retract unheard or unconvicted. Today I declare publicly that I am not conscious of having said anything contrary to Holy Scripture, the church fathers, or papal decretals or their correct meaning. All that I have said today seems to me to have been sensible, true, and catholic.

"Nevertheless, since I am a man who can err, I have submitted and now again submit to the judgment and the lawful conclusion of the holy church and of all who are better informed than I. In addition to this, however, I offer myself personally here or elsewhere to give an account also in public of all that I have said. But if this does not please the most reverend lord legate, I am even prepared to answer in writing the objections which he intends to raise against me, and to hear the judgment and opinion concerning these points of the doctors of the famed imperial universities of Basel, Freiburg, and Louvain, or, if this is not satisfactory, also of Paris, the parent of learning and from the beginning the university which was most Christian and most renowned in theology."

After I had said this, he again referred to yesterday's discussion concerning the first objection, for this one seemed to be very important from his point of view. When I was silent and then, in harmony with my protestation, promised to answer in writing, he again became self-confident. Yet, when he had agreed to the written response, we parted. The tenor and text of my response is the following.

Greetings to the most reverend father in Christ, Lord Thomas,[10] cardinal of the titular church of St. Sixtus, legate of the apostolic chair, from Friar Martin Luther, Augustinian.

That I do not refuse to answer and that I freely desire to give account for each individual statement of mine, most reverend father in Christ, in order to meet the objections which you raised yesterday and day before yesterday, this I wish to prove humbly in this letter. There are two things to which your majesty objected.

In the first place, I seem to deny in my theses[11] that *Extravagante* of Clement VI beginning with the word *Unigenitus* in which the treasury of indulgences appears to be identified with the merits of Christ and the saints.

I answer this objection in the following way: That *Extravagante* was not unknown to me when I was engaged in the preparation of my theses. Since I knew for certain, however, that it was the consensus of the entire church that the merits of Christ could not in spirit be entrusted to men or dispensed through men or by men, as the *Unigenitus* nevertheless seemed to imply, I preferred not to mention the bull and to leave it to better qualified persons to judge what great vexations and anguish I endured to save the honor of the pope.

---

[10] Jacopo de Vio of Gaeta assumed the names Thomas in honor of St. Thomas of Aquinas, and Cajetan, derived from Gaeta, the place of his origin.
[11] Cf. Theses 58 and 60, pp. 212, 228.

For it occurred to me and disturbed me, first of all, that the words of the pope alone would be an ineffective defense against a contentious or heretical person.[12] If one may say that it is scandalous if a secular prince speaks without support of the law, so, likewise, according to Zechariah [Mal. 2:7], not the words of men but the law of God is demanded from the mouth of a priest. Furthermore, it occurred to me that the *Unigenitus* twists the words of Scripture and abuses them by giving them another meaning, for what is said concerning justifying grace is applied to indulgences. For this reason it seemed merely to report, and by its pious impression to exhort people, rather than to prove something by a convincing demonstration.

Furthermore, the fact that it is quite possible that papal decretals occasionally are erroneous and militate against Holy Scriptures and Christian love also irritated me. For if one ought to obey the papal decretals as though they were the voice of St. Peter as it is stated in *distinctio* XIX,[13] nevertheless this is to be understood only of those decretals which are in agreement with Holy Scripture and the decretals of previous popes, as stated in the same authority.

Add to this the fact that Peter, when not walking in the truth of the gospel, is actually reprimanded by Paul in Gal. 2 [:14]. Therefore it does not seem strange if his successor has erred in some point or other, since indeed it is stated in Acts 15 [:1-19] that the teaching of Peter was not accepted until it had been accepted and approved by James the Less, the bishop of Jerusalem, and agreed to by the entire church. From this stems the legal principle that a law becomes established only when it is approved by those living according to its regulations.

Furthermore, how many early decretals are corrected by later ones! Therefore in time this decretal can also be corrected. Panormitanus,[14] too, in his edition of the *Decretals*, shows that in mat-

---

[12] Luther is thinking of the Hussites who, he believed, had gloated over the perversion of evangelical teaching in the Roman church.

[13] *Decretum Magistri Gratiani, Prima Pars,* dist. XIX. *Corpus Iuris Canonici,* I, cols. 58-64; Migne 187, 103-112.

[14] Nicholas of Tudesco, archbishop of Palermo, whose lectures on the *Decretals* Luther prized highly.

ters of faith not only is a general council above the pope, but also any believer, provided he uses better authority or reason than the pope, just as Paul does with Peter in Gal. 2 [:14]. This is confirmed also in the following statement in I Cor. 14 [:30]: "If a revelation is made to another sitting by, let the first be silent." Therefore the voice of Peter must be heard so that then the voice of Paul may be heard when he reprimands Peter. But the voice of Christ must be heard above all others.

I was most troubled, however, by the fact that the *Extravagante* appeared to me to contain certain most obviously false statements. First of all, it maintains that the merits of the saints constitute a treasure, despite the fact that the entire Scripture states that God rewards far beyond all our worth, as in Rom. 8 [:18]: "The sufferings of this present time are not worth comparing with the glory that is to be revealed to us." And St. Augustine says in chapter 19 [par. 3] of the first book of his *Retractations,* "The entire church prays, even to the end of the world, 'Forgive us our debts' [Matt. 6:12]. Therefore it cannot give others that which it itself lacks."[15] Even the wise virgins did not wish to share their oil with the foolish virgins [Matt. 25:9]. And St. Augustine says in the ninth book of his *Confessions,* "Woe unto the life of a man, however laudable, if it is judged without mercy."[16] And the prophet said, "Enter not into judgment with thy servant, for no man living is righteous before thee" [Ps. 143:2]. Likewise, the saints are saved, not by their merits, but alone by the mercy of God, as I have stated more fully in my *Explanations.*[17]

Indeed, I did not possess the extraordinary indiscretion so as to discard so many important clear proofs of Scripture on account of a single ambiguous and obscure decretal of a pope who is a mere human being. Much rather I considered it proper that the words of Scripture, in which the saints are described as being deficient in merits, are to be preferred to human words, in which the saints are said to have more merits than they need. For the pope is not above,

---

[15] Migne 32, 615.

[16] *Confessions,* book 9, chap. XIII, par. 34. Migne 32, 778.

[17] *Explanations of the Disputation Concerning the Value of Indulgences.* For Luther's explanation of Thesis 58, cf. p. 212.

but under the word of God, according to Gal. 1 [:8]: "Even if we, or an angel from heaven, should preach to you a gospel contrary to that which you received, let him be accursed." Furthermore, it was not unimportant to me that the bull stated that this treasure was committed to Peter, concerning which there is nothing either in the gospel or any part of the Bible.

Perturbed by these annoyances, I decided, as I have said, to remain silent and listen to others, for I believed that my theses were correctly stated, as I still believe to the present day. Now since I am urged to attempt that which I have a right to expect from others, especially from the pope, who alone can explain his own decretals, I will nevertheless, with all my ability and the grace of God and for the sake of the most holy truth, try to bring my theses into agreement with the *Extravagante* and preserve both in truth.

1. I shall assume that indulgences signify absolutely nothing (speaking metaphysically), for it is certain that they are merely remissions of satisfaction, that is, of good works such as giving alms, fasting, praying, and the like. Therefore it is also certain that indulgences constitute a negative good, since they only permit the remission of deserved punishments or the performing of burdensome works. From this it necessarily follows that no treasure is received in the proper sense of the term, for nothing positive is conferred. On the contrary, a person is merely permitted to do nothing.

2. It is certain that the pope does not have this treasure as it were in a purse or a moneychest, but that it consists of a statement connected with the office of the keys, for in dispensing the treasure he does not open a chest but makes known his will and thus grants the indulgence.

3. It therefore follows that the treasure of indulgences is the merits of Christ, not formally or properly but only in effect and figuratively. For the pope does not actually dispense the merits of Christ, but he grants indulgence through the merit of Christ, that is, through the office of the keys which was given to the church by Christ's merit, for it is by virtue of the office of the keys that satisfaction is remitted. Furthermore, it is clear that I correctly stated in Thesis 60 that the office of the keys of the church, given by the

CAREER OF THE REFORMER

merits of Christ, constitutes the treasure.[18] And in this sense it is true that the merits of Christ are the treasure of indulgences. To be sure, the treasure and the merits of Christ are to be understood figuratively. In this sense the agreement of the *Extravagante* with my thesis is apparent.

4. That this is the meaning of the pope in this *Extravagante* is proven by the pope's own words when he says that the treasure was committed to Peter and his successors by Christ. It is firmly established, however, that nothing was committed to Peter except the keys of the kingdom of heaven, which are the merits of Christ (that is, the keys were given by the merits of Christ); but they were given only figuratively and in effect, as I have stated. The other treasure which Christ gave Peter is the treasure of the Word, of which he said, "Feed, nourish, tend my sheep" [Cf. John 21:15-17].

5. It is certain, however, that this understanding of the treasure of indulgences is unknown and unrecognized among Christians, as my Thesis 56 states.[19] For these words, "treasure," "merit of Christ," and so on, are seldom used except figuratively and obscurely. Therefore Christians virtually believe that they themselves obtain an actual and positive good as if it were a gift or grace, when in fact they arrive at nothing but the office of the keys, by means of which the satisfaction for their sins is remitted. Thus they receive a negative good and a treasure that is not a treasure in the usual sense. That treasure is, to be sure, inexhaustible and infinite, because the office of the keys is inexhaustible. The office of the keys rests directly upon the merits of Christ, indulgences only indirectly. Therefore it can also be said that the merits of Christ are indirectly the treasure of indulgences.

6. Similarly, I might also admit that the merits of the saints constitute this treasure, however, in a figurative sense, since the merits of the saints are through their faith in Christ included and made one with his merits so that their merits are now the same and accomplish the same as the merits of Christ, because the life of the

---

[18] Cf. p. 228.
[19] Cf. p. 211.

righteous man is not his own but that of Christ living in him. According to Gal. 2 [:20], "It is no longer I who live, but Christ who lives in me," for the merits of the saints as saints would be of no value and damnable, as I have said above and as St. Augustine has said: "Where I am not, there I am the most blessed, because Christ and the church are two in one flesh."

7. It is nevertheless most certainly true that the merits of Christ are not synonymous with the treasure of indulgences either in an actual or a direct sense, as though they would confer something as uneducated people might understand it. If they convey an actual gift, they do so not as a treasure of indulgences but as a treasure of life-giving grace. Then they are given formally, actually, directly, without the office of the keys, without indulgences, alone by the Holy Spirit, but never by the pope. Because man is made one spirit with Christ through love, therefore he shares in all his benefits. And this is what my Thesis 58 stated: "Nor are they [the merits of indulgences] the merits of Christ and the saints, for, even without the pope, they always work grace for the inner man. . . ."[20]

Briefly, it is thus clear that the merits of Christ must of necessity be understood in a twofold sense if the *Extravagante* is to be retained as authoritative. On the one hand, according to the literal and formal sense, the merits of Christ are a treasure of the life-giving Spirit and, since they are his very own, the Holy Spirit apportions them to whomever he wills. On the other hand, according to the figurative sense, they only signify, according to the letter and the incidental consequences, a treasure created by the merits of Christ. And as the *Extravagante* quotes the Scriptures in a figurative sense, so also it understands the treasure, the merits of Christ, and all other concepts, in a figurative sense. For this reason it is ambiguous and obscure and affords a most proper occasion for debate. I, on the other hand, discussed this matter in a literal sense in my theses.

Whoever has a better understanding of this, let him give it to me, and I will retract. For it is not my duty to interpret the canons of the popes but to defend my theses lest they seem to be

---

[20] Cf. p. 212.

in opposition to the canons. In humility I expect that if the pope is of a different mind he will let it be known, and I am willing to comply.

All these things, nevertheless, I wish to have said out of reverence for the Apostolic See and the most reverend cardinal. If I am permitted to state my opinion publicly and freely, I contend and prove that this *Extravagante* is actually, directly, and obviously in opposition to the most reverend cardinal, for the wording of it expressly states that Christ acquired this treasure for the church. This word "acquired" clearly convinces one, and conclusively proves that the merits of Christ by which he acquired a treasure are something else than the treasure which he acquired, for the cause is one thing and the effect another, as the philosophers also teach. Therefore my thesis remains irrefutable, namely, that the merits of Christ are not the treasure of indulgences but have acquired it. Nevertheless, I submit this opinion to the judgment of the church, as I have stated above.

The other objection is that in Thesis 7[21] I stated that no one can be justified except by faith. Thus it is clearly necessary that a man must believe with firm faith that he is justified and in no way doubt that he will obtain grace. For if he doubts and is uncertain, he is not justified but rejects grace. My opponents wish to consider this theology new and erroneous.

This I answer by saying:

1. It is an infallible truth that no person is righteous unless he believes in God, as stated in Rom. 1 [:17]: "He who through faith is righteous shall live." Likewise, "He who does not believe is condemned already" [John 3:18] and dead. Therefore the justification and life of the righteous person are dependent upon his faith. For this reason all the works of the believer are alive and all the works of the unbeliever are dead, evil, and damnable, according to this passage: "A bad tree cannot bear good fruit. Every tree that does not bear good fruit is cut down and thrown into the fire" [Matt. 7:18-19].

2. Faith, however, is nothing else than believing what God

---

[21] Cf. p. 98.

promises and reveals, as in Rom. 4 [:3], "Abraham believed God, and he reckoned it to him as righteousness" [Cf. Gen. 15:6]. Therefore the Word and faith are both necessary, and without the Word there can be no faith, as in Isa. 55 [:11]: "So shall my word be that goes forth from my mouth; it shall not return to me empty."

3. I must now prove that a person going to the sacrament must believe that he will receive grace, and not doubt it, but have absolute confidence, otherwise he will do so to his condemnation.

I prove this first through the word of the Apostle in Heb. 11 [:6]: "For whoever would draw near to God must believe that he exists and that he rewards those who seek him." According to this it is clear that we dare not doubt but must firmly believe that God rewards those who seek him. If we must believe that God is one who rewards, then we must above all believe that he justifies man and gives his grace to those still living. Without grace he gives no reward.

Second, in the face of the peril of eternal damnation and the sin of unbelief, we must believe these words of Christ: "Whatever you loose on earth shall be loosed in heaven" [Matt. 16:19]. Therefore if you come to the sacrament of penance and do not firmly believe that you will be absolved in heaven, you come to your judgment and damnation because you do not believe that Christ speaks the truth when he says, "Whatever you loose," etc. [Matt. 16:19]. And with your doubt you make of Christ a liar, which is a horrible sin. If, however, you say, "What if I am unworthy and unfit for the sacrament?" I answer as I did above. Through no attitude on your part will you become worthy, through no works will you be prepared for the sacrament, but through faith alone, for only faith in the word of Christ justifies, makes a person alive, worthy, and well prepared. Without faith all other things are acts of presumption and desperation. The just person lives not by his attitude but by faith. For this reason you should not harbor any doubt on account of your unworthiness. You go to the sacrament because you are unworthy and so that you may be made worthy and be justified by him who seeks to save sinners and not the righteous [Cf. Luke 5:32]. When, however, you believe Christ's word, you honor it and thereby are righteous.

Third, he has commended this faith to us in many ways in the gospel. First, when he said to the woman of Canaan: "O woman, great is your faith! Be it done for you as you have believed" [Matt. 15:28].[22] This shows that not faith in general is meant here, but the special faith which was concerned with the daughter who was to be healed in answer to her mother's prayer. For she boldly believed that this would be done, that Christ could and would do it, and so her prayer was fulfilled. She never would have obtained this, however, if she had not believed. Therefore she was made worthy of this answer to her prayer, not by her attitude, but by faith alone.

Second, when Christ asked those blind men, "Do you believe that I am able to do this?" and they answered "Yes, Lord," he said, "According to your faith be it done to you" [Matt. 9:28-29]. See, they were certain that it would come to pass as they petitioned. Therefore it came to pass without any preparation on their part. If, however, they had doubted the outcome, they would not have prayed well or received what they had prayed for.

Third, the centurion said, "Only say the word, and my servant will be healed" [Matt. 8:8]. Certainly he believed in and obtained what was done for him in a specific, immediate concern, not according to a general faith.

Fourth, according to John 4 [:50]: The official "believed the word that Jesus spoke to him," that is, "Go; your son will live." By means of this faith he saved his son's life. So indeed every person approaching God should believe that he will receive what he requests, or he will not receive it.

Fifth, Christ says in Mark [11:24], "Verily I tell you, whatever you ask in prayer, believe that you receive it, and you will." Notice that he says "whatever," allowing for no exception. It is clear, however, that we ask for something in the sacrament, for no one goes to the sacrament unless he asks for grace. Therefore we must listen to Christ when he says, "Believe that you receive it, and you will." Otherwise all things in the church would waver and nothing would stand for certain, which is absurd.

Sixth, this passage: "If you have faith as a grain of mustard

---

[22] "As you have believed" has been substituted by Luther for the reading of the Greek and Vulgate text "as you desire."

seed, you will say to this mountain, 'Move hence to yonder place,' and it will move; and nothing will be impossible to you" [Matt. 17:20]. And if you look through the entire gospel you will find many other examples, all of which refer not to a general but to a particular faith and which pertain to achieving some immediate result. For this reason a firm faith is necessary if a person wishes to receive pardon, since the sacraments of the New Testament, according to the Teacher [Peter Lombard],[23] were instituted for motivating and activating our faith.

Seventh, for this reason the Lord often rebuked the disciples [Matt. 8:26], and especially Peter, for their lack of faith, not their lack of general faith, but of special faith concerning a specific, immediate need.

Eighth, James 1 [:5-8] says: "If any of you lacks wisdom, let him ask God. . . . let him ask in faith, with no doubting, for he who doubts is like the wave of the sea that is driven and tossed by the wind . . . for that person must not suppose that . . . [he] will receive anything from the Lord." That is certainly a most unequivocal statement, which also leads me to the conclusion that no one can receive grace or wisdom who doubts that he will receive it. Nor do I see what one can say against this conclusion.

Ninth, the holy Virgin would never have conceived the Son of God if she had not believed the annunciation of the angel. Thus she said, "Let it be to me according to your word" [Luke 1:38], just as Elizabeth proclaimed, "Blessed is she who believed that there would be a fulfilment of what was spoken to her from the Lord" [Luke 1:45]. Hence St. Bernard and the universal church marveled at her faith. Likewise Anna, the mother of Samuel, after she believed the word of Eli, went her way, "and her countenance was no longer sad" [I Sam. 1:18]. On the other hand, the children of Israel, because they did not believe the word of promise concerning the land of Canaan, perished in the wilderness.

Briefly, whatever remarkable thing we read about in the Old and New Testaments, we read that it was accomplished by faith, not by works or general faith, but by faith directed to the

---

[23] *Sentences.* Migne 192, 839-840.

accomplishment of an immediate end. Hence nothing else is so highly praised in Scripture as faith, especially that of Abraham, as in Rom. 4 [:1-5], which was a faith in the fact that a son Isaac was to be born to him. Nevertheless "it was reckoned to him as righteousness." Thus it is also with us in the sacrament: If we believe, we shall receive grace; if we do not believe, we shall go to our judgment.

Tenth, St. Augustine says in his treatment of the Gospel of St. John, "When the Word is coupled with the element, it becomes a sacrament, not because it becomes a sacrament, but because it is believed."[24] See, baptism cleanses one, not because it takes place, but because one believes that it cleanses. For this reason the Lord said in absolving Mary, "Your faith has saved you; go in peace" [Luke 7:50]. Hence this common saying: "Not the sacrament of faith, but faith in the sacrament, justifies." Without this faith it is impossible to have peace of conscience, as it is written in Rom. 5 [:1], "Therefore, since we are justified by faith, we have peace with God."

Eleventh, St. Bernard says in his first sermon on the annunciation, "You must above all believe that you cannot have forgiveness of sins except through the mercy of God." But add to this that you must believe and add this too, that your sins are forgiven by God. This is the testimony which the Holy Spirit brings forth in your heart, saying, "your sins are forgiven." For thus the Apostle concludes "that a man is justified by faith" [Rom. 3:28] out of grace. This is what St. Paul says.

These and many other explicit passages lead me inexorably to the opinion stated above.

For this reason, most reverend father in Christ, since you are blessed by divine favor with unusual gifts, especially with keen judgment, I humbly beg your most reverend highness to deal leniently with me, to have compassion with my conscience, to show me how I may understand this doctrine differently, and not to compel me to revoke those things which I must believe according to the testimony of my conscience. As long as these Scripture passages

---

[24] In Joannis evangelium, tract. 80, cap. 3. Migne 35, 1840.

stand, I cannot do otherwise, for I know that one must obey God rather than men [Acts 5:29].

May it please your highness to intercede with our most holy lord, Leo X, in my behalf so that he will not proceed against me with such stern rigor that he cast my soul into darkness, for I seek nothing but the light of truth and I am prepared to give up, change, or revoke everything if I am informed that these passages are to be understood in another sense. For I am neither arrogant nor so eager for vainglory that for this reason I would be ashamed to revoke ill-founded doctrines. Indeed, it will please me most of all if the truth is victorious. However, I do not want to be compelled to affirm something contrary to my conscience, for I believe without the slightest doubt that this is the meaning of Scripture. May the Lord Jesus direct and preserve you in eternity, most reverend father. Amen.

When I presented Cajetan with the above statement the next day, he at first considered it worthless and said that it consisted of mere words. But then he said that he would send it to Rome. Meanwhile he insisted that I retract, threatening me with the punishments which had been recommended to him, and said that if I did not retract I should leave him and stay out of his sight. When I heard this and realized that he was firm in his position and would not consider the Scripture passages, and since I had also determined not to retract, I left, with no hope of returning. Although he said, and now even glories in it, that he would act toward me as a father and not as a judge, I could not detect any such paternal attitude, except one which was sterner than any court of justice, since all he did was demand that I retract against my conscience. At least he did not show a desire or the ability to demonstrate where I was wrong or to convince me of error, for when he saw that I rejected the comments of the opinionated scholastics, he promised to take action against me on the basis of Holy Scripture and the canon law. What he meant by this, I do not know, for he never produced a syllable from the Holy Scriptures against me, and to the present day he could not do so, even if he were to put forth a special effort, since there is universal agreement that nothing is mentioned in the Holy Scriptures about indulgences. On the contrary, the Scriptures commend faith and are as devoid of references to indulgences as they are full of teaching concerning faith, so that it is impossible for the legate thereby to demolish either one of these two articles.

As a matter of fact, when I quoted the Scriptures to prove my points, that man began in a paternal way to conjure up glosses out of his own imagination. And while he so readily used the *Extravagante* against me, he cleverly pretended not to know that canon on the basis of which the church prohibits anyone from interpreting the Scriptures solely on his own authority. According to Hilary,[25] one should not read a meaning into the Holy Scriptures, but extract it from them. Nevertheless I was not overly annoyed with his distortion of the Bible, knowing that he had become accustomed to that kind of interpretation through his contacts with the long-established practice of the Roman Curia and the work of scholastic quibblers. It has long been believed that whatever the Roman church says, damns, or wants, all people must eventually say, damn, or want, and that no other reason need be given than that the Apostolic See and the Roman church hold that opinion. Therefore, since the sacred Scriptures are abandoned and the traditions and words of men are accepted, it happens that the church of Christ is not nourished by its own measure of wheat, that is, by the word of Christ, but is usually misled by the indiscretion and rash will of an unlearned flatterer. We have come to this in our great misfortune that these people begin to force us to renounce the Christian faith and deny Holy Scripture.

Furthermore, if that is what is involved in the revocation that is demanded of me, I foresee nothing else than that one revocation will be followed by another and so *ad infinitum*. For if I should answer one of his statements with a skill equal to his, he would quickly conjure up against me another idol out of his imagination (for Thomistic theology is remarkably fertile in producing subtle

---

[25] Hilary (300?-366) defended the Athanasian against the Arian Christians and was therefore exiled by Emperor Constantine. At Phrygia he become a mediator between the eastern and western theologians. Luther frequently refers to him.

distinctions, a veritable Proteus),[26] which I should be compelled
to submit to with another revocation. For since he wanders about,
not on solid rock, but on the sand of his own ideas, I should experience nothing but this business of perpetual revocation.

Therefore, having received the command not to return, I nevertheless remained there that day. Then Cajetan summoned my
reverend and most excellent father, Vicar Johann von Staupitz, and,
it is said, urged him to induce me to make a free revocation. I remained another day and received no orders. I remained a third day,
that is, Sunday [October 17], and sent a letter[27] but received no
answer. I remained a fourth day, and nothing happened. There was
the same silence on the fifth day. Finally, on the advice of my
friends and especially in view of the fact that Cajetan had previously announced that he had an order to throw me and the vicar
into jail, and since I had prepared my appeal for public posting,
I left, feeling that I had shown sufficient obedience despite my
dangerous position.

Now, my reader, you must listen to me again. I presented my
last response with great reverence and at the same time submitted
it to the judgment of the pope. You must not, however, believe
that I did this because I entertained any doubt concerning the
cause itself or that I should ever change my mind—for divine
truth is master also over the pope and I do not await the judgment of a man when I have learned the judgment of God—but
only because I needed to give reverence to him who acted as
the pope's representative, and because one should assert and
defend that which is undoubtedly true with humility and fear.

It makes no difference what you think of my first explanation,
for there is no danger involved whether it stands or falls. Indul-

---

[26] Proteus was a character from Greek mythology, a prophetic man of the sea
who knew the future as well as the past and present. He could be compelled
to divulge desired information only when surprised and bound. He would try
to avert capture by assuming various shapes. Luther thinks of him when he
describes the shifty scholastic debaters among his opponents who confused
issues by the introduction of extraneous materials. Cf. Homer *Odyssey* iv. 351;
Virgil *Georgics* iv. 386.

[27] Cf. Luther's letter to Cajetan, dated October 17, 1518. *WA*, Br 1, 220-221.

gences gain nothing in importance if that explanation is refuted and proven false, and they lose nothing if it is victorious and proven true, for it has little to do with the main issue at stake, unless an attempt is made to throw doubt upon my *Ninety-five Theses* as a whole by craftily bringing it up. If I had wished to act more haughtily in the presence of the legate, I could have refused to utter a single word, for I had already presented and explained the whole matter to the pope so that there was nothing more for me to do but to await his verdict.

In the latter answer, however, lies the whole summary of salvation. You are not a bad Christian because you do or do not know about the *Extravagante*. You are a heretic, however, if you deny faith in Christ's word. How much I repress and do not mention here, you, good reader, will surely not notice without a sigh.

One thing, however, I do not wish to conceal from you, namely, that I sought nothing in this hearing except the true meaning of Scripture, which those so-called holy decretals, if they do not actually corrupt, certainly obscure for us in many places with their distorted and malevolent words and hide as it were the brightest sun with a cloud. This I will some day treat in greater detail, especially if some Roman flatterer should oppose me. God willing, I will then distinguish myself as a jurist and theologian, even though I shall hardly please anyone, especially not the flatterers of the Roman Curia, for I have recently longed to play war with them, as Joshua waged war against the people of Ai [Josh. 8:3-29]. Meanwhile I am giving you a foretaste of what is to come, namely, that my conclusion is really in opposition to the *Extravagante*, which is in fact false and erroneous and should be revoked. For this reason I solemnly revoke it in this writing and pronounce it damned.

I also publicly declare that this writing was composed by me and now pleases me so much that I would compose it now if I had not already done so. In the second place, I reject, damn, and detest that *Extravagante* as false and erroneous, deserving of rejection. And I state that it would have been better if it had been put into other words, not because it misrepresents the meaning of its authors, but because it presents an erroneous theological meaning, for its words are used contrary to the most obvious meaning of Scripture.

See, that is my revocation. I hope that I have satisfied even my enemies. Do you, my reader, think that I am insane or drunk? I am not insane and speak with words of sobriety. To prove this, I will make clear even to the most unlearned that the popes are accustomed to doing violence to the Holy Scriptures in their decretals. The most reverend legate was most displeased with the fact that I had not even spared the holiness of the pope, as he wrote to the most illustrious Elector Frederick. And he added that I had said "things not deserving of repetition," because I accused the pope of twisting and abusing the Scriptures.[28] Therefore I must make it clear that he cannot deny that the pope forced the meaning of Scripture.

In the first place, the decretal *De Constitutionibus*,[29] beginning with the words, *Translato sacerdotio*, states that if the priesthood were changed, the law must also be changed. These are words of the Apostle to the Hebrews [7:12] to the effect that the temporal priesthood had ended and the law of Moses had been abrogated by the eternal priesthood of Christ which succeeded it. This is the true and genuine meaning of these words. But the meaning of this decretal is this: The priesthood of Christ is transferred from Moses to Christ and from Christ to Peter. For the jurists interpreted these words in this manner and the pope either permitted or approved it. Who, however, does not see that this is a distortion and abuse of the meaning of the words? It is indeed such a distortion that, if it is not modified with the greatest industry, it will be both unorthodox and impious. For it is most impious to say that the priesthood of Christ is abrogated and finished, so that Peter may be the priest and lawgiver while Christ is deposed. For this is what the word *translatio*, used by the Apostle, really means. I do not want Peter or Paul to be the priest, since each one is a sinner who has no

---

[28] Cajetan's letter to Elector Frederick of Saxony, dated Oct. 25, 1518. *WA*, Br 1,233; Enders, *ibid.*, I, 269.

[29] *Decretalium D. Gregorii Papae IX* Lib. i. tit. II, cap. 3. *Corpus Iuris Canonici*, II, col. 8.

sacrifice to offer for me or even for himself. I shall say nothing about the most abominable arrogance of which such an interpretation smells which maintains that the priesthood of Christ had without doubt been conferred upon Peter alone by Christ, as though the other apostles remained laymen or were ordained priests and apostles by Peter. Therefore, if I should now state my thesis as follows: "The priesthood of Christ was conferred neither upon Peter nor the pope," and the most reverend legate would then confront me with this decretal with his majestic bearing and thunderous eloquence and would demand that I revoke; and if I should answer that the pope twisted the Scriptures and abused its words, while my thesis was true in a theological sense and the decretal was perchance true in some other, distorted sense, do you think that I should be terrified by the threats of human words used to frighten me, as though I had said something which did not "deserve repetition" and had not spared the holiness of the pope? I will honor the holiness of the pope, but I will worship the holiness of Christ and of truth.

Likewise, if I should treat the passage in Matt. 16 [:18-19], "You are Peter, and I will give you the keys to the kingdom of heaven," and "Whatever you loose . . . " either in the classroom or in the pulpit, and should propound this thesis, "By these words one cannot prove that the Roman church has a higher rank than other churches in the entire world," and the most reverend legate would confront me—no doubt with commotion and indignation over what I had said—with distinctio XXI of Gratian's Decretals where Pope Pelagius[30] emphatically states that not by synodical decrees but by the word of the gospel—to be sure by the word but not the sense—was the Roman church given pre-eminence above all other churches, and if he would add to this the passage of the Apostle Matthew, do you believe that I should abandon the sense of the gospel and embrace the interpretation of Pelagius who boasts that he follows the word but not the sense of the gospel? Not that I condemn or deny the new rule of the Romans of our day, but I do not wish the power of Scripture to be reduced to mere words, and I reject the folly of certain very simple-minded men who would

---

[30] Pelagius II (578-590).

fix the church of Christ in time and place, whereas Christ said,
"The kingdom of God is not coming with signs to be observed"
[Luke 17:20]. And who dare deny that one can be a Christian
who does not submit to the pope and his decretals. Thus for more
than eight hundred years they have thrown out of the church of
Christ Christians in all the Orient and Africa who never were
under the pope or even understood the gospel in that sense. For
until the time of St. Gregory the Roman pope was not addressed as
the universal bishop. Even Gregory himself, although bishop of
Rome, attacks most vehemently the name of universal bishop and
pope of the entire church in more than six letters.[81] So he does not
hesitate to call this designation profane—he who alone in our time
is called most holy. Just as Peter did not create—for this is what or-
daining bishops is called today—the other apostles, so the successor
of Peter created no successor to the other apostles. Finally, other
bishops did not call the Roman pope anything but brother and
fellow bishop and colleague, as Cyprian addressed Cornelius and
Augustine addressed Boniface and others.[82]

Hence the church fathers did not understand Matthew's statement, "I give you . . ." [Matt. 16:19], in the sense of the above holy
canon, as though Christ addressed Peter in preference to the others,
but they say that "one" stands for "all" in order to express the
equality of all, while that which Peter answers, one and all answer.
Therefore Matthew also expresses the same meaning in the plural
in another place: "Whatever you bind . . . " [Matt. 18:18], so
what is said to one is said to all. Finally the Holy Spirit did not
descend upon Peter first on Pentecost [Acts 2], and we do not read
that he breathed upon Peter first [John 20:22-23]. If he had ac-

---

[81] Impressed by the humility and piety of Gregory I, the Great (590-604),
Luther erroneously inferred that he had refused to use the title of pope as head
of the entire church and that previous bishops had not used the title. As a
matter of fact Leo I (440-461) had demanded the title *episcopus universalis* at
the Council of Chalcedon in 451, but it had been denied him. Cf. MA³1, 451-
452.

[82] Cyprian (d. 258) was the bishop of Carthage who carried on a correspondence in connection with the Decian persecution with Cornelius, bishop of
Rome, from 251 to 252. St. Augustine (354-430) and St. Boniface I (418-422)
respectively occupied the same position.

tually done so, Peter would not for this reason have become a ruler in preference to the other apostles.

Therefore that canon may be true, I admit, but it is true in an improper sense. My thesis on the other hand is true in an evangelical and proper sense. If papal rule can be proven, it should be proven by that passage of the Apostle in Rom. 13 [:1]: "For there is no authority except from God, and those that exist have been instituted by God." By virtue of this, strictly speaking, I say, we are subjected to the Roman See as long as it pleases God, who alone, and not the Roman pontiff, changes and establishes authority.

Many such things, my reader, you will find in the sacred decretals, and also others, which, if you use the nose of the bride overlooking Damascus [Song of Sol. 7:4], that is, a nose of flesh and blood, you will often be offended by the smell.

I now say the following about the *Extravagante*: The merits of Christ are not a treasure of indulgences for they work grace without the pope. This statement is evangelical, for it is written in many places in the Bible that we are justified by the blood and obedience of Christ. Paul, for example, says in Rom. 5 [:19], "By one man's obedience [I believe this obedience to be the merits of Christ] many will be made righteous." No man is saved by indulgences, however. To maintain this concerning the merits of Christ is contrary to the clear meaning of the Scriptures. Therefore I do not care whether this statement is contrary to an *Extravagante* or an *Intravagante*. The truth of Scripture comes first. After that is accepted, one may determine whether the words of men can be accepted as true. I certainly would never dare to assert that people "become friends of God" through indulgences, as the *Extravagante* expressly states when, in referring to a passage in Proverbs concerning participation in eternal wisdom [Wisd. of Sol. 7:14], it applies this to participation in indulgences.

Those Scripture passages were authoritative long before the time of that *Extravagante*, from which they certainly did not obtain their authority. Moreover, one cannot say that they refer to indulgences, since everyone in the church knows that there is nothing in Scripture concerning indulgences. It necessarily follows that if certain passages are interpreted as referring to them, as is the case here, violence is done them and they are quoted improperly and erroneously. Nevertheless, I shall out of reverence admit that the *Extravagante* is true and attempt to maintain both meanings. Then I am told: "You must follow that meaning (the inferior one) and deny the other (the true one)." Therefore, if I am compelled to call my statement false, I shall do so, but at the same time I shall call the *Extravagante* false twice over. For if they accuse me of maintaining an opinion concerning indugences which is contrary to common belief, I clearly acknowledge this to be the case.

Furthermore, I admit that I have done this intentionally for the purpose of bringing up for discussion this common belief according to which the merits of Christ are called the treasure of merits. I knew that this was the common belief, but it sounded false. For this reason I formulated the thesis that the keys, given the church by virtue of the merits of Christ, constituted this treasure. Thus I did not entirely separate the merits of Christ from indulgences but interpreted the merits according to a sense other than that held by common opinion. If I had not wished in humility and reverence to contradict this common opinion, I should have refrained from saying that the keys were given by virtue of the merit of Christ, thereby completely excluding the merits of Christ from my discussion. Now, however, I have embodied them for the purpose of toning down my contradiction. I should not, however, have committed a mortal sin if I had boldly opposed the *Extravagante* and had quoted St. Jerome. Speaking of those who consider whatever they say to be the law of God, he said, "They disdain to know what the prophets and the apostles thought [note the word 'thought'], but accommodate unsuitable testimony to their own interpretation as though it were a grand and not a most vicious kind of teaching to distort passages and to bend the Scripture passage which opposes them to suit their wishes." This is certainly what the *Extravagante* does, for it applies words concerning the merits of Christ, by which sins are forgiven, to indulgences. I ask you to note the adaptation by means of which this is achieved.

The merits of Christ take away sins and increase the merits of the believer. Indulgences take away the merits and leave the sins. Can the same Scripture text be properly understood to apply to both? I believe that even Orestes[33] would deny this. Nevertheless I have out of reverence intentionally admitted it and, although I went too far, affirmed it. Finally, since the *Extravagante* is obscure and indeed wanders about[34] in its words, now saying that the merits of Christ are the treasure of indulgences and then that they have acquired them, I have made a statement which can at the same time constitute my opinion as opposed to the common one. And now in the face of such dubious twisting of the words of God and falsifying of meaning (as Jerome calls it), should I make a definite revocation when not convicted of my error? I will not do that. On the contrary, I consistently and confidently deny that the merits of Christ are in any way in the hands of the pope as the words [of the *Unigenitus*] state. Let the pope himself see how he understands his *Extravagante*.

May it suffice for the time being that I have shown that the true and proper meaning of Scripture is not found in all the papal decretals, that therefore one cannot, without doing injustice to them, say, maintain, or think otherwise than they prescribe since they themselves assign to the teachers of the church the function of interpreting Scripture and keep to themselves the right of judging between conflicting matters. Accordingly the juridical competence differs from the theological. Many things are permitted in the former which are prohibited in the latter. Jurists may emphasize their traditions, whereas we theologians preserve the purity of Scripture. We do this particularly because we in our time see evil flatterers appear who elevate the pope over the councils. The consequence is that one council is condemned by another until nothing certain remains for us and finally one man, the pope, can crush all things under foot since he is at the same time both above the

---

[33] Orestes, son of Agamemnon and Clytemnestra in Greek legend, was often used as an example of obedience. In some legends he is a human being burdened with sin but purified by the grace of the gods.

[34] A play on the meaning of the word *extravagante*.

council and within it. He is above it since he can condemn it, within it since he accepts from the council as from a higher power authority by means of which he becomes higher than the council.[35] There are also those who brazenly state in public that the pope cannot err and is above Scripture. If these monstrous claims were admitted, Scripture would perish and consequently the church also, and nothing would remain in the church but the word of man. These flatterers actually seek to arouse hatred for the church, then its ruin and destruction. For this reason, my reader, I declare before you that I cherish and follow the church in all things. I resist only those who in the name of the Roman church strive to erect a Babylon[36] for us and wish that whatever occurs to them—if only they could move the tongue enough to mention the Roman church —be accepted as the interpretation of the Roman church, as if Holy Scripture no longer existed, according to which (as Augustine says) we must judge all things, and against which the Roman church certainly never teaches or acts.

Numbered among those people, I believe, are those suave sycophants who dictated a certain apostolic breve against me, the contents of which I wish to publish so that you may see what clever tricks they used. For that it was composed in Germany and then with special assiduity sent to Rome and finally, perhaps at the suggestion of some important person of Rome, returned to Germany, I wish to prove, or at least to arouse a suspicion that this is the case, by means of the attached letter, for it also pertains to the account of my hearing.

---

[35] At the request of Emperor Maximilian I and Louis XII of France, a council was held in Pisa and Milan in 1511 and 1512 with the aim of reforming the head, in this case Pope Julius II, and members of the church. Although cited to appear before the council, Julius did not attend. Instead, Julius II called his own council, the Fifth Lateran Council, whose sessions were held in Rome at various intervals from 1512-1517. Ultimately, the papal council triumphed over its contemporary rival at Pisa and Milan so that Julius' successor, Leo X, was able to adjourn the sessions at Rome. Instead of being checked, papal prestige and authority were strengthened. Luther seems to have known about this most recent struggle for power between ecclesiastical and political authorities, and that in the end papal authority had asserted itself successfully.

[36] Cf. Luther's *Babylonian Captivity of the Church* (1520), WA 6, 381-469; PE 2, 170-293.

To our beloved Son Thomas, our cardinal priest of the titular church of St. Sixtus and our legate of the apostolic chair, from Pope Leo X.[37]

Our dear son, greeting and apostolic blessing. After we had learned that one Martin Luther, professor of the Order of Augustinian Eremites, harboring an evil doctrine, had asserted several ideas which are heretical and deviate from the doctrines of the Holy Roman Church, and in addition to this had dared to publish in several parts of Germany his theses and even scandalous pamphlets with extraordinary rashness and obstinacy, indifferent toward obedience and without consulting the Roman church, the mistress of faith, we, wishing to correct his rashness in a paternal manner, commissioned our Brother Jerome,[38] bishop of Ascoli, general auditor of the Apostolic Chamber of the Curia, to cite this Martin to appear personally before him and to be examined with respect to the above-mentioned accusations and to answer for his faith under threat of certain specified punishments. The said auditor, Jerome, has issued such a citation to the above-mentioned Martin, as we later learned.

Now, however, it has come to our attention that this Martin has abused our kindness and has become more insolent than ever, adding evil to evil and stubbornly persisting in his heresy. He has even gone so far as to publish certain other theses and infamous pamphlets in which there are additional heretical and erroneous doctrines. This, indeed, has perturbed us no little.

As it is incumbent upon us, according to our pastoral office, to counteract such beginnings, and since we wish to prevent a pest of this kind from spreading until it infects the souls of simple people, we command through this letter your circumspection (in which we place the greatest confidence in the Lord, on the one hand on account of your exceptional learning and experience, on the other

---

[37] For notes to and translation of Leo X's breve of August 23, 1518, to Cardinal Cajetan, cf. Preserved Smith, *Luther's Correspondence and other Contemporary Letters* (Philadelphia, 1913), pp. 101-104.

[38] Girolamo Ghinucci of Siena served as secretary to Julius II, by whom he was made bishop of Ascoli. Leo X made him auditor, i.e. Supreme Justice of the Papal Curia. In 1538 he was made cardinal, and died July 3, 1541.

because of your sincere devotion toward us and this holy chair, of which you are an honorable member) that you, as soon as you have received this letter and without any delay, since this matter is by report and also by established fact notorious and inexcusable among us, drive and compel the said Martin, declared a heretic by the said auditor, to appear personally before you. To accomplish this, secure the support of our most beloved sons in Christ, Maximilian, elected emperor of the Romans, as well as of the remaining German princes, cities, corporations, and other powers, ecclesiastical as well as secular. After he has been handed over to you, hold him in faithful custody until you have further order from us that he be brought before us and the apostolic chair.

If he should come before you of his own free will, seeking forgiveness for this rashness, and if after a change of heart he should show signs of repentance, we give you the authority to receive him into the unity of the holy mother church, which never closes its bosom to one who returns to her. If, however, he perseveres in his stubbornness and defies secular authority, we give you the authority to have him and all his adherents and followers branded in all parts of Germany through public edicts—like those which once upon a time were written on the praetor's bulletin board[39]—as heretics, excommunicates, anathematized, and damned and to be shunned as such by all faithful Christians. And that this disease be exterminated more quickly and easily, we give you authority to admonish and require of all prelates collectively and individually and other ecclesiastics, both secular and regular, of any order, including the mendicant orders, and also dukes, margraves, counts, barons, cities, corporations, and magistrates (with the exception of the said Maximilian, the elected emperor) by our authority and also under the threat of the sentence of excommunication and other punishments to be enumerated below, that they, if they desire to be considered believers, seize the said Martin and his adherents and followers and hand them over to you.

If, however, which God forbid and which we cannot believe

---

[39] The *Album praetorium* was the place where the praetor used to publish his edicts. Cf. Du Cange, *Glossarium Mediae et Infimae Latinitatis* (Paris, 1840). I, 171.

will happen, the said princes, cities, corporations, and magistrates collectively or individually should in any way receive the said Martin or his adherents and followers or give the same Martin aid, counsel, or public or secret favor, directly or indirectly, for any reason or in any manner whatsoever, we will place under the interdict of the church all the cities, towns, lands, and other places of those princes, cities, corporations, and magistrates, and also the cities, towns, lands, and other places to which the said Martin should go, as long as said Martin should remain there and three days thereafter, and nonetheless warn collectively and individually the said princes, cities, corporations, and magistrates that, in addition to the said punishment, as far as the ecclesiastics and the said regular clergy are concerned, they will be deprived of their churches, monasteries, and all ecclesiastical benefices and also be rendered incapable of holding these in the future, that they will also be deprived of their feudal holdings, as far as the laity are concerned (the emperor excepted), that they will be considered dishonorable and incapable of conducting legal business, and will be deprived of Christian burial and of the feudal holdings obtained from us and the Apostolic See or from any secular lords, incurring these punishments as far as they do not instantly follow your commands and exhortations without any reservation, contradiction, and opposition and do not abstain from giving any counsel, aid, favor, and asylum to those mentioned above.

On the other hand, we grant you by means of this letter the authority to give a plenary indulgence or any compensation or grace to those who are obedient according to your judgment. But you must take into account no obstructing exemptions, privileges, and favors, whether confirmed by oath, apostolic confirmation, or any other authority, or granted in any way to ecclesiastics and regulars of any order, that is, of mendicant orders, churches, monasteries, or communities, or to secular persons, even though it is expressly stipulated in these exemptions that the persons cannot in any way be excommunicated, suspended, or placed under interdict. The contents of these exemptions we expressly repeal and wish to have considered repealed by virtue of this present decree, despite all things to the contrary, just as though they were inserted word for word in the present decree which invalidates them. Given in Rome at St. Peter's under the ring of the fisherman on the 23rd day of August, 1518, the sixth year of our pontificate.

Jacopo Sadoleto[40]

THE REFLECTIONS OF FRIAR MARTIN LUTHER UPON THE PRECEDING BREVE

First, the supreme pontiff addresses all cardinals and bishops as his "venerable brethren." This cardinal priest of the titular church of St. Sixtus, however, he addresses as his "beloved son." This was observed so little that in this breve the remarkable author, forgetting his usual literary skill, writes that Bishop Jerome of Ascoli is called "venerable brother" by the pope. This talebearer should have taken to heart the proverb which states, "A liar must have a good memory."[41]

Furthermore, who told the pontiff that I had abused his kindness, for which reason he had me cited to appear before Cajetan through Jerome? Since at the time this breve was issued, or at least when I was supposed to have abused his good will, I had not yet heard anything about the citation, as you will see below. But a certain bungling magpie[42] in Germany, seeing my fidelity, croaked this loudly.

Then, that I stubbornly persisted in heresy after the citation and admonition of Jerome and published other pamphlets is an outright lie, for I had stopped publishing books, not only before the date of this breve, but also before the date of the admonition, with the exception of the *Resolutiones*,[43] which I had completed before being cited. But one can readily see that my popular defense[44] had displeased certain hooded fellows. When I made no concession to them, they conjured up for me a certain pope who

---

[40] Jacopo Sadoleto (1477-1547), a learned theologian, was secretary of Leo X.
[41] The first paragraph of these "Reflections" is found in WA 9, 205. The first paragraph of eight lines of the original copy of the manuscript was blacked out and illegible. For this reason the paragraph of a later copy was inserted here.
[42] An allusion to the black and white garb of the Dominican Order.
[43] Cf. *Explanations*, pp. 77-252.
[44] Luther refers to his *Eine Freiheit des Sermons päpstlichen Ablass und Gnade belangend*, published in June, 1518. Cf. WA 1, 380-393.

prophesies concerning the sequence of events and concerning no-toriety and inexcusability. That same Leo X whom they conjure up is perhaps born where there is talk about "the reason of the calculated thing and the reason of the calculating thing."[45]

Finally, and most delightful of all, this breve was issued August 23, but I was cited and admonished August 7. Therefore only sixteen days lapsed between the date of the breve and my receipt of the citation. Figure this out, my reader, and you will find that Jerome, bishop of Ascoli, had begun his process against me, had judged, condemned, and declared me a heretic either before the citation had been handed me or on the sixteenth day after that. So now I ask, where then are the sixty days allowed me in my citation, which began on August 7 and ended about October 7? Is that the custom and procedure of the Roman Curia that on the same day it cites, admonishes, accuses, judges, condemns, and declares one guilty, even one who is far from Rome and knows nothing of all this? What will they answer, unless that they had forgotten to purge themselves with hellabore[46] while they were preparing to fabricate this lie.

In conclusion, my reader, accept my admonition in faith: Whatever may happen to my theses and however much they may have emphasized indulgences, I advise you not to fall into my foolish error. For I once believed that the merits of Christ were actually given me through indulgences, and, proceeding in this foolish notion, I taught and preached to the people that, since indulgences were such valuable things, they should not fail to treasure them and not consider them cheap or contemptible. I, most stupid of all stupid people, did not notice that by such talk I virtually established a precept touching salvation, in any case an indispensable counsel, out of mere permissions, liberties, and relaxations. It was my reason which led me to this, since I was deceived by the obscure words of scholastic opinions and *Extravagantes*. I erred.

---

[45] Luther here makes sport of the hairsplitting dialectics and terminology of the scholastics.

[46] The dried roots of a plant of that name, used in classical times as a strong purgative to cure insanity.

Bear witness to this, my reader. I revoke. Bear witness to this, my reader.

However, when I saw with open eyes that all the teachers of the church agreed that it was better to dispense with indulgences than to obtain them and that those were more blessed who themselves rendered satisfaction than those who purchased indulgences, and that indulgences were nothing but the remission of good works by means of which the satisfaction was fulfilled, I soon saw from what followed that they could be despised, indeed, that it was the most salutary advice to abandon and consider them worthless. But to despise, ignore, and consider worthless the holy, precious, and inestimable merits of Christ (that is, indulgences) sounded horrible. Therefore I judged these words not so much as words of counsel but of mad irreverence.

This brought me to the conclusion that indulgences without reference to the merits of Christ were worthless; that only if they were equated with the merits of Christ were they made the most precious of all treasures; and that thus (alas!) the holy, incomparable merits of Christ might be used as a pretext for the filthiest and ugliest servitude to profit.

What Christian would not gladly give his life, not to mention his money, when the wounds, the blood, the sufferings of our sweetest Savior are described, to say nothing of when they are offered to him? On the other hand, what anguish would be yours if you should see that all this would only serve foul profit and that Christ would be sold not only once by one Judas, but repeatedly by innumerable Judases? Therefore may the name of Christ not deceive you. Remember the prophecy that many false Christs will come who in the name of Christ will do such wonders and signs that they will lead—if it is possible—even the elect into error [Matt. 24:24].

Let us assume that my thesis [58] is wrong, that the merits of Christ are the treasure of indulgences; but then think what necessarily follows from this assumption and what you must then say, namely, that the merits of Christ are to be ignored and considered worthless and that those people who do not buy the merits of Christ are more blessed than those who most devoutly seek to

291

obtain them. And since the merits of Christ according to their very nature impel one to do good works, they would in indulgences, nevertheless, exempt one from good works, which is self-contradictory. What by their nature and by the will of God they should accomplish, they would undo by the will of the pope.

I have done my duty, my reader. If you now err, you err without my being to blame. Farewell.

TWO KINDS OF RIGHTEOUSNESS

1519

Translated by Lowell J. Satre

INTRODUCTION

Luther's sermon on the *Two Kinds of Righteousness* is included in this volume to illustrate how, early in his career as a reformer, he applied his evangelical theology to the lives of his parishioners. Doctrines which were evolved by contemplation, exegetical and historical study, and in conflicts with learned opponents were stated in simple and practical terms in a direct manner. Luther's knowledge of the Bible was so extensive and had become so much a part of his life and thought that Scripture passages and applications constitute a harmonious unity. There is no introduction of extraneous materials to interfere with the development of the main theme, which is based on Phil. 2:5-6. Luther applies his doctrine of justification by faith to everyday living by effectively differentiating between Christ's righteousness by means of which he justifies, sanctifies, and redeems, and the righteousness of a believing Christian which is made possible by the righteousness of Christ.

It is not certain whether this sermon was preached late in 1518 or early in 1519. The text suggests that it was preached on Palm Sunday. This leads the editor of the sermon in the WA to date it 1519. The following translation was made from the edition of this printing in WA 2, 145-152. Georg Spalatin's translation into German was used in St. L. 10, 1262-1277.

An excellent account of Luther's preaching during his formative period is given by E. D. Kiessling in *The Early Sermons of Luther* (Grand Rapids, Mich., 1935).

TWO KINDS
OF RIGHTEOUSNESS

By
The Reverend Father
Martin Luther

Brethren, "have this mind among yourselves, which you have in Christ Jesus, who, though he was in the form of God, did not count equality with God a thing to be grasped" [Phil. 2:5-6].

There are two kinds of Christian righteousness, just as man's sin is of two kinds.

The first is alien righteousness, that is the righteousness of another, instilled from without. This is the righteousness of Christ by which he justifies through faith, as it is written in I Cor. 1 [:30]: "Whom God made our wisdom, our righteousness and sanctification and redemption." In John 11 [:25-26], Christ himself states: "I am the resurrection and the life; he who believes in me . . . shall never die." Later he adds in John 14 [:6], "I am the way, and the truth, and the life." This righteousness, then, is given to men in baptism and whenever they are truly repentant. Therefore a man can with confidence boast in Christ and say: "Mine are Christ's living, doing, and speaking, his suffering and dying, mine as much as if I had lived, done, spoken, suffered, and died as he did." Just as a bridegroom possesses all that is his bride's and she all that is his—for the two have all things in common because they are one flesh [Gen. 2:24]—so Christ and the church are one spirit [Eph. 5:29-32]. Thus the blessed God and Father of mercies has, according to Peter, granted to us very great and precious gifts in Christ [II Pet. 1:4]. Paul writes in II Cor. 1 [:3]: "Blessed be the God and Father of our Lord Jesus Christ, the Father of mercies and

God of all comfort, who has blessed us in Christ with every spiritual blessing in the heavenly places."[1]

This inexpressible grace and blessing was long ago promised to Abraham in Gen. 12 [:3]: "And in thy seed (that is, in Christ) shall all the nations of the earth be blessed."[2] Isaiah 9 [:6] says: "For to us a child is born, to us a son is given." "To us," it says, because he is entirely ours with all his benefits if we believe in him, as we read in Rom. 8 [:32]: "He who did not spare his own Son but gave him up for us all, will he not also give us all things with him?" Therefore everything which Christ has is ours, graciously bestowed on us unworthy men out of God's sheer mercy, although we have rather deserved wrath and condemnation, and hell also. Even Christ himself, therefore, who says he came to do the most sacred will of his Father [John 6:38], became obedient to him; and whatever he did, he did it for us and desired it to be ours, saying, "I am among you as one who serves" [Luke 22:27]. He also states, "This is my body, which is given for you" [Luke 22:19]. Isaiah 43 [:24] says, "You have burdened me with your sins, you have wearied me with your iniquities."

Through faith in Christ, therefore, Christ's righteousness becomes our righteousness and all that he has becomes ours; rather, he himself becomes ours. Therefore the Apostle calls it "the righteousness of God" in Rom. 1 [:17]: For in the gospel "the righteousness of God is revealed . . .; as it is written, 'The righteous shall live by his faith.'" Finally, in the same epistle, chapter 3 [:28], such a faith is called "the righteousness of God": "We hold that a man is justified by faith." This is an infinite righteousness, and one that swallows up all sins in a moment, for it is impossible that sin should exist in Christ. On the contrary, he who trusts in Christ exists in Christ; he is one with Christ, having the same righteousness as he. It is therefore impossible that sin should remain in him. This righteousness is primary; it is the basis, the cause, the source of all our own actual righteousness. For this is the righteousness given in

---

[1] The section "who has blessed, etc." is not from II Corinthians, as indicated by Luther, but from Eph. 1:3.
[2] Gen. 12:3 has "in thee" instead of "in thy seed." The quotation above is actually from Gen. 22:18 (A.V.). Cf. also Gal. 3:8.

place of the original righteousness lost in Adam. It accomplishes the same as that original righteousness would have accomplished; rather, it accomplishes more.

It is in this sense that we are to understand the prayer in Psalm 30 [Ps. 31:1]: "In thee, O Lord, do I seek refuge; let me never be put to shame; in thy righteousness deliver me!" It does not say "in my" but "in thy righteousness," that is, in the righteousness of Christ my God which becomes ours through faith and by the grace and mercy of God. In many passages of the Psalter, faith is called "the work of the Lord," "confession," "power of God," "mercy," "truth," "righteousness." All these are names for faith in Christ, rather, for the righteousness which is in Christ. The Apostle therefore dares to say in Gal. 2 [:20], "It is no longer I who live, but Christ who lives in me." He further states in Eph. 3 [14-17]: "I bow my knees before the Father . . . that . . . he may grant . . . that Christ may dwell in your hearts through faith."

Therefore this alien righteousness, instilled in us without our works by grace alone—while the Father, to be sure, inwardly draws us to Christ—is set opposite original sin, likewise alien, which we acquire without our works by birth alone. Christ daily drives out the old Adam more and more in accordance with the extent to which faith and knowledge of Christ grow. For alien righteousness is not instilled all at once, but it begins, makes progress, and is finally perfected at the end through death.

The second kind of righteousness is our proper righteousness, not because we alone work it, but because we work with that first and alien righteousness. This is that manner of life spent profitably in good works, in the first place, in slaying the flesh and crucifying the desires with respect to the self, of which we read in Gal. 5 [:24]: "And those who belong to Christ Jesus have crucified the flesh with its passions and desires." In the second place, this righteousness consists in love to one's neighbor, and in the third place, in meekness and fear toward God. The Apostle is full of references to these, as is all the rest of Scripture. He briefly summarizes everything, however, in Titus 2 [:12]: "In this world let us live soberly (pertaining to crucifying one's own flesh), justly (referring to one's neightbor), and devoutly (relating to God)."

This righteousness is the product of the righteousness of the first type, actually its fruit and consequence, for we read in Gal. 5 [:22]: "But the fruit of the spirit [i.e., of a spiritual man, whose very existence depends on faith in Christ] is love, joy, peace, patience, kindness, goodness, faithfulness, gentleness, self-control." For because the works mentioned are works of men, it is obvious that in this passage a spiritual man is called "spirit." In John 3 [:6] we read: "That which is born of the flesh is flesh, and that which is born of the Spirit is spirit." This righteousness goes on to complete the first for it ever strives to do away with the old Adam and to destroy the body of sin. Therefore it hates itself and loves its neighbor; it does not seek its own good, but that of another, and in this its whole way of living consists. For in that it hates itself and does not seek its own, it crucifies the flesh. Because it seeks the good of another, it works love. Thus in each sphere it does God's will, living soberly with self, justly with neighbor, devoutly toward God.

This righteousness follows the example of Christ in this respect [I Pet. 2:21] and is transformed into his likeness (II Cor. 3:18). It is precisely this that Christ requires. Just as he himself did all things for us, not seeking his own good but ours only—and in this he was most obedient to God the Father—so he desires that we also should set the same example for our neighbors.

We read in Rom. 6 [:19] that this righteousness is set opposite our own actual sin: "For just as you once yielded your members to impurity and to greater and greater iniquity, so now yield your members to righteousness for sanctification." Therefore through the first righteousness arises the voice of the bridegroom who says to the soul, "I am yours," but through the second comes the voice of the bride who answers, "I am yours." Then the marriage is consummated; it becomes strong and complete in accordance with the Song of Solomon [2:16]: "My beloved is mine and I am his." Then the soul no longer seeks to be righteous in and for itself, but it has Christ as its righteousness and therefore seeks only the welfare of others. Therefore the Lord of the Synagogue threatens through the Prophet, "And I will make to cease from the cities of Judah and from the streets of Jerusalem the voice of mirth and the voice of

gladness, the voice of the bridegroom and the voice of the bride"
[Jer. 7:34].

This is what the text we are now considering says: "Let this
mind be in you, which was also in Christ Jesus" [Phil. 2:5]. This
means you should be as inclined and disposed toward one another
as you see Christ was disposed toward you. How? Thus, surely, that
"though he was in the form of God, [he] did not count equality
with God a thing to be grasped, but emptied himself, taking the
form of a servant" [Phil. 2:6-7]. The term "form of God" here does
not mean the "essence of God" because Christ never emptied himself of this. Neither can the phrase "form of a servant" be said to
mean "human essence." But the "form of God" is wisdom, power,
righteousness, goodness—and freedom too; for Christ was a free,
powerful, wise man, subject to none of the vices or sins to which
all other men are subject. He was pre-eminent in such attributes
as are particularly proper to the form of God. Yet he was not
haughty in that form; he did not please himself (Rom. 15:3); nor
did he disdain and despise those who were enslaved and subjected
to various evils.

He was not like the Pharisee who said, "God, I thank thee that
I am not like other men" [Luke 18:11], for that man was delighted
that others were wretched; at any rate he was unwilling that they
should be like him. This is the type of robbery by which a man
usurps things for himself—rather, he keeps what he has and does
not clearly ascribe to God the things that are God's, nor does he
serve others with them that he may become like other men. Men
of this kind wish to be like God, sufficient in themselves, pleasing
themselves, glorying in themselves, under obligation to no one, and
so on. Not thus, however, did Christ think; not of this stamp was
his wisdom. He relinquished that form to God the Father and
emptied himself, unwilling to use his rank against us, unwilling to
be different from us. Moreover, for our sakes he became as one
of us and took the form of a servant, that is, he subjected himself
to all evils. And although he was free, as the Apostle says of himself also [I Cor. 9:19], he made himself servant of all [Mark 9:35],
living as if all the evils which were ours were actually his own.

Accordingly he took upon himself our sin and our punishment, and although it was for us that he was conquering those things, he acted as though he were conquering them for himself. Although as far as his relationship to us was concerned, he had the power to be our God and Lord, yet he did not will it so, but rather desired to become our servant, as it is written in Rom. 15 [:1, 3]: "We . . . ought . . . not to please ourselves . . . For Christ did not please himself; but, as it is written, 'The reproaches of those who reproached thee fell on me'" [Ps. 69:9]. The quotation from the Psalmist has the same meaning as the citation from Paul.

It follows that this passage, which many have understood affirmatively, ought to be understood negatively as follows: That Christ did not count himself equal to God means that he did not wish to be equal to him as those do who presumptuously grasp for equality and say to God, "If thou wilt not give me thy glory (as St. Bernard says), I shall seize it for myself." The passage is not to be understood affirmatively as follows: He did not think himself equal to God, that is, the fact that he is equal to God, this he did not consider robbery. For this interpretation is not based on a proper understanding since it speaks of Christ the man. The Apostle means that each individual Christian shall become the servant of another in accordance with the example of Christ. If one has wisdom, righteousness, or power with which one can excel others and boast in the "form of God," so to speak, one should not keep all this to himself, but surrender it to God and become altogether as if he did not possess it [II Cor. 6:10], as one of those who lack it.

Paul's meaning is that when each person has forgotten himself and emptied himself of God's gifts, he should conduct himself as if his neighbor's weakness, sin, and foolishness were his very own. He should not boast or get puffed up. Nor should he despise or triumph over his neighbor as if he were his god or equal to God. Since God's prerogatives ought to be left to God alone, it becomes robbery when a man in haughty foolhardiness ignores this fact. It is in this way, then, that one takes the form of a servant, and that command of the Apostle in Gal. 5 [:13] is fulfilled: "Through love be servants of one another." Through the figure of the members of the body Paul teaches in Rom. 12 [:4-5] and I Cor. 12 [:12-27] how the strong, honorable, healthy members do not glory over those that are weak, less honorable, and sick as if they were their masters and gods; but on the contrary they serve them the more, forgetting their own honor, health, and power. For thus no member of the body serves itself; nor does it seek its own welfare but that of the other. And the weaker, the sicker, the less honorable a member is, the more the other members serve it "that there may be no discord in the body, but that the members may have the same care for one another," to use Paul's words [I Cor. 12:25]. From this it is now evident how one must conduct himself with his neighbor in each situation.

And if we do not freely desire to put off that form of God and take on the form of a servant, let us be compelled to do so against our will. In this regard consider the story in Luke 7 [:36-50], where Simon the leper, pretending to be in the form of God and perching on his own righteousness, was arrogantly judging and despising Mary Magdalene, seeing in her the form of a servant. But see how Christ immediately stripped him of that form of righteousness and then clothed him with the form of sin by saying: "You gave me no kiss. . . . You did not anoint my head." How great were the sins that Simon did not see! Nor did he think himself disfigured by such a loathsome form as he had. His good works are not at all remembered.

Christ ignores the form of God in which Simon was superciliously pleasing himself; he does not recount that he was invited, dined, and honored by him. Simon the leper is now nothing but a sinner. He who seemed to himself so righteous sits divested of the glory of the form of God, humiliated in the form of a servant, willy-nilly. On the other hand, Christ honors Mary with the form of God and elevates her above Simon, saying: "She has anointed my feet and kissed them. She has wet my feet with her tears and wiped them with her hair." How great were the merits which neither she nor Simon saw. Her faults are remembered no more. Christ ignored the form of servitude in her whom he has exalted with the form of sovereignty. Mary is nothing but righteous, elevated into the glory of the form of God, etc.

In like manner he will treat all of us whenever we, on the ground of our righteousness, wisdom, or power, are haughty or angry with those who are unrighteous, foolish, or less powerful than we. For when we act thus—and this is the greatest perversion—righteousness works against righteousness, wisdom against wisdom, power against power. For you are powerful, not that you may make the weak weaker by oppression, but that you may make them powerful by raising them up and defending them. You are wise, not in order to laugh at the foolish and thereby make them more foolish, but that you may undertake to teach them as you yourself would wish to be taught. You are righteous that you may vindicate and pardon the unrighteous, not that you may only condemn, disparage, judge, and punish. For this is Christ's example for us, as he says: "For God sent the Son into the world, not to condemn the world, but that the world might be saved through him" (John 3:17). He further says in Luke 9 [:55-56]: "You do not know what manner of spirit you are of; for the Son of man came not to destroy men's lives but to save them."

But the carnal nature of man violently rebels, for it greatly delights in punishment, in boasting of its own righteousness, and in its neighbor's shame and embarrassment at his unrighteousness. Therefore it pleads its own case, and it rejoices that this is better than its neighbor's. But it opposes the case of its neighbor and wants it to appear mean. This perversity is wholly evil, contrary to love, which does not seek its own good, but that of another [I Cor. 13:5; Phil. 2:4]. It ought to be distressed that the condition of its neighbor is not better than its own. It ought to wish that its neighbor's condition were better than its own, and if its neighbor's condition is the better, it ought to rejoice no less than it rejoices when its own is the better. "For this is the law and the prophets" [Matt. 7:12].

But you say, "Is it not permissible to chasten evil man? Is it not proper to punish sin? Who is not obliged to defend righteousness? To do otherwise would give occasion for lawlessness."

I answer: A single solution to this problem cannot be given. Therefore one must distinguish among men. For men can be classified either as public or private individuals.

The things which have been said do not pertain at all to public individuals, that is, to those who have been placed in a responsible office by God. It is their necessary function to punish and judge evil men, to vindicate and defend the oppressed, because it is not they but God who does this. They are his servants in this very matter, as the Apostle shows at some length in Rom. 13 [:4]: "He does not bear the sword in vain, etc." But this must be understood as pertaining to the cases of other men, not to one's own. For no man acts in God's place for the sake of himself and his own things, but for the sake of others. If, however, a public official has a case of his own, let him ask for someone other than himself to be God's representative, for in that case he is not a judge, but one of the parties. But on these matters let others speak at other times, for it is too broad a subject to cover now.

Private individuals with their own cases are of three kinds. First, there are those who seek vengeance and judgment from the representatives of God, and of these there is now a very great number. Paul tolerates such people, but he does not approve of them when he says in I Cor. 6 [:12], "'All things are lawful for me,' but not all things are helpful." Rather he says in the same chapter, "To have lawsuits at all with one another is defeat for you" [I Cor. 6:7]. But yet to avoid a greater evil he tolerates this lesser one lest they should vindicate themselves and one should use force on the other, returning evil for evil, demanding their own advantages. Nevertheless such will not enter the kingdom of heaven unless they have changed for the better by forsaking things that are merely lawful and pursuing those that are helpful. For that passion for one's own advantage must be destroyed.

In the second class are those who do not desire vengeance. On the other hand, in accordance with the Gospel [Matt. 5:40], to those who would take their coats, they are prepared to give their cloaks as well, and they do not resist any evil. These are sons of God, brothers of Christ, heirs of future blessings. In Scripture therefore they are called "fatherless," "widows," "desolate"; because they do not avenge themselves, God wishes to be called their "Father" and "Judge" [Ps. 68:5]. Far from avenging themselves, if those in authority should wish to seek revenge in their behalf, they either do not desire it or seek it, or they only permit it. Or, if they are among the most advanced, they forbid and prevent it, prepared rather to lose their other possessions also.

Suppose you say: "Such people are very rare, and who would be able to remain in this world were he to do this?" I answer: This is not a discovery of today, that few are saved and that the gate is narrow that leads to life and those who find it are few [Matt. 7:14]. But if none were doing this, how would the Scripture stand which calls the poor, the orphans, and the widows "the people of Christ?" Therefore those in this second class grieve more over the sin of their offenders than over the loss or offense to themselves. And they do this that they may recall those offenders from their sin rather than avenge the wrongs they themselves have suffered. Therefore they put off the form of their own righteousness and put on the form of those others, praying for their persecutors, blessing those who curse, doing good to evil-doers, prepared to pay the penalty and make satisfaction for their very enemies that they may be saved [Matt. 5:44]. This is the gospel and the example of Christ [Luke 23:34].

In the third class are those who in persuasion are like the second type just mentioned, but are not like them in practice. They are the ones who demand back their own property or seek punishment to be meted out, not because they seek their own advantage, but through the punishment and restoration of their own things they seek the betterment of the one who has stolen or offended. They discern that the offender cannot be improved without punishment. These are called "zealots" and the Scriptures praise them. But no one ought to attempt this unless he is mature and highly experienced in the second class just mentioned, lest he mistake wrath for zeal and be convicted of doing from anger and impatience that which he believes he is doing from love of justice. For anger is like zeal, and impatience is like love of justice so that they cannot be sufficiently distinguished except by the most spiritual. Christ exhibited such zeal when he made a whip and cast out the sellers and buyers from the temple, as related in John 2 [:14-17]. Paul did likewise when he said, "Shall I come to you with a rod, or with love in a spirit of gentleness?" [I Cor. 4:21]. FINIS

THE LEIPZIG DEBATE

*Disputation and Defense of Brother Martin Luther
against the Accusations of Dr. Johann Eck*

AND

*Letter from Luther to Spalatin
Concerning the Leipzig Debate*

1519

Translated by Harold J. Grimm

INTRODUCTION

The indulgence controversy entered a new phase when Dr. Johann Eck became the chief aggressor against the new evangelical theology. Eck's real name was Maier, but he was generally known by the name of his birthplace, Eck, in Bavarian Swabia. Almost an exact contemporary of Luther, his polemics played an important role in the development of the Reformation. He failed, however, in influencing the religious movements of his day in a constructive way, for his chief weapon against Luther was the charge of heresy. Although he had a remarkable memory, he lacked the ability to apply his learning to the issues at hand in a convincing manner. He was an impressive debater, but he invariably irritated his opponents by his overbearing attitude.

Eck began a friendly exchange of letters with Luther early in 1517. Less than a year later, however, he suddenly terminated his friendship with Luther by the publication of his *Obelisks,* in which he attacked thirty-one of Luther's *Ninety-five Theses* in highly abusive language. Luther answered with his vehement *Asterisks* in March, 1518. The *Obelisks* were published for the first time after Eck's death together with Luther's *Asterisks* in the first volume of the Wittenberg edition of Luther's writings in 1545. They are printed in their original Latin form in WA 1, 281-314 and in German in *St. L.* 18, 536-589.

When Eck did not answer Luther's *Asterisks,* it seemed as though the polemics between the two would cease. Luther's colleague Karlstadt, however, at that time dean of the theological faculty at the University of Wittenberg, felt that his faculty had been insulted by Eck and wrote 370 theses in its defense. When Eck learned of this, he wrote Karlstadt, expressing regret over the fact that he had gone too far in his attack upon Luther in his *Obelisks* and requesting Karlstadt to drop the controversy. This request came too late, however, for Karlstadt had already published his theses and Eck's propositions were being debated in Wittenberg. Feeling that he could no longer remain silent, Eck published countertheses and challenged Karlstadt to a public disputation. He even visited Luther in Augsburg in October while the latter was having his hearings with Cajetan and discussed this matter with him.

Luther, Karlstadt, and Eck finally agreed that a disputation should be held at Leipzig. While negotiations were going on with the theological faculty at Leipzig, which was reluctant to agree to the holding of such a disputation in that city, Eck published on December 29 an announcement of the disputation between Karlstadt and him to be held at Leipzig, together with twelve theses which he would defend. Eleven of these theses dealt with indulgences. The twelfth introduced a new subject, the defense of papal supremacy, an attack upon Luther's explanation of Thesis 22 in his *Explanations* in which the latter had stated that the church of Rome had "had no jurisdiction over other churches" at the time of St. Gregory, "at least not over the Greek church." *

When Luther received a copy of these theses toward the end of January, 1519, he was surprised to note that Eck was actually challenging him, not Karlstadt, to the debate. Considering himself relieved of his promise to Miltitz† to discontinue the indulgence controversy provided his opponents did likewise, Luther published twelve countertheses which he sent to Spalatin early in February. The next month Eck published a second announcement of the coming disputation in which he made it clear that he was primarily concerned with attacking Luther. To his original twelve theses, however, he now added a thirteenth which concerned the freedom of the will, one of the main topics of dispute between Karlstadt and himself. This now became Thesis 7, and the one on papal authority became Thesis 13. Luther's response, his *Disputation and Defense . . . against the Accusations of Dr. Johann Eck,* published in May and translated into English in this volume, served as the basis of his debate with Eck at Leipzig, July 4-14.

Duke George of Saxony, who wanted the disputation held at Leipzig because he believed that it would bring prestige to his university, prevailed upon the theological faculty and the chancel-

---

* Cf. p. 152.
†Karl von Miltitz was a Saxon nobleman attached to the papal curia.

lor to accede to his wishes. The account of the arrival of Luther and Karlstadt, the preliminary arrangements, the disputation, and Eck's premature celebration of victory is given in words of disappointment and disillusionment by Luther himself in a letter to Spalatin written soon after the debate.

The chief emphasis in the disputation between Luther and Eck was upon Thesis 13 concerning the authority of the pope and the jurisdiction of the church of Rome. Although Luther was not historically accurate in maintaining that the jurisdiction of the church of Rome over the others was a product solely of the preceding four hundred years and of papal decretals, he was correct in holding that the claims made by Catholic tradition and defended by Eck were exaggerated. But he went far beyond the familiar medieval attacks upon the papacy by denying altogether the authority of the pope as contrary to the Bible. He maintained that Christ had not singled out Peter to give him alone jurisdiction (*potestas*) over the other apostles which could be transferred to his successors as bishops of Rome. The chief function of the church and the successors of the apostles, Luther said, was to feed Christ's sheep, that is, teach Christians the Word of God. The office of the keys thus was interpreted as being the command to preach the gospel. Christ, he stated, was present only there where the gospel was preached and the sacraments were administered according to his commands. Therefore the church owed its existence solely to Christ, its head. From this conviction stemmed Luther's growing animosity toward the conception of the church of Rome as a powerful ecclesiastical state.

The Leipzig Debate is of great significance in Luther's development as a reformer primarily because he on that occasion publicly stated his evangelical conception of the church in unmistakable terms and showed that in the last analysis his sole authority in matters of faith was the Word of God. Therefore he could state without reservations that not only the papacy but also church councils could err. This made reconciliation with the Roman church virtually impossible. It led inexorably to the threat of excommunication and finally to excommunication itself.

The original publication of Luther's thirteen theses against Eck served as the basis for the selection in WA 2, 158-161, which in turn has been translated into English in this volume. There are excellent German translations in St. L. 18, 718-721 and MA³ 1, 95-99. Luther's letter to Spalatin is contained in its original Latin in WA, Br 1, 420-424; in a German translation in MA³ 1, 100-105; and in an English translation in Preserved Smith, *The Life and Letters of Martin Luther* (Boston & New York, 1911), pp. 64-68. There are detailed accounts of the Leipzig Debate in E. G. Schwiebert, *Luther and His Times*, pp. 384-437 and R. H. Fife, *The Revolt of Martin Luther*, pp. 327-394.

THE LEIPZIG DEBATE

*Disputation and Defense of Brother Martin Luther
against the Accusations of Dr. Johann Eck
Brother Martin Luther Greets the Worthy Reader*

My dear Eck has become enraged, my kind reader, and has dedicated to the Apostolic See another scrap of paper with a disputation on it, full of his wrath and accusations against me. He has added to his former theses an exceptionally bitter one. It gives me a wonderful opportunity to answer his blasphemies once and for all, provided I do not fear that I might thereby place an obstacle in the way of the impending debate. But "for everything there is a season" [Eccles. 3:1]. For the present may the following suffice.

On the basis of a number of quotations from the holy church fathers, Eck accuses me of being an enemy of the church. Now note, my reader, that he means by the word "church" his own opinions and those of his heroes[1] who have worn themselves out in behalf of indulgences. He is a person who dedicates all things to the Apostolic See and talks according to the custom of his opinionated heroes who use the words of Scripture and the church fathers as Anaxagoras[2] does his elements. That is to say, as soon as they have dedicated them to the Apostolic See, these passages are transformed into words of their own choice and, strange to say, into any meaning whatsoever, even to the extent that they conveniently express that which they themselves dream in their fever or rave about in the impotence of their effeminate hatred.

Finally, they unhappily lose their skill to the extent that they do not at all correctly understand the good things which they have

---

[1] In the introduction to his theses against Luther, Eck had called attention to certain medieval theologians, his "heroes," whose views Luther had ignored.
[2] Anaxagoras (c. B.C. 500-428), a Greek philosopher who taught that the interaction of elements, directed by the divine mind, produced being. Since these elements could produce varying combinations Luther, by this reference, derides the fortuitous change of meaning in words when used by Eck.

learned, and, as the Apostle says, do not comprehend "what they are saying or the things about which they make assertions" [I Tim. 1:7]. That is to say, they cannot connect a predicate with a subject or a subject with a predicate in a categorical proposition. We hope that Eck will with similar dexterity provide us with other proofs in the coming debate, and not neglect to do so, so that even the children may laugh. I had hoped that Eck would lose his dulness by reading the letter of Erasmus,[3] the prince of letters, and Dr. Karlstadt's invincible *Apologia*.[4] But Eckian patience truly conquers everything. Even though he may displease all others, he is satisfied if he pleases at least himself and his heroes.

That he vilifies me as a heretic and a Bohemian,[5] however, saying that I rekindle old ashes etc., he does out of modesty and by virtue of his office of consecrator, according to which he consecrates everything by using no oil other than the venom of his tongue.

Since I cannot let this sort of name-calling pass unnoticed, you, my reader, must know that as far as the absolute authority of the Roman pontiff is concerned, I do not spurn the venerable consensus of all the faithful Christians in Italy, Germany, France, Spain, England, and other countries. But one thing I pray the Lord, namely, that he never permit me to say or believe anything which will please Eck as he now is; that I do not in behalf of the freedom of the will[6] hold up Christ, the Son of God, as a public spectacle and in behalf of the Roman church deny that Christ lives and rules in India and the Orient; or—so I may also give this merry maker of riddles a riddle—that I never reopen with Eck the Constantinopolitan sewer and celebrate the ancient murders in Africa as new martyrdoms of the church.[7]

---

[3] Letter of Erasmus to Eck dated May 15, 1518. P. S. Allen, *Opus epistolarum Des. Erasmi Roterodami* (11 vols.; Oxford, 1906-47), III, 330-338.

[4] Karlstadt's *Defensio . . . adversus eximii D. Joannis Eckii monomachiam* in which he accepted Eck's challenge to debate with him. *St.L.* 18, 632-710.

[5] In his *Obelisks* of January, 1518, Eck branded Luther as a follower of the Bohemian heretic, John Huss.

[6] Cf. Thesis 7, p. 317.

[7] Luther probably refers to the severe attacks on heretics in northern Africa during the fourth and fifth centuries.

So that you will not be harmed by the temptation of his poisonous riddle, my reader, you must know that among the articles of John Huss one among several is to be found in which he states that the pre-eminence of the papacy came from the emperor, as Platina plainly wrote.[8] I, however, undertook to prove that this power was derived, not from imperial, but from papal decrees. The Lateran Church itself in an inscription sings about the origin and the extent of its authority, stating that by papal and imperial decrees it is the mother of churches etc. These little verses[9] are well known. But what of it? It is necessary that the church itself also be Hussite to Eck and that he rekindle old ashes. Then by command of the pope and consent of the cardinals, the Lateran Church sings in this manner for all Rome and the universal church that it is no wonder that Eck loathes old ashes and according to his office of consecrator pants for a new holocaust to offer the Apostolic See, namely, to reduce the pope, the cardinals, and the Lateran Church itself to ashes anew. Thank God that then at least one person, Eck, will be left who has a Catholic taste, that most extraordinary persecutor of the most extraordinary, while all others are destroyed by the Bohemian virus. But it is strange that sophists of that kind are ignorant of history, when they do not even understand their own theses? I have indeed never dealt with this material or thought about making it a subject of debate. Eck, however, who for a long time had ulcerated very great hatred against me and knew that these theses were offensive to people, hoped that, since he had despaired of victory in other points, he could at least cause people to hate me, skilled as he is in beating the puppy in front of the lion, so to speak, and to make out of the disputation in search for truth a tragedy of hatred.

They may, however, make accusations as much as they wish and may consecrate the Apostolic See with their flattery, and con-

---

[8] Bartolomeo Platina (1421-1481), a humanist librarian of Sixtus IV who continued the account of the old *Liber pontificalis* or collection of biographies of the popes to 1471.
[9] Luther refers to well-known verses which express the headship of the church of Rome. The following is the one which he has in mind here: *Dogmate Papali datur et simul Imperiali Quod sim cunctarum Mater, Caput Ecclesiarum.* WA 2, 159, n. 2. The inscription was in front of the Lateran Church in Rome.

secrate the throne and the footstool, and consecrate even the
Apostolic money box, which, of course, is concerned most of all
with the indulgence affair and papal power; they may dance around
the altar of their Baal and shout with an ever louder voice so that
he awakens, for Baal is a god. Probably he will speak, or probably
he is on a journey or in an inn or asleep somewhere [I Kings 18:25-
29]. I am convinced that the Apostolic See neither wills nor can
do anything against Christ. Furthermore, in this matter I fear
neither the pope nor the name of the pope, much less those little
popes and puppets.[10] One thing only am I concerned about, namely,
that the despoiling of my Christian name does not bring with it
the loss of the most holy doctrine of Christ. In this matter I do
not want anyone to expect patience of me. I do not want Eck to
look for modesty either under the black or under the white hood.[11]
May the praise of that impious forbearance be damned which was
shown by Ahab when he set free Benhadad, the enemy of Israel
[I Kings 20]. For in this case I not only want to bite vehemently,
to the discomfiture of Eck, but I want to prove myself invincible
in devouring so that, to use Isaiah's phrase [Isa. 9:12], I could
swallow in one gulp all Sylvesters and Civesters, Cajetans and
Ecks[12] and the other brothers who are adversaries of Christian
grace. Let them terrify someone else with their flattery and conse-
crations; Martin despises the priests and consecrators of the Apostolic See. The other matters [which Eck brings up] I shall consider
during and after the disputation. Dr. Andreas Karlstadt, already
victor over Eck's errors, will also appear, and not as a fugitive
soldier. He will challenge in confidence this dead lion whom he has
already cast down. Until that time we shall permit this miserable
conscience to bask in its imagined hope of victory and the hollow
display of threats. For this reason I shall add to my theses a thirteenth against Eck's passionate anger. May it be from God that some

[10] This is a play on the Latin words *pappos et puppas.*

[11] The black hood was worn by the Augustinians, the white by the Dominicans.
Eck had previously stated that he had expected more wisdom and patience
under a black hood.

[12] Luther here refers to Sylvester Prierias (1456-1523), a Dominican scholar,
advisor to the pope, and grand inquisitor; "Civester," a fictitious name used in
a play on words to make this seem ridiculous; Cajetan, cf. p. 264, n. 10; Eck, cf.
p. xvi.

good comes from this disputation, which Eck pollutes with his evil hatred and slander. Farewell, my reader.

Martin Luther will defend the following theses against new and old errors at the University of Leipzig.

1. Every man sins daily, but he also repents daily according to Christ's teaching, "Repent" [Matt. 4:17], possibly with the exception of a person who has just been made righteous and who does not need repentance, although the heavenly vinedresser daily prunes the fruit-bearing vines [Cf. John 15:1-2].

2. To deny that man sins even when doing good; that venial sin is pardonable, not according to its nature, but by the mercy of God; or that sin remains in the child after baptism; that is equivalent to crushing Paul and Christ under foot.

3. He who maintains that a good work and penance begin with the hatred of sins and prior to the love of righteousness and that one no longer sins in doing good work, him we number among the Pelagian heretics;[13] but we also prove that this is a silly interpretation of his holy Aristotle.

4. God changes an eternal punishment into a temporary one, that is, the punishment of carrying the cross. Canons or priests have no power to burden one with the cross or to remove it, although, deceived by harmful flatterers, they presume that they can do this.

5. Every priest must absolve the penitent of punishment and guilt. If he does not, he sins. So does a higher prelate if he reserves secret matters without good reason, though the usage of the church, that is, of flatterers, opposes this.

6. Perhaps the souls in purgatory do render satisfaction for their sins. It is brazen rashness, however, to assert that God demands more of a dying person than a willingness to die since in no way can this assertion be proven.

7. He who babbles about the free will being the master of good or evil deeds shows he does not know what faith, contrition, or free will are; nor does he know who imagines that one is not justified alone by faith in the Word, or that faith is not lost in every mortal sin.

---

[13] Cf. p. 9, n. 1.

317

8. It is contrary to truth and reason to state that those who die unwillingly are deficient in love and must therefore suffer the horror of purgatory, but only if truth and reason are the same as the opinions of the would-be theologians.

9. We are familiar with the assertion of would-be theologians that the souls in purgatory are certain of their salvation and that grace is no longer increased in them; but we marvel at these very learned men that they can offer the uneducated no cogent reason for this their conviction.

10. It is certain that the merit of Christ is the treasure of the church and that this treasure is enhanced by the merits of the saints; but no one except a filthy flatterer or one who strays from the truth and embraces certain false practices and usages of the church pretends that the merits of Christ are the treasure of indulgences.

11. To say that indulgences are a blessing for a Christian is insane, for they are in truth a hindrance to a good work; and a Christian must reject indulgences because of their abuse, for the Lord says, "I, I am He who blots out your transgressions for my own sake" [Isa. 43:25], not for the sake of money.

12. Completely unlearned sophists and pestiferous flatterers dream that the pope can remit every punishment owed for sins in this and the future life and that indulgences are helpful to those who are not guilty. But they cannot prove this with so much as a gesture.

13. The very callous decrees of the Roman pontiffs which have appeared in the last four hundred years prove that the Roman church is superior to all others. Against them stand the history of eleven hundred years, the test of divine Scripture, and the decree of the Council of Nicaea, the most sacred of all councils.

In the year 1519

LETTER FROM LUTHER TO SPALATIN CONCERNING THE LEIPZIG DEBATE

Wittenberg, July 20, 1519.

To the Illustrious Georg Spalatin, Court Chaplain and

Librarian of His Highness the Elector of Saxony, His Friend in Christ.

Greetings! That our highness the prince and you all have returned safely pleases me, my dear Spalatin.[14] May Christ claim the soul of Pfeffinger,[15] Amen. I should have written you long ago about our famous debate, but I did not know where or about what. Certain people of Leipzig, neither sincere nor upright, are celebrating victory with Eck. It is from this nonsense that rumor has spread, but the truth of the matter will bring everything to light.

Almost at the very moment of our arrival, even before we had gotten out of our wagon, the *Inhibition* of the bishop of Merseburg was affixed to the doors of the churches to the effect that the debate should not be held, together with that newly published explanation concerning this matter of indulgences.[16] This *Inhibition* was disregarded and the person who had posted it was thrown into jail by the city council because he had acted without its knowledge.

Since our enemies got nowhere with this trick, they tried another. Having called Andreas Karlstadt to meet alone with them, they tried hard to get him to agree to hold the debate orally, according to Eck's wishes, without stenographers taking down the proceedings in writing. Eck hoped that he might carry off the victory by his loud shouting and impressive delivery, means which he had long used to his advantage. Karlstadt, however, opposed this and insisted that they proceed according to a previous agreement,[17] that is, that the statements of the disputants be written down by stenographers. Finally, to attain this, he was compelled to agree that the account of the debate made by the stenographers should not be published prior to a hearing by a court of judges.

At this point a new dispute arose over the choice of the judges.

---

[14] Elector Frederick the Wise had been in Frankfurt am Main at the election of the emperor from June 11 to July 4.

[15] Degenhard Pfeffinger, who had long been in the service of Elector Frederick the Wise, had died July 3, a victim of a plague.

[16] The papal decree on indulgences of November 9, 1518. Apparently a copy of this decretal had been sent to Bishop Adolph of Merseburg who believed that this decretal had decided the questions for debate.

[17] Cf. Luther's letter to Eck, *WA* Br. 1, 230-231.

At length they compelled him also to consent to postpone coming to an agreement concerning the judges until after the debate had been concluded. Otherwise they did not wish to permit the debate. Thus they attacked us with the syllogistic horns of a dilemma, so that we should be confounded by both alternatives, whether we gave up the debate or placed the outcome into the hands of unfair judges. So you see how barbarous was their cunning, by means of which they robbed us of the freedom which had been agreed upon. For it is certain that the universities and the pope[18] will never make a pronouncement, or they would make one against us, and this is what they want.

The next day they called me to appear before them and proposed the same thing. Suspecting, however, the pope as the instigator of this procedure, I refused to accept these conditions, having been persuaded to do so by my colleagues. Then they proposed other universities as judges, without the pope. I requested that the freedom upon which we had agreed be respected. When they were unwilling to do this, I became reluctant and repudiated the debate. Then the rumor spread that I did not want to risk participating in the debate and, what is particularly unfair, that I wished to have no judges. All these accusations were hatefully and malignantly hurled at me and were interpreted in such a way that now they were turning even our best friends against us; and already permanent disgrace to our university was in prospect. After this, upon the advice of friends,[19] I went to them and indignantly accepted their conditions. I did this in such a way and with the exclusion of the Roman Curia so that my power of appeal would be safeguarded and my case would not be prejudged.

Eck and Karlstadt at first debated for seven days over the freedom of the will. With God's help Karlstadt advanced his arguments and explanations excellently and in great abundance from books which he had brought with him. Then when Karlstadt had also been given the opportunity of rebuttal, Eck refused to debate unless the books were left at home. Andreas [Karlstadt] had used the books to demonstrate to Eck's face that he had correctly quoted

---

[18] Luther assumed that they would constitute the judges.
[19] Cf. p. 323, n. 26.

the words of Scripture and the church fathers, that he had not done violence to them as Eck was now shown to have done. This marked the beginning of another uproar until at length it was decided to Eck's advantage that the books should be left at home. But who was not aware of the fact that if the debate were concerned with the cause of truth, it would be advisable to have all possible books at hand? Never did hatred and ambition show themselves more impudently than here.

Finally this deceitful man conceded everything that Karlstadt had asserted, although he had vehemently attacked it, and agreed with him in everything, boasting that he had led Karlstadt to his own way of thinking. He accordingly rejected Scotus and the Scotists and Capreolus and the Thomists, saying that all other scholastics had thought and taught the same as he.[20] So Scotus and Capreolus toppled to the ground, together with their respective schools, the two celebrated divisions of scholasticism.

The next week Eck debated with me, at first very acrimoniously, concerning the primacy of the pope. His proof rested on the words "You are Peter . . ." [Matt. 16:18] and "Feed my sheep, . . . follow me" [John 21:17, 22], and "strengthen your brethren" [Luke 22:32], adding to these passages many quotations from the church fathers. What I answered you will soon see.[21] Then, coming to the last point, he rested his case entirely on the Council of Constance[22] which had condemned Huss's article alleging that papal authority derived from the emperor instead of from God. Then Eck stamped about with much ado as though he were in an arena, holding up the Bohemians before me and publicly accusing me of the heresy and support of the Bohemian heretics,[23] for he is a sophist, no less impudent

---

[20] On Scotus, cf. p. 9, n. 2. Capreolus (d. 1444) was a leading late scholastic theologian who strengthened the *via antiqua* of Thomas Aquinas in opposition to the *via moderna* of Duns Scotus.

[21] It may have been Luther's intention to send Spalatin a copy of the proceedings of the debate. Cf. WA, Br. 1, 426.

[22] The Council of Constance (1414-1418) had condemned Huss to death at the stake for heresy in 1415.

[23] This was a clever trick, for the Bohemian followers of Huss had caused Duke George of Saxony much trouble. Furthermore, the University of Leipzig had come into being when the German section withdrew from the University of Prague.

than rash. These accusations tickled the Leipzig audience more than the debate itself.

In rebuttal I brought up the Greek Christians during the past thousand years, and also the ancient church fathers, who had not been under the authority of the Roman pontiff, although I did not deny the primacy of honor due the pope. Finally we also debated the authority of a council. I publicly acknowledged that some articles had been wrongly condemned [by the Council of Constance], articles which had been taught in plain and clear words by Paul, Augustine, and even Christ himself. At this point the adder swelled up, exaggerated my crime, and nearly went insane in his adulation of the Leipzig audience. Then I proved by the words of the council itself that not all the articles which it condemned were actually heretical and erroneous. So Eck's proofs had accomplished nothing. There the matter rested.

The third week Eck and I debated penance, purgatory, indulgences, and the power of a priest to grant absolution, for Eck did not like to debate with Karlstadt and asked me to debate alone with him. The debate over indulgences fell completely flat, for Eck agreed with me in nearly all respects and his former defense of indulgences came to appear like mockery and derision, whereas I had hoped that this would be the main topic of the debate. He finally acknowledged his position in public sermons so than even the common people could see that he was not concerned with indulgences. He also is supposed to have said that if I had not questioned the power of the pope, he would readily have agreed with me in all matters. Then he said to Karlstadt, "If I could agree with Martin in as many points as I do with you, I could be his friend." He is such a fickle and deceitful person that he is ready to do anything. Whereas he conceded to Karlstadt that all the scholastics agreed in their teaching, in debating with me he rejected Gregory of Rimini[24] as one who alone supported my opinion against all other scholastics. Thus he does not seem to consider it wrong to affirm

---

[24] Gregory of Rimini (d. 1358), an Augustinian like Luther, who became a well known nominalist scholastic, teacher at the Sorbonne, and general of the order. With his emphasis upon the theology of Augustine, he had a strong influence upon Luther.

and deny the same thing at different times. The people of Leipzig do not see this, so great is their stupidity. Much more fantastic was the following: He conceded one thing in the disputation hall but taught the people the opposite in church. When confronted by Karlstadt with the reason for his changeableness, the man answered without blinking an eye that it was not necessary to teach the people that which was debatable.

When I had concluded my part of the disputation, Eck debated once more with Karlstadt on new topics during the last three days, again making concessions in all points, agreeing that it is sin to do that which is in one, that free will without grace can do nothing but sin, that there is sin in every good work, and that it is grace itself which enables man to do what is in him in preparing for the reception of grace. All these things the scholastics deny. Therefore virtually nothing was treated in the manner which it deserved except my thirteenth thesis. Meanwhile Eck is pleased with himself, celebrates his victory, and rules the roost; but he will do so only until we have published our side of the debate. Because the debate turned out badly, I shall republish my *Explanations Concerning the Value of Indulgences.*[25]

The citizens of Leipzig neither greeted nor called on us but treated us as though we were their bitterest enemies. Eck, however, they followed around town, clung to, banqueted, entertained, and finally presented with a robe and added a chamois-hair gown. They also rode horseback with him. In short, they did whatever they could to insult us. Furthermore they persuaded Caesar Pflug [the official host] and the prince [Duke George] that this pleased all concerned. One thing they did for us; they honored us, according to custom, with a drink of wine, which it would not have been safe for them to overlook. Those who were well disposed toward us, on the other hand, came to us in secret. Yet Dr. Auerbach, a very fair and just man, and Pistorious the younger, professor in ordinary, invited us. Even Duke George invited the three of us together on one occasion.[26]

---

[25] Cf. above, p. 81.

[26] Dr. Heinrich Stromer of Auerbach (1482-1542), professor of medicine at Leipzig and court physician to Duke George (1471-1539); Simon Pistorious (1497-1562), professor of law at Leipzig.

The most illustrious prince also called me to visit him alone and talked with me at length about my writings, especially my exposition of the Lord's Prayer. He stated that the Bohemians were greatly encouraged by me and also that with my Lord's Prayer I had caused confusion among many conscientious people who complained that they would not be able to pray one Lord's Prayer in four days if they were compelled to listen to me, and much of a similar nature. But I was not so dull that I could not distinguish between the pipe and the piper. I was grieved that such a wise and pious prince was open to the influence of others and followed their opinions, especially when I saw and experienced how like a prince he spoke when he spoke his own thoughts.

The most recent exhibition of hatred was this: When on the day of Peter and Paul [June 29] I was summoned by our lord rector, the duke of Pomerania,[27] to preach a sermon before his grace in the chapel of the castle, the report of this quickly filled the city, and men and women gathered in such numbers that I was compelled to preach in the debating hall, where all our professors and hostile observers had been stationed by invitation. The Gospel for this day [Matt. 16: 13-19] clearly embraces both subjects of the debate, so that I was compelled to explain the content of the entire debate. I got little thanks from the people of Leipzig.

Then Eck, stirred up against me, preached four sermons in different churches,[28] publicly twisting and cutting to pieces what I had said. The would-be theologians had urged him to do this. No further opportunity was given me to preach, however, no matter how many people requested it. I could be accused and incriminated but not cleared. This is the way my enemies also acted in the debate, so that Eck, even though he represented the negative, always had the last word, which I did not have an opportunity to refute.

Finally, when Caesar Pflug heard that I had preached (he had not been present), he said, "I wish that Dr. Martin had saved his

---

[27] Barnim XI (1501-1573) who in 1534 entrusted Johann Bugenhagen, a native of Pomerania and principal co-worker of Luther's, with the responsibility of introducing evangelical Christianity in his territories. Cf. *Allgemeine Deutsche Biographie* (Leipzig, 1875) II, 79ff.

[28] At the time of the writing of this letter Eck had only preached twice. Later Luther corrected this error. Cf. WA Br. 1, 428.

sermon for Wittenberg." In short, I have experienced hatred before, but never more shameless or more impudent.

So here you have the whole tragedy. Dr. Johannes Plawnitzer[29] will tell you the rest, for he himself was also present and helped not a little in preventing the debate from being a complete fiasco. Since Eck and the people of Leipzig sought their own glory and not the truth at the debate, it is no wonder that it began badly and ended worse. Whereas we had hoped for harmony between the people of Wittenberg and Leipzig, they acted so hatefully that I fear that it will seem that discord and dislike were actually born here. This is the fruit of human glory. I, who really restrain my impetuosity, am still not able to dispel all dislike of them, for I am flesh and their hatred was very shameless and their injustice was very malicious in a matter so sacred and divine.

Farewell and commend me to the most illustrious prince.

Your

Martin Luther

Wednesday, July 20, 1519.

I met the honorable Vicar Staupitz in Grimma.

---

[29] Plawnitzer, or Hans von der Planitz (d. 1535), a counsellor of Frederick the Wise's court, had attended the Leipzig Debate. It is he who asked Pflug to request the debaters to refrain from personal abuse.

THE FREEDOM
OF A CHRISTIAN

1520

Translated by W. A. Lambert

Revised by Harold J. Grimm

INTRODUCTION

After the Leipzig Debate Luther returned to Wittenberg, where he resumed his heavy responsibilities and at the same time devoted a large amount of time to study and writing. The list of his publications alone was phenomenal. In addition to writing much devotional literature, often at the request of the elector and his court, he produced sermons, lectures, and polemical tracts. Within six months, in 1520, he published three important Reformation tracts which clarified his new evangelical theology for his ever-increasing following.

In *The Address to the German Nobility*, published August 18, he attacked the authority of the papacy over secular rulers, denied that the pope was the final interpreter of Scripture, assailed the corruption of the Roman Curia, enunciated his important doctrine of the universal priesthood of believers, and called for a drastic reform of the church. In *The Babylonian Captivity of the Church*, published October 6, he attacked the sacramental system of the church by means of which the ecclesiastical hierarchy had gained its control over all Christians. *The Freedom of a Christian*, published early in November, differed from the preceding two pamphlets in that it was written in a conciliatory spirit. Yet it contained a positive and unequivocal statement of Luther's evangelical theology as applied to Christian life. It owed its origin to a final attempt on the part of Miltitz* to prevent a rift in the church.

Despite the fact that Miltitz' first meeting with Luther had failed to end the indulgence controversy, and animosities had been increased by the Leipzig Debate, Miltitz had a second interview with Luther at Liebenwerda on October 9, 1519, at which time the Reformer agreed to present his case before the archbishop of Trier. This also failed. Miltitz did not, however, give up his attempt to counteract the tactics of Eck, even after the Roman Curia had

---

° Cf. above, pp. xvii-xix.

issued the *Exsurge Domine* on June 15, 1520.[†] On August 28 he attended a chapter meeting of the Augustinians at Eisleben where he conferred with Johann von Staupitz, who retired from his office as vicar general at that time, and Wenceslaus Link, his successor. He persuaded these two to visit Luther and- to induce him to write a friendly letter to Leo X, assuring the pope that he had never intended to attack him personally. This they did September 6, and Luther agreed to comply with their wishes. Miltitz, however, wanting to make certain that the letter would be written in the proper spirit, had another interview with Luther on October 12, 1520, this time at Lichtenberg. There Luther agreed to write a conciliatory letter and a devotional booklet to accompany it, and even to date the letter September 6 to indicate that he was not motivated by the publication in Germany of the *Exsurge Domine.*

Luther immediately began writing his open letter to Leo and *The Freedom of a Christian,* both, of course, in Latin. It is not known whether the pope received these two documents. If he did, he must have been shocked by the fact that Luther now wrote him as an equal, offered him advice as though he were the papal father confessor, and expressed his evangelical views without a sign of retraction. Although the tract breathed the spirit of late-medieval mysticism and was favorably commented upon by a number of papal supporters, it makes clear that a believing Christian is free from sin through faith in God, yet bound by love to serve his neighbor.

Soon after the completion of the open letter to Leo and *The Freedom of a Christian,* Luther made a free translation of the latter into German and sent it to Hermann Mühlphordt of Zwickau. Although this German version is the most widely read, the clearer and more complete Latin text given in WA 7, 49-73, and translated into English in PE 2, 312-348, is included in this volume with minor revisions. A recent English translation of the German text in WA 7, 20-38, is given in Bertram Lee Woolf, *Reformation Writings of Martin Luther,* I, 356-379. The open letter to Leo X was published separately in Wittenberg before November 4, 1520. The translation

---

[†] Cf. Carl Mirbt, *Quellen zur Geschichte des Papsttums und des roemischen Katholizimus* (2d ed.; Tübingen and Leipzig, 1901), pp. 183-185.

of it in *PE* 2, 301-311, revised for this volume, was based on the Latin in *WA* 7, 42-49. The most detailed English account of the three important pamphlets of 1520 is that of Mackinnon, *Luther and the Reformation*, II, 222-270.

THE FREEDOM
OF A CHRISTIAN

LETTER OF DEDICATION TO MAYOR MÜHLPHORDT

To the learned and wise gentleman, Hieronymus Mühlphordt,[1] mayor of Zwickau, my exceptionally gracious friend and patron, I, Martin Luther, Augustinian, present my compliments and good wishes.

My learned and wise sir and gracious friend, the venerable Master Johann Egran, your praiseworthy preacher, spoke to me in terms of praise concerning your love for and pleasure in the Holy Scripture, which you also diligently confess and unceasingly praise before all men. For this reason he desired to make me acquainted with you. I yielded willingly and gladly to his persuasion, for it is a special pleasure to hear of someone who loves divine truth. Unfortunately there are many people, especially those who are proud of their titles, who oppose the truth with all their power and cunning. Admittedly it must be that Christ, set as a stumbling block and a sign that is spoken against, will be an offense and a cause for the fall and rising of many [I Cor. 1:23; Luke 2:34].

In order to make a good beginning of our acquaintance and friendship, I have wished to dedicate to you this treatise or discourse in German, which I have already dedicated to the people in Latin, in the hope that my teachings and writings concerning the papacy will not be considered objectionable by anybody. I commend myself to you and to the grace of God. Amen. Wittenberg, 1520.[2]

---

[1] The given name of Mühlphordt was Hermann, not Hieronymus, as Luther has it.

[2] In place of the German version of the treatise which Luther sent to Mühlphordt, the Latin version dedicated to the pope is used as the basis of the English translation in this volume.

AN OPEN LETTER TO POPE LEO X

To Leo X, Pope at Rome, Martin Luther wishes salvation in Christ Jesus our Lord. Amen.

Living among the monsters of this age with whom I am now for the third year waging war, I am compelled occasionally to look up to you, Leo, most blessed father, and to think of you. Indeed, since you are occasionally regarded as the sole cause of my warfare, I cannot help thinking of you. To be sure, the undeserved raging of your godless flatterers against me has compelled me to appeal from your see to a future council, despite the decrees of your predecessors Pius and Julius, who with a foolish tyranny forbade such an appeal. Nevertheless, I have never alienated myself from Your Blessedness to such an extent that I should not with all my heart wish you and your see every blessing, for which I have besought God with earnest prayers to the best of my ability. It is true that I have been so bold as to despise and look down upon those who have tried to frighten me with the majesty of your name and authority. There is one thing, however, which I cannot ignore and which is the cause of my writing once more to Your Blessedness. It has come to my attention that I am accused of great indiscretion, said to be my great fault, in which, it is said, I have not spared even your person.

I freely vow that I have, to my knowledge, spoken only good and honorable words concerning you whenever I have thought of you. If I had ever done otherwise, I myself could by no means condone it, but should agree entirely with the judgment which others have formed of me; and I should do nothing more gladly than recant such indiscretion and impiety. I have called you a Daniel in Babylon; and everyone who reads what I have written knows how zealously I defended your innocence against your defamer Sylvester.[3] Indeed, your reputation and the fame of your blameless life, celebrated as they are throughout the world by the

---

[3] Sylvester Mazzolini (1456-1523), usually called Prierias after Prierio, the city of his birth, had published three books against Luther. In these he had exaggerated the authority of the papacy.

writings of many great men, are too well known and too honorable
to be assailed by anyone, no matter how great he is. I am not so
foolish as to attack one whom all people praise. As a matter of fact,
I have always tried, and will always continue, not to attack even
those whom the public dishonors, for I take no pleasure in the
faults of any man, since I am conscious of the beam in my own
eye. I could not, indeed, be the first one to cast a stone at the
adulteress [John 8:1-11].

I have, to be sure, sharply attacked ungodly doctrines in general, and I have snapped at my opponents, not because of their bad
morals, but because of their ungodliness. Rather than repent this
in the least, I have determined to persist in that fervent zeal and
to despise the judgment of men, following the example of Christ
who in his zeal called his opponents "a brood of vipers," "blind
fools," "hypocrites," "children of the devil" [Matt. 23:13, 17, 33;
John 8:44]. Paul branded Magus [Elymas, the magician] as the
"son of the devil, . . . full of all deceit and villainy" [Acts 13:10],
and he calls others "dogs," "deceivers," and "adulterers" [Phil 3:2;
II Cor. 11:13; 2:17]. If you will allow people with sensitive feelings
to judge, they would consider no person more stinging and unrestrained in his denunciations than Paul. Who is more stinging than
the prophets? Nowadays, it is true, we are made so sensitive by
the raving crowd of flatterers that we cry out that we are stung
as soon as we meet with disapproval. When we cannot ward off
the truth with any other pretext, we flee from it by ascribing it to
a fierce temper, impatience, and immodesty. What is the good of
salt if it does not bite? Of what use is the edge of a sword if it
does not cut? "Cursed is he who does the work of the Lord deceitfully . . ." [Jer. 48:10].

Therefore, most excellent Leo, I beg you to give me a hearing
after I have vindicated myself by this letter, and believe me when
I say that I have never thought ill of you personally, that I am the
kind of a person who would wish you all good things eternally,
and that I have no quarrel with any man concerning his morals
but only concerning the word of truth. In all other matters I will
yield to any man whatsoever; but I have neither the power nor the
will to deny the Word of God. If any man has a different opinion

concerning me, he does not think straight or understand what I have actually said.

I have truly despised your see, the Roman Curia, which, however, neither you nor anyone else can deny is more corrupt than any Babylon or Sodom ever was, and which, as far as I can see, is characterized by a completely depraved, hopeless, and notorious godlessness. I have been thoroughly incensed over the fact that good Christians are mocked in your name and under the cloak of the Roman church I have resisted and will continue to resist your see as long as the spirit of faith lives in me. Not that I shall strive for the impossible or hope that by my efforts alone anything will be accomplished in that most disordered Babylon, where the fury of so many flatterers is turned against me; but I acknowledge my indebtedness to my Christian brethren, whom I am duty-bound to warn so that fewer of them may be destroyed by the plagues of Rome, at least so that their destruction may be less cruel.

As you well know, there has been flowing from Rome these many years—like a flood covering the world—nothing but a devastation of men's bodies and souls and possessions, the worst examples of the worst of all things. All this is clearer than day to all, and the Roman church, once the holiest of all, has become the most licentious den of thieves [Matt. 21:13], the most shameless of all brothels, the kingdom of sin, death, and hell. It is so bad that even Antichrist himself, if he should come, could think of nothing to add to its wickedness.

Meanwhile you, Leo, sit as a lamb in the midst of wolves [Matt. 10:16] and like Daniel in the midst of lions [Dan. 6:16]. With Ezekiel you live among scorpions [Ezek. 2:6]. How can you alone oppose these monsters? Even if you would call to your aid three or four well learned and thoroughly reliable cardinals, what are these among so many? You would all be poisoned[4] before you could begin to issue a decree for the purpose of remedying the situation. The Roman Curia is already lost, for God's wrath has relentlessly fallen upon it. It detests church councils, it fears a reformation, it cannot allay its own corruption; and what was

---

[4] An attempt to poison Leo X had been made in the summer of 1517.

said of its mother Babylon also applies to it: "We would have cured Babylon, but she was not healed. Let us forsake her" [Jer. 51:9].

It was your duty and that of your cardinals to remedy these evils, but the gout of these evils makes a mockery of the healing hand, and neither chariot nor horse responds to the rein [Virgil, *Georgics* i. 514]. Moved by this affection for you, I have always been sorry, most excellent Leo, that you were made pope in these times, for you are worthy of being pope in better days. The Roman Curia does not deserve to have you or men like you, but it should have Satan himself as pope, for he now actually rules in that Babylon more than you do.

Would that you might discard that which your most profligate enemies boastfully claim to be your glory and might live on a small priestly income of your own or on your family inheritance! No persons are worthy of glorying in that honor except the Iscariots, the sons of perdition. What do you accomplish in the Roman Curia, my Leo? The more criminal and detestable a man is, the more gladly will he use your name to destroy men's possessions and souls, to increase crime, to suppress faith and truth and God's whole church. O most unhappy Leo, you are sitting on a most dangerous throne. I am telling you the truth because I wish you well.

If Bernard felt sorry for Eugenius[5] at a time when the Roman See, which, although even then very corrupt, was ruled with better prospects for improvement, why should not we complain who for three hundred years have had such a great increase of corruption and wickedness? Is it not true that under the vast expanse of heaven there is nothing more corrupt, more pestilential, more offensive than the Roman Curia? It surpasses beyond all comparison the godlessness of the Turks so that, indeed, although it was once a gate of heaven, it is now an open mouth of hell, such a mouth that it cannot be shut because of the wrath of God. Only one thing can

---

[5] Bernard of Clairvaux wrote a devotional book, *On Consideration,* to Pope Eugenius III (1145-53), in which he discussed the duties of the pope and the dangers connected with his office. Migne 182, 727-808.

we try to do, as I have said:[6] we may be able to call back a few from that yawning chasm of Rome and save them.

Now you see, my Father Leo, how and why I have so violently attacked that pestilential see. So far have I been from raving against your person that I even hoped I might gain your favor and save you if I should make a strong and stinging assault upon that prison, that veritable hell of yours. For you and your salvation and the salvation of many others with you will be served by everything that men of ability can do against the confusion of this wicked Curia. They serve your office who do every harm to the Curia; they glorify Christ who in every way curse it. In short, they are Christians who are not Romans.

To enlarge upon this, I never intended to attack the Roman Curia or to raise any controversy concerning it. But when I saw all efforts to save it were hopeless, I despised it, gave it a bill of divorce [Deut. 24:1], and said, "Let the evildoer still do evil, and the filthy still be filthy" [Rev. 22:11]. Then I turned to the quiet and peaceful study of the Holy Scriptures so that I might be helpful to my brothers around me. When I had made some progress in these studies, Satan opened his eyes and then filled his servant Johann Eck, a notable enemy of Christ, with an insatiable lust for glory and thus aroused him to drag me unawares to a debate, seizing me by means of one little word which I had let slip concerning the primacy of the Roman church. Then that boastful braggart,[7] frothing and gnashing his teeth, declared that he would risk everything for the glory of God and the honor of the Apostolic See. Puffed up with the prospect of abusing your authority, he looked forward with great confidence to a victory over me. He was concerned not so much with establishing the primacy of Peter as he was with demonstrating his own leadership among the theologians of our time. To that end he considered it no small advantage to triumph over Luther. When the debate ended badly for the sophist, an unbelievable madness overcame the man, for he believed that it was his fault alone which was responsible for my disclosing all the infamy of Rome.

---

[6] Cf. p. 336, par. 1.

[7] Thraso, in the original, is the name of a braggart soldier in Terence's *Eunuch*.

Allow me, I pray, most excellent Leo, this once to plead my cause and to indict your real enemies. You know, I believe, what dealings your legate, cardinal of St. Sisto,[8] an unwise and unfortunate, or rather, an unreliable man, had with me. When out of reverence for your name I had placed myself and my cause in his hands, he did not try to establish peace. He could easily have done so with a single word, for at that time I promised to keep silent and to end the controversy, provided my opponents were ordered to do likewise. As he was a man who sought glory, however, and was not content with such an agreement, he began to defend my opponents, to give them full freedom, and to order me to recant, even though this was not included in his instructions. When matters went fairly well, he with his churlish arbitrariness made them far worse. Therefore Luther is not to blame for what followed. All the blame is Cajetan's, who did not permit me to keep silent, as I at that time most earnestly requested him to do. What more should I have done?

There followed Karl Miltitz,[9] also a nuncio of Your Holiness, who exerted much effort and traveled back and forth, omitting nothing that might help restore the order which Cajetan had rashly and arrogantly disturbed. He finally, with the help of the most illustrious prince, the Elector Frederick, managed to arrange several private conferences with me.[10] Again I yielded out of respect for your name, was prepared to keep silent, and even accepted as arbiter either the archbishop of Trier or the bishop of Naumburg. So matters were arranged. But while this arrangement was being followed with good prospects of success, behold, that other and greater enemy of yours, Eck, broke in with the Leipzig Debate which he had undertaken against Dr. Karlstadt. When the new question of the primacy of the pope was raised, he suddenly turned his weapons against me and completely upset our arrangement for maintaining peace. Meanwhile Karl Miltitz waited. The debate was held and judges were selected. But again no decision was

---

[8] Cardinal Cajetan, cf. p. 264, n. 10.
[9] Karl von Miltitz had induced Luther to be silent with respect to the indulgence controversy, provided his opponents did likewise. Cf. above, p. 310 and p. 329.
[10] At Altenburg on January 5 or 6, 1519.

reached, which is not surprising, for through Eck's lies, tricks, and wiles everything was stirred up, aggravated, and confused worse than ever. Regardless of the decision which might have been reached, a greater conflagration would have resulted, for he sought glory, not the truth. Again I left undone nothing that I ought to have done.

I admit that on this occasion no small amount of corrupt Roman practices came to light, but whatever wrong was done was Eck's fault, who undertook a task beyond his capacities. Striving insanely for his own glory, he revealed the shame of Rome to all the world. This man is your enemy, my dear Leo, or rather the enemy of your Curia. From his example alone we can learn that no enemy is more pernicious than a flatterer. What did he accomplish with his flattery but an evil which not even a king could have accomplished? The name of the Roman Curia is today a stench throughout the world, papal authority languishes, and Roman ignorance, once honored, is in ill repute. We should have heard nothing of all this if Eck had not upset the peace arrangements made by Karl [von Miltitz] and myself. Eck himself now clearly sees this and, although it is too late and to no avail, he is furious that my books were published. He should have thought of this when, like a whinnying horse, he was madly seeking his own glory and preferred his own advantage through you and at the greatest peril to you. The vain man thought that I would stop and keep silent out of fear for your name, for I do not believe that he entirely trusted his cleverness and learning. Now that he sees that I have more courage than that and have not been silenced, he repents of his rashness, but too late, and perceives—if indeed he does finally understand—that there is One in heaven who opposes the proud and humbles the haughty [I Pet. 5:5; Jth. 6:15].

Since we gained nothing from this debate except greater confusion to the Roman cause, Karl Miltitz, in a third attempt to bring about peace, came to the fathers of the Augustinian Order assembled in their chapter and sought their advice in settling the controversy which had now grown most disturbing and dangerous. Because, by God's favor, they had no hope of proceeding against me by violent means, some of their most famous men were sent to me. These men asked me at least to show honor to the person of Your Blessedness and in a humble letter to plead as my excuse your innocence and mine in the matter. They said that the affair was not yet in a hopeless state, provided Leo X out of his innate goodness would take a hand in it. As I have always both offered and desired peace so that I might devote myself to quieter and more useful studies, and have stormed with such great fury merely for the purpose of overwhelming my unequal opponents by the volume and violence of words no less than of intellect, I not only gladly ceased but also joyfully and thankfully considered this suggestion a very welcome kindness to me, provided our hope could be realized.

So I come, most blessed father, and, prostrate before you, pray that if possible you intervene and stop those flatterers, who are the enemies of peace while they pretend to keep peace. But let no person imagine that I will recant unless he prefer to involve the whole question in even greater turmoil. Furthermore, I acknowledge no fixed rules for the interpretation of the Word of God, since the Word of God, which teaches freedom in all other matters, must not be bound [II Tim. 2:9]. If these two points are granted, there is nothing that I could not or would not most willingly do or endure. I detest contentions. I will challenge no one. On the other hand, I do not want others to challenge me. If they do, as Christ is my teacher, I will not be speechless. When once this controversy has been cited before you and settled, Your Blessedness will be able with a brief and ready word to silence both parties and command them to keep the peace. That is what I have always wished to hear.

Therefore, my Father Leo, do not listen to those sirens who pretend that you are no mere man but a demigod so that you may command and require whatever you wish. It will not be done in that manner and you will not have such remarkable power. You are a servant of servants,[11] and more than all other men you are in a most miserable and dangerous position. Be not deceived by those who pretend that you are lord of the world, allow no one

---

[11] *Servus servorum* was the usual title of the pope.

to be considered a Christian unless he accepts your authority, and prate that you have power over heaven, hell, and purgatory. These men are your enemies who seek to destroy your soul [I Kings 19:10], as Isaiah says: "O my people, they that call thee blessed, the same deceive thee" [Isa. 3:12]. They err who exalt you above a council and the church universal. They err who ascribe to you alone the right of interpreting Scripture. Under the protection of your name they seek to gain support for all their wicked deeds in the church. Alas! Through them Satan has already made much progress under your predecessors. In short, believe none who exalt you, believe those who humble you. This is the judgment of God, that ". . . he has put down the mighty from their thrones and exalted those of low degree" [Luke 1:52]. See how different Christ is from his successors, although they all would wish to be his vicars. I fear that most of them have been too literally his vicars. A man is a vicar only when his superior is absent. If the pope rules, while Christ is absent and does not dwell in his heart, what else is he but a vicar of Christ? What is the church under such a vicar but a mass of people without Christ? Indeed, what is such a vicar but an antichrist and an idol? How much more properly did the apostles call themselves servants of the present Christ and not vicars of an absent Christ?

Perhaps I am presumptuous in trying to instruct so exalted a personage from whom we all should learn and from whom the thrones of judges receive their decisions, as those pestilential fellows of yours boast. But I am following the example of St. Bernard in his book, *On Consideration*,[12] to Pope Eugenius, a book every pope should know from memory. I follow him, not because I am eager to instruct you, but out of pure and loyal concern which compels us to be interested in all the affairs of our neighbors, even when they are protected, and which does not permit us to take into consideration either their dignity or lack of dignity since it is only concerned with the dangers they face or the advantages they may gain. I know that Your Blessedness is driven and buffeted about in Rome, that is, that far out at sea you are threatened on all sides

---

[12] Cf. p. 337, n. 5.

by dangers and are working very hard in the miserable situation so that you are in need of even the slightest help of the least of your brothers. Therefore I do not consider it absurd if I now forget your exalted office and do what brotherly love demands. I have no desire to flatter you in so serious and dangerous a matter. If men do not perceive that I am your friend and your most humble subject in this matter, there is One who understands and judges [John 8:50].

Finally, that I may not approach you empty-handed, blessed father, I am sending you this little treatise[13] dedicated to you as a token of peace and good hope. From this book you may judge with what studies I should prefer to be more profitably occupied, as I could be, provided your godless flatterers would permit me and had permitted me in the past. It is a small book if you regard its size. Unless I am mistaken, however, it contains the whole of Christian life in a brief form, provided you grasp its meaning. I am a poor man and have no other gift to offer, and you do not need to be enriched by any but a spiritual gift. May the Lord Jesus preserve you forever. Amen.

Wittenberg, September 6, 1520.

MARTIN LUTHER'S TREATISE ON CHRISTIAN LIBERTY
[THE FREEDOM OF A CHRISTIAN]

Many people have considered Christian faith an easy thing, and not a few have given it a place among the virtues. They do this because they have not experienced it and have never tasted the great strength there is in faith. It is impossible to write well about it or to understand what has been written about it unless one has at one time or another experienced the courage which faith gives a man when trials oppress him. But he who has had even a faint taste of it can never write, speak, meditate, or hear enough concerning it. It is a living "spring of water welling up to eternal life," as Christ calls it in John 4 [:14].

As for me, although I have no wealth of faith to boast of and

---

[13] *The Freedom of a Christian.*

know how scant my supply is, I nevertheless hope that I have attained to a little faith, even though I have been assailed by great and various temptations; and I hope that I can discuss it, if not more elegantly, certainly more to the point, than those literalists and subtile disputants have previously done, who have not even understood what they have written.

To make the way smoother for the unlearned—for only them do I serve—I shall set down the following two propositions concerning the freedom and the bondage of the spirit:

A Christian is a perfectly free lord of all, subject to none.

A Christian is a perfectly dutiful servant of all, subject to all.

These two theses seem to contradict each other. If, however, they should be found to fit together they would serve our purpose beautifully. Both are Paul's own statements, who says in I Cor. 9 [:19], "For though I am free from all men, I have made myself a slave to all," and in Rom. 13 [:8], "Owe no one anything, except to love one another." Love by its very nature is ready to serve and be subject to him who is loved. So Christ, although he was Lord of all, was "born of woman, born under the law" [Gal. 4:4], and therefore was at the same time a free man and a servant, "in the form of God" and "of a servant" [Phil. 2:6-7].

Let us start, however, with something more remote from our subject, but more obvious. Man has a twofold nature, a spiritual and a bodily one. According to the spiritual nature, which men refer to as the soul, he is called a spiritual, inner, or new man. According to the bodily nature, which men refer to as flesh, he is called a carnal, outward, or old man, of whom the Apostle writes in II Cor. 4 [:16], "Though our outer nature is wasting away, our inner nature is being renewed every day." Because of this diversity of nature the Scriptures assert contradictory things concerning the same man, since these two men in the same man contradict each other, "for the desires of the flesh are against the Spirit, and the desires of the Spirit are against the flesh," according to Gal. 5 [:17].

First, let us consider the inner man to see how a righteous, free, and pious Christian, that is, a spiritual, new, and inner man, becomes what he is. It is evident that no external thing has any influence in producing Christian righteousness or freedom, or in producing unrighteousness or servitude. A simple argument will furnish the proof of this statement. What can it profit the soul if the body is well, free, and active, and eats, drinks, and does as it pleases? For in these respects even the most godless slaves of vice may prosper. On the other hand, how will poor health or imprisonment or hunger or thirst or any other external misfortune harm the soul? Even the most godly men, and those who are free because of clear consciences, are afflicted with these things. None of these things touch either the freedom or the servitude of the soul. It does not help the soul if the body is adorned with the sacred robes of priests or dwells in sacred places or is occupied with sacred duties or prays, fasts, abstains from certain kinds of food, or does any work that can be done by the body and in the body. The righteousness and the freedom of the soul require something far different since the things which have been mentioned could be done by any wicked person. Such works produce nothing but hypocrites. On the other hand, it will not harm the soul if the body is clothed in secular dress, dwells in unconsecrated places, eats and drinks as others do, does not pray aloud, and neglects to do all the above-mentioned things which hypocrites can do.

Furthermore, to put aside all kinds of works, even contemplation, meditation, and all that the soul can do, does not help. One thing, and only one thing, is necessary for Christian life, righteousness, and freedom. That one thing is the most holy Word of God, the gospel of Christ, as Christ says, John 11 [:25], "I am the resurrection and the life; he who believes in me, though he die, yet shall he live"; and John 8 [:36], "So if the Son makes you free, you will be free indeed"; and Matt. 4 [:4], "Man shall not live by bread alone, but by every word that proceeds from the mouth of God." Let us then consider it certain and firmly established that the soul can do without anything except the Word of God and that where the Word of God is missing there is no help at all for the soul. If it has the Word of God it is rich and lacks nothing since it is the Word of life, truth, light, peace, righteousness, salvation, joy, liberty, wisdom, power, grace, glory, and of every incalculable blessing. This is why the prophet in the entire Psalm [119] and in many other places yearns and sighs for the Word of God and uses so many names to describe it.

On the other hand, there is no more terrible disaster with which the wrath of God can afflict men than a famine of the hearing of his Word, as he says in Amos [8:11]. Likewise there is no greater mercy than when he sends forth his Word, as we read in Psalm 107 [:20]: "He sent forth his word, and healed them, and delivered them from destruction." Nor was Christ sent into the world for any other ministry except that of the Word. Moreover, the entire spiritual estate—all the apostles, bishops, and priests—has been called and instituted only for the ministry of the Word.

You may ask, "What then is the Word of God, and how shall it be used, since there are so many words of God?" I answer: The Apostle explains this in Romans 1. The Word is the gospel of God concerning his Son, who was made flesh, suffered, rose from the dead, and was glorified through the Spirit who sanctifies. To preach Christ means to feed the soul, make it righteous, set it free, and save it, provided it believes the preaching. Faith alone is the saving and efficacious use of the Word of God, according to Rom. 10 [:9]: "If you confess with your lips that Jesus is Lord and believe in your heart that God raised him from the dead, you will be saved." Furthermore, "Christ is the end of the law, that every one who has faith may be justified" [Rom. 10:4]. Again, in Rom. 1 [:17], "He who through faith is righteous shall live." The Word of God cannot be received and cherished by any works whatever but only by faith. Therefore it is clear that, as the soul needs only the Word of God for its life and righteousness, so it is justified by faith alone and not any works; for if it could be justified by anything else, it would not need the Word, and consequently it would not need faith.

This faith cannot exist in connection with works—that is to say, if you at the same time claim to be justified by works, whatever their character—for that would be the same as "limping with two different opinions" [I Kings 18:21], as worshiping Baal and kissing one's own hand [Job 31:27-28], which, as Job says, is a very great iniquity. Therefore the moment you begin to have faith you learn that all things in you are altogether blameworthy, sinful, and damnable, as the Apostle says in Rom. 3 [:23], "Since all have sinned and fall short of the glory of God," and, "None is righteous, no, not one; . . . all have turned aside, together they have gone wrong" (Rom. 3:10-12). When you have learned this you will know that you need Christ, who suffered and rose again for you so that, if you believe in him, you may through this faith become a new man in so far as your sins are forgiven and you are justified by the merits of another, namely, of Christ alone.

Since, therefore, this faith can rule only in the inner man, as Rom. 10 [:10] says, "For man believes with his heart and so is justified," and since faith alone justifies, it is clear that the inner man cannot be justified, freed, or saved by any outer work or action at all, and that these works, whatever their character, have nothing to do with this inner man. On the other hand, only ungodliness and unbelief of heart, and no outer work, make him guilty and a damnable servant of sin. Wherefore it ought to be the first concern of every Christian to lay aside all confidence in works and increasingly to strengthen faith alone and through faith to grow in the knowledge, not of works, but of Christ Jesus, who suffered and rose for him, as Peter teaches in the last chapter of his first Epistle (I Pet. 5:10). No other work makes a Christian. Thus when the Jews asked Christ, as related in John 6 [:28], what they must do "to be doing the work of God," he brushed aside the multitude of works which he saw they did in great profusion and suggested one work, saying, "This is the work of God, that you believe in him whom he has sent" [John 6:29]; "for on him has God the Father set his seal" [John 6:27].

Therefore true faith in Christ is a treasure beyond comparison which brings with it complete salvation and saves man from every evil, as Christ says in the last chapter of Mark [16:16]: "He who believes and is baptized will be saved; but he who does not believe will be condemned." Isaiah contemplated this treasure and foretold it in chapter 10: "The Lord will make a small and consuming word upon the land, and it will overflow with righteousness" [Cf. Isa. 10:22]. This is as though he said, "Faith, which is a small and perfect fulfilment of the law, will fill believers with so great a righteousness that they will need nothing more to become righteous." So Paul says, Rom. 10 [:10], "For man believes with his heart and so is justified."

Should you ask how it happens that faith alone justifies and offers us such a treasure of great benefits without works in view of the fact that so many works, ceremonies, and laws are prescribed in the Scriptures, I answer: First of all, remember what has been said, namely, that faith alone, without works, justifies, frees, and saves; we shall make this clearer later on. Here we must point out that the entire Scripture of God is divided into two parts: commandments and promises. Although the commandments teach things that are good, the things taught are not done as soon as they are taught, for the commandments show us what we ought to do but do not give us the power to do it. They are intended to teach man to know himself, that through them he may recognize his inability to do good and may despair of his own ability. That is why they are called the Old Testament and constitute the Old Testament. For example, the commandment, "You shall not covet" [Exod. 20:17], is a command which proves us all to be sinners, for no one can avoid coveting no matter how much he may struggle against it. Therefore, in order not to covet and to fulfil the commandment, a man is compelled to despair of himself, to seek the help which he does not find in himself elsewhere and from someone else, as stated in Hosea [13:9]: "Destruction is your own, O Israel: your help is only in me." As we fare with respect to one commandment, so we fare with all, for it is equally impossible for us to keep any one of them.

Now when a man has learned through the commandments to recognize his helplessness and is distressed about how he might satisfy the law—since the law must be fulfilled so that not a jot or tittle shall be lost, otherwise man will be condemned without hope—then, being truly humbled and reduced to nothing in his own eyes, he finds in himself nothing whereby he may be justified and saved. Here the second part of Scripture comes to our aid, namely, the promises of God which declare the glory of God, saying, "If you wish to fulfil the law and not covet, as the law demands, come, believe in Christ in whom grace, righteousness, peace, liberty, and all things are promised you. If you believe, you shall have all

348

things; if you do not believe, you shall lack all things." That which is impossible for you to accomplish by trying to fulfil all the works of the law—many and useless as they all are—you will accomplish quickly and easily through faith. God our Father has made all things depend on faith so that whoever has faith will have everything, and whoever does not have faith will have nothing. "For God has consigned all men to disobedience, that he may have mercy upon all," as it is stated in Rom. 11 [:32]. Thus the promises of God give what the commandments of God demand and fulfil what the law prescribes so that all things may be God's alone, both the commandments and the fulfilling of the commandments. He alone commands, he alone fulfils. Therefore the promises of God belong to the New Testament. Indeed, they are the New Testament.

Since these promises of God are holy, true, righteous, free, and peaceful words, full of goodness, the soul which clings to them with a firm faith will be so closely united with them and altogether absorbed by them that it not only will share in all their power but will be saturated and intoxicated by them. If a touch of Christ healed, how much more will this most tender spiritual touch, this absorbing of the Word, communicate to the soul all things that belong to the Word. This, then, is how through faith alone without works the soul is justified by the Word of God, sanctified, made true, peaceful, and free, filled with every blessing and truly made a child of God, as John 1 [:12] says: "But to all who . . . believed in his name, he gave power to become children of God."

From what has been said it is easy to see from what source faith derives such great power and why a good work or all good works together cannot equal it. No good work can rely upon the Word of God or live in the soul, for faith alone and the Word of God rule in the soul. Just as the heated iron glows like fire because of the union of fire with it, so the Word imparts its qualities to the soul. It is clear, then, that a Christian has all that he needs in faith and needs no works to justify him; and if he has no need of works, he has no need of the law; and if he has no need of the law, surely he is free from the law. It is true that "the law is not laid down for the just" [I Tim. 1:9]. This is that Christian liberty, our faith, which does not induce us to live in idleness or wickedness but makes the law and works unnecessary for any man's righteousness and salvation.

This is the first power of faith. Let us now examine also the second. It is a further function of faith that it honors him whom it trusts with the most reverent and highest regard since it considers him truthful and trustworthy. There is no other honor equal to the estimate of truthfulness and righteousness with which we honor him whom we trust. Could we ascribe to a man anything greater than truthfulness and righteousness and perfect goodness? On the other hand, there is no way in which we can show greater contempt for a man than to regard him as false and wicked and to be suspicious of him, as we do when we do not trust him. So when the soul firmly trusts God's promises, it regards him as truthful and righteous. Nothing more excellent than this can be ascribed to God. The very highest worship of God is this that we ascribe to him truthfulness, righteousness, and whatever else should be ascribed to one who is trusted. When this is done, the soul consents to his will. Then it hallows his name and allows itself to be treated according to God's good pleasure for, clinging to God's promises, it does not doubt that he who is true, just, and wise will do, dispose, and provide all things well.

Is not such a soul most obedient to God in all things by this faith? What commandment is there that such obedience has not completely fulfilled? What more complete fulfilment is there than obedience in all things? This obedience, however, is not rendered by works, but by faith alone. On the other hand, what greater rebellion against God, what greater wickedness, what greater contempt of God is there than not believing his promise? For what is this but to make God a liar or to doubt that he is truthful?—that is, to ascribe truthfulness to one's self but lying and vanity to God? Does not a man who does this deny God and set himself up as an idol in his heart? Then of what good are works done in such wickedness, even if they were the works of angels and apostles? Therefore God has rightly included all things, not under anger or lust, but under unbelief, so that they who imagine that they are fulfilling the law by doing the works of chastity and mercy required by the law (the civil and human virtues) might not be saved. They are included under the sin of unbelief and must either seek mercy or be justly condemned.

When, however, God sees that we consider him truthful and by the faith of our heart pay him the great honor which is due him, he does us that great honor of considering us truthful and righteous for the sake of our faith. Faith works truth and righteousness by giving God what belongs to him. Therefore God in turn glorifies our righteousness. It is true and just that God is truthful and just, and to consider and confess him to be so is the same as being truthful and just. Accordingly he says in I Sam. 2 [:30], "Those who honor me I will honor, and those who despise me shall be lightly esteemed." So Paul says in Rom. 4 [:3] that Abraham's faith "was reckoned to him as righteousness" because by it he gave glory most perfectly to God, and that for the same reason our faith shall be reckoned to us as righteousness if we believe.

The third incomparable benefit of faith is that it unites the soul with Christ as a bride is united with her bridegroom. By this mystery, as the Apostle teaches, Christ and the soul become one flesh [Eph. 5:31-32]. And if they are one flesh and there is between them a true marriage—indeed the most perfect of all marriages, since human marriages are but poor examples of this one true marriage—it follows that everything they have they hold in common, the good as well as the evil. Accordingly the believing soul can boast of and glory in whatever Christ has as though it were its own, and whatever the soul has Christ claims as his own. Let us compare these and we shall see inestimable benefits. Christ is full of grace, life, and salvation. The soul is full of sins, death, and damnation. Now let faith come between them and sins, death, and damnation will be Christ's, while grace, life, and salvation will be the soul's; for if Christ is a bridegroom, he must take upon himself the things which are his bride's and bestow upon her the things that are his. If he gives her his body and very self, how shall he not give her all that is his? And if he takes the body of the bride, how shall he not take all that is hers?

Here we have a most pleasing vision not only of communion but of a blessed struggle and victory and salvation and redemption. Christ is God and man in one person. He has neither sinned nor

351

died, and is not condemned, and he cannot sin, die, or be condemned; his righteousness, life, and salvation are unconquerable, eternal, omnipotent. By the wedding ring of faith he shares in the sins, death, and pains of hell which are his bride's. As a matter of fact, he makes them his own and acts as if they were his own and as if he himself had sinned; he suffered, died, and descended into hell that he might overcome them all. Now since it was such a one who did all this, and death and hell could not swallow him up, these were necessarily swallowed up by him in a mighty duel; for his righteousness is greater than the sins of all men, his life stronger than death, his salvation more invincible than hell. Thus the believing soul by means of the pledge of its faith is free in Christ, its bridegroom, free from all sins, secure against death and hell, and is endowed with the eternal righteousness, life, and salvation of Christ its bridegroom. So he takes to himself a glorious bride, "without spot or wrinkle, cleansing her by the washing of water with the word" [Cf. Eph. 5:26-27] of life, that is, by faith in the Word of life, righteousness, and salvation. In this way he marries her in faith, steadfast love, and in mercies, righteousness, and justice, as Hos. 2 [:19-20] says.

Who then can fully appreciate what this royal marriage means? Who can understand the riches of the glory of this grace? Here this rich and divine bridegroom Christ marries this poor, wicked harlot, redeems her from all her evil, and adorns her with all his goodness. Her sins cannot now destroy her, since they are laid upon Christ and swallowed up by him. And she has that righteousness in Christ, her husband, of which she may boast as of her own and which she can confidently display alongside her sins in the face of death and hell and say, "If I have sinned, yet my Christ, in whom I believe, has not sinned, and all his is mine and all mine is his," as the bride in the Song of Solomon [2:16] says, "My beloved is mine and I am his." This is what Paul means when he says in I Cor. 15 [:57], "Thanks be to God, who gives us the victory through our Lord Jesus Christ," that is, the victory over sin and death, as he also says there, "The sting of death is sin, and the power of sin is the law" [I Cor. 15:56].

From this you once more see that much is ascribed to faith,

352

namely, that it alone can fulfil the law and justify without works. You see that the First Commandment, which says, "You shall worship one God," is fulfilled by faith alone. Though you were nothing but good works from the soles of your feet to the crown of your head, you would still not be righteous or worship God or fulfil the First Commandment, since God cannot be worshiped unless you ascribe to him the glory of truthfulness and all goodness which is due him. This cannot be done by works but only by the faith of the heart. Not by the doing of works but by believing do we glorify God and acknowledge that he is truthful. Therefore faith alone is the righteousness of a Christian and the fulfilling of all the commandments, for he who fulfils the First Commandment has no difficulty in fulfilling all the rest.

But works, being inanimate things, cannot glorify God, although they can, if faith is present, be done to the glory of God. Here, however, we are not inquiring what works and what kind of works are done, but who it is that does them, who glorifies God and brings forth the works. This is done by faith which dwells in the heart and is the source and substance of all our righteousness. Therefore it is a blind and dangerous doctrine which teaches that the commandments must be fulfilled by works. The commandments must be fulfilled before any works can be done, and the works proceed from the fulfilment of the commandments [Rom. 13:10], as we shall hear.

That we may examine more profoundly that grace which our inner man has in Christ, we must realize that in the Old Testament God consecrated to himself all the first-born males. The birthright was highly prized for it involved a twofold honor, that of priesthood and that of kingship. The first-born brother was priest and lord over all the others and a type of Christ, the true and only first-born of God the Father and the Virgin Mary and true king and priest, but not after the fashion of the flesh and the world, for his kingdom is not of this world [John 18:36]. He reigns in heavenly and spiritual things and consecrates them—things such as righteousness, truth, wisdom, peace, salvation, etc. This does not mean that all things on earth and in hell are not also subject to him—otherwise how could he protect and save us from them?

353

—but that his kingdom consists neither in them nor of them. Nor does his priesthood consist in the outer splendor of robes and postures like those of the human priesthood of Aaron and our present-day church; but it consists of spiritual things through which he by an invisible service intercedes for us in heaven before God, there offers himself as a sacrifice, and does all things a priest should do, as Paul describes him under the type of Melchizedek in the Epistle to the Hebrews [Heb. 6-7]. Nor does he only pray and intercede for us but he teaches us inwardly through the living instruction of his Spirit, thus performing the two real functions of a priest, of which the prayers and the preaching of human priests are visible types.

Now just as Christ by his birthright obtained these two prerogatives, so he imparts them to and shares them with everyone who believes in him according to the law of the above-mentioned marriage, according to which the wife owns whatever belongs to the husband. Hence all of us who believe in Christ are priests and kings in Christ, as I Pet. 2 [:9] says: "You are a chosen race, God's own people, a royal priesthood, a priestly kingdom, that you may declare the wonderful deeds of him who called you out of darkness into his marvelous light."

The nature of this priesthood and kingship is something like this: First, with respect to the kingship, every Christian is by faith so exalted above all things that, by virtue of a spiritual power, he is lord of all things without exception, so that nothing can do him any harm. As a matter of fact, all things are made subject to him and are compelled to serve him in obtaining salvation. Accordingly Paul says in Rom. 8 [:28], "All things work together for good for the elect," and in I Cor. 3 [:21-23], "All things are yours whether ... life or death or the present or the future, all are yours; and you are Christ's. . . ." This is not to say that every Christian is placed over all things to have and control them by physical power—a madness with which some churchmen are afflicted—for such power belongs to kings, princes, and other men on earth. Our ordinary experience in life shows us that we are subjected to all, suffer many things, and even die. As a matter of fact, the more Christian a man is, the more evils, sufferings, and deaths he must endure, as we see in

Christ the first-born prince himself, and in all his brethren, the saints. The power of which we speak is spirtual. It rules in the midst of enemies and is powerful in the midst of oppression. This means nothing else than that "power is made perfect in weakness" [II Cor. 12:9] and that in all things I can find profit toward salvation [Rom. 8:28], so that the cross and death itself are compelled to serve me and to work together with me for my salvation. This is a splendid privilege and hard to attain, a truly omnipotent power, a spiritual dominion in which there is nothing so good and nothing so evil but that it shall work together for good to me, if only I believe. Yes, since faith alone suffices for salvation, I need nothing except faith exercising the power and dominion of its own liberty. Lo, this is the inestimable power and liberty of Christians.

Not only are we the freest of kings, we are also priests forever, which is far more excellent than being kings, for as priests we are worthy to appear before God to pray for others and to teach one another divine things. These are the functions of priests, and they cannot be granted to any unbeliever. Thus Christ has made it possible for us, provided we believe in him, to be not only his brethren, co-heirs, and fellow-kings, but also his fellow-priests. Therefore we may boldly come into the presence of God in the spirit of faith [Heb. 10:19, 22] and cry "Abba, Father!" pray for one another, and do all things which we see done and foreshadowed in the outer and visible works of priests.

He, however, who does not believe is not served by anything. On the contrary, nothing works for his good, but he himself is a servant of all, and all things turn out badly for him because he wickedly uses them to his own advantage and not to the glory of God. So he is no priest but a wicked man whose prayer becomes sin and who never comes into the presence of God because God does not hear sinners [John 9:31]. Who then can comprehend the lofty dignity of the Christian? By virtue of his royal power he rules over all things, death, life, and sin, and through his priestly glory is omnipotent with God because he does the things which God asks and desires, as it is written, "He will fulfil the desire of those who fear him; he also will hear their cry and save them" [Cf.

Phil. 4:13]. To this glory a man attains, certainly not by any works of his, but by faith alone.

From this anyone can clearly see how a Christian is free from all things and over all things so that he needs no works to make him righteous and save him, since faith alone abundantly confers all these things. Should he grow so foolish, however, as to presume to become righteous, free, saved, and a Christian by means of some good work, he would instantly lose faith and all its benefits, a foolishness aptly illustrated in the fable of the dog who runs along a stream with a piece of meat in his mouth and, deceived by the reflection of the meat in the water, opens his mouth to snap at it and so loses both the meat and the reflection.[14]

You will ask, "If all who are in the church are priests, how do these whom we now call priests differ from laymen?" I answer: Injustice is done those words "priest," "cleric," "spiritual," "ecclesiastic," when they are transferred from all Christians to those few who are now by a mischievous usage called "ecclesiastics." Holy Scripture makes no distinction between them, although it gives the name "ministers," "servants," "stewards" to those who are now proudly called popes, bishops, and lords and who should according to the ministry of the Word serve others and teach them the faith of Christ and the freedom of believers. Although we are all equally priests, we cannot all publicly minister and teach. We ought not do so even if we could. Paul writes accordingly in I Cor. 4 [1], "This is how one should regard us, as servants of Christ and stewards of the mysteries of God."

That stewardship, however, has now been developed into so great a display of power and so terrible a tyranny that no heathen empire or other earthly power can be compared with it, just as if laymen were not also Christians. Through this perversion the knowledge of Christian grace, faith, liberty, and of Christ himself has altogether perished, and its place has been taken by an unbearable bondage of human works and laws until we have become, as the Lamentations of Jeremiah [1] say, servants of the vilest men on earth who abuse our misfortune to serve only their base and shameless will.

---

[14] Luther was fond of Aesop's Fables, of which this is one.

To return to our purpose, I believe that it has now become clear that it is not enough or in any sense Christian to preach the works, life, and words of Christ as historical facts, as if the knowledge of these would suffice for the conduct of life; yet this is the fashion among those who must today be regarded as our best preachers. Far less is it sufficient or Christian to say nothing at all about Christ and to teach instead the laws of men and the decrees of the fathers. Now there are not a few who preach Christ and read about him that they may move men's affections to sympathy with Christ, to anger against the Jews, and such childish and effeminate nonsense. Rather ought Christ to be preached to the end that faith in him may be established that he may not only be Christ, but be Christ for you and me, and that what is said of him and is denoted in his name may be effectual in us. Such faith is produced and preserved in us by preaching why Christ came, what he brought and bestowed, what benefit it is to us to accept him. This is done when that Christian liberty which he bestows is rightly taught and we are told in what way we Christians are all kings and priests and therefore lords of all and may firmly believe that whatever we have done is pleasing and acceptable in the sight of God, as I have already said.

What man is there whose heart, upon hearing these things, will not rejoice to its depth, and when receiving such comfort will not grow tender so that he will love Christ as he never could by means of any laws or works? Who would have the power to harm or frighten such a heart? If the knowledge of sin or the fear of death should break in upon it, it is ready to hope in the Lord. It does not grow afraid when it hears tidings of evil. It is not disturbed when it sees its enemies. This is so because it believes that the righteousness of Christ is its own and that its sin is not its own, but Christ's, and that all sin is swallowed up by the righteousness of Christ. This, as has been said above,[15] is a necessary consequence on account of faith in Christ. So the heart learns to scoff at death and sin and to say with the Apostle, "O death, where is thy victory? O death, where is thy sting? The sting of death is sin, and the power of sin is the law. But thanks be to God, who gives us the

---

[15] Cf. p. 352.

victory through our Lord Jesus Christ" [I Cor. 15:55-57]. Death is swallowed up not only in the victory of Christ but also by our victory, because through faith his victory has become ours and in that faith we also are conquerors.

Let this suffice concerning the inner man, his liberty, and the source of his liberty, the righteousness of faith. He needs neither laws nor good works but, on the contrary, is injured by them if he believes that he is justified by them.

Now let us turn to the second part, the outer man. Here we shall answer all those who, offended by the word "faith" and by all that has been said, now ask, "If faith does all things and is alone sufficient unto righteousness, why then are good works commanded? We will take our ease and do no works and be content with faith." I answer: not so, you wicked men, not so. That would indeed be proper if we were wholly inner and perfectly spiritual men. But such we shall be only at the last day, the day of the resurrection of the dead. As long as we live in the flesh we only begin to make some progress in that which shall be perfected in the future life. For this reason the Apostle in Rom. 8 [:23] calls all that we attain in this life "the first fruits of the Spirit" because we shall indeed receive the greater portion, even the fulness of the Spirit, in the future. This is the place to assert that which was said above, namely, that a Christian is the servant of all and made subject to all. Insofar as he is free he does no works, but insofar as he is a servant he does all kinds of works. How this is possible we shall see.

Although, as I have said, a man is abundantly and sufficiently justified by faith inwardly, in his spirit, and so has all that he needs, except insofar as this faith and these riches must grow from day to day even to the future life; yet he remains in this mortal life on earth. In this life he must control his own body and have dealings with men. Here the works begin; here a man cannot enjoy leisure; here he must indeed take care to discipline his body by fastings, watchings, labors, and other reasonable discipline and to subject it to the Spirit so that it will obey and conform to the inner man and faith and not revolt against faith and hinder the inner man, as it is the nature of the body to do if it is not held in check. The inner man, who by faith is created in the image of God, is both joyful and happy because of Christ in whom so many benefits are conferred upon him; and therefore it is his one occupation to serve God joyfully and without thought of gain, in love that is not constrained.

While he is doing this, behold, he meets a contrary will in his own flesh which strives to serve the world and seeks its own advantage. This the spirit of faith cannot tolerate, but with joyful zeal it attempts to put the body under control and hold it in check, as Paul says in Rom. 7 [:22-23], "For I delight in the law of God, in my inmost self, but I see in my members another law at war with the law of my mind and making me captive to the law of sin," and in another place, "But I pommel my body and subdue it, lest after preaching to others I myself should be disqualified" [I Cor. 9:27], and in Galatians [5:24], "And those who belong to Christ Jesus have crucified the flesh with its passions and desires."

In doing these works, however, we must not think that a man is justified before God by them, for faith, which alone is righteousness before God, cannot endure that erroneous opinion. We must, however, realize that these works reduce the body to subjection and purify it of its evil lusts, and our whole purpose is to be directed only toward the driving out of lusts. Since by faith the soul is cleansed and made to love God, it desires that all things, and especially its own body, shall be purified so that all things may join with it in loving and praising God. Hence a man cannot be idle, for the need of his body drives him and he is compelled to do many good works to reduce it to subjection. Nevertheless the works themselves do not justify him before God, but he does the works out of spontaneous love in obedience to God and considers nothing except the approval of God, whom he would most scrupulously obey in all things.

In this way everyone will easily be able to learn for himself the limit and discretion, as they say, of his bodily castigations, for he will fast, watch, and labor as much as he finds sufficient to repress the lasciviousness and lust of his body. But those who presume to be justified by works do not regard the mortifying of the lusts, but only the works themselves, and think that if only they have done as many and as great works as are possible, they have done well and have become righteous. At times they even addle their brains and destroy, or at least render useless, their natural strength with their works. This is the height of folly and utter ignorance of Christian life and faith, that a man should seek to be justified and saved by works and without faith.

In order to make that which we have said more easily understood, we shall explain by analogies. We should think of the works of a Christian who is justified and saved by faith because of the pure and free mercy of God, just as we would think of the works which Adam and Eve did in Paradise, and all their children would have done if they had not sinned. We read in Gen. 2 [:15] that "The Lord God took the man and put him in the garden of Eden to till it and keep it." Now Adam was created righteous and upright and without sin by God so that he had no need of being justified and made upright through his tilling and keeping the garden; but, that he might not be idle, the Lord gave him a task to do, to cultivate and protect the garden. This task would truly have been the freest of works, done only to please God and not to obtain righteousness, which Adam already had in full measure and which would have been the birthright of us all.

The works of a believer are like this. Through his faith he has been restored to Paradise and created anew, has no need of works that he may become or be righteous; but that he may not be idle and may provide for and keep his body, he must do such works freely only to please God. Since, however, we are not wholly recreated, and our faith and love are not yet perfect, these are to be increased, not by external works, however, but of themselves.

A second example: A bishop, when he consecrates a church, confirms children, or performs some other duty belonging to his office, is not made a bishop by these works. Indeed, if he had not first been made a bishop, none of these works would be valid. They would be foolish, childish, and farcical. So the Christian who is consecrated by his faith does good works, but the works do not make him holier or more Christian, for that is the work of faith alone. And if a man were not first a believer and a Christian, all his works would amount to nothing and would be truly wicked and damnable sins.

The following statements are therefore true: "Good works do not make a good man, but a good man does good works; evil works do not make a wicked man, but a wicked man does evil works." Consequently it is always necessary that the substance or person himself be good before there can be any good works, and that good works follow and proceed from the good person, as Christ also says, "A good tree cannot bear evil fruit, nor can a bad tree bear good fruit" [Matt. 7:18]. It is clear that the fruits do not bear the tree and that the tree does not grow on the fruits, also that, on the contrary, the trees bear the fruits and the fruits grow on the trees. As it is necessary, therefore, that the trees exist before their fruits and the fruits do not make trees either good or bad, but rather as the trees are, so are the fruits they bear; so a man must first be good or wicked before he does a good or wicked work, and his works do not make him good or wicked, but he himself makes his works either good or wicked.

Illustrations of the same truth can be seen in all trades. A good or a bad house does not make a good or a bad builder; but a good or a bad builder makes a good or a bad house. And in general, the work never makes the workman like itself, but the workman makes the work like himself. So it is with the works of man. As the man is, whether believer or unbeliever, so also is his work —good if it was done in faith, wicked if it was done in unbelief. But the converse is not true, that the work makes the man either a believer or an unbeliever. As works do not make a man a believer, so also they do not make him righteous. But as faith makes a man a believer and righteous, so faith does good works. Since, then, works justify no one, and a man must be righteous before he does a good work, it is very evident that it is faith alone which, because of the pure mercy of God through Christ and in his Word, worthily and sufficiently justifies and saves the person. A Christian has no need of any work or law in order to be saved since through faith he is free from every law and does everything out of pure liberty and freely. He seeks neither benefit nor salvation since he already abounds in all things and is saved through the grace of God because in his faith he now seeks only to please God.

Furthermore, no good work helps justify or save an unbeliever. On the other hand, no evil work makes him wicked or damns him; but the unbelief which makes the person and the tree evil does the evil and damnable works. Hence when a man is good or evil, this is effected not by the works, but by faith or unbelief, as the Wise Man says, "This is the beginning of sin, that a man falls away from God" [Cf. Sirach 10:14-15], which happens when he does not believe. And Paul says in Heb. 11 [:6], "For whoever would draw near to God must believe. . . ." And Christ says the same: "Either make the tree good, and its fruit good; or make the tree bad, and its fruit bad" [Matt. 12:33], as if he would say, "Let him who wishes to have good fruit begin by planting a good tree." So let him who wishes to do good works begin not with the doing of works, but with believing, which makes the person good, for nothing makes a man good except faith, or evil except unbelief.

It is indeed true that in the sight of men a man is made good or evil by his works; but this being made good or evil only means that the man who is good or evil is pointed out and known as such, as Christ says in Matt. 7 [:20], "Thus you will know them by their fruits." All this remains on the surface, however, and very many have been deceived by this outward appearance and have presumed to write and teach concerning good works by which we may be justified without even mentioning faith. They go their way, always being deceived and deceiving [II Tim. 3:13], progressing, indeed, but into a worse state, blind leaders of the blind, wearying themselves with many works and still never attaining to true righteousness [Matt. 15:14]. Of such people Paul says in II Tim. 3 [5, 7], "Holding the form of religion but denying the power of it . . . who will listen to anybody and can never arrive at a knowledge of the truth."

Whoever, therefore, does not wish to go astray with those blind men must look beyond works, and beyond laws and doctrines about works. Turning his eyes from works, he must look upon the person and ask how he is justified. For the person is justified and saved, not by works or laws, but by the Word of God, that is, by the promise of his grace, and by faith, that the glory may remain God's, who saved us not by works of righteousness which we have done [Titus 3:5], but by virtue of his mercy by the word of his grace when we believed [I Cor. 1:21].

From this it is easy to know how far good works are to be rejected or not, and by what standard all the teachings of men concerning works are to be interpreted. If works are sought after as a means to righteousness, are burdened with this perverse leviathan,[16] and are done under the false impression that through them one is justified, they are made necessary and freedom and faith are destroyed; and this addition to them makes them no longer good but truly damnable works. They are not free, and they blaspheme the grace of God since to justify and to save by faith belongs to the grace of God alone. What the works have no power to do they nevertheless—by a godless presumption through this folly of ours—pretend to do and thus violently force themselves into the office and glory of grace. We do not, therefore, reject good works; on the contrary, we cherish and teach them as much as possible. We do not condemn them for their own sake but on account of this godless addition to them and the perverse idea that righteousness is to be sought through them; for that makes them appear good outwardly, when in truth they are not good. They deceive men and lead them to deceive one another like ravening wolves in sheep's clothing [Matt. 7:15].

But this leviathan, or perverse notion concerning works, is unconquerable where sincere faith is wanting. Those work-saints cannot get rid of it unless faith, its destroyer, comes and rules in their hearts. Nature of itself cannot drive it out or even recognize it, but rather regards it as a mark of the most holy will. If the influence of custom is added and confirms this perverseness of nature, as wicked teachers have caused it to do, it becomes an incurable evil and leads astray and destroys countless men beyond all hope of restoration. Therefore, although it is good to preach and write about penitence, confession, and satisfaction, our teaching is unquestionably deceitful and diabolical if we stop with that and do not go on to teach about faith.

---

[16] Probably a reminiscence of Leviathan, the twisting serpent, in Isa. 27:1.

Christ, like his forerunner John, not only said, "Repent" [Matt. 3:2; 4:17], but added the word of faith, saying, "The kingdom of heaven is at hand." We are not to preach only one of these words of God, but both; we are to bring forth out of our treasure things new and old, the voice of the law as well as the word of grace [Matt. 13:52]. We must bring forth the voice of the law that men may be made to fear and come to a knowledge of their sins and so be converted to repentance and a better life. But we must not stop with that, for that would only amount to wounding and not binding up, smiting and not healing, killing and not making alive, leading down into hell and not bringing back again, humbling and not exalting. Therefore we must also preach the word of grace and the promise of forgiveness by which faith is taught and aroused. Without this word of grace the works of the law, contrition, penitence, and all the rest are done and taught in vain.

Preachers of repentance and grace remain even to our day, but they do not explain God's law and promise that a man might learn from them the source of repentance and grace. Repentance proceeds from the law of God, but faith or grace from the promise of God, as Rom. 10 [:17] says: "So faith comes from what is heard, and what is heard comes by the preaching of Christ." Accordingly man is consoled and exalted by faith in the divine promise after he has been humbled and led to a knowledge of himself by the threats and the fear of the divine law. So we read in Psalm 30 [:5]: "Weeping may tarry for the night, but joy comes with the morning."

Let this suffice concerning works in general and at the same time concerning the works which a Christian does for himself. Lastly, we shall also speak of the things which he does toward his neighbor. A man does not live for himself alone in this mortal body to work for it alone, but he lives also for all men on earth; rather, he lives only for others and not for himself. To this end he brings his body into subjection that he may the more sincerely and freely serve others, as Paul says in Rom. 14 [:7-8], "None of us lives to himself, and none of us dies to himself. If we live, we live to the Lord, and if we die, we die to the Lord." He cannot ever in this life be idle and without works toward his neighbors, for he will necessarily speak, deal with, and exchange views with men, as Christ also, being made in the likeness of men [Phil. 2:7], was found in form as a man and conversed with men, as Baruch 3 [:38] says.

Man, however, needs none of these things for his righteousness and salvation. Therefore he should be guided in all his works by this thought and contemplate this one thing alone, that he may serve and benefit others in all that he does, considering nothing except the need and the advantage of his neighbor. Accordingly the Apostle commands us to work with our hands so that we may give to the needy, although he might have said that we should work to support ourselves. He says, however, "that he may be able to give to those in need" [Eph. 4:28]. This is what makes caring for the body a Christian work, that through its health and comfort we may be able to work, to acquire, and lay by funds with which to aid those who are in need, that in this way the strong member may serve the weaker, and we may be sons of God, each caring for and working for the other, bearing one another's burdens and so fulfilling the law of Christ [Gal. 6:2]. This is a truly Christian life. Here faith is truly active through love [Gal. 5:6], that is, it finds expression in works of the freest service, cheerfully and lovingly done, with which a man willingly serves another without hope of reward; and for himself he is satisfied with the fullness and wealth of his faith.

Accordingly Paul, after teaching the Philippians how rich they were made through faith in Christ, in which they obtained all things, thereafter teaches them, saying, "So if there is any encouragement in Christ, any incentive of love, any participation in the Spirit, any affection and sympathy, complete my joy by being of the same mind, having the same love, being in full accord and of one mind. Do nothing from selfishness or conceit, but in humility count others better than yourselves. Let each of you look not only to his own interests, but also to the interests of others" [Phil. 2:1-4]. Here we see clearly that the Apostle has prescribed this rule for the life of Christians, namely, that we should devote all our works to the welfare of others, since each has such abundant riches in his faith that all his other works and his whole life are a surplus with which he can by voluntary benevolence serve and do good to his neighbor.

As an example of such life the Apostle cites Christ, saying, "Have this mind among yourselves, which you have in Christ Jesus, who, though he was in the form of God, did not count equality with God a thing to be grasped, but emptied himself, taking the form of a servant, being born in the likeness of men. And being found in human form he humbled himself and became obedient unto death" [Phil. 2:5-8]. This salutary word of the Apostle has been obscured for us by those who have not at all understood his words, "form of God," "form of a servant," "human form," "likeness of men," and have applied them to the divine and the human nature. Paul means this: Although Christ was filled with the form of God and rich in all good things, so that he needed no work and no suffering to make him righteous and saved (for he had all this eternally), yet he was not puffed up by them and did not exalt himself above us and assume power over us, although he could rightly have done so; but, on the contrary, he so lived, labored, worked, suffered, and died that he might be like other men and in fashion and in actions be nothing else than a man, just as if he had need of all these things and had nothing of the form of God. But he did all this for our sake, that he might serve us and that all things which he accomplished in this form of a servant might become ours.

So a Christian, like Christ his head, is filled and made rich by faith and should be content with this form of God which he has obtained by faith; only, as I have said, he should increase this faith until it is made perfect. For this faith is his life, his righteousness, and his salvation: it saves him and makes him acceptable, and bestows upon him all things that are Christ's, as has been said above, and as Paul asserts in Gal. 2 [:20] when he says, "And the life I now live in the flesh I live by faith in the Son of God." Although the Christian is thus free from all works, he ought in this liberty to empty himself, take upon himself the form of a servant, be made in the likeness of men, be found in human form, and to serve, help, and in every way deal with his neighbor as he sees that God through Christ has dealt and still deals with him. This he should do freely, having regard for nothing but divine approval.

He ought to think: "Although I am an unworthy and condemned man, my God has given me in Christ all the riches of righteousness and salvation without any merit on my part, out of pure, free mercy, so that from now on I need nothing except faith which believes that this is true. Why should I not therefore freely, joyfully, with all my heart, and with an eager will do all things which I know are pleasing and acceptable to such a Father who has overwhelmed me with his inestimable riches? I will therefore give myself as a Christ to my neighbor, just as Christ offered himself to me; I will do nothing in this life except what I see is necessary, profitable, and salutary to my neighbor, since through faith I have an abundance of all good things in Christ."

Behold, from faith thus flow forth love and joy in the Lord, and from love a joyful, willing, and free mind that serves one's neighbor willingly and takes no account of gratitude or ingratitude, of praise or blame, of gain or loss. For a man does not serve that he may put men under obligations. He does not distinguish between friends and enemies or anticipate their thankfulness or unthankfulness, but he most freely and most willingly spends himself and all that he has, whether he wastes all on the thankless or whether he gains a reward. As his Father does, distributing all things to all men richly and freely, making "his sun rise on the evil and on the good" [Matt. 5:45], so also the son does all things and suffers all things with that freely bestowing joy which is his delight when through Christ he sees it in God, the dispenser of such great benefits.

Therefore, if we recognize the great and precious things which are given us, as Paul says [Rom. 5:5], our hearts will be filled by the Holy Spirit with the love which makes us free, joyful, almighty workers and conquerors over all tribulations, servants of our neighbors, and yet lords of all. For those who do not recognize the gifts bestowed upon them through Christ, however, Christ has been born in vain; they go their way with their works and shall never come to taste or feel those things. Just as our neighbor is in need and lacks that in which we abound, so we were in need before God and lacked his mercy. Hence, as our heavenly Father has in Christ freely come to our aid, we also ought freely to help our neighbor through our body and its works, and each one should become as it were a

Christ to the other that we may be Christs to one another and Christ may be the same in all, that is, that we may be truly Christians.

Who then can comprehend the riches and the glory of the Christian life? It can do all things and has all things and lacks nothing. It is lord over sin, death, and hell, and yet at the same time it serves, ministers to, and benefits all men. But alas in our day this life is unknown throughout the world; it is neither preached about nor sought after; we are altogether ignorant of our own name and do not know why we are Christians or bear the name of Christians. Surely we are named after Christ, not because he is absent from us, but because he dwells in us, that is, because we believe in him and are Christs one to another and do to our neighbors as Christ does to us. But in our day we are taught by the doctrine of men to seek nothing but merits, rewards, and the things that are ours; of Christ we have made only a taskmaster far harsher than Moses.

We have a pre-eminent example of such a faith in the blessed Virgin. As is written in Luke 2 [:22], she was purified according to the law of Moses according to the custom of all women, although she was not bound by that law and did not need to be purified. Out of free and willing love, however, she submitted to the law like other women that she might not offend or despise them. She was not justified by this work, but being righteous she did it freely and willingly. So also our works should be done, not that we may be justified by them, since, being justified beforehand by faith, we ought to do all things freely and joyfully for the sake of others.

St. Paul also circumcised his disciple Timothy, not because circumcision was necessary for his righteousness, but that he might not offend or despise the Jews who were weak in the faith and could not yet grasp the liberty of faith. But, on the other hand, when they despised the liberty of faith and insisted that circumcision was necessary for righteousness, he resisted them and did not allow Titus to be circumcised Gal. 2 [:3]. Just as he was unwilling to offend or despise any man's weak faith and yielded to their will for a time, so he was also unwilling that the liberty of faith should be offended against or despised by stubborn, work-righteous men. He chose a middle way, sparing the weak for a time, but always withstanding the stubborn, that he might convert all to the liberty of faith. What we do should be done with the same zeal to sustain the weak in faith, as in Rom. 14 [:1]; but we should firmly resist the stubborn teachers of works. Of this we shall say more later.

Christ also, in Matt. 17 [:24-27], when the tax money was demanded of his disciples, discussed with St. Peter whether the sons of the king were not free from the payment of tribute, and Peter affirmed that they were. Nonetheless, Christ commanded Peter to go to the sea and said, "Not to give offense to them, go to the sea and cast a hook, and take the first fish that comes up, and when you open its mouth you will find a shekel; take that and give it to them for me and for yourself." This incident fits our subject beautifully for Christ here calls himself and those who are his children sons of the king, who need nothing; and yet he freely submits and pays the tribute. Just as necessary and helpful as this work was to Christ's righteousness or salvation, just so much do all other works of his or his followers avail for righteousness, since they all follow after righteousness and are free and are done only to serve others and to give them an example of good works.

Of the same nature are the precepts which Paul gives in Rom. 13 [:1-7], namely, that Christians should be subject to the governing authorities and be ready to do every good work, not that they shall in this way be justified, since they already are righteous through faith, but that in the liberty of the Spirit they shall by so doing serve others and the authorities themselves and obey their will freely and out of love. The works of all colleges,[17] monasteries, and priests should be of this nature. Each one should do the works of his profession and station, not that by them he may strive after righteousness, but that through them he may keep his body under control, be an example to others who also need to keep their bodies under control, and finally that by such works he may submit his will to that of others in the freedom of love. But very great care must always be exercised so that no man in a false confidence imagines that by such works he will be justified or acquire merit

---

[17] The word "college" here denotes a corporation of clergy supported by a foundation and performing certain religious services.

or be saved; for this is the work of faith alone, as I have repeatedly said.

Anyone knowing this could easily and without danger find his way through those numberless mandates and precepts of pope, bishops, monasteries, churches, princes, and magistrates upon which some ignorant pastors insist as if they were necessary to righteousness and salvation, calling them "precepts of the church," although they are nothing of the kind. For a Christian, as a free man, will say, "I will fast, pray, do this and that as men command, not because it is necessary to my righteousness or salvation; but that I may show due respect to the pope, the bishop, the community, a magistrate, or my neighbor, and give them an example. I will do and suffer all things, just as Christ did and suffered far more for me, although he needed nothing of it all for himself, and was made under the law for my sake, although he was not under the law." Although tyrants do violence or injustice in making their demands, yet it will do no harm as long as they demand nothing contrary to God.

From what has been said, everyone can pass a safe judgment on all works and laws and make a trustworthy distinction between them and know who are the blind and ignorant pastors and who are the good and true. Any work that is not done solely for the purpose of keeping the body under control or of serving one's neighbor, as long as he asks nothing contrary to God, is not good or Christian. For this reason I greatly fear that few or no colleges, monasteries, altars, and offices of the church are really Christian in our day—nor the special fasts and prayers on certain saints' days. I fear, I say, that in all these we seek only our profit, thinking that through them our sins are purged away and that we find salvation in them. In this way Christian liberty perishes altogether. This is a consequence of our ignorance of Christian faith and liberty.

This ignorance and suppression of liberty very many blind pastors take pains to encourage. They stir up and urge on their people in these practices by praising such works, puffing them up with their indulgences, and never teaching faith. If, however, you wish to pray, fast, or establish a foundation in the church, I advise you to be careful not to do it in order to obtain some benefit, whether temporal or eternal, for you would do injury to your faith which alone offers you all things. Your one care should be that faith may grow, whether it is trained by works or sufferings. Make your gifts freely and for no consideration, so that others may profit by them and fare well because of you and your goodness. In this way you shall be truly good and Christian. Of what benefit to you are the good works which you do not need for keeping your body under control? Your faith is sufficient for you, through which God has given you all things.

See, according to this rule the good things we have from God should flow from one to the other and be common to all, so that everyone should "put on" his neighbor and so conduct himself toward him as if he himself were in the other's place. From Christ the good things have flowed and are flowing into us. He has so "put on" us and acted for us as if he had been what we are. From us they flow on to those who have need of them so that I should lay before God my faith and my righteousness that they may cover and intercede for the sins of my neighbor which I take upon myself and so labor and serve in them as if they were my very own. That is what Christ did for us. This is true love and the genuine rule of a Christian life. Love is true and genuine where there is true and genuine faith. Hence the Apostle says of love in I Cor. 13 [:5] that "it does not seek its own."

We conclude, therefore, that a Christian lives not in himself, but in Christ and in his neighbor. Otherwise he is not a Christian. He lives in Christ through faith, in his neighbor through love. By faith he is caught up beyond himself into God. By love he descends beneath himself into his neighbor. Yet he always remains in God and in his love, as Christ says in John 1 [:51], "Truly, truly, I say to you, you will see heaven opened, and the angels of God ascending and descending upon the Son of man."

Enough now of freedom. As you see, it is a spiritual and true freedom and makes our hearts free from all sins, laws and commands, as Paul says, I Tim. 1 [:9], "The law is not laid down for the just." It is more excellent than all other liberty, which is external, as heaven is more excellent than earth. May Christ give us this liberty both to understand and to preserve. Amen.

Finally, something must be added for the sake of those for

whom nothing can be said so well that they will not spoil it by misunderstanding it. It is questionable whether they will understand even what will be said here. There are very many who, when they hear of this freedom of faith, immediately turn it into an occasion for the flesh and think that now all things are allowed them. They want to show that they are free men and Christians only by despising and finding fault with ceremonies, traditions, and human laws; as if they were Christians because on stated days they do not fast or eat meat when others fast, or because they do not use the accustomed prayers, and with upturned nose scoff at the precepts of men, although they utterly disregard all else that pertains to the Christian religion. The extreme opposite of these are those who rely for their salvation solely on their reverent observance of ceremonies, as if they would be saved because on certain days they fast or abstain from meats, or pray certain prayers; these make a boast of the precepts of the church and of the fathers, and do not care a fig for the things which are of the essence of our faith. Plainly, both are in error because they neglect the weightier things which are necessary to salvation, and quarrel so noisily about trifling and unnecessary matters.

How much better is the teaching of the Apostle Paul who bids us take a middle course and condemns both sides when he says, "Let not him who eats despise him who abstains, and let not him who abstains pass judgment on him who eats" [Rom. 14:3]. Here you see that they who neglect and disparage ceremonies, not out of piety, but out of mere contempt, are reproved, since the Apostle teaches us not to despise them. Such men are puffed up by knowledge. On the other hand, he teaches those who insist on the ceremonies not to judge the others, for neither party acts toward the other according to the love that edifies. Wherefore we ought to listen to Scripture which teaches that we should not go aside to the right or to the left [Deut. 28:14] but follow the statutes of the Lord which are right, "rejoicing the heart" [Ps. 19:8]. As a man is not righteous because he keeps and clings to the works and forms of the ceremonies, so also will a man not be counted righteous merely because he neglects and despises them.

Our faith in Christ does not free us from works but from false opinions concerning works, that is, from the foolish presumption that justification is acquired by works. Faith redeems, corrects, and preserves our consciences so that we know that righteousness does not consist in works, although works neither can nor ought to be wanting; just as we cannot be without food and drink and all the works of this mortal body, yet our righteousness is not in them, but in faith; and yet those works of the body are not to be despised or neglected on that account. In this world we are bound by the needs of our bodily life, but we are not righteous because of them. "My kingship is not of this world" [John 18:36], says Christ. He does not, however, say, "My kingship is not here, that is, in this world." And Paul says, "Though we live in the world we are not carrying on a worldly war" [II Cor. 10:3], and in Gal. 2 [:20], "The life I now live in the flesh I live by faith in the Son of God." Thus what we do, live, and are in works and ceremonies, we do because of the necessities of this life and of the effort to rule our body. Nevertheless we are righteous, not in these, but in the faith of the Son of God.

Hence the Christian must take a middle course and face those two classes of men. He will meet first the unyielding, stubborn ceremonialists who like deaf adders are not willing to hear the truth of liberty [Ps. 58:4] but, having no faith, boast of, prescribe, and insist upon their ceremonies as means of justification. Such were the Jews of old, who were unwilling to learn how to do good. These he must resist, do the very opposite, and offend them boldly lest by their impious views they drag many with them into error. In the presence of such men it is good to eat meat, break the fasts, and for the sake of the liberty of faith do other things which they regard as the greatest of sins. Of them we must say, "Let them alone; they are blind guides." According to this principle Paul would not circumcise Titus when the Jews insisted that he should [Gal. 2:3], and Christ excused the apostles when they plucked ears of grain on the sabbath [Matt. 12: 1-8]. There are many similar instances. The other class of men whom a Christian will meet are the simple-minded, ignorant men, weak in the faith, as the Apostle calls them, who cannot yet grasp the liberty of faith, even if they were willing to do so [Rom. 14:1]. These he must take care not to offend. He must yield to their weakness until they are more fully instructed. Since they do and think as they do, not because they are stubbornly wicked, but only because their faith is weak, the fasts and other things which they consider necessary must be observed to avoid giving them offense. This is the command of love which would harm no one but would serve all men. It is not by their fault that they are weak, but by that of their pastors who have taken them captive with the snares of their traditions and have wickedly used these traditions as rods with which to beat them. They should have been delivered from these pastors by the teachings of faith and freedom. So the Apostle teaches us in Romans 14: "If food is a cause of my brother's falling, I will never eat meat" [Cf. Rom. 14:21 and I Cor. 8:13]; and again, "I know and am persuaded in the Lord Jesus that nothing is unclean in itself; but it is unclean for any one who thinks it unclean" [Rom. 14:14].

For this reason, although we should boldly resist those teachers of traditions and sharply censure the laws of the popes by means of which they plunder the people of God, yet we must spare the timid multitude whom those impious tyrants hold captive by means of these laws until they are set free. Therefore fight strenuously against the wolves, but for the sheep and not also against the sheep. This you will do if you inveigh against the laws and the lawgivers and at the same time observe the laws with the weak so that they will not be offended, until they also recognize tyranny and understand their freedom. If you wish to use your freedom, do so in secret, as Paul says, Rom. 14 [:22], "The faith that you have, keep between yourself and God"; but take care not to use your freedom in the sight of the weak. On the other hand, use your freedom constantly and consistently in the sight of and despite the tyrants and the stubborn so that they also may learn that they are impious, that their laws are of no avail for righteousness, and that they had no right to set them up.

Since we cannot live our lives without ceremonies and works, and the perverse and untrained youth need to be restrained and saved from harm by such bonds; and since each one should keep his body under control by means of such works, there is need that the minister of Christ be far-seeing and faithful. He ought so to govern and teach Christians in all these matters that their conscience and faith will not be offended and that there will not spring up in them a suspicion and a root of bitterness and many will thereby be defiled, as Paul admonishes the Hebrews [Heb. 12:15]; that is, that they may not lose faith and become defiled by the false estimate of the value of works and think that they must be justified by works. Unless faith is at the same time constantly taught, this happens easily and defiles a great many, as has been done until now through the pestilent, impious, soul-destroying traditions of our popes and the opinions of our theologians. By these snares numberless souls have been dragged down to hell, so that you might see in this the work of Antichrist.

In brief, as wealth is the test of poverty, business the test of faithfulness, honors the test of humility, feasts the test of temperance, pleasures the test of chastity, so ceremonies are the test of the righteousness of faith. "Can a man," asks Solomon, "carry fire in his bosom and his clothes and not be burned?" [Prov. 6:27]. Yet as a man must live in the midst of wealth, business, honors, pleasures, and feasts, so also must he live in the midst of ceremonies, that is, in the midst of dangers. Indeed, as infant boys need beyond all else to be cherished in the bosoms and by the hands of maidens to keep them from perishing, yet when they are grown up their salvation is endangered if they associate with maidens, so the inexperienced and perverse youth need to be restrained and trained by the iron bars of ceremonies lest their unchecked ardor rush headlong into vice after vice. On the other hand, it would be death for them always to be held in bondage to ceremonies, thinking that these justify them. They are rather to be taught that they have been so imprisoned in ceremonies, not that they should be made righteous or gain great merit by them, but that they might thus be kept from doing evil and might more easily be instructed to the righteousness of faith. Such instruction they would not endure if the impulsiveness of their youth were not restrained.

Hence ceremonies are to be given the same place in the life of a Christian as models and plans have among builders and artisans. They are prepared, not as a permanent structure, but because without them nothing could be built or made. When the structure is complete the models and plans are laid aside. You see, they are not despised, rather they are greatly sought after; but what we despise is the false estimate of them since no one holds them to be the real and permanent structure.

If any man were so flagrantly foolish as to care for nothing all his life long except the most costly, careful, and persistent preparation of plans and models and never to think of the structure itself, and were satisfied with his work in producing such plans and mere aids to work, and boasted of it, would not all men pity his insanity and think that something great might have been built with what he has wasted? Thus we do not despise ceremonies and works, but we set great store by them; but we despise the false estimate placed upon works in order that no one may think that they are true righteousness, as those hypocrites believe who spend and lose their whole lives in zeal for works and never reach that goal for the sake of which the works are to be done, who, as the Apostle says, "will listen to anybody and can never arrive at a knowledge of the truth" [II Tim. 3:7]. They seem to wish to build, they make their preparations, and yet they never build. Thus they remain caught in the form of religion and do not attain unto its power [II Tim. 3:5]. Meanwhile they are pleased with their efforts and even dare to judge all others whom they do not see shining with a like show of works. Yet with the gifts of God which they have spent and abused in vain they might, if they had been filled with faith, have accomplished great things to their own salvation and that of others.

Since human nature and natural reason, as it is called, are by nature superstitious and ready to imagine, when laws and works are prescribed, that righteousness must be obtained through laws and works; and further, since they are trained and confirmed in this opinion by the practice of all earthly lawgivers, it is impossible that they should of themselves escape from the slavery of works and come to a knowledge of the freedom of faith. Therefore there is need of the prayer that the Lord may give us and make us *theodidacti*, that is, those taught by God [John 6:45], and himself, as he has promised, write his law in our hearts; otherwise there is no hope for us. If he himself does not teach our hearts this wisdom hidden in mystery [I Cor. 2:7], nature can only condemn it and judge it to be heretical because nature is offended by it and regards it as foolishness. So we see that it happened in the old days in the case of the apostles and prophets, and so godless and blind popes and their flatterers do to me and to those who are like me. May God at last be merciful to them and to us and cause his face to shine upon us that we may know his way upon earth [Ps. 67:1-2], his salvation among all nations, God, who is blessed forever [II Cor. 11:31]. Amen.

WHY THE BOOKS OF THE POPE AND HIS DISCIPLES WERE BURNED

1520

Translated by Lewis W. Spitz

INTRODUCTION

The bull, *Exsurge Domine,** threatening Luther with excommunication, also included a demand to burn his books. The official publication of the bull in Rome on June 15, 1520, was accompanied by the burning of Luther's books. Owing to a rising tide of sympathy for Luther's cause in Germany and the Netherlands, official publication of the bull in these countries did not take place until the papal nuncio, Jerome Aleander, was given the special assignment to enforce compliance with the Roman Curia's decision and demand. Shortly upon his arrival at the imperial court of Charles V in the Netherlands the bull was published officially and accompanied by a burning of Luther's books in Louvain before the middle of October, 1520. At the instigation of Aleander similar bonfires were lit at Cologne and Mainz. Eck, who accompanied Aleander on his way from Rome to the Netherlands, incited similar actions at Ingolstadt and perhaps at Leipzig and Merseburg. As the threat of burning his books came nearer to Wittenberg, Luther was determined to fight fire with fire.

On December 10, upon Melanchthon's announcement, a crowd of students and lovers of evangelical truth gathered at nine o'clock in the morning at the chapel of the Holy Cross and from there proceeded to a place outside the Elster gate in Wittenberg. There Luther cast into the fire volumes of the canon law, the papal decretals, and scholastic philosophy. Then Luther, deeply agitated, stepped from the crowd and consigned a small document to the mounting flames, the papal bull threatening him with excommunication. This was the solemn moment which in a sense marked the irrevocable and formal break with Rome.

Luther was keenly conscious of the meaning of his act. The next day he spoke of it in class before beginning his lecture on the Psalms. To justify this daring deed publicly, he wrote in German

---

* Cf. Carl Mirbt, *Quellen zur Geschichte des Papsttums und des roemischen Katholizimus* (2d ed.; Tübingen and Leipzig, 1901), pp. 183-185.

during the course of the next two weeks the treatise, *Why the Books of the Pope and His Disciples Were Burned by Doctor Martin Luther*. It was published for Luther by Johann Grünenberg. While the translation in this volume is based on the German in WA 7, 161-182, readings of the parallel Latin version have been taken into account.

WHY THE BOOKS OF THE POPE AND HIS DISCIPLES WERE BURNED

BY DOCTOR MARTIN LUTHER

Let whoever wishes also declare why they have burned Doctor Luther's books.

Jesus

God grant grace and peace to all who love Christian truth.

I, Martin Luther, called a doctor of Holy Scripture, an Augustinian of Wittenberg, notify all men that by my will, advice, and help the books of the pope of Rome and some of his disciples were burned on the Monday after Saint Nicholas[1] in the year 1520. If somebody wondering about this should ask, as I indeed foresee, on what ground or mandate I have done it, let this be his answer.

In the first place, it is an ancient traditional practice to burn poisonous evil books, as we read in chapter nineteen of the Acts of the Apostles. There they burned books for five thousand pennies [fifty thousand pieces of silver], according to the account of St. Paul [Acts 19:19].

Secondly, I am, however unworthy, a baptized Christian, in addition a sworn doctor of Holy Scripture, and beyond that a preacher each weekday whose duty it is on account of his name, station, oath, and office, to destroy or at least to ward off false, corrupt, unchristian doctrine. And even though many more who are similarly duty-bound nevertheless do not wish or like to do the same, perhaps as a result of a lack of understanding or frail fear, I would still not be justified in letting someone's example stop

---

[1] In 1520 the day of St. Nicholas, observed on December 6, fell on a Thursday.

me, if my conscience were sufficiently instructed and my spirit, awakened by God's grace, bold enough.

Thirdly, for all that I still would not have attempted an undertaking of this kind, had I not experienced and observed that the pope and the papal seducers do more than err and lead astray. Even after the many instructions which I gave in vain, they are so completely obdurate and callous in their unchristian error and corruption of the soul that they do not want to be guided or taught. Rather, with closed ears and eyes they blindly damn and burn evangelical teaching in order to confirm and preserve their antichristian, devilish doctrine.

Fourthly, I also do not believe that they have the command from Pope Leo X, so far as his person is concerned, unless I shall learn differently. I also hope that such books as I burned were not pleasing to him, even though they belonged to his predecessors. And if they pleased him, it is still a matter of indifference to me. I know, too, and have reliable information that the people of Cologne and Louvain who boast they have his Imperial Majesty's permission and command to burn my little books are sparing of the truth, for they have bought their way into such a project from several magistrates with bribes worth many thousand gulden.

Fifthly, since, then, through their kind of book burning great damage to truth and a false delusion among the plain common people might result, to the destruction of many souls, I have on the prompting of the Spirit (as I hope), in order to strengthen and preserve the same, burned the books of the adversaries in turn, since their improvement is not to be hoped for.

Therefore let no one be impressed by the lofty titles, names, and prestige of the papal estate, of canon law, and by the use of these burned books, which is of long standing. Rather listen and look first at what the pope teaches in his books, what poisonous and frightful doctrines are contained in the holy canon law, and what until the present time we have worshipped instead of the truth, and then judge freely whether I have burned these books justly or unjustly.

Articles and Errors in the Canon Law and
Papal books on account of which they are
rightly to be burned and shunned.

1

The pope and his men are not bound to be subject and obedient to God's commands.

He records this atrocious teaching clearly in the chapter[2] where he explains the words of St. Peter, who says, "Be subject to every human institution," [I Pet. 2:13] thus: St. Peter did not thereby refer to himself or his successors, but rather to his subjects.

2

It is not a command, but a counsel, of St. Peter, where he teaches that all Christians should be subject to kings [I Pet. 2:13].[3]

3

The sun symbolizes the papal, the moon the secular power in Christendom.[4]

4

The pope and his see are not bound to be subject to Christian councils and decrees.[5]

5

The pope has in his heart full power over all laws.[6]

---

[2] *Solitae, Decretalium Gregorii IX* i. tit. XXXIII: *De maioritate et obedientia,* cap. 6. *Corpus Iuris Canonici,* ed. Aemilius Friedberg (Graz, 1955), II, cols. 196-198.

[3] *Ibid.*

[4] *Ibid.*

[5] *Significasti, Decretalium Gregorii IX* i. tit. VI: *De electione et electi potestate,* cap. 4. *Corpus Iuris Canonici,* II, cols. 45-50.

[6] Luther has: *in prologo Sexti.* Cf. *Decretalium Gregorii IX* i. tit. II: *De Constitutionibus. Corpus Iuris Canonici,* II, cols. 7-16.

6

From this it follows that the pope has the power to break up, change, and establish all councils and all decrees, as he does daily, so that no power or usefulness remains for councils and Christian orders.

7

The pope has the right to demand oath and fealty of the bishops for their pallium.[7]

The saying of Jesus, "You received without pay, give without pay" [Matt. 10:8] is opposed to this.

8

Even if the pope were so wicked that he would lead innumerable people in great masses to the devil, nevertheless, no one would be permitted to punish him for it.[8]

This article alone would be enough cause for burning all the pope's books. What devilish unchristian thing would they not undertake, if they shamelessly hold and teach such frightful things? See there, Christian, what canon law teaches you.

9

Next to God the salvation of all Christendom depends on the pope.[9]

The statement, "I believe in one holy church, etc," is opposed to this. All Christians, then, would have to perish as often as the pope is wicked.

10

No one on earth can judge the pope. Also, no one can

---

[7] The pallium is a circular band of white wool with pendants, worn by archbishops over the chasuble, the outer vestments of the celebrant at mass. Luther refers the reader once again to the chapter, *Significasti*. Cf. note 5 above.

[8] *Decreti Prima Pars*, dist. XL, cap. 6: *Si Papa Suae. Corpus Iuris Canonici*, I, col. 146.

[9] *Ibid.*

*judge his decision. Rather, he is supposed to judge all
people on earth.*[10]

This is the main article. In order that it may become deeply im-
bedded, it is always quoted again and again through many chapters
and almost through the whole canon law, so that it indeed appears
as though the canon law were devised only in order that the pope
could freely do and leave what he wished, to give permission to
sin, and to be a hindrance to good. If this article stands, then Christ
and his Word are defeated. But if it does not stand, then the whole
canon law, together with the pope and see, is defeated.

However, it cannot stand, for St. Peter commands in I Pet. 6
[5:5], "Clothe yourself with humility toward one another." And
St. Paul wrote in Rom. 12 [:10], "Outdo one another in showing
honor." And Christ often says: "Whoever would be great among
you must be your servant" [Matt. 20:26-27; 23:11]. In the same
way St. Paul chastises St. Peter, Gal. 2 [:11-21], that his actions
are not in accord with the gospel. And in Acts 8 [:14] St. Peter
was sent out with St. John by the other apostles as a subordinate.
Therefore it is not and can not be true that the pope is subject to
or to be judged by no one, but he shall be subject to and judged
by every man, inasmuch as he wishes to be supreme. And the
canon law, because this is its foundation and whole essence, contends in all its parts against the gospel.

It is indeed true that the secular power shall not be subject
to its inferiors, but Christ reverses and changes that order, saying:
"You shall not be as the secular overlords" [Cf. Luke 22:25-26].
And he desires that the leaders of his people should be subject to
every man and should allow judgment from them. As he says in
Luke 22 [:25-26], "The kings of the gentiles exercise lordship over
them. But not so with you; rather let the greatest among you become as the youngest, and the leader as one who serves." How
can he be beneath anyone, if he does not want to let anyone
judge him?

If one wants to distort the words of Christ (as some do),
namely, that he ought to regard himself as the lowliest in his heart

---

[10] *Decreti Secunda Pars,* causa IX, ques. III, cap. 17: *Cuncta per mundum
nouit ecclesia. Corpus Iuris Canonici,* I, col. 611.

and not show it outwardly, then one must also infer that he ought to regard himself in his heart as superior and not show it outwardly. Thus one must either hold both spiritually in the heart or show outwardly, so that Christ's words can stand.

This is the article from which all misfortune has come into all the world. Therefore the canon law is rightly to be destroyed and rejected as a poisonous thing. For from it follows, as it actually has happened, and is evident to everyone, that one can check no evil, can demand no good, and we have to let the gospel and the faith go under before our very eyes.

11

The Roman see indeed imparts authority and power to all laws, but it is subject to none of them.[11]

That is as much as to say that what he wants is right, yet he is bound to keep none of them. Even as Christ says in Matt. 23 [:4] of the Jewish Pharisees, "They bind heavy burdens on men's shoulders, but they themselves will not move them with their finger." Against this St. Paul says in Gal. 6 [5:1], "Stand fast in your freedom and do not submit again to a yoke of slavery."

12

The rock on which Christ builds his church, Matt. 16 [:18], is called the Roman see,[12] *although Christ alone is that very rock, I Cor. 10 [4].*

13

The keys are given to St. Peter alone, even though in Matt. 18 [:18] Christ gives them to the whole congregation.

---

[11] *Decreti Secunda Pars,* causa XXV, ques. I. cap. 1: *Confidimus.* See *Corpus Iuris Canonici,* I, col. 1007. Cf. also ques. I. cap. 16: *Ideo permittente. Corpus Iuris Canonici,* I, col. 1010.

[12] Luther's reference is to dist. XIX, *Ita Dominus.* Cf. *Decreti Prima Pars,* dist. XIX, cap. 7. *Corpus Iuris Canonici,* I, col. 62. Cf. also dist. XXI, cap. 2: *In novo testamento, Corpus Iuris Canonici,* I, cols. 69f.; dist. XXI, cap. 3: *Quamvis universae, Corpus Iuris Canonici,* I, col. 70; and dist. XXII, cap. 2: *Sacrosancta Romano, Corpus Iuris Canonici,* I, cols. 73f.

14

Christ's priesthood was transferred from him to St. Peter.[13]

Against this David in Psalm 109 [110:4] and Paul in the Epistle to the Hebrews [5:6; 6:20; 7:21-28] say that Christ is a unique, eternal priest whose priesthood would never be transferred.

15

The pope has the power to make laws for the Christian church.[14]

Against this St. Paul says in Gal. 5 [:13]: "You were called by God to freedom."

16

He interprets the passage, "Whatsoever you shall bind, etc." [Matt. 16:19], *to mean that he has the power to burden all Christendom with his wanton laws. Christ intends nothing else thereby than to drive sinners to punishment and penance and not at all to burden the other innocent ones with laws, as the words clearly read.*

17

Under threat of excommunication and of committing sin, the pope has commanded not to eat meat, eggs, butter, and other miscellaneous things on certain days.

He has no authority to do this but rather should only admonish people in a friendly manner to heed his advice, leaving each man to act with complete freedom and without pressure.

18

He has forbidden marriage to the whole priesthood.

He thereby increases many sins and scandals without cause, contrary to God's command and Christian freedom.

---

[13] *Translato, Decretalium Gregorii IX* i. tit. II: *De Constitutionibus*, cap. 3. *Corpus Iuris Canonici*, II, col. 8.

[14] *Decreti Secunda Pars* causa XXV, ques. I, cap. 16: *Ideo permittente. Corpus Iuris Canonici*, I, col. 1010.

19

Pope Nicholas the third or fourth proposed among the many bad articles in his antichristian decretal that Christ has given to St. Peter and his successors power over the heavenly and earthly kingdom together with the keys.

Everyone well knows how Christ fled from the earthly kingdom [John 6:15] and that all priests have the keys, even though they are not all emperors of heavenly and earthly kingdoms.

20

He holds to be true and fosters the great unchristian lie that Emperor Constantine has given him Rome, land, empire, and power on earth.[15]

Against this Christ says, Matt. 6 [:19], "Do not lay up for yourselves treasures on earth;" likewise, "You cannot serve God and mammon" [Matt. 6:24].

21

He boasts he is the heir of the Roman empire,[16] *although everyone well knows that the spiritual and secular realms do not get along well with each other.*

And St. Paul enjoins that a bishop should serve the word of God [Cf. Titus 1:9].

22

He teaches that it is right for a Christian to defend himself against force with force.

This is contrary to and above what Christ says in Matt. 5 [:40]: "If anyone take your coat, let him have your cloak as well."

---

[15] Luther gives no reference here to canon law, but cf. *Decreti Prima Pars,* dist. XCVI, cap. 13: *Constantinus imperator,* and cap. 14: *Constantinus imperator quarta. Corpus Iuris Canonici,* I, col. 342.

[16] *Pastoralis, Clementinarum* ii. tit. XI: *De sententia et re iudicata,* cap. 2. *Corpus Iuris Canonici,* II, cols. 1151-1153.

23

Subjects can be disobedient to their overlords and the pope can depose the kings, as he writes in many places and has often done, against and above God.

24

He claims to have the power to dissolve all oaths, alliances, and obligations arranged between the higher and lower estates.

This is against and above God, who ordered every man to keep faith with the other [Zech. 8:16].

25

The pope has the power to dissolve and alter vows made to God.[17]

That is also against and above God.

26

Whoever delays fulfilling his vow upon the command of the pope is not guilty of breaking the vow.[18]

That is as much as to say, "the pope is above God."

27

No one who is married is able to serve God, even though Abraham and many saints have been married and God himself established marriage without a doubt.

Thus the Antichrist again rises above God.

28

He makes his useless laws equal to the gospels and to Holy Scripture, as he repeatedly indicates in the decretal.

---

[17] *De peregrinationis* quoque *votis, Decretalium Gregorii* IX iii. tit. XXXIV: *De voto et voti redemptione,* cap. 1. *Corpus Iuris Canonici,* II, col. 589.

[18] *Ibid.,* cap. 5: *Non est voti. Corpus Iuris Canonici,* II, col. 590.

29

The pope has the power to interpret and to teach Holy Scripture according to his will and allows no one to interpret it otherwise than he wants.

He thereby puts himself above God's word, dismembers and destroys it, as St. Paul says in I Cor. 14 [:30], the superior should yield to the revelation of the inferior.

30

The pope does not derive authentic existence, strength, and dignity from Scripture, but Scripture from him, which is one of the main articles.

Therefore, as a true Antichrist he deserves to have Christ from heaven itself destroy him together with his government, as Paul predicted [II Thess. 1:7-10].

These and similar articles which are without number—all of them aim at exalting the pope above God and man. Everyone, even God and the angels, is subject to him, while he is subject to no one, so that even his disciples say he is an extraordinary creature, being neither God nor man (perhaps the devil himself). So now the saying of Paul is fulfilled, "the man of lawlessness is revealed, the son of perdition, who opposes and exalts himself against every so-called god or object of worship . . . by the activity of Satan," and so on [II Thess. 2:3-12]. When he calls him a man of lawlessness and a son of perdition, he does not mean his person alone, for that would cause little damage, but rather that his government is nothing else than sin and perdition and that he will rule only to lead all the world to sin and hell. It can readily be observed, then, and is clear from such articles that nothing except sin and perdition have come into the world through the pope, and more keeps coming daily.

Those very men who observe canon law, although in out-of-the-way places, have confessed that it smells of nothing but greed and power. That is true indeed, and whoever does not want to lie must admit it. For if you want to know in a few words what the canon law contains, then listen. It is, to put it briefly, the following:

The pope is a god on earth over everything heavenly, earthly, spiritual, and secular, and all is his own. No one is permitted to say to him: "What are you doing?"

That is the abomination and stench of which Christ speaks in Matt. 24 [:15]: "So when you see the desolating sacrilege spoken of by the prophet Daniel [Dan. 9:27; 12:11], standing in the holy place (let the reader understand)," etc. And St. Paul writes: "He will take his seat in the temple of God (that is, in Christendom), proclaiming himself to be God" [Cf. II Thess. 2:4].

Now the fact that no one or few people have been permitted to speak out to the pope about his abomination is not amazing, for it has been announced that he will have all those burned who oppose him and that he will have the consent of all the kings and princes. If the seduction of the Antichrist were so gross that everyone could notice it, or so trifling that the kings and big-wigs would not be most distinguished men in it, then the prophets and apostles would have cried out and written so much and so earnestly in vain.

When Christ was on earth, many people who heard his word and saw his work spoke against those who did not want to let him be Christ: "When the Christ appears, will he do more signs than this man has done?" [John 7:31]. Even now that mumbling goes on in similar fashion: "Even if the Antichrist appears, what greater evil can he do than the pope's rule has done and does daily?" For it is simply inconceivable that if his government were from God, he should allow so much corruption and sin to come out of it and let the evil spirit rule in it so powerfully. Yet we do not believe it until we are lost, and we all too slowly recognize the Antichrist.

Likewise from the beginning of all creatures the greatest evil has always come from the best, for in the highest choir of angels, where God had worked most mightily, Lucifer sinned and did great harm. In paradise, the greatest sin and harm occurred in the first, best man. According to Gen. 6 [:4] the giants and tyrants came from none other than the holy children of God. And Christ, the Son of God, was crucified nowhere else than in the holy city of Jerusalem where he had been honored most of all and where he had done many miracles, and by none other than the princes and chief priests and the most learned and holy. And Judas also had to compromise not simply a humble station in life, but the position of an apostle. Thus God has also blessed no city on earth with so much grace and so many saints as Rome and did more for her than for any other. Therefore she, too, like Jerusalem, in gratitude to God, must do the greatest harm and give the world the true and most destructive Antichrist who does more harm than the good which Christ has done before. That is the way it happens. And it must all transpire in the name and under the pretext of Christ and of God, so that no one believes it until Christ himself comes and enlightens such darkness with the light of his advent, as St. Paul says [II Thess. 2:8; I Cor. 4:5].

These articles must suffice this time. If, however, someone is the pope's ally and is itching to undertake to protect and defend the same, then I shall indeed paint them more clearly for him and bring up much more of the same sort. These articles are to be only the beginning of dealing seriously with matters pertaining to the pope, because until now I have only toyed and played with them. I have begun it in God's name. I hope the time has come for the cause to move forward in his name without me. Hereby I also wish to embrace all the articles as Christian and true which were damned and burned in the last bull by the nuncio of Antichrist now come from Rome and on the other hand to charge just as many articles of the pope with being antichristian and unchristian as the number of my articles which have been condemned.[19] If they are allowed to burn my articles, in which there is more gospel and more of the true substance of Holy Scripture (which I can say truthfully without boasting, and prove also) than in all the pope's books, then I am justified much more in burning their unchristian law books in which there is nothing good. But even if there were some good in them, as I must acknowledge of the decretal, nevertheless everything is so distorted as to do harm and strengthen the pope in his antichristian rule. In addition, none of it is observed with very much diligence except to retain what is evil and harmful in it.

I am willing to let everyone have his own opinion. I am moved

---

[19] The papal bull *Exsurge Domine* was signed by the papal chancery on June 15, 1520 and brought north by Aleander, papal nuncio. Cf. also p. 381.

most by the fact that the pope has never once refuted with Scripture or reason anyone who has spoken, written, or acted against him, but has at all times suppressed, exiled, burned, or otherwise strangled him with force and bans, through kings, and other partisans, or with deceit and false words, of which I shall convince him from history. Nor has he ever been willing to submit to a court of justice or judgment, but at all times bawled that he was above Scripture, judgment, and authority.

Now it is always true that truth and righteousness do not shun judgment, yes, love nothing more than light and judgment, gladly permit themselves to be examined and tried. The apostles in Acts 4 [:19] granted the right of judgment to their enemies and said: "Whether it is right to listen to you rather than to God, you must judge." So certain was the truth. But the pope wants to blind everyone's eyes, let no one judge, but alone judge everyone. That is how uncertain and fearful he is for his cause and affairs. This dealing in the darkness and shying away from the light has the effect that, if the pope were nothing but a pure angel, I still could not believe anything that came from him. Every man rightly hates dark dealings and loves the light. Amen.

In all this I offer to give an account in the
presence of every man.
Samson, Judges 15 [:11]:
"As they did to me, so have I done to them."

395

INDEXES

INDEX OF NAMES AND SUBJECTS

INDEX TO SCRIPTURE PASSAGES

415

Type used in this book
Body, 10 on 13 Caledonia
Display, Bulmer and Caledonia
Paper: Standard White Antique